P9-CEA-785

the ultimate
RICE COOKER
cookbook

the **ultimate**
RICE COOKER
cookbook

250 No-Fail Recipes for Pilafs, Risotto,
Polenta, Chilis, Soups, Porridges, Puddings,
and More, from Start to Finish
in Your Rice Cooker

BETH HENSPERGER
and JULIE KAUFMANN

THE HARVARD COMMON PRESS
Boston, Massachusetts

THE HARVARD COMMON PRESS

535 Albany Street
Boston, Massachusetts 02118
www.harvardcommonpress.com

Printed in the United States of America

Printed on acid-free paper

Library of Congress Cataloging-in-Publication Data

Hensperger, Beth.
　　The ultimate rice cooker cookbook : 250 no-fail recipes for pilafs, risotto, polenta, chilis, soups, porridges, puddings, and more from start to finish in your rice cooker / Beth Hensperger and Julie Kaufmann.
　　　　p. cm.
　　　ISBN 1-55832-202-7 (hc : alk. paper)
　　　1. Cookery (Rice) I. Kaufmann, Julie. II. Title.

TX809.R56.H44 2002
641.6'318—dc21　　　　　　　　　　　　　　　2001039603

Special bulk-order discounts are available on this and other Harvard Common Press books. Companies and organizations may purchase books for premiums or resale, or may arrange a custom edition, by contacting the Marketing Director at the address above.

10　9　8　7　6　5　4　3　2　1

Jacket design by Night & Day Design
Book design by Marysarah Quinn
Text illustration by Michael Cox

These recipes were tested at sea level. If you are cooking at an altitude of over 3,000 feet, you may need to add additional liquid, especially when cooking brown rices.

for GUHAN TOM DAVIS
heart-to-heart and a bowl of Thai jasmine

for MAX, MAYA, MOM, and BEN, who started it all

contents

acknowledgments

The rice angel is a guardian for people who appreciate rice. We met a lot of angels disguised as humans who not only appreciate, but unabashedly love rice and their rice cookers, while working on this book.

Thank-you's to the following for contributing their time and expertise to this work: food writer Lynn Alley; "Aunt Joan" Billheimer; Naoko Boerger; Matthew Bunson; Michelle Camerlengo and Jim Rogers of Panasonic/Matsushita Consumer Electronics Company; California Cooperative Rice Research Foundation, Inc., Biggs, California; Paul Cha; barley lover Jean Clem of Western Trails Food Products; Jesse Cool; restaurateurs and culinary intelligentsia Elaine Corn and David SooHoo of Bamboo Restaurant, Sacramento, California; Joyce Gemperlein; Joyce Goldstein, for her generous information on Italian rices; Barbara Grunes; Glenda Hildon of Rice Specialty, Inc.; Judith Dunbar Hines; Hitachi America Limited; Ming-man Hsieh; Atsuko Ishii; Sharon Jones, for the big burlap bag of Daawat basmati; Asian food specialist and *San Francisco Chronicle* columnist Joyce Jue; Carolyn Jung; Caryl Levine and Ken Lee of Lotus Foods; Grace Liu; Deborah Locke of RiceTec, Inc.; Amanda Lorenzo of Aroma; Jacquie McMahan, the matriarch of California rancho and Mexican cooking; plant breeder John Neal of Lundberg Family Farms; Tamera Moore, for critiquing all the rices; Marianne New of Zojirushi America Corporation; Sharon Noguchi; Mexican culinary tour guide Marge Poore; Toni Ramsaur of Gibbs Wild Rice; food writer Rick Rogers; Kimberly Park of the USA Rice Federation, Houston, Texas; Diana of Sanyo Electronics Company; creative consultant Julia Scannel; Hiroko Shimbo; U.S. Department of Agriculture Agricultural Research Center, Beaumont, Texas; Mary Weide, for sharing all that Thai jasmine; Andrew Whitfield, who taught Beth how to cook short-grain brown rice; Williams-Sonoma; Feng-Chih "Lucy" Wuchen; Martin and Susan Yan. And to all of the members, past and present, of the English Conversation Club at Escondido Elementary School for so generously opening their kitchens and their hearts.

Our thanks also go to Pam Hoenig and Julie Stillman for their marvelous editing; Valerie Cimino, managing editor; the sales, marketing, production, and publicity managers and assistants at Harvard Common Press; and Martha Casselman, our stalwart and dedicated literary agent, who loves leftover rice in her soup.

it all started with
a grain of rice

Hajimé choro choro
Naka pa ppa
Akago naité mo
Futa toru na.

At first it bubbles
And then it hisses
Even if the baby is crying
Don't remove the lid.

Japanese nursery rhyme on how to cook rice
translated by Elizabeth Andoh

Once upon a time, rice was just rice—in our lives anyway. You planned a meal and rice seemed to be the right starch to serve with it. You placed the saucepan on the stove, measured some water into it, pulled down the bag of rice, measured it into the cup, and poured it into the boiling water. As the water came back to a boil, on went the cover and, when the timer beeped, you ate the rice.

That was before we met the rice cooker. Since then, the world of rice—the amazing array of rice available on every supermarket and specialty grocery shelf, where it grows, its lore and history, sharing recipes, the writing of this book—has become an everyday part of our lives.

To an American cook, the electric rice cooker has been, up to now, a take-it-or-leave-it kitchen appliance. I mean, what's a stove for? But to many Asian-American cooks and cooks throughout Asia, the rice cooker is an absolutely essential appliance for everyday meal preparation. It is the method of choice for cooking rice in Japanese and Chinese restaurants (most of the rice cooker manufacturers have a commercial division). Since in many of these diets rice is eaten three times a day, the rice cooker is always on in every home. There are even small ones with a handle to carry while traveling on vacations and business trips. Well, why eat less-than-perfect rice when you don't have to?

Rice cookers appeal to a busy cook for a number of reasons, the first being you may have heard one of your friends tell you how great it is. It is an appliance well suited to a limited cooking space (it is the cooking tool of choice in college dorms and is great up at the ski cabin) and boasts easy cleanup. It is a closed-environment, slow-cook method that has ended up a cross between a countertop slow cooker, an oven clay pot, and a stove-top saucepan. Since it is a one-button technology, there is virtually no maintenance.

There is not much written about rice cookers in general. "I will be interested in seeing what you can do with the rice cooker," Janice Cole, professional cook and editor of *Cooking Pleasures* magazine, told us. "I have never made anything but plain rice in mine." This is the sentiment shared by the majority of cooks we talked to. Beyond the slim pamphlet enclosed with the unit, not much information on how to use it exists in print. "In Asia, a rice cooker is part of a normal household," Julie explained during one of our early discussions about the appliance. "It is like an iron or a toaster here. Why write a book about how to use an iron or toaster? Everybody just knows."

So, here is a book that fills that gap. How to use your rice cooker to make foolproof everyday basic rice, recipes for the new rices on the market, and beautiful pilafs make up the core of the book. But there is a host of other possibilities, from risottos and hot breakfast cereals to incredible desserts, made start to finish in your rice cooker. Dim sum and sushi rice, often intimidating, are within the grasp of even the novice cook. But if all you want is to make some good plain rice, this book is also for you. All instructions are presented as simply, but also as comprehensively, as possible, to be of practical use in every type and size of machine.

In every section there are plenty of step-by-step instructions, hints about the machine itself, and delicious recipes, from plain everyday "I don't have time to think about it" to boldly seasoned. Your rice cooker is a versatile, convenient kitchen appliance that embraces a style of cooking that emphasizes health and natural ingredients. The basic principles of the venerable cooking centers of the world are represented—France, Mexico, and Italy, as well as India, Japan, and China. Rices from around the world, every one available on the market today, are covered in depth—where they come from, how to cook them, and ways to incorporate them into your meals.

Whether you are buying a new rice cooker or are an accomplished cook with an old model, may these recipes bring you as much gustatory pleasure as they have to us.

SCIENCE, MYTHOLOGY, AND THE ORIGINS OF RICE

The role that rice plays as an essential food in the Eastern Hemisphere, along with being one of the first gathered wild grains in the prehistoric Neolithic era, associates the grain with both powerful spiritual symbolism and physical nourishment. It has been postulated that the very act of planting the first seeds was a magico-religious act to appease the local reigning gods, although scientifically speaking, far less is known about the beginnings of rice than any other cereal grains. There is a romantic saying that rice was the first food plant cultivated after the loss of Paradise when heaven and earth became separate worlds. One scientific source has rice growing wild on the ancient supercontinent of Gondwanaland, which split into Africa, Australia, Southeast Asia, South America, and Antarctica. The first cultivation of rice is proven by archaeological remains in Southeast Asia between India and China, and in India.

The worship of food plants is known to have been an integral part of religions, coming down through the millennia to become an aspect of modern world formal religions, as well as folklore. Rice is intertwined with the powerful presence of Shiva, the ancient Indian god who is the father of the Hindu panopoly of deities. Failing to create the perfect food to tempt the Shakti (enlivening female force or consort) of his affections, she died a virgin and from the bowers of her tomb sprang the perfect food, rice. Whether the Indonesian Samyan Sri, Thai rice goddess Maeae Posop, Indonesian Dewie Sri, or Chinese-Taoist Tou Mu (the Mother of the Rice Measure, keeping the divine records of life and death), all rice goddesses are virgin deities, their gift to mankind, associating the grain with fertility, abundance, and purity. The mysteries associated with cultivating rice have existed for so many centuries (archaeological discoveries in the Indus River valley have unearthed rice dating back to 4530 B.C.) that these mythological stories have become interrelated with the actual grain right up into our present time.

The Indian cultures of antiquity were all built around rice-growing areas, and rice, the ideal plant for the humid tropics, is still the most extensively cultivated of any food grain. Rice is mentioned in ancient Chinese scrolls (there are recipes and references to *fan* from the eighth century B.C.), and is known as "the good grain of life." It is the staple food of over half the world's population from India throughout Indonesia and the Philippines to China, Korea, and Japan, and all the islands from Taiwan to Madagascar. It can be planted in aquatic paddies, our most familiar vision of rice, but also as an upland crop called hill paddy rice, in tropical areas with lots of rainfall.

The traditional rituals that accompany every step of the cultivation and harvest acknowledge a belief system that a soul lies within each and every grain. Rice is always considered female in Eastern cultures, and while men can prepare the land and irrigation system, it is the women who plant seedlings, harvest, and winnow. Harvests were not considered joyous, but were often accompanied by lamentations as the body of the "spirit" was reaped. In ceremonial plantings, seeds are returned to the gods via the soil. Even today, there are hand-carved "demons" dotting the rural Indian countryside positioned to guard the life-giving fields of rice from invisible forces. Rice dolls, fashioned from the sacred first cuttings, give the precious spirit of the rice a home until the next planting. In Sri Lanka, astrologers and geomancers are consulted to determine the heavenly logistics of when to plant the rice.

Although the Japanese culture is intertwined with the importance of rice as a basic food, rice did not reach Japan until the second century B.C. The emperor, regarded as a direct descendant of the sun, planted his own personal paddy field of rice on the palace grounds. In Japan the rice deity is Inari, the rice-bearer, and miniature shrines to him are scattered throughout the rural countryside and villages. On February 12, the Japanese celebrate a popular folk festival, Hatsuuma, in the presence of the Inari shrines to pray for a good rice crop.

the rice cooker
MACHINE

Congratulations on your purchase of an electric or electronic rice cooker. It's versatile and reliable, a very nifty little bit of technology. It can make perfect rice and, as you are about to find out, much more. The electric rice cooker is a kitchen appliance that was born in the climate of postwar Japan. Available since the early 1950s, when the first machines were manufactured by Toshiba, the rice cooker is a contemporary of the electric blender, part of the surge for faster, more convenient food preparation with the aid of the widespread availability of electricity as a relatively cheap power source. The current variety available is astonishing: The smallest, simplest models can be had for about $15; large, sleek, technologically advanced versions easily run into the hundreds of dollars.

At its simplest, the rice cooker machine is a round, removable, aluminum bowl that sits atop a metal heating element. The heating element looks like a solid metal spring the size of a quarter. It automatically can "sense" when the water is boiled off by the temperature inside the pot (the amount of water added determines the length of the cooking time, not the amount of rice) and automatically shuts the unit off. It has a round metal or glass lid with a knob handle. The bowl has a rim or handles for lifting it in and out of the appliance housing. There is a switch to push down for turning on the appliance. The switch pops up when the machine turns off. Today's models are remarkably similar in style to those first ones made by the major Japanese companies still in business today: Hitachi, Zojirushi, Sanyo, Toshiba, and Panasonic/National. Newcomers include Aroma, Rival, and DuPont.

The shape of the rice cooker bowl was designed to mimic the shape of the *okama*, the traditional Japanese metal pot for cooking rice, with a curved bottom and wooden lid (daily rice is called *okame*). The slightly curved bottom is well known as an efficient heat conductor as far as cooking pots are concerned. It enables food to be cooked efficiently within the confines of the pot using the least amount of fuel. The *okama* was used for many centuries over an open fire or on top of a wood-burning stove. With the gradual modernization of Japanese homes, first in the cities and then in the outlying rural villages, housewives adopted cooking in the electric rice cooker as a simple alternative to using up limited space on their new electric or gas stoves. Half a century later, the electric rice cooker is a commonplace appliance in every Japanese home.

If you eat rice more than a couple of times a week, a rice cooker is a sensible investment. It does an exceptional job of cooking rice and other whole grains, as well as being very durable.

TYPES OF RICE COOKERS

There are two basic categories of rice cookers available on the market today: on/off and fuzzy logic. Within these categories there are five types of machines: cook-and-shut-off, cook-and-reduce-heat, deluxe electronic, basic fuzzy logic, and induction heating. These range from simple to sophisticated, each reflecting a step in the evolution of the rice cooker. You can recognize the types not only by the range of features, but by the price. Choose your rice cooker by first analyzing what type of cooking you want to do with it. If you make only white rice and steam a few vegetables, go for a simpler machine. If you want the full range of timing and cooking capabilities, from porridge to brown rice, go for a more elaborate model, but realize that you won't be able to use it as a steamer. Models are labeled for what the cooker will do, such as Rice Cooker/Warmer or Rice Cooker/Steamer/Warmer. If you do

a lot of steaming or make multicomponent steamed meals, look for a model with a large steamer tray or a set of baskets; this feature is not included in fuzzy logic cookers. We are not going to recommend any particular models since technology is constantly being updated and model numbers change often. Just stay with one of the reliable brands and shop for the features you desire.

Rice cookers come in standard sizes: the 3- or 4-cup capacity (small), 5- or 6-cup (medium), and 8- or 10- or 14-cup (large) models. Many manufacturers have models that can hold up to 20 cups for home use. The jumbo rice cooker, or deluxe cooker, has a capacity of 15 to 30 cups. This is a cook-and-reduce-heat type machine that is great for large families, entertaining, and small cottage businesses. It is available in restaurant supply stores.

Look for safety features such as thermal fuse protection and an automatic cord reel. All models come with a 6-ounce measuring cup (see Measuring Up, page 12) and handy heat-resistant plastic rice paddle. Many come with a small steaming plate insert. If the model is designed to be portable, there will be a conveniently designed carrying handle.

On/Off Rice Cookers

The two most basic types of rice cookers are the cook-and-shut-off cooker and the cook-and-reduce-heat cooker/warmer. Each has a round metal housing with a removable aluminum rice bowl; the carrying handles are on the outer housing and there is a switch on the front of the machine. This on/off mechanism, while seemingly simple compared to the newer fuzzy logic machines, contains the same efficient heating elements without the digital options. In addition to making rice, it is a superior machine for steaming purposes. The cook-and-reduce-heat cooker/warmer models can keep rice hot and ready to eat for several hours.

The third type of on/off rice cooker is the deluxe electronic model, which is fitted with an electronic sensor unit and retains the round housing style of the other on/off cookers.

Some manufacturers also have a model called the Persian-style rice cooker, designed specifically for making *chelo* with *tahdig* and *kateh*, the slow-cooked Middle Eastern daily rice preparations that create their own bottom crust.

Cook-and-Shut-Off Rice Cooker The cook-and-shut-off cooker, marketed simply as a rice cooker, is fast and safe. Toshiba Corporation of Japan invented the first cook-and-shut-off rice cooker in 1955. Matsushita Corporation introduced its own model soon after and brought the rice cooker to the U.S. market in 1957. You push down the switch and the machine turns on. It automatically shuts off when the rice is done (when the water boils off or if the pot is removed). If you are nearby, you will hear the switch pop up.

This machine is the most basic (it is designed to make only white rice, although it does a credible job with brown rice, too, if you follow our instructions) and is very inexpensive. It is fitted with a plain aluminum cooking pot and a tempered glass or metal lid. There is no indicator light to tell you when the rice is done; if you don't hear the click as it shuts itself off, you can tell by examining the position of the switch. This is the only model that comes in a mini-size of 1 cup, for the single rice eater. You can find small models for $15 to $20.

Cook-and-Reduce-Heat Rice Cooker The cook-and-reduce-heat rice cooker (also known as the keep warm cooker), automatically adjusts the heating element to low when the thermostat senses that the water has boiled off and the rice is done. The two heat settings are On/Off and Keep Warm, which is basically very low heat. This type of machine will keep the rice warm for up to four hours before forming a thick crust on the bottom of the pan. There is an indicator light to let you know if the cooker is cooking or in keep warm mode. To turn off this rice cooker, you must unplug it.

Top-of-the-line models designed for the steaming option have one or two clear plastic steaming baskets with slatted tiers, which imitate the Chinese bamboo steamer baskets; this is a wonderful option that does a superior job. There is a tight-fitting, see-through tempered glass lid, which we consider essential. Less expensive models are fitted with plain aluminum cooking pots and metal lids, the more expensive (still comparatively inexpensive) ones have a Teflon non-stick rice bowl coating and glass lid. This machine usually comes with a perforated metal steamer tray that fits into the top of the rice bowl, allowing for other foods to be steamed as the rice is cooking. The cheaper models have a small tray that fits into the bottom of the bowl so that steaming is done only an inch above the element.

These are very reasonably priced machines; models sell for $40 to $75. A great deal and a good first machine.

Deluxe Electronic Rice Cooker The electronic machine, designed in the 1980s, was the next big jump in rice cooker technology—it cooks and keeps the rice warm and moist for up to 12 hours. The temperature is controlled by a thermal-read switch (note that the fuzzy logic machine senses by weight rather than by temperature). This is the type of cooker to get if you want to hold large quantities of rice for extended periods. The heating elements are located not only on the bottom, but on the sides as well, so the rice stays an even consistency and you won't get a thick crust or dry spots on the bottom of the pan. These machines are great if your family eats lots of rice and they do it at different times (for instance, if you want to make rice once a day and eat it all day long, as is done in many Asian households). You lift the lid, scoop some rice, and walk away, knowing that the next person will have access to warm, moist rice. There is an indicator light to let you know if the cooker is cooking or on the Keep Warm cycle.

These machines usually cost $100 to $150; they do a great job and normally come with a Teflon nonstick rice bowl coating. Many of the deluxe electronic machines are portable.

Fuzzy Logic Rice Cookers

The fuzzy logic rice cookers—the basic fuzzy logic and the induction heating machine—are immediately recognizable by their digital face, multiple-choice function buttons, and elongated housing shape that Beth has dubbed "Queen Mum's Hatbox." Note that these machines are not usually set up for steaming (you could use an expandable steamer basket, but it might scratch the bowl lining).

Basic Fuzzy Logic Cooker The fuzzy logic cooker (also called neuro fuzzy), which hit the market in the early 1990s, is the next step up from the electronic models. Fuzzy logic technology enables the rice cooker to judge and calculate the amount of rice by weight, automatically adjusting the cooking time. Fuzzy logic rice cookers are very popular in the Asian-American food community and for good reason: They make fantastic rice. If you can afford the price and eat rice regularly, this is the machine to invest in; they are great. The first ones on the market were designed to handle white rice, especially the medium- and short-grain white rice preferred in Japan. They have evolved to incorporate multiple menus, choice of what texture you want your rice to have (soft or hard), a Porridge (or Soup) setting, and a Brown Rice setting. At this writing, Williams-Sonoma carried a lovely medium-size National brand fuzzy logic rice cooker complete with a Sushi cycle (signaling a machine made for the Japanese market), which is a nice touch, though not essential if you want to make sushi at home.

With a bit of fiddling, we got long-grain white rice and brown rice to turn out as well as the medium-grain rices (see the rice cooking charts, pages 34, 42, and 50) in fuzzy logic machines without special cycles. The beautiful spherical DuPont SilverStone coated cooker bowl that is made from a combination of stainless steel and high-grade aluminum (the shape is a fantastic heat conductor) is so easy to clean you will wish every pan you own was just like it. There is a hinged cover. There are various settings, like the Quick Cook cycle (reduces the cooking time by 20 minutes by eliminating the soak rest at the beginning) and the gentle Porridge cycle. The cooking process includes brief soaking at the beginning and steaming at the end. The digital 24-hour clock with timer brings freedom to the cooking process, so you can program the time you want the rice to start or finish cooking. Place the ingredients in the pot, set the timer, and the rice or meal is ready when you are. After the food is cooked, the unit automatically switches to the Keep Warm function, which keeps foods moister than in conventional models, warming it for up to 12 hours.

The prices on these machines range from $170 to $200 and up. You can't have everything, though, and these models are not designed for steaming.

Induction Heating Rice Cooker The induction heating cooker is fitted with state-of-the-art microm technology designed for sensitive sensor timing and temperature detection. It does everything the earlier model of fuzzy logic machine does, plus it delivers a finished product that is the most evenly cooked of any method available because of the accuracy of the microm technology controlled by a microcomputer (think microchip). Also known as the microm rice cooker, these models have been introduced into the mainstream appliance market during the last seven years in Japan. This machine is described as "the thinker." The technology in the sensor unit can compensate for improper measuring since it judges the temperature and detects moisture proportions, allowing for multiple functions, especially important in rices other than white, such as wild rice and brown rices. The induction heating rice cooker uses the highest amount of wattage of all the machines.

These are the most expensive machines, though the price is coming down; they start at about $200, with the top models at about $400.

TIPS FOR BUYING A **RICE COOKER ABROAD**

Planning a trip? If you are traveling to or through many of the major airports in Asia, you'll find a large selection of high-end rice cookers in the duty-free electronics shops. Julie's beloved Sanyo fuzzy logic rice cooker came from the Tokyo airport. At the time, there were about 15 rice cookers to choose from, priced from $80 to more than $400 for the large fuzzy logic models. Obviously these are not the under-$20 models found in many American variety stores, but serious machines for serious cooks.

important note: Before you buy abroad, double-check to make sure the machine runs on U.S. current, has a U.S.-style plug, and comes with English-language instructions and English-language buttons (Julie's is labeled in English and Chinese). Generally speaking, if you're visiting Asia, you'll be better off shopping for your rice cooker at the airport instead of in town. The airport is the best place to find rice cookers meant for the English-speaking consumer.

HOW THE RICE COOKER WORKS (THE SCIENTIFIC SCOOP)

The rice cooker has taken all the guesswork out of cooking rice. Well, sort of. First you have to figure out how to use it and what it does. While you don't have to know what and when, you most certainly have to know the recipe, the proportions of rice to water, and the parameters of what the machine can or cannot do to get the best possible results. Then it is automatic. This is a machine that will grow on you as you use it (be prepared; each machine has its own personality) and the steps involved will become second nature. We guarantee it.

The best rice is achieved by the following steps: washing or rinsing, soaking, boiling, and steaming. It is a variation of stovetop cooking, a boil-steam method known as the Canton style.

Washing or Rinsing the Rice

The washing or rinsing (depending on what type of rice you have) is done by hand before you place the rice in the cooker. Almost all serious consumers of rice rinse the rice thoroughly before cooking, but it is a step that is purely optional. There are good reasons to do so. Cooking instructions in the United States instruct you not to rinse the rice because, by law, rice meant for the American consumer has been fortified with powdered vitamins that are removed during rinsing. If you want the vitamins (which are not necessary if you have a well-balanced diet), then do not wash or rinse. If you want the best quality cooked rice, then washing helps by removing much of the loose surface starch, and will reduce excess stickiness.

The difference is subtle, but a real rice eater can tell the difference: The flavor is cleaner, the whiteness improves, and the rice is less sticky when cooked. (This is preferred even for sticky-type *japonica* rices.) And, of course, the subtle flavors of the vitamins are removed. See our section on how to wash rice (page 45).

The exception to this is that Arborio and other risotto-style rices are never washed before using, because the starch is what makes the risotto creamy.

Soaking the Rice

Soaking white rice for about an hour before cooking allows moisture to get to the center of the kernel, reduces cooking time, and improves the final texture. During the boiling phase, the heat will transfer quicker to the center and the rice will be done six to eight minutes faster, causing the least amount of damage to the outside of the delicate kernels. Soaking can be done outside the cooker, or in the rice cooker bowl with the cover closed before turning on the machine. In fuzzy logic machines, a short soak period is automatically timed in all but the Quick Cook cycle.

Boiling the Rice

Rice needs to cook in hot water in order to get additional moisture into the rice and transfer the heat necessary to gelatinize the starch in rice. When you turn on your rice cooker, it begins to slowly heat the contents of the rice bowl. Soon the water boils and the grains of rice begin absorbing water; you will hear the rice and water start to bubble in the machine. (In fuzzy logic rice cookers, there is a built-in Soak cycle for the rice, designed to help it absorb water better. In that case, it may appear to take a long time for the water to boil. Don't worry. When the time is right, the cooker will kick into high gear and boil the water.)

It takes about 15 minutes in boiling water to get water and heat absorbed into the center of the rice kernel. If you look inside the cooker during this period, you will see semi-cooked rice with steam holes over the surface. These are caused by pockets of water vapor that were formed on the pan bottom and have risen to the surface. The water bubbles in the cooker until the temperature exceeds 212°F, then the cooker shuts off. The temperature of water cannot exceed 212°F, so the cooker knows all the water is gone when the temperature hits a few degrees higher. (This is the secret to how the cooker knows the rice is ready.) Do not remove the cover at this time.

Steaming the Rice

In the new on/off and fuzzy logic cookers, the steaming period is built into the regular cooking cycle, and the Keep Warm cycle is an extended low-heat steaming period. In simpler models, you set a timer or note the time. The rice cooker switches from the cooking cycle to the Keep Warm cycle (or, in simple on/off machines, simply shuts off). But your rice isn't finished yet. Now is when the all-important steaming process takes place.

Steaming is a key part of the cooking process. It allows further cooking of the rice without any swelling damage to the starch inside the grain. Ten minutes of steaming is adequate for most models of rice cooker and most rices; if your rice still seems wet at the end of 10 minutes, wait and check at 5-minute intervals. When the steaming period ends, uncover the rice cooker and stir or fluff the rice thoroughly but gently with a wooden or plastic rice paddle or wooden spoon. Replace the cover if you are not serving the rice immediately. Rice is not done until the center of each grain is completely cooked, which is achieved during the final steaming period. The result: perfectly cooked rice. Most rice is perfectly cooked when its moisture content is between 58 and 64 percent, though the final moisture content is a matter of preference and differs with every type of rice. Some fuzzy logic machines have a setting for regular, soft, and firm textures, varying the amount of moisture in the rice. The more water per cup of rice, the longer the machine will cook the rice.

Machines without a Keep Warm cycle just turn off when the regular cycle is finished. You let the rice steam for the specified time after the machine shuts off. There is enough retained heat to accomplish the steaming. You can hold the rice in the machine for as long as it stays warm, certainly for an hour, but the exact time depends on the machine, its size, and how full it is. This is a place where you have to use your judgment.

On the front of each rice cooker body is the cooking control panel. There are only two distinctly different faces to the multitude of rice cookers: One is the simple on/off machine that has a manual cooking indicator switch and prominent power indicator light; the other is the digital face of the fuzzy logic cookers, which has a clock and buttons in place of the switch used in the cook-and-shut-off cookers, cook-and-keep-warm cookers, and electronic cookers. Here is a simplified guide to these controls. As always, carefully read your manufacturer's manual to familiarize yourself with your particular machine.

On/Off Cookers

The on/off cookers have a switch that can be clicked into an up or down position—down being the On or Cook cycle and up being the Off or Keep Warm cycle. Both positions snap securely into place. Cook and Keep Warm both deliver a constant heat, although at two different temperatures: On is the high temperature and Keep Warm is the low temperature.

The power indicator light is lit as soon as the machine is plugged in, and the machine immediately heats up depending on which position the switch is in. There may be a secondary indicator light labeled Cook or Keep Warm, the easy visual for identifying immediately where the switch is set. The Cook position equates to the regular cycle in the fuzzy logic machines. To cook rice, you must press the switch down to Cook; when the cooker senses the rice is done, it will automatically snap to the up, or Keep Warm, position. It will hold on the Keep Warm position until you unplug the machine (which you must do to turn it off). Note that the least expensive cookers do not have a Keep Warm feature.

Digital-Face Cookers

You can immediately recognize the modern digital face and display clock of the fuzzy logic and induction heating rice cookers. The digital control panel, manipulated with buttons (also referred to as keys), will vary slightly from brand to brand, but they all have basically the same features. You will have a main Cooking/Reheat button, one for Keep Warm (which can be used to reset the program by stopping the cycle at any point). You may have a button for an Extended Keep Warm cycle on models in which the regular Keep Warm is designed for only the first three hours after rice is made. The Timer button can be used to trigger the memory capabilities of the machine and preset the timer for starting the machine automatically. Refer to your manufacturer's manual for the specific steps for setting the timer. Remember that your rice will be soaking while waiting for the machine to turn on. To prevent spoilage, never leave rice soaking in a meat or poultry broth or with perishable ingredients.

All the buttons/keys have their own indicator lamp to visually cue you where the machine is in the cycle. Only one indicator lamp will be lit at one time. The first few times you might be a bit awkward getting the sequence to program the keys, but once you get the hang of setting the controls on your machine, you will find it a smooth and almost automatic procedure.

Keep Warm Cycle

When the rice is done, both the on/off and fuzzy logic machines will automatically switch to the constant low temperature of the Keep Warm mode, designed to be a nice temperature for serving. On the fuzzy logics, there may be a digital record of how long the rice has been on Keep Warm from the end of the cooking cycle, given in units of hours. In machines with a two-cycle Keep Warm function, the Keep Warm cycle will automatically shut off after three hours, or you can stop the machine by pressing the button (the light will go out). In these machines, the light for the Keep Warm goes out at the end of the time period, the Extended Keep Warm clicks in, and an even lower set temperature will take over for an additional eight hours. In some machines, at the end of the eight hours, the machine will automatically switch back to the Keep Warm cycle. You can press Extended Keep Warm at any time and press Keep Warm to prepare the rice for eating. In the on/off machines, the Keep Warm is on until you unplug the machine.

These cycles are based on cooking medium-grain white rice. Be sure to refer to specific recipes for the recommended amount of time to safely keep warm various types of rice and more complex rice preparations. Even white rice will dry out or spoil when left for extended periods on Keep Warm. Dishes that include any type of meat, fish, beans, or vegetables should always be eaten as soon as possible after the cooking cycle is completed to avoid spoilage. Brown rice can sour when left on Keep Warm for more than an hour (especially in hot weather), and glutinous rice loses its desirable texture. The Keep Warm cycle also automatically clicks in after the Porridge cycle (see pages 10 and 11) has completed, but rice porridge, such as congee, should not be left on Keep Warm.

Menu

The Menu button is the first button you will press to make your choices for how your machine will cook your rice. It is automatically set for a white rice cycle. You select the desired texture (Regular—sometimes called Normal—Softer, Harder, Porridge, Quick Cook), and an audio signal will beep and a visual indicator signal will rotate counterclockwise through these positions as you press the button. The white rice button is sometimes labeled White/Brown, but some machines have separate settings for both brown rice and sushi rice, which need to be cooked to textures very different than regular white rice.

Regular/Softer/Harder

The machine is automatically set for regular (or normal) when the machine is plugged in. If you want something other than that, you will use the Menu button to set it. Regular is usually the setting for cooking white rice, brown rice, mixed rice, and glutinous rice. Softer is a good setting if you like your white rice a softer consistency. Harder is a good setting for rice that will be used in rice salads and other preparations, such as stuffings, where the rice will be further cooked with other ingredients.

Quick Cook Cycle

Some fuzzy logic rice cookers have a Quick Cook cycle as well as a regular cycle. The Quick Cook cycle bypasses the regular cycle's built-in soak time and is very convenient when you want rice in a hurry. It is also handy in one other situation: when you are sautéing ingredients in the rice cooker bowl. In this case, you want to program the cooker for the Quick Cook cycle when you are heating the oil or butter and sautéing the ingredients. Then when you are finished sautéing and are ready to add the liquid and proceed with the recipe, you have a choice. You may cancel the Quick Cook cycle and program whatever cycle is required for the recipe, the regular cycle or the Porridge cycle, for instance. Or, if the recipe does not require the Porridge cycle, you may simply let the Quick Cook cycle complete. In the Quick Cook mode, you cannot select the texture of the rice, so the texture may be slightly different than when you cook on the regular cycle.

Porridge Cycle

The fuzzy logic machines all offer a Porridge cycle designed to cook the staple savory rice breakfast porridge enjoyed throughout Asia. It has a medium-low, constant set temperature different than that for the regular cycle for white rices and the Keep Warm cycle. The on/off machines do not have this feature. For more information on the Porridge cycle capabilities, see the following page.

Reheat

Some fuzzy logic machines have a Reheat mode. The Reheat mode is on the same button as the main button for turning on the machine, labeled Cooking. It can be used to bring the rice that has been kept on the Keep Warm cycle, or leftover or refrigerated rice, back up to a hot serving temperature. (On machines without this feature, Keep Warm is serving temperature.) The machine will beep as soon as the right temperature is reached, usually about 5 to 10 minutes, then switch automatically to the Keep Warm mode. Most rice on Reheat, especially cold rice, needs a tablespoon or two of water per cup drizzled over it to rehydrate properly to a soft consistency. We recommend that you eat the rice as soon as the Reheat cycle indicates it is done rather than leave on Keep Warm (possibly for a second time) for the best consistency and to prevent a tough bottom layer from forming due to drying out.

THE PORRIDGE CYCLE

We had a big surprise during the testing of recipes in the electronic fuzzy logic rice cooker—we love the Porridge cycle. It is incredibly versatile. It was developed for perfect "rice porridge," a versatile and nourishing dish that is a staple in Asia, yet hardly prepared at all in Western kitchens. The gentle heat of the 45-minute cycle works well for the soupy Italian rice called risotto and for mushes like polenta, grits, and hominy, as well as hot breakfast cereals.

But the Porridge cycle is not limited to these savory preparations. It makes knockout applesauce, creamy tapioca, and rice pudding right in the rice bowl, as well as exceptional fruit desserts that are poached in a liquid bath. We think you will be pleasantly surprised.

While these foods are traditionally prepared on the stovetop, being able to make them in the rice cooker extends its capabilities to a more all-around appliance, a real boon if you are in a situation where you want to do your own cooking and there is no kitchen available. The other consideration is that this is a type of cooking that is completely unattended, with little risk of burning or overcooking. Consider the rice cooker in this capacity as a faster slow cooker. If all you have is the basic kind of rice cooker with the on/off switch, you can still make many of the recipes in this book that call for the Porridge cycle, with a bit more attention paid to the timing of the cooking process.

The Porridge cycle is easily set for a second time to extend cooking time when necessary. This eliminates the need to use the automatic timer. If you need only a portion of the cycle, just set a kitchen timer and then cancel the program. The cooking process will stop immediately and you can serve your wonderful dish.

RICE COOKER BASICS

Here are a few tips and basic pieces of information that will help you get the most from your rice cooker.

Our first bit of advice is to carefully review and read the manufacturer's little booklet that came with your rice cooker. Brands do differ. Orient yourself to the parts of the machine and the list of safety precautions. Then review the manufacturer's recipes for any that appeal to you. You can use the manufacturer's recipes, a recipe designed for the rice cooker on a package of rice or one using our convenient rice charts (pages 34, 42, and 50), or recipes from this book.

Measuring Up

Measuring the rice correctly is of crucial importance to achieving success in your rice cooker. Please read this section carefully before making your first pot of rice.

1. Don't throw away the little plastic measuring cup that came with your rice cooker. That measuring cup is the standard unit of measurement for your machine. When the little booklet that came with your rice cooker says to put in 2 cups of rice and add water to the "2-cup" level on the bowl, that means you are supposed to measure the rice *with that little cup*, not with one of your regular measuring cups. This is very important. *Throughout this book, we will refer to this unit of measurement as a "rice cooker cup."*

We must say we were a bit surprised by these measuring cups. Even the ones that come with very expensive rice cookers are made from thin, translucent plastic and seem almost like an afterthought. Don't be fooled. These measuring cups are essential. A rice cooker cup measures out to 180 milliliters (about 6 ounces or ¾ of a U.S. cup) and a standard U.S. cup holds 240 milliliters, so there is a difference. Measuring with this special cup may seem awkward at first, but you will quickly get used to it.

2. In this book, many of our recipes, especially the Asian-style ones and the measurement charts for plain rice, use the rice cooker cup form of measurement. Other recipes use standard U.S. cups. We always specify the difference. But even when we measure rice with the rice cooker cup, we measure liquids using the U.S. standard cups and ounces. Why? We've found it most convenient to keep our rice cooker cups clean, dry, and ready to use with rice and other grains. It's also difficult to measure liquids (especially larger quantities) precisely with the little cups.

3. Rice cooker directions are beginning to appear on the back of packages of rice, especially on brands that are marketed to Asian-American consumers. In all of the examples that we found, the directions were given in terms of rice cooker cups, even if the directions just said "cups". This is frequently also the case for rice cooker recipes that you find on the Internet.

4. In case you lose your special rice cooker measuring cup, or prefer otherwise, you can measure both your raw rice and water with a standard U.S. measuring cup with excellent results. This is the case with many of the more complex rice recipes in this book.

5. If a friend shares a rice cooker recipe with you, it's a good idea to ask, in the case of both solid and liquid ingredients, "Is this in rice cooker cups or regular U.S. cups?"

Making That First Pot of Rice in Your Rice Cooker

Your first look at the rice cooker can be a bit confusing, especially with the digital face on a fuzzy logic machine. But the procedure is exactly the same with all models: Choose a recipe, assemble your ingredients, measure and wash the rice, load the rice bowl, add the water, close the cover, plug it in, and press the button. Here are the details.

1. Measure the desired amount of rice. Don't mound the rice in the measuring cup—level it off with a sweep of your finger or a table knife. For reference, 1 pound of raw rice is equal to a bit more than 3 rice cooker cups.

2. Some cooks swear by coating the rice bowl with a film of nonstick cooking spray or 1 teaspoon vegetable oil to prevent sticking and keep the rice grains a bit more separate (especially brown rices); while some of our recipes call for this step when applicable, it is purely optional.

3. If desired, rinse or wash the rice, or follow the instructions in each specific recipe for any presoaking, depending on the type of rice. Many cooks wash the rice right in the rice cooker bowl, even though the instructions that come with many machines say not to. (If you choose to do this, and we frequently do, we promise not to tell.)

4. Place the drained rice in the bowl of your rice cooker; if the rice is wet, you may need a rubber spatula to get all of the grains out of the bowl. Place the bowl into the body of the rice cooker machine. With your hand or your rice spatula, spread out the rice into a fairly flat layer over the entire bottom surface of the bowl. This helps it cook evenly.

5. Measure and add the required amount of cold liquid to the bowl. Use bottled or filtered water rather than tap water for the best tasting rice. You can use the lines on the inside of the rice cooker bowl as a guide. If you have put in 1 rice cooker cup of rice, add water to the "1" line. More elaborate rice cookers (especially the fuzzy logic models) often have several sets of lines on the bowl, indicating the amount of water needed for regular rice, "soft" rice, "hard" rice, brown rice, sushi rice, or rice porridge. Follow the correct line for the type of rice you are making. If you choose to measure the rice in U.S. dry measuring cups, of course the lines on the bowl will not apply. You will add liquid measured in a U.S. measuring cup according to the recipe you have selected.

Many people, especially those raised in Asian households, swear by the finger-measuring method. Plop in the desired amount of rice, smooth it out, and add water until the level comes to the first knuckle on your index finger, with your fingertip just touching the surface of the rice. Many experienced rice cooks measure in this manner, a relatively constant level (about ½ inch) of water above the level of the rice, regardless of the quantity of rice.

Some people like their rice a little bit softer; some, a little bit harder. As you become an experienced rice cooker owner, you will develop your own preferences. If you want softer rice, you'll add a bit more water; for firmer rice, you'll add a bit less.

Add salt, if called for in the recipe, give the mixture a swirl with your finger or a rice paddle, and close the cover.

6. Plug in the unit and arrange the cooker on your counter away from the wall and out from under the cabinets so the steam can escape the vent without hindrance.

7. On fuzzy logic machines, choose the regular White Rice/Brown Rice cycle, then press Cooking/Cook. On the cook-and-keep-warm or cook-and-shut-off machines, simply press down on the switch. No peeking, please! The hot steam inside the machine is what is cooking the rice; open the cover and the moisture is lost as the steam evaporates, and the moderate pressure and heat that have naturally built up will dissipate in an instant cloud. The rice cooker uses the same principles and process of cooking as a covered pot on the stove: You boil the mixture until all of the water is evaporated or absorbed. The main advantage of a rice cooker is that it knows when to stop cooking automatically, thanks to a sensitive built-in thermostat rather than your judgment, and prevents the scorching normally associated with stovetop methods.

8. The steaming period at the end of the cooking cycle is *crucial* to your success. It is the time when the rice "rests" and any extra liquid is absorbed. In fuzzy logic cookers, this period is often automatically programmed in. When the finish "beep" sounds, the rice is really done, steaming and all. In on/off cookers, you must listen for the "click" when the machine switches off the cooking cycle and into its Keep Warm cycle. (In very inexpensive on/off cookers, there is no Keep Warm mode. The rice will rest, covered, for the specified time in the machine.) Set a timer or note the time on a piece of paper. For the best textured rice, it is advisable to let the cooked rice rest for 10 to 15 minutes after the cooking cycle has ended with a small or medium rice cooker,

15 to 20 minutes with a large one. This rest period gives the rice time to settle and absorb a bit more moisture, softening the starch a bit further.

9. When the "resting" period is over, open the cooker cover and stir the rice thoroughly but gently with a wooden or plastic rice paddle, or a wooden spoon. If you are not ready to serve the rice, re-cover or close the lid immediately to keep it warm on the Keep Warm cycle, if your model has one.

10. Enjoy eating your perfectly cooked rice!

Cleanup

It is recommended that all parts of the rice cooker be washed by hand, not in a dishwasher. Even with cooked-on rice, a quick soak in cold water has always been all that is needed to quickly clean the bowl. The most simple machines have an uncoated aluminum bowl. If your bowl has a Teflon or SilverStone nonstick coating, use a sponge or plastic scrubber that will not scratch its surface. The machine housing only needs a sponge-down after unplugging; it should never be immersed in water.

HOW TO USE THIS BOOK

This is a book dedicated to recipes that can be made in electric rice cooker machines. It is important to note that there are many models of rice cookers but just two basic styles: the on/off and fuzzy logic machines. Many of the following recipes can be made in either type of machine, but some can be made only in one or the other. If you are not sure what type of machine you have, refer to page 2. Before starting a recipe, please check to make sure you have the type

A special feature in the more sophisticated on/off and fuzzy logic machines is that after the machine has run a complete cycle, it will automatically switch to a Keep Warm cycle, which is a lower temperature than the Cook cycle. While this is not a feature of the simplest on/off machines, the more elaborate ones do have it. However, remember that to turn off the machine, you must unplug it or remove the rice bowl.

While this is a purely optional step, it is convenient if you have not heard the beep signaling the end of the cycle, or you are not quite ready to serve your rice. The booklet that came with your rice cooker will tell you how long you may hold plain rice on the Keep Warm cycle. On most models, it will be 4 to 12 hours. (There may be an Extended Keep Warm button as well.) Plain white rice can take the full period no problem, but some specialty brown rices (like Riz Rouge, page 55) should not be held longer than one hour, as they will begin to sour. Most of our recipes call for a rest at the end of the entire cooking cycle; we find the extra time makes for a better bowl of rice. If you turn off the machine and leave the rice in the cooker with the cover closed, the rice will still stay gently warm for a couple of hours.

of machine recommended for that recipe. For more information on the cycles, refer to page 8.

A note about machine sizes: In addition to information about machine type, each recipe is labeled with a size of rice cooker: small (4-cup), medium (6-cup), or large (10-cup). The size given is the one that works best for the recipe. In many cases, though, you can adjust the recipe for a smaller or larger rice cooker by increasing or decreasing ingredients. However, do not exceed the manufacturer's stated capacity for your machine.

The Regular Cycle

In the recipes, the regular cycle refers to the basic cooking program for the on/off and fuzzy logic machines. To begin the regular cycle in the on/off machine, you press or flip the switch to the Cook position. To begin the regular cycle in the fuzzy logic machines, you program for the regular/Brown Rice cycle by pressing that button. The Quick Cook program is an abbreviated cycle of the regular cycle on the fuzzy logic machines.

The recipes in the following chapters can be made in both types of machines, but for the best results, be sure to check the key information at the top of the recipe regarding the machine size and Keep Warm limits.

The Perfect Pot of Rice
Simple Everyday Rices and Little Meals
The Family of Pilafs
The Whole-Grain Cooker
Sushi
Beans and Legumes

The Porridge Cycle

The Porridge cycle is an exclusive feature of the fuzzy logic machines. While we have found that many of the recipes in the chapters listed below can be made in the on/off machines using the regular cycle on the Cook position (check each recipe), the results are not as satisfactory as on the Porridge cycle. This is because the on/off machines run at a higher temperature that maintains a full rolling boil and, if there is a lot of liquid in the recipe, such as for risotto, the machine will not automatically turn off. The Porridge cycle has a longer, more gentle simmer. For the best results, be sure to check the key information at the top of the recipe regarding machine size to avoid boilover.

Risotto

Polenta, Grits, and Hominy

Hot Breakfast Cereals and Porridges

Sweet Puddings and Fruit Desserts

Steaming in the Rice Cooker

Unless foods are placed directly on top of the rice, steaming is a feature that works best in the on/off machines. We recommend the large (10-cup) cooker fitted with a steamer plate in the bottom of the bowl, an insert tray, or a set of stacked steamer baskets for most of these recipes.

The fuzzy logic machines with their attached covers do not have the wide range of steamer capabilities of the on/off machines. For the best results, please carefully read the hints for successful steaming on page 7 before making the recipes in the following chapters.

Vegetables in the Rice Cooker

Whole-Meal Steam Cuisine

Dim Sum, Dolmas, and Tamales:
    Little Bites

Custards and Steamed Puddings

the perfect
POT OF RICE

Buddha is said to have existed on one grain of cooked rice per day while on his early ascetic path. His mendicant disciples are given the credit for the spread of the rice culture, along with its cooking pots, making rice basic fare throughout Southeast Asia and China. For the Buddhists, this set the atmosphere to imbue the grain with the power for supernatural nourishment (thus making rice the food of alms throughout Asia) as well as a simply wholesome foodstuff (the first food an Indian bride serves her new husband). Japanese Zen Buddhists have lent the name "little Buddha" to each grain in their rice bowls; children love the association.

The gentleman-scholar Confucius, a contemporary of Buddha, was known as the apostle of virtuous living and a gourmet. He is said to have established the philosophical basis for today's Chinese cuisine: food that combines the attributes of fine sensory aesthetics with inner harmony. His meticulously prepared daily rice bowl, always perfectly white, would be the background for the jewel-like colors of contrasting or similarly hued complementary foods, served in a bowl that was also a work of notable artistry. This is the ancestry of the rice, cooked in basically the same manner, that graces our tables today.

Rice, the most popular grain in the world, comes in a wide variety of textures, colors, sizes, and tastes. It is grown in every temperate and tropical zone on this earth. The explosion of interest in traditional ethnic cuisines, from Asian to Middle Eastern cooking, has introduced a staggering array of different types of rices to the home cook. After cooking, some rices are dry, with each grain delightfully separate, while others are moist and sticky. All types can be cooked successfully in a rice cooker. Of all existing species of rice in the plant world, only two types have been cultivated. One is native to the African continent and the other, *Oryza sativa*, is indigenous to Asia. This latter species is the rice that the world eats, knows, and loves. There have been tens of thousands of varieties, cultivated and cross-cultivated off the early ones, over a multitude of centuries.

There are two distinctly different shapes of *Oryza sativa*. One is long and slender, known as *indica*, or long-grain rice. The other is short, plump, and more translucent, known as *japonica*, or short-grain. Once you have these two types set in your mind, you have the key to knowing the basics about rice. Within each type of rice, there are many varieties. While some people think that rice is just rice, so very many traditional dishes call for a specific rice in their preparation. *Indica* (for India) is the grain of choice for pilafs, a favorite Western rice dish. It is low-starch rice and cooks up dry, with each grain separate from the others. This is the preferred rice for salads and a pile of plain old hot rice and butter for dinner. Long-grain rice can be rather bland, like extra-long Carolina gold, or aromatic, like Thai jasmine and Indian basmati. Long-grain rice always requires more liquid to cook properly than medium- and short-grain white rices. Long-grain rices are popular in all cuisines of the Western world and are the rice of choice in India, China, and the Philippines.

Japonica (for Japan) includes short- and medium-grain rices. While Americans make a distinction between short- and medium-grain rices, please note that outside the United States these rices are both known as short-grain rice. These are the rices grown in Southeast Asia, Korea, and Japan and are generally not exported. The University of California at Davis developed the variety of medium-grain rice so beloved by Japanese-Americans, called Calrose, and a good portion of the California rice-growing land north of Sacramento is devoted to this and similar varieties of rice. The finest short- and medium-grain domestic rices are such superior rices that we were told they are brought as house gifts when visiting in Japan.

Short-grain rice is known for its clumpy, clingy nature, perfect for eating with chopsticks, and often eaten only when dining at a Japanese restaurant. It is beautifully made at home in the rice cooker, giving your sushi or Japanese recipes that wonderful authentic touch. There is also a short-grain sticky rice, also known as sweet rice (it is not sugar-sweet) or glutinous rice. This is a specialty rice eaten in Japan, parts of southern China, and the mountainous northern areas of Indonesia, Thailand, and Vietnam, where it is rolled into balls and popped into the mouth. This type of rice is usually steamed, rather than boiled like other rices, because it is mercilessly sticky otherwise. It is also used in rice desserts and porridge.

Different varieties of *japonica* rice are grown in northern Italy, France, and Spain. These have plenty of the starch amylopectin and are featured in traditional dishes of each area, risotto and paella respectively. Medium-grain rice is the rice of choice in the Caribbean, Central America, and Japan. Medium- and short-grain rices are nice for rice pudding, giving it a thick, naturally creamy consistency.

Rices are further categorized by how each is processed. Plain white rice, whether long-, medium-, or short-grained, is processed, or milled, by a procedure called polishing. The bran and germ are removed (hulled) to make the grain more digestible and faster to cook. It is then enriched by spraying it with thiamine, which is lost when the bran is discarded. Thiamine is needed for the proper metabolizing of carbohydrates and iron.

Brown, or unhulled, rice is a whole grain, with its bran and outer layer of fiber intact. It has all the vitamins and minerals rice has to offer. Because of the oil-rich bran, it is best kept refrigerated or frozen, rather than on the cupboard shelf, where it can go rancid. Brown rice will always take at least twice the amount of time to cook as white rice.

In the United States, more and more specialty rice varieties are being grown for niche markets. There are several varieties of rice that have been developed to perform like the imported white Thai jasmine and

Indian basmati. There are several varieties of rice that have unusual bran colors like Wehani, red rice, and black rice, all technically considered brown rices.

Converted rice is long-grain white rice that has been parboiled and dried before refining. It is an excellent, firm white rice; do not confuse it with instant rice. We don't usually use minute rice or instant rice, which is completely precooked and dehydrated. Cooking up quite mushy, instant rice just cannot compare with fresh-cooked white rice. But if you are backpacking or traveling (and cooking in your motel room), instant rice has its place.

There is a place for every type of rice in the home kitchen. No rice is better or worse than another; it is totally dependent on your own palate. "Rice is a live thing," says Ken Lee, co-owner of Lotus Foods, a specialty rice import company with its headquarters in El Cerrito, California. "You have to pay attention since every rice can vary from time to time." This accounts for the rice you make every day looking, behaving, and tasting just that little bit different, even though you made it the same way you always do. If you buy rice in bulk, note the proportions of liquid to rice that worked best for that batch and be prepared to reassess the recipe when you buy your next batch of rice. Variables include the time of year, how old the rice is, what grade you bought, and how the rice was stored; it changes all the time.

When buying or evaluating rice, you want to look at the color of the grains; they should be pearly (for white rice) or shiny (for red or black rice) or evenly tan (for brown rice). The grains should be the same size, without a lot of broken grains or milling bits in the bag (and certainly no bugs!). Judge the aroma of both the uncooked and cooked grain; every single rice will have a different fragrance, from floral, grassy, nutty, or herbaceous to earthy and musty. The aroma will blossom and intensify after cooking into a bouquet of sorts. Some rices lose their aroma as they cool. Then there is the final texture, which is dictated by the amount of water absorbed during the cooking; some people like chewy rice, others like it mushy. And, finally, judge the overall flavor of each rice. Sweet and nutty to wholesome and bland, each rice is an adventure to the palate.

Every recipe in this book will specify what type of rice is needed, so you won't have to wonder when a recipe says "rice" what it means. Keep your cupboard stocked with different rices and, before you know it, you will be a bona fide rice lover with a vast repertoire of different rices that are less than an hour away from serving.

LONG-GRAIN RICES

The kernel of long-grain rice is slender and about four times as long as it is wide.

Carolina Long-Grain Rice

Carolina gold, America's long-grain *indica* rice, was first grown in the waterlands of North and South Carolina during the eighteenth century. It is also known as southern long-grain. Dozens of varieties of this rice have been developed. This is the most common type of rice consumed in the United States—and the world—as a table rice, beloved for its dry, separate grains and bland sweet-grain flavor. After the destruction of the Civil War, growing shifted to

Every time you cook a pot of rice, you are making mental notes about amylose and amylopectin, the two components of starch found in rice, even though you probably don't know it. Long-grain rices like Carolina and basmati, with a dry texture, have a high level of amylose and low levels of amylopectin; amylose is a waxy starch that sets up into a stiff gel in the grain during cooking, so you end up with dry, separate grains. The raw grains of long-grain rices look translucent; a bit of light shines through.

Medium- and short-grain rices have the opposite balance; they are low in amylose and high in amylopectin (think "pectin" like the plant substance that helps fruits jell). Rices low in amylose are sticky and creamy when cooked, like Arborio and Calrose, because the starch does not set up during the cooking; when you look at the raw grains they have a more solid, opaque, pearly essence.

Between the shape and the color, with a little practice, you can identify every rice, even if it's not in its identifying packaging.

Texas on the Gulf of Mexico, Arkansas, the Missouri riverbeds, and the Louisiana Mississippi delta, all areas with a specific type of soil and moisture perfect for rice growing, where its cultivation flourishes to this day. The top producers are Arkansas, then Texas, and the northern Central Valley of California. Some brands will have the state of origin on the bag (look at the address in the small print on the side of the bag), others will be generically labeled "long-grain rice." There are slight differences among varieties, and many varieties are kept separate for special processing like parboiling (converted rice), while similar rices are mixed and packaged under the generic label by super-companies like Uncle Ben's and Riviana (Mahatma). American long-grain rice is good for casseroles, side dishes, curries, pilafs, jambalaya, salads, chili, stuffings, and waffles.

Asian Long-Grain Rice

Part of the royal duties of Chinese princes was to plant the first grains of rice at the beginning of each growing season. In China, rice growing has been an agricultural passion for millennia, rivaling that of India. In Mandarin, a bowl of plain rice is known as *fan*, or rice bowl rice. Asian long-grain rice is a slightly moist rice, but not sticky like Japanese medium- or short-grain, or dry and separate, like Indian basmati or converted rice. It is never aromatic. It is pure, simple rice at its most basic.

Inspect a pile of rice sacks in the corner of your Asian specialty market, labeled in Chinese, and this will be Asian-style long-grain rice. This is the rice called for in Chinese recipes, served in Chinese restaurants and for fried rice. It is the preferred rice in China, Taiwan, and parts of Southeast Asia. Little of this rice is exported, so unless you shop in Asian grocery stores, any type of Carolina rice can be substituted.

Aromatic Long-Grain Rice

Known for their authentic floral-incense scents emitted during cooking, aromatic rices are exceptionally popular now for all-around cooking purposes. They were once served to Asian royalty and reserved for religious holidays. Varieties are now being grown domestically, but connoisseurs seek out the imported brands.

Basmati rice, which translates to the "queen of fragrance," is imported from the Indian Himalayan foothills of the Ganges Valley and Pakistan. Its distinctive flavor is an integral part of the cuisine of India and is said to be the result of the combination of the Himalayan headwaters and the soil of the Punjab, the famous ancient valleys of the Indus River and its tributaries (the best grade still comes from this region). Fine basmati commands high prices. This rice has a high amylose content and a firm, almost dry, texture when properly cooked. The raw kernel is long and slender like southern long-grain, but is slightly smaller, and the kernels increase in length by more than three times when cooked to produce a very long, slender cooked grain. The best Indian basmati has been aged for at least one year (with no broken grains in the bag) to increase the firmness of the cooked texture and increase the elongation achieved in cooking. It is simply one of the finest rices grown, with a rich flavor, and is perfect for pilafs, curry, *biryani*, casseroles, and sweet puddings. It is a great all-purpose rice. Excellent brands include Pari, Daawat, and Tilda, although if you shop in Indian gro-

ceries, the bags can also be labeled by the area in which the rice is grown.

Thai jasmine has a lovely muted floral quality akin to the scent of tropical flowers (hence the name) and is more nut-sweet than basmati; it is the second most popular aromatic rice in America. While classified as a long-grain rice and looking much like Carolina rice before and after cooking, it contains the same amount of moisture as medium-grain rice and cooks up more similar to that type. The national rice of Thailand, it is ever so slightly sticky and tender compared to basmati. The rice is best consumed after the new crop is harvested, as the rice hardens in texture and loses aroma with time. There are many varieties being grown in the United States in imitation of this unique type of rice, with Jasmati being the best offshoot of the lot. There is now a Texas-grown domestic organic jasmine (both white and brown) available from Lowell Farms that is a must for jasmine rice lovers. The first American-grown jasmine is marketed in cloth sacks by Della, and grown in the delta areas of Arkansas and Missouri. For a lovely salad, steep a jasmine tea bag in the cooking water for a few minutes before you make a pot of jasmine rice. Jasmine is not the traditional Chinese rice, but today many Chinese-American consumers are making the switch. Good brands are Mahatma, Pacific International (formerly Homai), and Tilda, labeled Riz Parfumé.

Calmati, Texmati, Kasmati, and *Jasmati* are all domestic offshoots of the wonderful but more intensely flavored aromatics. Calmati is an Indian basmati crossed with regional varieties of Carolina long-grain grown in California. Texmati, a Texas long-grain basmati adapted to the area, was bred twenty years ago by RiceTec, Inc., and was the first grain in their line of hybrids. Texmati is part of RiceSelect's Royal Blend, a combination of white and brown Texmati with scarified wild rice, so that all the types cook in the same amount of time. Kasmati rice has a stronger aroma and firmer center of the grain, which is visible upon inspecting the individual grains. These three rices have basmati's viscosity and cooking style, but smaller individual grains. Jasmati is Texas-grown Carolina long-grain rice crossed with Thai jasmine rice and our favorite of these aromatic offshoots; it cooks up softer, is snowy white, fragrant, and stays moist longer under refrigeration. It is recommended for rice puddings. All of these rices cook very quickly, like other long-grain white rices, with some rest time on the Keep Warm steam cycle at the end to set the starch. Look for RiceSelect brand, the marketing arm of RiceTec, Inc., formerly the Farms of Texas Company, the largest private rice research and plant breeding company in the United States. Located in the "rice belt" south of Houston, which covers an area from El Campo to Beaumont on the Gulf of Mexico, RiceTec contracts with small local farmers to grow their proprietary seed (the farms are in various locations to avoid total crop devastation in case of tropical storms). A 14-ounce box contains 2 cups of raw rice.

Della rice is our homegrown American aromatic basmati grown in Arkansas, the landlocked area that is not a river delta but the Mississippi River basin, a prairie that is known for how well it holds water, irrigated by extensive ground wells. Decades ago, Lehman Fowler of the Southern Rice Marketing company planted a variety of Indian basmati seed that he adapted for growing conditions in the United States. It is marketed as a white and brown rice under the Della Gourmet trademark of Specialty Rice, Inc. (an offshoot of the now defunct Southern Marketing), along with domestic Arkansas jasmine, Texas Arborio, and domestic Koshi Hikari Japanese rice. Della basmati cooks up nice and dry with distinct grains and is a popular variety to cross with other rices (the different seed stock relatives of Della all have names like Delmont and Delrose, with slightly different characteristics). It is subtle, but still has that nutty basmati taste that is easy to eat alone. Della basmati has been nicknamed "popcorn rice." The most notable American rice offshoots from the Della seed stock are Wild Pecan rice and Louisiana popcorn rice, both with the same faint characteristic perfume.

SHORT- AND MEDIUM-GRAIN RICES

The kernel of medium-grain rice is oblong and two to three times as long as it is wide. This is the standard rice to use for dessert rice puddings. The kernel of short-grain rice is almost round, but slightly oval, and almost as long as it is wide. It is also referred to as pearl rice. Short-grain white rice is rare to find. When the topic is Asian-style rices, the terms "medium-grain" and "short-grain" are used almost interchangeably. These rices are a must for sushi and rice balls.

American Rice

California-grown Calrose, a medium-grain *japonica* type rice, is the most commonly available medium-grain variety on the West Coast; in the East, southern medium-grain rice from Carolina is on store shelves.

Calrose is typically the lowest priced Japanese-style rice, but its popularity stems from more than its affordability. Like other Japanese-style rices, it has a smooth, moist texture that holds together nicely for chopsticks, and its soothing, mild flavor goes well with spicy foods. This is the rice some people make three times a day fresh for meals, eaten alone, without flavoring. In terms of a bland, clean taste, this rice is probably the best in the world. The kernels cling together and have

RICE AND OTHER COMMERCIAL GRAIN MIXES IN THE RICE COOKER

The number and variety of commercial rice and grain mixes on the shelf of the average American supermarket is astonishing and, in many cases, so is their high quality. Almost every producer of rice has a line of rice plus flavoring mixtures designed for "extra-quick" meals. You can have a mellow pilaf, a robust brown rice blend, or even a satisfyingly spicy jambalaya on the table in the amount of time it takes to cook plain rice, with no chopping and only minimal cleanup.

We tested a dozen of the more than 100 rice and grain mixes we found at a local market. All cooked up beautifully in the rice cooker, except a risotto mix that spattered all over the counter when made on the regular cycle. If you want to make a risotto mix in the rice cooker, do so only on the Porridge cycle of a fuzzy logic machine.

Here are some of our favorite brands and flavor offerings:

■ **Zatarain's New Orleans Style Jambalaya Mix**, which was spicy and satisfyingly hearty. We followed a suggestion on the package and added a pound of sliced smoky sausage (we used turkey sausage).

■ **Near East Toasted Almond Pilaf Mix**, an old favorite that includes orzo pasta, pearled wheat, and almonds along with the rice. This one is buttery and mildly spiced, and it's a bit chewy because of the wheat.

■ **Casbah Nutted Pilaf Mix**, which enriches plain rice with a surprisingly extravagant variety of nuts: cashews, almonds, pine nuts, and pistachios.

■ The San Francisco Treat, **Rice-A-Roni**, in Herb and Butter flavor. This mellow rice and pasta mix is flecked with parsley. The package directions call for two extra steps: a short sauté of the rice and pasta before the water is added and stirring in the seasonings at the end. We sautéed right in the rice cooker bowl and stirred in the seasonings before the steaming period.

■ We liked the bright color, aroma, and flavor of **Mahatma Saffron Yellow Seasonings & Long Grain Rice**, which is sold in a yellow foil tube. But a comforting tongue appeal. In a pinch, Calrose can be used for sushi (the better brands of Calrose rice can be quite good). One we like, with wide distribution, is Pacific International (formerly Homai).

Calrose was the first Japanese-style rice available in this country, developed by the Rice Development research specialists of the University of California at Davis. It is one of two or three similar varieties grown in California. This rice needs a special temperate climate and is grown only in a few places in the world, including Japan, Korea, Australia, and some countries around the

that bright yellow color left a ring on the bowl of one of our inexpensive cookers. This mix did not stain bowls with nonstick coatings.

Here are some tips for preparing rice and grain mixes in the rice cooker:

■ When using a medium (6-cup) rice cooker, use the *same* amount of water called for on the package. In a small rice cooker (2- to 4-cup), start with $1/4$ cup *less* liquid; in a large cooker (10-cup), start with $1/4$ cup *more* liquid.

■ Put the water, rice, any butter or oil, and any seasonings from a separate packet into the rice cooker bowl. Program for the regular or Quick Cook cycle, remembering to let the rice steam for 15 minutes on the Keep Warm cycle before fluffing it with a wooden or plastic rice paddle or a wooden spoon. Some mixes (like Rice-A-Roni) call for adding the seasonings at the end of the cooking instead of the beginning; do this by stirring them in when the cooker shuts off or switches to Keep Warm.

■ If the resulting product is too chewy, add $1/4$ cup more water next time; if it is too wet for your taste, use $1/4$ cup less water next time. Keep a record of what works best for your favorite mixes. (If your rice cooker has a Keep Warm cycle, you can fix chewy rice on the spot. Just sprinkle the additional water over the rice, close the cover, and let the rice stay on Keep Warm for about 15 minutes more while the water is absorbed. Fluff the rice, then serve.)

■ If the mix you have selected has a sautéing step (like Rice-A-Roni), you can do this right in the rice cooker. Program the cooker for the regular or Quick Cook program and add the specified amount of butter or oil. When the butter is melted or the oil is hot, add the rice and sauté as directed on the package. Then add the liquid and allow the cooking cycle to complete as usual.

■ To cook two rice mixes at the same time, you will not need to quite double the water. Use $1/4$ cup less water for the second mix.

■ As noted above, cook risotto mixes on the Porridge cycle only. You may need an additional $1/4$ cup water to achieve the desired degree of creaminess.

Mediterranean Sea (see Italian Rice). There is no effort to keep the varieties separate during milling and storage in California, so each bag contains a mixture of California rices.

In Asian markets in the United States, where the customers really know rice, price is a good general guide to quality. In fact, at some specialty Asian markets in our own San Francisco Bay Area, the prices of different brands of rice are written on a white board, erased, and rewritten as the market changes. Picky Japanese-American cooks now have many more varieties from which to choose. At the top of the line are Tamaki Gold (our favorite!), Tamanishiki, and other "premium" brands; even in large bags, they can cost about $1 a pound. They are great for sushi or special meals. As your rice palate develops, buy a bag of this premium rice to see if you can taste the difference.

Next come popular but more everyday brands with more moderate prices. Kokuhu Rose, Konriko, Nishiki, and other "new variety" rices are delicious examples. The term "new variety" (not the same as "new crop") means it is a high-quality variety of American-grown Japanese-style rice. Many say "new variety" rice is better tasting than Calrose.

If you visit a Japanese market (in the U.S.) during the fall and winter months, you are likely to come across a display of banners proclaiming "New Crop Rice Is In." New crop rice is just what it sounds like: the fresh rice from the new harvest. This rice contains more of its natural moisture; use less water to cook it. How much less? Every bag is different, and your first cup of rice from every bag will be your test batch. A general guide is to start off with water about ¼ inch below the correct line on your rice cooker bowl (about 1 to 2 tablespoons less water per rice cooker cup of rice; 2 to 3 tablespoons less per U.S. cup of rice). If your rice ends up mushy, reduce the water further; if it's still too chewy at the core, increase the water.

Two coveted and expensive short-grain artisanal rices that were perfected in Japan over two thousand years ago, Koshi Hikari and Akita Komachi, have been planted successfully domestically. Koshi Hikari is being grown in Texas and marketed as sushi rice by RiceSelect and Della Gourmet. If you are a sushi lover or lover of fine Japanese food, you will want to try these short-grain rices. For more information, see Japanese Rice.

Southern medium-grain rice *appears* to be the same as California medium-grain rice, since its shape and amylose content are the same. But it is not, because it is an *indica* variety, rather than a *japonica*, hence the protein content is a little higher, and it takes longer to cook. If you prefer the Japanese-style medium-grain rices, you will find southern medium-grain rices unacceptable since they cook up drier. Southern medium-grain rice is not as white, not as moist or sticky, and not as clean tasting. This is the type of rice eaten in the southern United States, Louisiana, some parts of Latin America, and Puerto Rico, with black beans, jerked meats, and spicy Caribbean sauces. Good brands include Riceland Plump, Tender Southern Star, Water Maid, and Uncle Ben's Medium Grain (not a converted rice).

Italian Rice
Happily, Italian rice is widely imported today from the Po River region in northern

Italy, so an excellent risotto is moments away. Risotto must be made with an Italian-type rice to achieve the proper texture. The rice is intentionally overcooked (by more than 15 minutes). The resulting product has a creamy, starchy surface but a firm bite through the center. Don't rinse or wash Italian rice before cooking; the surface starch contributes to the creamy consistency of risottos, paellas, and puddings.

The most common Italian rice is Arborio, but there are two other lesser known regional varieties, Carnaroli and Vialone nano. Prevean Carnaroli, estate grown and milled in Argentina by the Preve Family of the Po River valley since 1905, is now being imported under the Lotus Foods brand. Arborio has a bigger kernel than regular medium-grain rice, with a distinct chalky center. Carnaroli is the most expensive of the triad and the most difficult to grow. Two domestic brands of Arborio, CalRiso by Lotus Foods and California Arborio by Lundberg, are grown in the Central Valley of California from *superfino* Arborio seed, and they are both delightfully delicious. Look for the word *superfino* on the package; it is the top grade.

Japanese Rice

Japanese rice is not usually exported but there is no lack of Japanese-style rices, since the American-grown varieties of these rices, like Calrose, are very popular and widely available. In California today there are several Japanese medium- and short-grain varieties being grown that are comparable to two of the most famous and coveted Japanese rices, Akita Komachi and Koshi Hikari, the seeds of which are now being cultivated in small crops in the United States as well (see page 26).

Just when we had resigned ourselves to the fact that there was no Japanese rice exported, Beth had a sighting at one of our local Japanese markets of the artisanal rice Koshi Hikari, which poetically translates to "rice offering to the gods." The price was steep: $30 for two kilograms (a little more than four pounds), about twice the price of Koshi Hikari rice in Japan. But, of course, we had to test it out in our rice cookers and have a taste.

Often called the best rice in Japan, Koshi Hikari is the name of the variety, and it is truly an artisan product, tended and processed with extra care in lots as small as three acres so as to protect the variety's reputation. A short-grain rice, it is grown in Nigata prefecture, a small coastal area in central Japan on the Sea of Japan that is renowned for the quality of its rice. We found beautiful rice-paper bags of Koshi Hikari rice for sale around January and New Year's, a prime season for gift-giving. It was delicious, a beautiful pearlescent oval, and very similar in flavor, texture, and style to our favorite U.S.-grown Japanese-style brand, Tamaki Gold. It is prepared in exactly the same way as other Japanese-style short- and medium-grain rices and is excellent for eating rice bowl style and for sushi.

If you want to try some of the world's best imported Koshi Hikari sushi rice, you can mail-order it from Williams-Sonoma under the label of Kumai Harvest.

Spanish Rice

Spanish-grown rice is labeled paella or Valencia rice *(arroz a la Valenciana)*. Cultivated on the Mediterranean coast of Spain in Valencia and the Ebro River delta, it is increasingly available in this country. Other medium-grain rices can be substituted beautifully for this rice.

The other well-known Spanish rice is the unique Calasparra. A large-grained *japonica* called *bomba*, because of its size, it is now readily available from Williams-Sonoma. It is expensive because it is grown only in one small region outside of Valencia, stamped with a *denominación del origin*, a region of origin, like the rices imported from Japan. It is considered an artisanal rice by gourmet standards and is used to make paella. Be prepared for it to soak up a lot of liquid, more than you have ever seen a rice absorb, needed to soften the grains.

Indian Rice

When shopping in an Indian foods market, we found an astonishing array of miniature grain rices imported from various areas of India. While unfamiliar to most American cooks, these rices have their own charm and uses in regional cooking. Kalijira is a miniature basmati-type medium-grain white rice imported exclusively by Lotus Foods, and is the diminutive rice that has crossed over into specialty supermarkets. Like all true basmatis, its little needle-like grain elongates as it cooks, but plumps like a medium-grain rice at the same time. It is an ancient strain grown in Bangladesh and is so expensive that it is reserved only for holiday meals in that country. It is also grown across the border in Bengal, India, where it is known as *gobindavog*. Use Kalijira for special pilafs and dessert puddings.

Egyptian Rice

Egyptian-grown rice is a medium-grain *japonica* cultivated in the marshy Nile waters and is used for Turkish-style pilafs. While the grains are smaller than those of Arborio, they look similar, but cook up more like Japanese-style medium-grain rice. Use the same proportions as for Wild Pecan Rice (page 55) and cook as for a pilaf using olive oil instead of butter. It is sold in Middle Eastern specialty food stores.

Sweet Rice

Sweet rice, also known as sticky, waxy, glutinous, pearl, or California mochi rice (it is known as *mochi gome* in Japan), is a real specialty item. These names are deceptive since sweet rice is only slightly sweeter than conventional rice, so most palates would not detect any sweetness. The nature of the starch is that it contains almost pure amylopectin (see page 21), so the rice is very sticky indeed. Sweet rice is a *japonica* rice and a small number of acres in California is dedicated to this variety. It is usually steamed and used to make Asian-style desserts, stuffings, and cakes. It is made into noodles and sake, or is ground into flour. A good brand is Honen sweet rice, which can be found in Asian markets and larger supermarkets.

BROWN RICES

Brown rice is the earthy sibling of white rice. It is the same grain as white rice, but is simply left unhulled, so it looks tan. Brown rice always takes at least twice the amount of time to cook as white rice and a bit more water since the grains needs to absorb more to soften. The thick bran layer is coated with

THE LUNDBERG FAMILY RICE FARM

Throughout this book you will see references to Lundberg rices. Lundberg Family Farms is situated in the northern Central Valley of California, smack-dab in the center of rice country in the shadow of Sutter Buttes. California is known for its remarkable rice crop yields, 25 percent higher than in any of the southern states, and Lundberg is the living proof of this; it operates on a relatively small total acreage of rice-growing land and produces a staggering amount of really good, consistently dependable rice. Still family owned and operated, the company sells some of the best tasting, and most diverse, rices in the country.

The company started in the late 1960s by selling 50-pound bags of their Natural Short-Grain Brown Rice off the back of a flatbed truck parked on the side of the road under the label of Wehah Farms (a combination of initials of the four brothers, Harlan, Weldon, Homer, Eldon, with their father). This same nutra-farmed short-grain brown rice is still their best seller today, along with their delicious long-grain brown rice. The brown rices are also available organically grown.

Harlan Lundberg is known for dabbling in exotic rices and has taken many rice-tasting trips to India. Obtaining seed of an Indian red rice from the seed bank in Aberdeen, Idaho (where 30,000 varieties of rice can sit waiting to be adopted for up to 20 years under refrigeration), he set to perfecting the rice marketed today as Wehani, an offshoot of the original farm name. He then went on to create the Black Japonica using parent stock from the Rice Research Station in Biggs, California, a seed bank owned by the California rice producers. His latest project is a speckled rice, still known as SP2, that looks like a pinto bean, a tasty red rice crossed with domestic southern long-grain. We can't wait to try it.

a waxy layer that is very difficult for moisture to penetrate; requirements for cooking and soaking times are dramatically increased, though the boiling/steaming cooking process remains the same. Because of these bran layers, brown rice has more fiber, which makes it chewy, with a great, distinctive flavor. Because of its retention of natural vitamins and minerals, this is the rice called for in special high-fiber and vegetarian diets. Since any pesticides and fungicides that are used during the growing remain as residue in the bran layer, many cooks seek out organic brands.

Natural brown rice comes in long-, medium-, and short-grain varieties, as well as a number of specialty and heirloom varieties. We found most aromatic varieties, like Wild Pecan rice and imported brown basmati, taste quite similar, while the California-grown brown rices are less complex but nuttier, although every bit as satisfying.

Short-grain brown rices include Lundberg's California-grown Natural Short-Grain

At this writing, there is no federal standard for organic rice. But there are several nonprofit and private organizations that certify rice, such as the California Certified Organic Farmers (CCOF). They have strict requirements and the public has learned to trust and respect their logos on organic products. The number of acres devoted to organic rice in the United States is very small in proportion to the number devoted to regular rice-growing practices, but is steadily growing. The field yields for organic rice are small and unpredictable, due to damage by insects and weeds, and average about half those of conventionally grown rice. Unless an artisan rice, most imported rices from Asia or India are not organic.

For rice to be certified organic by organizations such as the CCOF, the field used must be clean of the use of pesticides, herbicides, fertilizers, or any chemicals for three years before being marketed as an organic crop after harvest. Then the crop must be grown, harvested, stored, and milled under organic conditions, which means no nonorganic rice is processed at that facility without stringent cleaning of the equipment and separate storage units. It is very difficult to store organic rice and avoid insect problems without some sort of pesticide control. The final cost of milled organic rice is about three times that of conventional rice, but for purists, this is no deterrent. Since pesticide and fungicide residues would be found in the bran layer, brown rice is the most desirable crop for being organic. Polishing,

Brown Rice, Kokuho Rose Brown Rice, Calrose, and Hinode Brown Rice. Long-grain brown rices include imported brown basmati, domestic brown jasmine (from Lowell Farms), Lundberg Long-Grain Brown Rice, and brown Della and Texmati rices. Pacific International (formerly Homai) markets both California-grown grades. While the Japanese traditionally eat only white rice (given rations of brown rice, "poor people's rice," after World War II, locals polished the rice with their home milling equipment rather than eat brown rice), this is changing. At our last shopping visit to the Japanese market, there were stacks of 10- and 20-pound plastic bags of both long- and medium-grain organic California-grown brown rices, simply labeled as such.

Short- and medium-grain brown rices are good for casseroles, salads, dinner rice, stuffings, unorthodox sushi, and stir-fries. Long-grain brown rices are good in casseroles, fried rice, salads, soups, waffles and pancakes, side dishes, and pilafs.

Red Rice

There are dozens of red rices grown around the world, but they are relatively new to the American gourmet rice eater. Though technically a brown rice, instead of a brown hull, red rices have a pink to red to mahogany hull. Red rices cook in a manner similar to the process that makes white rice, disposes of the bran layer, leaving the pristine, undisturbed heart of the grain.

Enter sustainable agriculture. Sustainable agriculture practices growing foods without synthetic chemicals (insecticides, fungicides, and herbicides) and the soil is replenished with nutrients during the growing process. The new references to heirloom grain conservation describe the intentional cultivation and fostering of lesser known varieties of grain suited for human food by private plant breeders and mini-farmers with the goal of maintaining diversity. Having different characteristics than high-yield crops developed for long storage and mechanized harvesting techniques, heirloom crops are products of deliberately cultivated living gardens, often more flavorful and of different coloring and shape. Their gene pool is naturally resistant to disease and has adapted in the framework of a natural evolutionary cycle. These crops are described in terms of nutrition-per-acre rather than yield-per-acre. This is a language and way of looking at food production that will be gaining in acceptance and practice into the twenty-first century.

Despite these obstacles, we will be seeing a lot more delicious, organic rices, both white and brown, in the future, as the demand for untarnished foodstuffs continues to increase. Agricultural reform, in hand with a growing demand for these tasty, smaller yield heirloom grains, has made way for the Grain Revolution to flourish in your home kitchen. Seeds for Change Incan crop specialist Emigdio Ballon of New Mexico says it best: "The earth and the seeds, they represent life."

that of other brown or medium-grain rices, have a distinct nutty, almost popcorn-like aroma, and a distinct nutty flavor.

Wehani (an Indian red rice hybrid developed by Lundberg) is a plump long-grain red rice that has been improved to cook up less sticky than regular brown rices. Wehani and a rice called Richvale Red are mixed to make Lundberg's Christmas Blend. Lotus Foods imports a red rice from Bhutan and in some specialty markets you can find Thai red rice, South Indian red rice (*rosematta*), Vietnamese (cargo) red rice, and Himalayan red rice.

French red rice has a gourmet following and is often served in three-star restaurants. Planted in 1942 by the Chinese and Madagascarean military troops fighting in France, the marshy lands on the Mediterranean have been desalinated and developed into an artisan rice colony, with both medium-grain red and organic brown rices grown; at this writing, these rices are rarely imported. If you are traveling in Provence, France, you may encounter a red rice grown in the Rhône delta of the Camargue, *riz rouge de Camargue*.

Black Rice

Black and purple-black rices are considered brown rices because they are unhulled (underneath the hull they are white when polished), leaving the colored hull layers intact. While this color rice is highly unusual in America, there are hundreds of varieties of black rice in Asia. They are common in southern China, the highlands of Southeast Asia, Bali, and parts of Indonesia. Black rice is a *japonica*, so it cooks up sticky and is eaten with the fingers. It is also a familiar temple and festival offering for special religious holidays. Domestic Black Japonica (from Lundberg) was the first recognizable black rice in America; it has an assertive flavor, like that of wild rice. For that reason, Lundberg mixes it into blends such as Wild Blend and Gourmet Blend of 7 Brown Rices; they are not only delicious, but work beautifully in the rice cooker. Thai black rice, which is not really sticky, is not often seen in the United States; it is mixed with white rice and dyes the whole pot purple-black. Thai black rice is especially good for desserts. The newest black rice to be marketed in the U.S. is Forbidden Rice (China black), grown in Zhezhiang in northern China and imported by Lotus Foods. It has become popular as an alternative to regular white rice in California-style cuisine and restaurants. It is not a sticky rice, which makes this rice unique. It is a rice bowl rice and used to make congee, the beloved Chinese savory breakfast porridge.

A RECIPE FORMULA FOR EVERY RICE

The rice cooker is, in most cases, used exclusively for making plain white rices cooked in water. While experienced cooks can dump some rice into a pot and estimate the amount of water by eye or "knuckle deep" feel (½ inch above the rice by "eye"), some of us need a bit more help, such as a proportion chart and measuring cup. Every home cook, as well as professional cooks, agrees that getting the proportions right is often a challenge (sometimes even the proportions on the bag are not quite right). We have provided them here, for every type of rice, for your convenience.

Each of the three charts on the following pages has amounts suitable for all three sizes of machines: 3- to 4-cup (known as "small"), 5- to 6-cup (known as "medium"), and 8- to 10-cup (known as "large"). While there are rice cookers that are downright gigantic and used in restaurants, we have

JUST ADD WATER?

Described as one of the chemical protagonists of the cooking process, indeed, water is the most important ingredient in the cooking of rice. It is a general consensus that if your tap water is good enough to drink, it will be good enough to cook with. But many cooks wouldn't consider using tap water to make their rice. They use bottled or spring water or filtered water systems attached to their tap, since municipal sources and deep wells often contain hard minerals, chlorination, fluoride, or foreign material. Milk, fruit and vegetable juices, beer, wine, meat and vegetable stocks, and coconut milk may all be used as liquid substitutes in recipes, adding food value and a variety of flavor.

focused on the sizes available to the home cook. There is a chart for each category of rice: long (page 34), medium (page 42), and brown rice (page 50).

We recommend that when you first make rice in your rice cooker, you use the amounts and guidelines stated in the manual accompanying your machine. If you are not happy with the results, then refer to our charts. We were astonished to find that *every* rice cooker cooked rice just a little bit differently, and each cook likes his or her rice just so, so plan on a bit of experimentation to get your rice just as you like it.

How much to make and in what size machine? If you live alone, a small rice cooker is perfect. For 2 to 6 people, use a 5- to 6-cup model (it cooks even 1 rice cooker cup of raw rice perfectly), and if you have a larger family or make rice for company and large salads, get a large 10-cup cooker. The 10-cup model does not make 1 cup of raw rice efficiently; you must make 2 cups minimum or it will cook up too dry. Some rice cooker aficionados own two sizes.

A basic guide when deciding how much rice to make is to remember that rice doubles or triples in volume after cooking, so 1 cup of raw rice cooks up into 2 to 3 cups of cooked rice. How much you need will be determined by how you will be eating. Will it be a side dish, part of the main dish with a topping, or the main dish itself? Is it for a salad and do you want leftovers?

How to Use the Rice Charts

The most common use of the rice cooker is to cook plain rice, and most people, most of the time, will be cooking long-grain white rice, medium-grain white rice, or brown rice. Each of these types takes different amounts of water, and the amounts can vary based on the size of the rice cooker since rice cooks differently in every type of cooking vessel (depth and width of the pot, weight of the material the pot is made out of, and how tight the cover is are all factors). That's why we put together these charts—to help you make perfect rice, whatever your favorite variety and whatever the size of your rice cooker.

In every case, we recommend starting out with the amounts of water and rice suggested by the manufacturer of your rice cooker. If you are dissatisfied, try the measurements here. In our testing, we found that those handy calibrations on the rice cooker bowls are not always correct, or at least they didn't always correspond to the way we liked the rice cooked. If the rice is still not to your liking, continue to tinker, adding or reducing the water about ¼ cup at a time until your cooker is turning out rice that is perfectly suited to your tastes, jotting down the results. If your rice is too chewy, increase the amount of water; if it's too mushy or soggy, decrease the water. Some do like it chewier, some like it softer. And in the end, your preferences are the ones that matter.

Also, please be aware that increasing and decreasing rice proportions is downright tricky. Short- and medium-grain rices always need less water than long-grain. And as the amount of rice increases, the proportion of necessary water or cooking liquid decreases. You will be able to use our charts to help determine correct proportions for the recipes in this book.

Looking at the chart, first determine how many servings of rice you want to make. The amounts of rice in the charts are listed first in rice cooker cups, with the equivalent measurement in U.S. cups shown in the next column, so you can measure either way. Then read across the chart to find the amount of water to add under the size of your machine. The water is measured in U.S. cups (8 fluid ounces = 1 cup). Please measure the water carefully, at eye level, in a liquid measuring cup (the kind with a handle and pouring spout and calibrations on the side, usually made of Pyrex rather than metal).

Notice that the amount of water differs based on the size of the rice cooker, because of the amount of surface evaporation, with the larger cooker obviously having the most surface area. Cooking small amounts of rice in the large machine is not advised; it will end up too dry and tough. Add the water to the rice in the rice cooker. Then close the rice cooker and turn it on. When the machine finishes cooking, be sure to let the rice steam for 10 to 15 minutes on the Keep Warm cycle (or in the closed rice cooker, if you have the on/off type) before opening the cooker, stirring the rice with the rice paddle, and serving. (In fuzzy logic rice cookers, the steaming period is built in, but a short rest on Keep Warm is still recommended.)

American Long-Grain White Rice

The Japanese-made rice cooker was developed specifically to cook the rices most often cooked in their cuisine: medium- and short-grain white rices. So long-grain white rice is sometimes a bit of a challenge to get just right in the rice cooker. Long-grain rice is preferred in Chinese diets, as well as most of the other rice-oriented cuisines, such as in the Philippines, India, and South America. American cooks also prefer long-grain rices.

American Long-Grain White Rice

| SERVES | RICE | | WATER (in U.S. cups) | | |
	Rice Cooker Cups	(Equivalent in U.S. cups)	Small (4-cup) Rice Cooker	Medium (6-cup) Rice Cooker	Large (10-cup) Rice Cooker
2	1	$3/4$	$1^1/4$	$1^1/4$	$1^1/4$
4	2	$1^1/2$	$2^1/8$	$2^1/8$	$2^1/4$
6	3	$2^1/4$	3	$3^1/8$	$3^1/4$
8	4	3	$3^2/3$	$3^3/4$	4
10	5	$3^3/4$		$4^1/2$	$4^3/4$
12	6	$4^1/2$		$5^1/2$	$5^1/2$
14	7	$5^1/4$			$6^1/2$
16	8	6			$7^1/2$
18	9	$6^3/4$			$8^1/2$
20	10	$7^1/2$			$9^1/2$

american long-grain white rice

This recipe is for regular domestic long-grain white rice, brands like Mahatma and Pacific International, and the non-aromatic Indian extra-long-grain white rice (look for the finest grade, called *Patna*, for the region in which it is grown). The rice will indicate it is grown in Texas, Arkansas, or California, our main regions for growing the offshoots of our original Carolina gold strain of rice. Domestic long-grain white rice does not have to be washed or soaked before cooking, but the extra-long-grain Indian rice should have one rinse. (Note: This recipe is *not* for imported aromatic rices like basmati or jasmine.)

MACHINE: Medium (6-cup) rice cooker; fuzzy logic or on/off
CYCLE: Regular
YIELD: Serves 3 to 4

1 cup long-grain white rice
1 1/2 cups water
1/4 teaspoon salt
1 to 2 tablespoons unsalted butter, margarine, olive oil, or nut oil (optional)

1. Place the rice in the rice cooker bowl. Add the water and salt; swirl to combine. Close the cover and set for the regular cycle.
2. When the machine switches to the Keep Warm cycle, let the rice steam for 10 minutes. Fluff the rice with a wooden or plastic rice paddle or wooden spoon. This rice will hold on Keep Warm for hours.
3. Before serving, stir in the butter or oil, if using. Serve hot.

chinese-style plain rice

Ancient Chinese cooks were given the same social rank as esteemed painters and poets, and one especially important dish they had to make was *fan*, or Chinese white rice, to be served alongside multiple savory dishes. Besides long-grain white rice, Chinese recipes can call for long-grain brown rice (as an alternative to white rice in stir-fries and as an everyday rice), glutinous sticky rice (for stuffings and dumplings), or short-grain white rice, for everyday eating and the savory breakfast porridge, congee. Beth loves this plain rice, for its consistency on the tongue and barely clumping in the bowl, perfect for fried rice of any sort. (Julie thought it had a bit too much bite at the core of the kernel for her palate.) It is always made without salt to properly complement the soy sauce and other complex flavoring condiments in the food. Please note that the rice is not finished cooking until after sitting for 15 minutes on the Keep Warm cycle.

MACHINE: Medium (6-cup) rice cooker; fuzzy logic or on/off
CYCLE: Regular
YIELD: Serves 3 to 4

1 cup long-grain white rice
1 1/4 cups water

1. Place the rice in a bowl, rinse with cold water, and pour the water off, taking care to keep the rice in the bottom of the bowl. Rinse one to three more times, if desired.

2. Coat the rice cooker bowl with nonstick cooking spray or a film of vegetable oil. Place the rice in the rice bowl. Add the water, close the cover, and set for the regular cycle.

3. When the machine switches to the Keep Warm cycle, let the rice steam for 15 minutes. Fluff the rice with a wooden or plastic rice paddle or wooden spoon. This rice will hold on Keep Warm for hours. Serve hot.

chinese jasmine rice: Place the water in the rice cooker bowl. Add 1 teaspoon loose jasmine tea leaves and a dash of salt to the water; let stand for 3 minutes to steep. Add the rinsed and drained rice, swirl to evenly distribute, and cook the rice as directed. You could also use a jasmine tea bag and remove it before you begin cooking the rice, but the bits of tea leaves in the cooked rice are very nice. Great with soy-and-ginger-marinated chicken or fish.

chinese restaurant rice: Coat the rice bowl with 1 teaspoon Asian sesame oil. Substitute 1/4 cup short-grain rice for 1/4 cup of the long-grain rice (the ratio is 3 parts long-grain white rice to 1 part short-grain rice).

converted rice

Parboiling rice is a technique that was invented in ancient India (and still preferred in the humid areas of southern India and Bangladesh). Rice is boiled still in its husk, which keeps it from swelling, kills the microscopic larva in the germ of every grain, and pushes the nutrients in the outer layers into the center of the grain. The grain hardens slightly (making it easy to polish by hand) and is sterilized. The process even mends cracks in the rice (the starch glues broken rice back together), making for a higher yield. The rice is then dried unhusked (known as paddy rice), and passed through a standard milling process to remove the hull and bran. Once milled, the rice can be safely stored for long periods without losing any of its inherent nutrition and is resistant to bugs.

In this country, parboiled rice is known as converted rice. Converted rice, under the trademark of Uncle Ben's, is long-grain white rice that has been parboiled by steaming it under pressure, and then is refined by removing the hull, bran, and germ. It was developed for use in the overseas armed forces kitchens during World War II. It is the only type of rice that can withstand the harsh treatment of most industrial processes that involve cooking and then freezing, canning, or drying and, for that reason, it is the rice used in most boxed mixes. It has more nutrition than plain white rice, since it is enriched, and takes longer to cook than regular white rice because the starch is slightly hardened and needs more liquid to soften.

While most cooks say, "No, thank you," to converted rice because so many other long-grain white rices are available, we love it for certain dishes. It cooks up perfectly, with the most distinct grains and the least amount of stickiness of any of the rices. Because of this, converted rice is excellent for use in rice salads, absorbing dressings and not becoming mushy. It is the rice of choice of restaurateurs like Paul Prudhomme of New Orleans for dishes such as jambalaya. It is good in pilafs and, to our great surprise, is the most used rice in Paris after imported Thai jasmine.

Here is a guide to making converted rice in your rice cooker, from 2 to 22 servings, since the rice/liquid proportions vary so drastically and this is the perfect rice to make in quantity.

MACHINE: Small (4-cup) rice cooker; fuzzy logic or on/off
CYCLE: Regular
YIELD: Serves 2

1/2 cup converted rice
1 cup plus 2 tablespoons water
2 teaspoons unsalted butter (optional)
Pinch of salt

MACHINE: Small (4-cup) or medium (6-cup) rice cooker; fuzzy logic or on/off
YIELD: Serves 4

1 cup converted rice
2 cups water
1 tablespoon unsalted butter (optional)
1/3 teaspoon salt

MACHINE: Medium (6-cup) rice cooker; fuzzy logic or on/off
YIELD: Serves 6

1 1/2 cups converted rice
3 cups water
1 1/2 tablespoons unsalted butter (optional)
3/4 teaspoon salt

MACHINE: Medium (6-cup) or large (10-cup) rice cooker: fuzzy logic or on/off
YIELD: Serves 12

note: This is the largest volume of cooked rice that will fit in the medium rice cooker.

3 cups converted rice
5 cups water
2 1/2 tablespoons unsalted butter (optional)
1 1/2 teaspoons salt

MACHINE: Large (10-cup) rice cooker; fuzzy logic or on/off
YIELD: Serves 22

6 cups converted rice
9 1/2 cups water
5 tablespoons unsalted butter (optional)
1 tablespoon salt

1. Place the rice in the rice cooker bowl. Add the water, butter, if using, and salt; swirl to combine. Close the cover and set for the regular cycle.
2. When the machine switches to the Keep Warm cycle, let the rice steam for 10 minutes. Fluff the rice with a wooden or plastic rice paddle or wooden spoon. This rice keeps perfectly on Keep Warm for at least 2 hours.

basmati rice

One taste and imported white basmati rice will become your favorite—we guarantee it. We have many friends who go from store to store looking for a brand they picked up on a whim, fell in love with, and want to find again. It can be packaged in boxes, plastic bags, even burlap sacks. Basmati is ever so delightfully delicate both in texture and flavor. It gives credence to the label "aromatic" rice. The best grades are Dehraduni and Patna basmati, but just look in the box: the rather small, needle-like grains should all be whole, rather than broken. Basmati is aged from six months to a year in burlap sacks layered with neem leaves—an ancient tree native to East India that is a natural insecticide—to dry it out and develop its flavor; basmati should never smell musty. As it cooks, the grain elongates up to three times its length, rather than plumping out. Basmati cooks in a very short time, around 30 minutes usually, depending on the freshness of the rice (older rice will take longer). This is also the recipe to use for domestic Della white basmati, Lundberg white basmati, and the lesser known imported Indian Tohfa and Kohinoor basmatis.

MACHINE: Medium (6-cup) rice cooker; fuzzy logic or on/off
CYCLE: Regular
YIELD: Serves 4

1 cup basmati rice
1¹/₂ cups water
¹/₄ teaspoon fine sea salt

1. Place the rice in a bowl and fill with cold water. Swish it around with your fingers. Bits of grain will float to the top; the water will foam around the edges and become murky. Carefully pour off the water and rinse a second time. If the rice water is still murky, rinse and drain again; basmati usually takes two to four rinsings. Discard the rinse water. An optional step is to let the basmati air-dry in the strainer for 30 minutes or to soak it in a bowl, covered with cold water, for 30 minutes. Drain well. (Traditional recipes call for the basmati to be cooked in its soaking liquid. If you'd like, you can pour this off into a measuring cup and use it for cooking.)

2. Place the rice in the rice cooker bowl. Add the water and salt; swirl to combine. Close the cover and set for the regular cycle.

3. When the machine switches to the Keep Warm cycle, let the rice steam for 10 minutes. Fluff the rice with a wooden or plastic rice paddle or wooden spoon. This rice will hold on Keep Warm for hours. Serve hot.

kalijira rice

Kalijira white rice is a cute baby basmati imported by Lotus Foods. It needs to be handled just like basmati, with multiple rinsings and a relatively short steaming period. While it can be made in 10 minutes on the stovetop, the rice cooker gives a short soak time and ever so slowly cooks the rice to perfection for a bit longer. We like a rest at the end also. Kalijira ends up with the dry, very separate soft grains marked by the distinct perfumey aroma that is so characteristic of basmati rice. The big difference is the tongue feel, which is so different because of the miniature size of the grains. Babies will love it. A wonderful daily or special occasion rice.

This is also the proportion guide to use for other miniature Indian white rices like Idli and Ponni, available in specialty Indian grocery stores.

MACHINE: Medium (6-cup) rice cooker; fuzzy logic or on/off
CYCLE: Regular
YIELD: Serves 3 to 4

1 cup Kalijira rice
1¹/₄ cups water
1 tablespoon unsalted butter or margarine
¹/₈ teaspoon salt

1. Place the rice in a bowl and fill with cold water. Swish it around with your fingers. Bits of grain will float to the top; the water will foam around the edges and become murky. Carefully pour off the water and rinse a few more times until the water is clear. Kalijira usually takes four full rinsings. Discard the rinse water.

2. Coat the rice cooker bowl with nonstick cooking spray or a film of vegetable oil. Place the rice in the rice bowl. Add the water, butter, and salt; swirl to combine. Close the cover and set for the regular cycle.

3. When the machine switches to the Keep Warm cycle, let the rice steam for 10 minutes. Fluff the rice with a wooden or plastic rice paddle or wooden spoon. This rice will hold on Keep Warm for hours. Serve hot.

american jasmine rice

American jasmine rice is exclusively grown for and distributed by Lotus Foods under the Lowell Farms label. We got this recipe from the company founder, Caryl Levine, who not only searches out exceptional imported and domestic rices, but eats rice every day out of her 10-cup rice cooker. The organic jasmine rice grown in El Campo, Texas, is a variety developed by the International Rice Institute in the Philippines and Texas A & M University. American jasmine is less processed than imported Thai jasmine, so it will take a bit more time to cook and, as you will note from the proportions, a bit more water. Caryl always likes a bit of salt. "It brings out the best in rice," she says. A great everyday rice you just might end up liking better than the imported variety.

MACHINE: Medium (6-cup) rice cooker; fuzzy logic or on/off
CYCLE: Regular
YIELD: Serves 6 to 8

2 cups domestic white jasmine rice
3 cups water
Large pinch of fine sea salt (optional)

1. Place the rice in a fine strainer or bowl, rinse with cold water, and drain once.

2. Coat the rice cooker bowl with nonstick cooking spray or a film of vegetable oil. Place the rice in the rice bowl. Add the water and salt, if using; swirl to combine. Close the cover and set for the regular cycle.

3. When the machine switches to the Keep Warm cycle, let the rice steam for

15 minutes. Fluff the rice with a wooden or plastic rice paddle or wooden spoon. This rice will hold on Keep Warm for hours. Serve hot.

thai jasmine rice

The word for rice in Thai is *kao* and the type of rice found all over the country is a pearl white long-grain rice labeled Thai jasmine. It has a plump, elongated shape, not round like short-grain rice or thin and long like American long-grain. The rice cooks up fluffy and moist, with a delicate floral aroma that is a favorite with many cooks in many nations. Many brands are labeled Riz Parfumé. Considered the most delicate grain of all the rices, it is harvested in December during the dry months and is marketed fresh. Thai jasmine loses its fragrance as the raw rice ages, so often it is stored in the refrigerator.

Many cooks complain that their jasmine rice is too gummy after cooking; that is because they are cooking it in too much water. Thai jasmine is not the same as long-grain Thai sticky rice, *kao neuw*, which is eaten in the north of the country, steamed in a spittoon-shaped rice pot, and eaten only with the hands.

MACHINE: Medium (6-cup) rice cooker; fuzzy logic or on/off
CYCLE: Regular
YIELD: Serves 6 to 8

2 cups Thai jasmine rice
2$^1/_4$ cups water
$^1/_4$ teaspoon salt

1. Place the rice in a fine strainer or bowl, rinse with cold water twice, and drain twice.
2. Coat the rice cooker bowl with nonstick cooking spray or a film of vegetable oil. Place the rice in the rice bowl. Add the water and salt; swirl to combine. Close the cover and set for the regular cycle.
3. When the machine switches to the Keep Warm cycle, let the rice steam for 15 minutes. Fluff the rice with a wooden or plastic rice paddle or wooden spoon. This rice holds nicely on Keep Warm for up to 3 hours. Serve hot.

note: If the cooked rice seems too dry, add a bit more water (up to 2 to 3 tablespoons) and leave it on the Keep Warm cycle for 15 minutes to continue steaming.

white jasmine blend

Cooked by itself, jasmine rice can be very soft and tender, almost sticky. In combination with a domestic long-grain white rice, it will have a lovely nutty fragrance and drier texture. It's especially nice with Chinese food; in fact, one restaurateur of our acquaintance says he serves only jasmine rice (made in a 55-cup gas-powered rice cooker!) because he loves the way it makes the restaurant smell. If you use domestic-grown American jasmine rice, increase the water to 1$^3/_4$ cups.

MACHINE: Medium (6-cup) rice cooker; fuzzy logic or on/off
CYCLE: Regular
YIELD: Serves 3 to 4

½ cup long-grain white rice

½ cup Thai jasmine rice

1½ cups water

¼ teaspoon salt

1. Place the rices in a fine strainer or bowl, rinse with cold water, and drain twice.
2. Coat the rice cooker bowl with nonstick cooking spray or a film of vegetable oil. Place the rices in the rice bowl. Add the water and salt; swirl to combine. Close the cover and set for the regular cycle.
3. When the machine switches to the Keep Warm cycle, let the rice steam for 10 to 15 minutes. Fluff the rice with a wooden or plastic rice paddle or wooden spoon. This rice will hold on Keep Warm for hours. Serve hot.

jasmati rice

We thought Jasmati rice was a combination of jasmine and basmati, but that is not the case. Grown in Texas, Jasmati is a combination of Thai jasmine and Carolina long-grain white rice from RiceSelect. The aroma of the un-cooked rice is as intoxicating a perfume as the best jasmine, but the aroma becomes muted during cooking. The soft, tender cooked rice is a great alternative to regular bland white rice or one of the imported aromatics. It cooks up snowy white, gets ever so slight a curl on some grains, and tastes like jasmine rice with-out any of the stickiness. This is rated one of our favorite rices and we think you will agree. Jasmati can be substituted for any long-grain white rice or basmati in the pilaf recipes on pages 97–124. Store in the refrigerator.

MACHINE: Medium (6-cup) rice cooker; fuzzy logic or on/off
CYCLE: Regular
YIELD: Serves 3 to 4

1 cup Jasmati rice

1½ cups water

2 tablespoons unsalted butter or margarine

⅛ teaspoon salt (optional)

1. Place the rice in the rice cooker bowl. Add the water, butter, and salt, if using; swirl to combine. Close the cover and set for the regular cycle.
2. When the machine switches to the Keep Warm cycle, let the rice steam for 15 minutes. Fluff the rice with a wooden or plastic rice paddle or wooden spoon. This rice will hold on Keep Warm for hours. Serve hot.

kasmati rice

After Texmati, the next rice developed by RiceSelect was their Kasmati, with a stronger aromatic fragrance and firmer center of the grain than the Texmati. Adapted from basmati seedstock in a manner like Della and Louisi-ana popcorn rice, Texas-grown Kasmati looks exactly like a scaled-down basmati grain with similar opaque viscosity. Kasmati is far more aromatic and is tasty, indeed. Beth originally thought that since Kasmati was similar to Jasmati they would cook and taste the same; not so. It has rather dense grains, so it needs a preliminary soaking to cook properly; with-out soaking it is very firm (which is okay for fried rice). The needle-like grains elongate considerably, especially with the presoak. Kasmati is a lovely rice that quickly became a dinner favorite and is definitely delightfully unique compared to other American aromatics. Store the raw rice in the refrigerator.

MACHINE: Medium (6-cup) rice cooker; fuzzy logic or on/off

CYCLE: Regular

YIELD: Serves 3 to 4

1 cup Kasmati rice
1³/₄ cups water
Small pinch of salt (optional)

1. Place the rice and water in the rice cooker bowl. Close the cover and let the rice soak for 30 minutes to 1 hour. At the end of the soaking period, add the salt, if using, swirl to combine, and set for the regular cycle.

2. When the machine switches to the Keep Warm cycle, let the rice steam for 10 minutes. Gently but thoroughly fluff the rice with a plastic or wooden rice paddle or wooden spoon. This rice will hold on Keep Warm for hours. Serve hot.

Medium-Grain White Rice

The right cooking pot has always been a very important issue in cooking rice, and the rice cooker is downright infallible when cooking medium-grain white rices. Medium-grain white rice is perfect for a plain side dish, but expect a moister, more tender grain than with long-grain rice; it should never be mushy. If you're buying rice labeled for Japanese-American consumers, it may be labeled short-grain. The terms are used interchangeably in Asia; the United States is the only country with a separate class for medium-grain. When you inspect the grain, note that it is shorter and slightly plumper than long-grain. It requires less water to cook than long-grain rice. You may use this rice in pilafs, as well as in paella.

Medium-Grain White Rice

| SERVES | RICE | | WATER (in U.S. cups) | | |
	Rice Cooker Cups	(Equivalent in U.S. cups)	Small (4-cup) Rice Cooker	Medium (6-cup) Rice Cooker	Large (10-cup) Rice Cooker
2	1	³/₄	1¹/₄	1¹/₄	1¹/₂
4	2	1¹/₂	2	2	2¹/₈
6	3	2¹/₄	2³/₄	3	3
8	4	3	3¹/₂	3²/₃	3²/₃
10	5	3³/₄		4¹/₄	4¹/₃
12	6	4¹/₂		5¹/₄	5¹/₄
14	7	5¹/₄			6
16	8	6			7
18	9	6³/₄			8
20	10	7¹/₂			9

medium-grain white rice

This is the recipe to use for basic steamed rice or the Japanese daily rice, *okame*, made from the white rice known as *seihakumai*. Remember, if you bought a bag of rice labeled "new crop," *shinmai* (which is fresh every autumn), you will decrease the ratio of water to rice to 1:1 (that will be 1 cup of water here). The method of washing described below is characteristically Japanese and more extensive than what many rushed cooks actually do. Certainly, if you're pressed for time, just swish and drain a few times. This recipe is geared to domestic medium-grain white rice, all of which is grown either in California or Arkansas (the climate is not right anywhere else in the country for it). Use brands like Nishiki, Homai, Botan, Konriko, Tamaki Classic, and southern medium-grain brands, *not* domestic or imported Arborios. These are the same proportions to use for *haigamai*, partially polished white rice. For 1½ cups rice, use 2 cups water.

MACHINE: Medium (6-cup) rice cooker; fuzzy logic or on/off

CYCLE: Regular

YIELD: Serves 3 to 4

1 cup medium-grain white rice

1⅓ cups water

¼ teaspoon salt (optional)

1. Wash the rice. Place the rice in a bowl and fill the bowl about half-full with cold water. Swirl the rice in the water with your hand. Carefully pour off most of the water, through a mesh strainer or by holding one cupped hand under the stream to catch any grains of rice that are carried away with the water. Holding the bowl steady with one hand, use the other to rub and squeeze the wet rice, turning the bowl as you go so that all the rice is "scrubbed." The small amount of water in the bowl will turn chalky white. Now, run cold water into the bowl, give the rice a quick swish, and carefully drain off the water as before. Repeat the scrubbing and pouring-off process twice more. By the third time, the water you pour off will be nearly clear.

2. Place the rice in the rice cooker bowl. Add the water and salt, if using; swirl to combine. Let the rice soak for 30 minutes to 1 hour with the cover shut, time permitting. At the end of the soaking period, set for the regular cycle.

3. When the machine switches to the Keep Warm cycle, let the rice steam for 15 minutes. Gently but thoroughly fluff the rice with a plastic or wooden rice paddle or wooden spoon. This rice will hold on Keep Warm for hours. Serve hot.

japanese white rice with umeboshi and sesame

Tart and salty, pinky red umeboshi pickled plums are an acquired taste to some. To others, it is just another comfort food along with miso. Anyone who has taken a macrobiotic cooking class gets hooked on umeboshi. On a visit to Japantown, our lunch boxes always have a bright, shriveled pickled plum plunked into the mound of fresh white rice. Prepare the condiments while the rice is cooking; you want to be ready to serve as soon as the rice has finished on the Keep Warm cycle. Umeboshi plums are sold in Asian groceries and natural foods stores. This recipe—inspired by Hiroko Shimbo, author of *The Japanese Kitchen* (Harvard Common Press, 2000)—has quickly become a favorite quick lunch on the run.

YIELD: Serves 2 to 3

2 umeboshi plums, pitted and minced
2 tablespoons minced fresh Italian parsley
    leaves
1 1/2 tablespoons toasted Japanese sesame
    seeds (page 145)
3 cups hot cooked medium-grain white
    rice
Sesame oil (not toasted), for drizzling
Tamari (a thick, strong soy sauce;
    reduced-sodium, if desired),
    for drizzling

1. Place the umeboshi, parsley, and sesame seeds in separate small, shallow serving bowls.
2. Place the rice in a medium-size serving bowl, sprinkle it with the condiments, and drizzle with some sesame oil and tamari. Serve immediately.

note: Japanese sesame seeds are sold toasted; you can toast them again in a dry skillet for more flavor.

riso

Riso is Italian for rice, and Italian rice is domestic or imported Arborio, Carnaroli, or Vialone nano. While these rices are commonly cooked into a risotto, the side dish that is like a creamy savory rice pudding, "everyday" rice is cooked so that the grains are dry and separate, more like a pilaf than a risotto. Home recipes for *riso* require the cook to measure the same amount of dry rice and water plus 1/2 cup extra water for the cooking pot. We found the measurements ran true when translating the recipe to the rice cooker. This rice takes a long time to cook for white rice, a full hour. Be prepared for the rice to be ever-so-slightly chewy in a percentage of the grains. One look and you will recognize the perfect example of a plumped medium-sized grain of rice. It is slightly moist, but dry on the tongue, and very tasty without being sweet. Serve with butter and Parmesan cheese as a side like any other rice bowl rice, or as a bed for sautéed meat and onions. This is the rice to make for stuffed peppers, stuffings, rice omelets, fritters, and Italian rice and vegetable salads dressed with olive oil and lemon juice.

MACHINE: Medium (6-cup) rice cooker;
fuzzy logic or on/off
CYCLE: Regular
YIELD: Serves 4 (about 3 1/2 cups)

1 1/4 cups Arborio, Carnaroli, or Vialone
    nano rice
1 3/4 cups water
1 tablespoon olive oil
Small pinch of salt

1. Place the rice in the rice cooker bowl. Add the water, olive oil, and salt; swirl to combine. Close the cover and set for the regular cycle.

2. When the machine switches to the Keep Warm cycle, let the rice steam for 10 minutes. Fluff the rice gently with a wooden or plastic rice paddle or wooden spoon. This rice will hold on Keep Warm for hours. Serve hot.

TO WASH OR NOT TO WASH

This is one of the places where rice asks to be treated with respect. While washing rice or not is a personal preference, the general rule is to wash or rinse imported rices and not to wash domestic rices, which are well cleaned and dried before packaging. Imported rices can have plenty of clinging starch left over from the processing, and your cooked rice will be downright gluey if you don't wash it off prior to cooking.

However, don't wash Arborio or the other Italian-style risotto rices; the starch makes the risotto creamy. And many Asian cooks would not think of cooking unwashed rice; it would defy tradition. Domestically produced Japanese-style rice is coated with powdered glucose or rice powder (talc in days of old). It's perfectly safe to eat, but washing off this whitish powder does improve the flavor. Indian basmati must be rinsed; recipes often call for up to nine or ten rinsings. Boxed and packaged rices usually do not need washing or maybe just one rinse. Converted rice does not need rinsing.

To wash rice, place the measured rice in a bowl of cold tap water and swish it around with your hand until the water becomes cloudy. It will often be foamy around the edges. Tilt the bowl and carefully pour the water off or pour through a fine strainer. Rinse and return the rice to the bowl, if need be, and add more cold water. Repeat until the water stays clear, or nearly so. Most rices need at least two rinsings, but each batch of rice will be different; we have seen some basmatis take four. Purists wash for minutes and really use some muscle power to rub the rice grains, especially for Japanese rices. You can dump the clump of wet, washed rice directly into the rice bowl or spread the wet rice out to dry on a clean tea towel until cooking time.

Some recipes call for soaking the rice in cold water after washing and before cooking to soften the outer cell walls. This is a traditional technique in Turkish, Persian, and Indian cuisines. Some newer models of rice cookers have a built-in soaking cycle. You can soak rice in the sink, in a separate bowl, or in the rice cooker bowl, or leave the drained rice right in a mesh strainer for 10 to 30 minutes and let the grains soak up the water that is clinging to the grains.

short-grain white rice

Japanese-style short-grain white rice is about 5 percent of the rice grown in the United States. Since half of it is exported, there is not much around. You might say it is a real specialty item. Short-grain rice makes the best sushi. It is also called pearl rice, especially in dessert recipes. Traditional cooking methods require soaking to get a nice soft texture. There is a lot of starch in short-grain rice, so it really sticks together after cooking, but deliciously so. It is a type of rice that tastes better with every bite. Our favorite brand of Japanese-style rice, Tamaki Gold, is labeled short-grain. "What were the proportions to get that Tamaki Gold so perfect?" asked Beth of Julie one day. "Three rice cooker cups and water to the line that says 3 on the bowl, just the way the machine was designed to cook." This recipe gives measurements in U.S. cups, but if you use the white rice recipe from the manufacturer's pamphlet, measurements will be in rice cooker cups. This is the recipe to use for imported and domestic Koshi Hikari.

MACHINE: Medium (6-cup) rice cooker; fuzzy logic or on/off
CYCLE: Regular
YIELD: Serves 3 to 4

1 1/2 cups (2 rice cooker cups) short-grain white rice
1 2/3 cups cold water
1/4 teaspoon salt (optional)

1. Place the rice in a bowl and fill about half-full with cold water. Swirl the rice in the water with your hand. Carefully pour off most of the water, through a mesh strainer or by holding one cupped hand under the stream to catch any grains of rice that are carried away with the water. Holding the bowl steady with one hand, use the other to rub and squeeze the wet rice, turning the bowl as you go so that all the rice is "scrubbed." The small amount of water in the bowl will turn chalky white. Now, run cold water into the bowl, give the rice a quick swish, and carefully drain off the water as before. Repeat the scrubbing and pouring-off process twice more. By the third time, the water you pour off will be nearly clear.

2. Place the rice in the rice cooker bowl. Add the water (to line 2) and salt, if using; swirl to combine. Let the rice soak for 30 minutes to 1 hour in the bowl with the cover shut, time permitting. When the soaking period is finished, set for the regular cycle.

3. When the machine switches to the Keep Warm cycle, gently but thoroughly fluff the rice with a plastic or wooden rice paddle or wooden spoon. Let the rice steam for 10 to 15 minutes. This rice will hold on Keep Warm for hours. Serve hot.

Sticky Rice

Sticky rice, also known as glutinous rice or sweet rice (even though it isn't sweet at all), is a staple in the Asian culinary repertoire and a frequent ingredient in stuffings and desserts. Japanese cooks combine it with small red adzuki beans for a savory, pink-tinted side dish that is often served at festive meals, topped with sesame seeds and salt. Chinese cooks mix sticky rice with sweet or savory tidbits for stuffings, hearty one-pot meals, or

Salt is a flavor enhancer. In the environment of the rice cooker, when salt is added as one of the ingredients, it is absorbed into each grain of rice during the cooking. We have detected that some rices, especially brown rices and the aromatic rices, can get a bit of a bitter edge from the salt, masking the delicate flavor of the rice. To salt or not to salt is a decision that you will have to make in your own kitchen, based on your own palate. The addition of salt to rice is purely personal preference and also varies depending on how you plan to serve it. For instance, if you are serving the rice with roasted meat, you might want to salt it to taste. If the rice will be served with a spicy curry or salty stir-fry, you wouldn't need the salt.

We have specified salt in some of the recipes that follow, but you may choose to eliminate it without affecting the recipe adversely. If you do add salt, add it with the water and swirl a few times to evenly distribute. If you are using a stock that already has salt added, or miso, the rice will not need salt. Some unhulled rices, such as Wehani, are minimally processed and are always cooked without salt in order to ensure the most tender results.

Types of Salt

Salt is not just a blue box with a little girl in a raincoat and umbrella anymore; there are fine, downright exquisite, salts on the market.

Fine iodized table salt (mechanically removed from rock salt deposits, with potassium iodine and magnesium silicate added to prevent caking) and fine sea salt (from saline deposits at the edge of the sea) can be used interchangeably. Sun-evaporated, unrefined sea salts retain their complementary minerals, calcium, potassium, and magnesium, which give a distinct flavor reminiscent of the sea. We use La Baleine, an iodized sun-evaporated fine sea salt from the Mediterranean that contains no preservatives or anticaking agents (you'll find it at the supermarket), or Japanese sea salt, which we buy at the Asian market. If you buy regular sea salt, you want fine-crystal, which is finer than table salt, or medium-crystal, which is ground like table salt. Kosher salt (which is mined, but contains no additives) is preferred by many cooks for its purity and milder flavor.

Coarse salts, usually for sprinkling after a food is cooked, must be ground in a salt grinder before being added to the cooking water. Ducros of Provence markets sea salt in its own disposable grinder. Celtic Sea Salt, touted by the macrobiotic community for its health-giving properties, is pale gray. Fleur de Sel de Guerande, from Brittany and available from King Arthur, is hand-harvested. *Fleur de sel*, the "flower of salt" that is the top layer in sun-evaporation pans, is so coveted that the pretty white crystals are simply sprinkled over hot rice with some sweet butter. Take a chance and experiment with the flavor of salt as you would with any other premium ingredient.

sweet puddings. It is the rice of choice in Thailand, where it is eaten with the fingers.

Sticky rice must be soaked before cooking, for several hours at least, to cook properly, though overnight soaking is the most common recommendation. During the soaking time, the grains swell and soften, and will crumble easily between your teeth or fingernails.

Once it has soaked, there are three ways to cook sticky rice. There is the traditional method, steaming, and two modern ones: the microwave and the fuzzy logic rice cooker boil/steam method. Since the on/off rice cookers are easy-to-use, reliable steamers, we highly recommend this method. Some fuzzy logic rice cookers also are designed to cook sticky rice and have a cycle or button specifically for it. If your rice cooker is designed to cook sticky rice, it will say so in the booklet that came with it. You will notice that sticky rice takes less water than other types of rice and that the cooker's sticky rice capacity is somewhat less than for regular white medium- and short-grain rices. (Julie's medium-size Sanyo fuzzy logic cooker makes 3 rice cooker cups of sticky rice, versus making 5½ rice cooker cups of regular white rice.)

To make sticky rice in a fuzzy logic rice cooker, just follow the manufacturer's instructions. Sticky rice made in a fuzzy logic machine is fine for some uses, such as when it will be combined with other ingredients, as in Sticky Rice in Lotus Leaves (page 270), but overall it is wetter, softer, and not as appealing as steamed sticky rice. You can also mix sticky rice with regular long-grain rice in mixed dishes such as Rainbow Rice in a Pot (page 83). To do so, you can substitute one-quarter to one-half sticky rice for long-grain.

Machine-made sticky rice should never be held on the Keep Warm cycle. When the regular cycle completes, turn the rice out into a bowl and fan it (or use an electric fan or a hair dryer set on cool) for a few minutes. Then serve it.

steamed sticky rice

These instructions for steamed sticky rice come courtesy of Hiroko Shimbo, author of the encyclopedic and accessible book *The Japanese Kitchen* (Harvard Common Press, 2000). Not everyone salts their sticky rice before cooking; feel free to leave out the salt if you wish. Hiroko notes that sticky rice is often served for special occasions, topped with a sprinkle of *gomasio*, the addictive sesame seed and salt condiment. She explains that you can make your own by toasting 3 tablespoons black sesame seeds in a small skillet over low heat until fragrant. If you wish, you can release more of the seeds' fragrance and flavor by partly grinding them with a mortar and pestle or the Japanese ridged *suribachi*, made for precisely that purpose. Add 2 teaspoons sea salt to the sesame seeds and let the mixture cool.

You need an on/off rice cooker with a steamer basket or tray that fits into the top of the cooker. When steaming sticky rice, the steamer basket or tray must be lined with a piece of cloth, which is then folded over to enclose the rice. You can use a double or triple layer of cheesecloth, a square of muslin, or a cloth made especially for this purpose, which is sold in Japanese markets. We have also used a clean linen handkerchief with great success. If you love rice, treat yourself to making this rice and enjoy the texture achieved by the steaming.

MACHINE: Medium (6-cup) or large (10-cup) rice cooker; on/off only
CYCLE: Regular
YIELD: Serves 4 to 6

2¹/₄ cups (3 rice cooker cups) sticky rice
1 teaspoon salt

1. Wash the rice. Place the rice in a bowl (or use the bowl of your rice cooker) and fill the bowl about half-full with cold tap water. Swirl the rice in the water with your hand. Carefully pour off most of the water, holding one cupped hand under the stream to catch any grains of rice that are carried away with the water. Holding the bowl steady with one hand, use the other to rub and squeeze the wet rice, turning the bowl as you go, so that all the rice is "scrubbed." The small amount of water in the bowl will turn chalky white. Now, run cold water into the bowl, give the rice a quick swish, and carefully drain off the water as before. Repeat the scrubbing and pouring-off process two more times. By the third time, the water you pour off will be nearly clear.

2. Place the drained rice in a bowl and add cold water to cover by several inches. Let the rice soak at room temperature for at least 3 hours, and overnight if possible.

3. Drain the rice, discarding the water. Add the salt to the rice and toss it gently to mix. Fill the rice cooker bowl about half-full of water. Close the cover and set for the regular cycle. When the water comes to a full boil, you are ready to begin.

4. Lay the cloth or a double or triple layer of cheesecloth in the steamer basket or tray. Pour the rice onto the cloth and spread it out as evenly as possible. Make a shallow depression 2 inches in diameter in the center of the rice. This allows the steam to circulate and cook the rice evenly. Fold the corners of the cloth over the rice to cover it completely. Place the steamer basket in the rice cooker and close the cover. Set a timer for 40 minutes. After 15 minutes of cooking, open the cover, taking care to avoid steam burns, and fold back the cloth. Sprinkle ⅓ cup water over the rice. Re-cover the rice with the cloth, close the cover, and proceed with the steaming. Repeat the water-sprinkling process once or twice during the cooking. When the timer sounds, open the cover and taste some rice. It should be tender. If it's not,

REHEATING RICE IN THE RICE COOKER

Some cooks make extra rice and have it for a day or two in the refrigerator, ready for quick meals. Other cooks would never think of using day-old rice. In case you need to reheat some rice, here's how.

Place the cold rice in the rice cooker bowl. Add 1 to 2 tablespoons water (old rice will need a bit more water, new rice less) and break up the stiff clumps of cold rice. Cover and program for regular cycle. Steam until the timer sounds, about 10 minutes. Eat immediately and do not reheat again.

or if you are not sure, let the rice steam for 10 minutes more.

5. Transfer the cooked rice to a large bowl and fan it to cool the rice quickly.

6. Serve the rice immediately or, if you are making it ahead of time, cover it with a clean, dry tea towel and store it at cool room temperature. (If you have made the rice a day ahead, refrigerate it, tightly covered.) You can reheat sticky rice in the steamer or microwave oven.

Medium- and Long-Grain Brown Rice

Most rice cookers are not really engineered with brown rice in mind, although some sophisticated models have a setting for it. Nevertheless, all rice cookers can and will do a wonderful job of cooking it, as long as you keep a few basic points in mind. (If your machine is one of the relatively few models with a Brown Rice cycle, then by all means use it according to the manufacturer's instructions.)

Brown rice takes longer to cook than white rice because its protective outer bran layer is intact. It also requires more water. Your brown rice will taste better if you have time to let the rice and water soak for about an hour before cooking, but this is not necessary. (Some fuzzy logic rice cookers have a soaking cycle built in.)

After much testing and deliberation, we came up with a rule of thumb for adapting the basic stovetop recipe for brown rice to the rice cooker. For white rices you adapt by using ¼ cup less water than the package says; for brown rices, start with ¼ cup *more* water.

As with white rice, the long-grain brown cooks up fluffier with the individual grains more separate, while the medium-grain is a bit stickier and moister. Wash the rice first, if you wish; washing will reduce stickiness by rinsing off some of the surface starch.

If you have the time, do soak your brown rice for 30 minutes to an hour before you cook it. This allows the rice to cook more evenly and quickly. If you don't have time or you forget, don't worry. Just push the button and go. Your brown rice will still be fine.

Use the proportions in the chart below as a guide; you may need to make adjustments for your rice cooker or for a particularly dry or moist bag of rice. Of course, personal taste varies, too. If you like softer rice, add more water; for firmer rice, use less. If the water boils over while you are cooking, try reducing the amount of water slightly (start with 2 tablespoons less water, and continue in 2-tablespoon increments). Note your adjustment on the chart to jog your memory the next time.

Brown Rice (Medium-Grain or Long-Grain)

SERVES	RICE Rice Cooker Cups	(Equivalent in U.S. cups)	WATER (in U.S. cups) Small (4-cup) Rice Cooker	Medium (6-cup) Rice Cooker	Large (10-cup) Rice Cooker
2	1	³/₄	1³/₄	1³/₄	2¹/₄
4	2	1¹/₂	2¹/₂	2¹/₂	3¹/₃
6	3	2¹/₄	3²/₃	3²/₃	4¹/₂
8	4	3		4²/₃	5¹/₃
10	5	3³/₄			6¹/₂
12	6	4¹/₂			7¹/₂

You will notice that the standard brown rice capacity of rice cookers is lower than their capacity for white rice. This is because brown rice must cook longer to become tender, and therefore you must start off with more water than for white rices. If you overload your rice cooker, you'll face a messy boil over.

If your machine has a Brown Rice cycle, use it. But because most rice cookers do not have one, we put together these charts using the regular cycle.

During testing, we learned two surprising things about cooking brown rice. The first is that long- and medium-grain brown rice require the same amount of water. (On the stove, long-grain rice takes more water.) The second thing we discovered almost by accident: It is possible to exceed the brown rice capacities listed in the brown rice cooking chart. In fact, you can cook as much brown rice in your rice cooker as you can white rice; 4 cups in a 4-cup cooker, 6 cups in a 6-cup cooker, 10 cups in a 10-cup cooker. What about those messy boilovers we mentioned above? The trick we discovered is detailed in the chart below, Stretching the Brown Rice Capacity of Your Rice Cooker. When the rice has finished steaming, open the cover, fluff the rice, and re-cover the rice to keep it warm. Do not leave brown rice on the Keep Warm cycle for longer than 1 or 2 hours, as it has a tendency to begin fermenting.

Stretching the **Brown Rice** Capacity of Your Rice Cooker*

SERVES	RICE Cooker Cups	(Equivalent in U.S. cups)	WATER (in U.S. cups) Small (4-cup) Rice Cooker	Medium (6-cup) Rice Cooker	Large (10-cup) Rice Cooker
8	4	3	4		
10	5	3³/₄		5¹/₄	
12	6	4¹/₂		6¹/₄	
14	7	5¹/₄			7
16	8	6			8
18	9	6³/₄			8³/₄
20	10	7¹/₂			9¹/₂

*important note: When stretching the brown rice capacity of your rice cooker, you must use the special technique developed to go along with this chart or you will experience a messy boilover. Add water and rice to the rice cooker as usual, but when the water boils, SHUT OFF THE RICE COOKER. Set a timer for 30 minutes. After 30 minutes, turn the cooker on again and let the regular cycle complete as usual. Be sure to allow the full 15 minutes of steaming time after the rice cooker has switched to Keep Warm.

long- or medium-grain brown rice

There are lots of long-grain brown rices, most sold in generic-looking bags. They come in a range of natural colors, from creamy to dark tan, with a flavor palate to match. We find long-grain brown rice has its own special sweetness, a far different flavor from medium- or short-grain. Brown rice takes more water and a longer time to cook than white rice, so plan your meal accordingly. You will use this same proportion scale for medium-grain brown rice.

MACHINE: Medium (6-cup) rice cooker; fuzzy logic or on/off
CYCLE: Regular/Brown Rice
YIELD: Serves 4

1 cup domestic long-grain brown rice
2 cups plus 1 tablespoon water

1. Place the rice in a fine strainer or bowl, rinse with cold water twice, and drain twice.
2. Place the rice in the rice cooker bowl. Add the water, swirl to combine, close the cover, and set for the regular/Brown Rice cycle.
3. When the machine switches to the Keep Warm cycle, let the rice steam for 10 to 15 minutes. Fluff the rice with a wooden or plastic rice paddle or wooden spoon. This rice will hold on Keep Warm for 1 to 2 hours. Serve hot.

short-grain brown rice

Short-grain brown rice is beloved by vegetarians, health food advocates, macrobiotics, Somersizers, and everyone else who loves chewy, flavorful brown rice. Short-grain brown rice is not as smoothly sweet as long-grain and makes a perfect side dish with a bit of butter or sprinkled with *gomasio* (page 65), a sesame salt condiment very popular in Japanese cuisine. If you want a brown rice risotto (don't tell the purists) or a dessert pudding, this would be the rice to use.

MACHINE: Medium (6-cup) rice cooker; fuzzy logic or on/off
CYCLE: Regular/Brown Rice
YIELD: Serves 4

1 cup short-grain brown rice
2¼ cups cold water

1. Place the rice in a fine strainer or bowl, rinse with cold water twice, and drain twice.
2. Place the rice in the rice cooker bowl. Add the water; swirl to combine. If you have the time, soak the rice in its cooking water for 30 minutes to 1 hour. Close the cover and set for the regular/Brown Rice cycle.
3. When the machine switches to the Keep Warm cycle, let the rice steam for 10 to 15 minutes. Fluff the rice with a wooden or plastic rice paddle or wooden spoon. This rice will hold on Keep Warm for 1 to 2 hours. Serve hot.

Some rices come in boxes, others in sealed bags, and others in bulk bins or large sacks. The latter require that you transfer the rice to a storage container. We recommend that you label your raw rices; even on a good day, short-grain Tamaki Gold can look a lot like Carnaroli, and short-grain and medium-grain brown rices are almost indistinguishable. Different types of long-grain brown rice are identical. Make a batch of the rice, write down the water-to-rice proportion, and keep it with the batch for quick reference; the rest of the batch should consistently cook up just like that first batch. Store white and wild rices at room temperature indefinitely, although remember that rice will dry out over time and need a bit more water to cook, especially Thai jasmine. Brown rices and some specialty rices like Jasmati are best stored refrigerated after a month.

Store cooked rice in the refrigerator for up to five days in a tightly covered container; if you just cover it with plastic wrap, it will dry out a lot faster (scientifically known as retrogradation, the degree to which the starch hardens as the rice chills) and lose its taste. Cooled cooked rice can be frozen for six to eight months in plastic freezer bags, waiting for your next fried rice session or spur-of-the-moment rice salad. You can defrost rice at room temperature or in the refrigerator. We remove frozen rice the day before using.

brown basmati rice

Considering how aromatic white basmati rice is, you will have a shock if you expect the imported brown unhulled basmati to taste and smell the same. It doesn't. It might as well be an entirely different rice. First, the dark tan rice is a lot less foamy while washing. The aroma is distinctly grassy and the flavor delicately nutty. It takes fully twice the amount of time to cook as the white long-grain basmati. You can use these proportions for the domestic brown basmati developed by Lundberg, which is a delicious, milder rice all around.

MACHINE: Medium (6-cup) rice cooker; fuzzy logic or on/off
CYCLE: Regular/Brown Rice
YIELD: Serves 4

1 cup imported Indian brown basmati rice
2 cups water
1 tablespoon unsalted butter
1/4 teaspoon salt

1. Place the rice in a fine strainer or bowl, rinse with cold water twice, and drain twice.
2. Coat the rice cooker bowl with nonstick cooking spray or a film of vegetable oil. Place the rice in the rice bowl. Add the water, butter, and salt; swirl to combine.

Close the cover and set for the regular/ Brown Rice cycle.

3. When the machine switches to the Keep Warm cycle, let the rice steam for 10 minutes. Fluff the rice with a wooden or plastic rice paddle or wooden spoon. This rice will hold on Keep Warm for 1 to 2 hours. Serve hot.

brown jasmine rice

Brown jasmine rice is grown in the marshy river delta area south of Galveston, Texas, by a third generation of rice growers. It is sold by Lotus Foods under the label of Lowell Farms. It is a pale tan, long-grain rice that we found cooks up very much like white rice because the bran and germ layers are so thin. But be prepared; it is a bit moist, like regular jasmine rice, rather than dry, like other long-grain brown rices. We found this had the most appealing aroma of all the brown rices, delicate and slightly nutty. The flavor is equally light and not overly sweet like other brown rices. We do not add salt during cooking; it is too strong and can be detected in the final flavor. This rice became a fast favorite.

MACHINE: Medium (6-cup) rice cooker; fuzzy logic or on/off
CYCLE: Regular/Brown Rice
YIELD: Serves 4

1 cup domestic brown jasmine rice
2 cups water
1 tablespoon unsalted butter

1. Coat the rice cooker bowl with nonstick cooking spray or a film of vegetable oil. Place the rice in the rice bowl. Add the water and butter, swirl to combine, close the cover, and set for the regular/Brown Rice cycle.

2. When the machine switches to the Keep Warm cycle, let the rice steam for 15 minutes. Fluff the rice with a wooden or plastic rice paddle or wooden spoon. This rice will hold on Keep Warm for 1 to 2 hours. Serve hot.

wehani rice

Wehani rice, which is a russet color and somewhere between a long- and medium-grain brown rice, is a specialty rice developed by the Lundberg brothers in the upper Sacramento delta in central California. This rice is served as the house rice at one of our local gourmet restaurants, with everything from grilled seafood to game hens. Let the rice sit for 15 minutes longer if it is too moist. You don't want a big clump of rice, but know that it tends to look moist, even if it will be delicate on the tongue. Don't add salt while Wehani is cooking; it will toughen the grain. This rice is delicious and one of our favorites in the brown rice genre (try it as a fried rice).

MACHINE: Medium (6-cup) rice cooker; fuzzy logic or on/off
CYCLE: Regular/Brown Rice
YIELD: Serves 4

1 cup Wehani rice
1³/₄ cups plus 2 tablespoons water
1 tablespoon unsalted butter (optional)

1. Coat the rice cooker bowl with nonstick cooking spray or a film of vegetable oil. Place the rice in the rice bowl. Add the water and butter, if using, swirl to combine, close the cover, and set for the regular/Brown Rice cycle.

2. When the machine switches to the Keep Warm cycle, open and dry the inside of the cover. Crumple a clean paper towel and place over the surface of the rice to absorb excess moisture. Close the cover and let the rice steam for 15 minutes. Remove the paper towel. Fluff the rice with a wooden or plastic rice paddle or wooden spoon. This rice will hold on Keep Warm for 1 to 2 hours. Serve hot.

riz rouge

Riz rouge de Camargue is a red rice from the marshy Camargue region of southern France, adjacent to the French Riviera. It is imported as an artisanal rice by Made in France, Inc., of San Francisco and is really a special find since friends in Paris don't seem to be able to get it! It is a beautiful, earthy-colored russet rice with pointed ends and intact hull, technically making it a brown rice. The rice is so visually delicate that immediately our instincts were to use proportions as for a white rice rather than a brown rice, which ended up being accurate. The rice plumps and elongates, cooking into a mass of dark rice with lots of white grains scattered throughout.

It has a milder flavor than other red rices that deepens as it sits on the Keep Warm cycle. It is the longest grain of all the red rices and the least sticky. Serve as a side dish with roast meats and rosy dark sauces.

MACHINE: Medium (6-cup) rice cooker; fuzzy logic or on/off
CYCLE: Regular/Brown Rice
YIELD: Serves 4

1 cup riz rouge
1³/₄ cups water
1 tablespoon unsalted butter (optional)

1. Coat the rice cooker bowl with nonstick cooking spray or a film of vegetable oil. Place the rice in the rice bowl. Add the water and butter, if using. Close the cover and set for the regular/Brown Rice cycle.

2. When the machine switches to the Keep Warm cycle, let the rice steam for 10 minutes. Fluff the rice with a wooden or plastic rice paddle or wooden spoon. This rice will hold on Keep Warm for 1 to 2 hours. Serve hot.

wild pecan rice

Wild Pecan aromatic rice is a hearty-flavored long-grain brown rice with a gently woodsy aroma that cooks up slightly moist. It is a local regional specialty, grown only in Iberia Parish in the Acadian counties of the South Louisiana bayous. Developed by Louisiana

State University, Wild Pecan rice is a cross between Carolina long-grain and several varieties of Indochine aromatic rices. It is milled with almost all the bran layers intact, hence the creamy color of the brown rice with some dark grains dispersed; portions of the cooked rice will curl, or butterfly. It is available in the rice section of the supermarket in 7-ounce boxes. If there is a lot of creamy dust in the bag, give it a rinse to clean off the dry bran layers that have fallen off while aging on the shelf. Serve with poultry, game, and shrimp dishes.

MACHINE: Medium (6-cup) rice cooker; fuzzy logic or on/off
CYCLE: Regular/Brown Rice
YIELD: Serves 4

One 7-ounce package Wild Pecan rice
1³/₄ cups water
2 tablespoons unsalted butter
1 teaspoon salt

1. Coat the rice cooker bowl with nonstick cooking spray or a film of vegetable oil. Place the rice in the rice bowl. Add the

AN IMPORTANT NOTE ABOUT MEASUREMENT

Every rice cooker comes with a small plastic measuring cup. This cup holds ³/₄ of a U.S. cup, 6 ounces, or 180 milliliters. When the manual that comes with your cooker says to put 1 cup rice in the rice cooker bowl and add water to the 1-cup line, this is the cup you are supposed to use. This can be very confusing for American cooks, whose cooking instincts have been honed on the standard 8-ounce U.S. cup (which is equal to 240 milliliters).

When we began using the rice cooker, and adapting recipes for it, we were befuddled by this new standard of measurement. In the end, we took different paths, but fortunately both paths led to perfect rice. Beth has stuck with U.S. cups for all applications. Julie uses U.S. cups for "dressed-up" rices like risottos and pilafs, but for Asian recipes, or for ordinary plain rice, Julie likes the convenience of the rice cooker cups, which allow her to pour water directly into the rice cooker bowl, according to the calibrations on its side. Beth doesn't mind the extra step of measuring water. Until some enterprising manufacturer begins to calibrate a rice cooker for the American market using standard U.S. cups, you, too, will have to find your own path. Whether you choose one method or the other, or a combination of both, your rice cooker will work perfectly, as long as you use the correct amount of liquid. The charts on pages 34, 42, and 50 are designed to help you.

Throughout this book, we use the term "rice cooker cup" to distinguish these little 6-ounce cups from the standard 8-ounce U.S. cup. For consistency, most of the recipes in this book have been developed using U.S. cups. Some exceptions to this are the sushi rice and the rice cooking charts, which give both measurements for your convenience. If a recipe is designed for rice cooker cup proportions, it will be labeled such (1 rice cooker cup). If there is no designation (1 cup), that will always mean a U.S. cup.

water, 1 tablespoon of the butter, and the salt; swirl to combine. Close the cover and set for the regular/Brown Rice cycle.

2. When the machine switches to the Keep Warm cycle, let the rice steam for 10 minutes. Fluff the rice with a wooden or plastic rice paddle or wooden spoon. This rice will hold on Keep Warm for 1 to 2 hours. Serve hot, with the remaining 1 tablespoon butter nestled on top.

b h u t a n e s e
r e d   r i c e

Heirloom, unhulled short-grain red rice (*eue chum*) is an ancient grain from the remote and beautiful Himalayan kingdom of Bhutan, and has been a staple daily grain in that country for centuries. It is imported exclusively by Lotus Foods. It is as colorful as it is flavorful, a lovely salmon red after cooking. Naturally colored, red rice is served at festive occasions. Red is the color of the rajas, bearers of a title of nobility in India. The red color is a long-standing Hindu and Buddhist symbol for creativity and the energy of life. We found the rice to have an aroma like that of a robust brown rice. It is a slightly moist rice, so be sure to let it rest for 10 minutes after cooking to firm up a bit.

MACHINE: Medium (6-cup) rice cooker; fuzzy logic or on/off
CYCLE: Regular/Brown Rice
YIELD: Serves 4

1 cup red rice
1³/₄ cups water
¹/₄ teaspoon salt

1. Place the rice in a fine strainer or bowl, rinse with cold water twice, and drain twice. The water will be foamy and a dull red.

2. Coat the rice cooker bowl with nonstick cooking spray or a film of vegetable oil. Place the rice in the rice bowl. Add the water and salt; swirl to combine. Close the cover and set for the regular/Brown Rice cycle.

3. When the machine switches to the Keep Warm cycle, let the rice steam for 10 minutes. Fluff the rice with a wooden or plastic rice paddle or wooden spoon. This rice will hold on Keep Warm for up to 1 hour. Serve hot.

b l a c k   r i c e

Forbidden Black Rice is a Chinese black rice. This rice was the first grain to be imported by the fledgling company that would be called Lotus Foods. While traveling in China, owners Caryl Levine and Ken Lee went on a marketing tour of the upper Mekong area, Laos, and Burma. In an area populated by 26 autonomous tribes, they ate this rice bowl rice at every village they visited. This rice is unusual because black rice is usually sticky; Forbidden Rice is not. It is known as having medicinal qualities. Because it still has its colorful bran layer, it turns an intriguing purple-black color when cooked. It is a sweet, rather moist rice with an ever so slight crunch and is perfectly addicting. Note: This rice will stain the sides of your mouth for a short while, just like blueberries. Serve under stir-fries and with grilled poultry.

MACHINE: Medium (6-cup) rice cooker;
fuzzy logic or on/off
CYCLE: Regular/Brown Rice
YIELD: Serves 4

1 cup Forbidden Black Rice (China black
  rice)
1³/₄ cups water
¹/₄ teaspoon salt (optional)

1. Place the rice in a fine strainer or bowl,
rinse with cold water twice, and drain
twice. The water will turn grayish.
2. Coat the rice cooker bowl with nonstick
cooking spray or a film of vegetable oil.
Place the rice in the rice bowl. Add the
water and salt, if using; swirl to combine.
Close the cover and set for the regular/
Brown Rice cycle.
3. When the machine switches to the Keep
Warm cycle, open and dry the inside of the
cover. Crumple a clean paper towel and
place it over the rice to absorb excess
moisture. Close the cover and let the rice
steam for 15 minutes. Remove the paper
towel. Fluff the rice with a wooden or
plastic rice paddle or wooden spoon. This
rice will hold on Keep Warm for 1 to 2
hours. Serve hot.

black
japonica rice

Black Japonica is another specialty rice
developed by the Lundberg brothers in the
upper Sacramento delta in central California.
It is an unhulled, unmilled blend of a medium-
grain red rice and a short-grain black rice; it
cooks just like brown rice. When fresh, the
rice has an attractive natural sheen and very
earthy smell. This rice turns a dark mahogany
color and ends up with a bit of a bite after it is
cooked, so don't expect it to be soft or mushy
on the tongue even though it is quite moist.
This is an assertively flavored rice, much like
pure wild rice, with a strong vegetable/grain
taste that is almost mossy. Serve with roast
venison, prime rib, or as part of a stuffing.

MACHINE: Medium (6-cup) rice cooker;
fuzzy logic or on/off
CYCLE: Regular/Brown Rice
YIELD: Serves 4 to 6

1 cup Black Japonica rice
2¹/₃ cups water

1. Place the rice in a fine strainer or bowl,
rinse with cold water twice, and drain
twice. The water will be dull reddish.
2. Coat the rice cooker bowl with nonstick
cooking spray or a film of vegetable oil
(this is important with this rice). Place the
rice in the rice bowl. Add the water; swirl
to combine. Close the cover and set for the
regular/Brown Rice cycle.
3. When the machine switches to the Keep
Warm cycle, open and dry the inside of the
cover. Close the cover and let the rice rest
for 30 to 45 minutes. Fluff the rice a few
times with a wooden or plastic rice paddle
or wooden spoon. This rice will hold on
Keep Warm for 1 to 2 hours. Serve hot.

This section of recipes includes our "throw-all-the-ingredients-at-once-into-the-pot" rice dishes. These are the recipes we make most when we need a rice side dish for dinner or a quick lunch or supper. They are the staples of the everyday cook's repertoire and are great alongside roasted and sautéed meats, poultry, fish, sausages, and game. Some of the recipes are very simple, such as the saffron or lemon rice. There are ethnic specialties, such as a Mexican-style green rice and a rice with dried fruit, and others are more complex, with a bit of meat and vegetables, such as Rainbow Rice in a Pot, designed to be a one-dish meal. Other dishes are outright compositions of rice with a topping that have multiple preparations, such as the Indonesian Rice Bowl or Paella Sauté. Japanese rice balls are lunch box staples. For a simple meal, have one of our rices, a crisp green salad, and a piece of fruit.

saffron rice

Plain long-grain white rice with a pinch of saffron—the bright orange stigmas from the flowering bulb *Crocus sativus*—added to the cooking water is a favorite rice from the British Isles to Poland. The rice takes on a lovely pale yellow cast. Use a tiny pinch of powdered saffron or crush a stigma or two between your fingers. It is important that it is no more than a pinch; you want only the faintest hint of the pungent spice in the cooked rice. Serve with roast lemon chicken or pork loin with prunes.

MACHINE: Medium (6-cup) rice cooker; fuzzy logic or on/off
CYCLE: Regular
YIELD: Serves 3 to 4

1 cup long-grain white rice, such as basmati, Texmati, or Carolina
1 1/2 cups water
1/3 teaspoon salt
Small 2-finger pinch of saffron

1. If using basmati, place the rice in a fine strainer or bowl, rinse with cold water twice, and drain twice.
2. Coat the rice cooker bowl with nonstick cooking spray or a film of vegetable oil. Place the rice in the rice bowl. Add the water, salt, and saffron; swirl just to combine, close the cover, and set for the regular cycle.
3. When the machine switches to the Keep Warm cycle, let the rice steam for 15 minutes. Fluff the rice with a wooden or plastic rice paddle or wooden spoon. This rice

will hold for 2 to 3 hours on Keep Warm. Serve hot.

saffron rice with cherries: Add ³/₄ cup coarsely chopped pitted sweet cherries (unsweetened, fresh or thawed frozen) to the rice in step 2. Hold on Keep Warm for up to 1 hour.

lemon rice

Beth's mom makes this fresh-tasting rice to serve with chicken sautés and grilled prawns. It is a favorite.

MACHINE: Medium (6-cup) rice cooker; fuzzy logic or on/off
CYCLE: Regular
YIELD: Serves 3 to 4

1 cup long-grain white rice, such as basmati or Carolina
1¹/₂ cups chicken stock
Pinch of salt
1 large clove garlic
2 teaspoons grated lemon zest
2 tablespoons unsalted butter
2 tablespoons chopped fresh Italian parsley leaves

1. If using basmati rice, place the rice in a fine strainer or bowl, rinse with cold water twice, and drain twice.
2. Place the rice in the rice cooker bowl. Add the stock and salt, stir just to combine, then place the garlic in the center on top of the rice. Close the cover and set for the regular cycle.

3. When the machine switches to the Keep Warm cycle, add the lemon zest, butter, and parsley; stir to combine. Close the cover and let the rice steam for 10 minutes. Fluff the rice with a wooden or plastic rice paddle or wooden spoon. This rice will hold on Keep Warm for 1 to 2 hours. Before serving, remove the garlic and discard. Serve hot.

asian multigrain rice

In Chinese specialty markets you can find an easy-to-use, inexpensive, and delicious grain blend that adds a sweetish, nutty flavor, fiber, and nutrition to your plain rice. It also adds color; the cooked grain blend will be tinted a light lavender. Greenmax Fine Multi Grains are imported from Taiwan. Look in the rice section for a small plastic bag containing a wide variety of grains, including two kinds of barley, four kinds of rice, buckwheat groats, fox-nuts, whole millet, wheat, and oats. As you can imagine, this blend is quite assertively flavored. We like it best combined with regular white rice to mute the flavors. Be sure to soak the mixture for an hour before cooking to soften the whole grains.

MACHINE: Medium (6-cup) rice cooker; fuzzy logic or on/off
CYCLE: Regular
YIELD: Serves 4 to 6

1 1/2 cups (2 rice cooker cups) Japanese-
　　style short- or medium-grain white rice
3/4 cup (1 rice cooker cup) multigrain
　　blend
3 3/4 cups water

1.Wash the rice. Place the rice in a bowl
(or use the bowl of your rice cooker) and
fill the bowl about half-full with cold tap
water. Swirl the rice in the water with your
hand. Carefully pour off most of the
water, holding one cupped hand under the
stream to catch any grains of rice that are
carried away with the water. Holding the
bowl steady with one hand, use the other
to rub and squeeze the wet rice, turning
the bowl as you go, so that all the rice is
"scrubbed." The small amount of water in
the bowl will turn chalky white. Now, run
cold water into the bowl, give the rice a
quick swish, and carefully drain off the
water as before. Repeat the scrubbing and
pouring-off process two more times. By
the third time, the water you pour off will
be nearly clear.

2.Place the rice and multigrain blend in the
rice cooker bowl. Add the water; swirl to
combine. Let the grains soak for 1 hour.

3.Close the cover and set for the regular
cycle. When the machine switches to the
Keep Warm cycle, let the grains steam for
15 minutes. Fluff the grains with a wooden
or plastic rice paddle or wooden spoon.
This rice will hold on Keep Warm for 1 to
2 hours. Serve hot.

julia's aromatic basmati rice

From excellent cook and new friend Julia
Scannel, here is her quick weekday-night
fluffy rice, which she learned when working
on a book of recipes, *Cooking with the Spices of
India* (Culinary Alchemy, 1995). The whole
spices add a gentle scent and subtle flavor
to the rice, especially apparent in the rice
close to the spices. You will need to go to
a specialty grocery to purchase the whole
green cardamom pods, a member of the
ginger family, which are different than the
bleached white ones that are used in Scan-
dinavian cuisine. The spices are left whole
during serving, but are not eaten. Serve
with yogurt-marinated tandoori chicken
and chutney.

MACHINE: Medium (6-cup) rice cooker;
fuzzy logic or on/off
CYCLE: Regular
YIELD: Serves 3

1 cup white basmati rice
1 1/2 cups water
1/4 teaspoon salt
One 4-inch stick cinnamon
3 green cardamom pods

1.Place the rice in a fine strainer or bowl,
rinse with cold water, and drain.

2.Place the rice, water, salt, and spices in
the rice cooker bowl; swirl to combine.
Close the cover and set for the regular
cycle.

3. When the machine switches to the Keep Warm cycle, let the rice steam for 15 minutes. Fluff the rice with a wooden or plastic rice paddle or wooden spoon. This rice will hold on Keep Warm for 3 to 4 hours. Serve hot.

raisins and rice

Dried fruits, especially raisins, are used extensively in rice dishes. We love the combination of rice, nuts, and plump raisins, especially when everything goes in the pot at once. Fast and simple, with a sweet edge, for dinner.

MACHINE: Medium (6-cup) rice cooker; fuzzy logic or on/off
CYCLE: Regular
YIELD: Serves 3 to 4

1/2 cup golden raisins
3 tablespoons dry sherry
1 cup long-grain white rice or white basmati rice
1 cup chicken stock
1/3 cup water
1/4 teaspoon salt
2 tablespoons unsalted butter, cut into pieces
1/3 cup chopped unsalted macadamia nuts

1. Combine the raisins and sherry in a small bowl. Let stand on the kitchen counter for 1 hour to macerate.
2. Place the rice, stock, water, salt, and raisin-sherry mixture in the rice cooker

bowl; stir just to combine. Close the cover and set for the regular cycle.
3. When the machine switches to the Keep Warm cycle, dot the rice with the butter and sprinkle with the nuts. Close the cover and let the rice steam for 15 minutes. Fluff the rice with a wooden or plastic rice paddle or wooden spoon. This rice will hold on Keep Warm for 1 to 2 hours. Serve hot.

rice with mushrooms

Although this recipe is designed for use with mild domestic button mushrooms (also known as the "youngsters"), if you are a mushroom lover, feel free to use another type. Look in the produce section of your supermarket or farmer's market for cremini mushrooms, shiitakes, or chanterelles.

MACHINE: Medium (6-cup) rice cooker; fuzzy logic or on/off
CYCLE: Regular
YIELD: Serves 3 to 4

1 cup long-grain white rice
1 1/2 cups chicken or vegetable stock
1/2 teaspoon salt, plus more for seasoning
2 tablespoons unsalted butter
6 ounces fresh mushrooms, sliced
Freshly ground black pepper

1. Coat the rice cooker bowl with nonstick cooking spray or a film of vegetable oil. Place the rice in the rice bowl. Add the stock and 1/2 teaspoon salt; swirl just to

combine. Close the cover and set for the regular cycle.

2. When the machine switches to the Keep Warm cycle, prepare the mushrooms. In a medium-size sauté pan, melt the butter over medium-high heat. Add the mushrooms and cook, stirring, until tender and slightly browned around the edges. Season to taste with salt and pepper and add the mushrooms to the cooked rice. Stir to combine, close the cover, and let the rice steam for 15 minutes. Fluff the rice with a wooden or plastic rice paddle or wooden spoon. This rice will hold on Keep Warm for 1 to 2 hours. Serve hot.

julia's mexican green rice

Another great recipe from creative consultant and recipe writer Julia Scannel, learned while she traveled in Mexico to help write *Cooking with the Chiles & Spices of Mexico* (Culinary Alchemy, 1996). It's wonderful to serve with enchiladas and chiles rellenos. Cilantro, also known as fresh coriander, is an herb characteristic of Mexican cooking. Don't consider reducing the amount called for here; it is perfect as designed.

MACHINE: Medium (6-cup) rice cooker; fuzzy logic or on/off
CYCLE: Regular/Brown Rice
YIELD: Serves 3 to 4

1 tablespoon unsalted butter
1/2 small white onion, chopped
1 cup long-grain white rice
1 1/2 cups water
1/2 teaspoon salt
1/2 cup minced fresh cilantro leaves

1. Set the rice cooker for the Quick Cook or regular/Brown Rice cycle. Place the butter in the rice bowl. When melted, add the onion. Cook, stirring a few times, until the onion is translucent and softened, about 5 minutes.

2. Add the rice, water, salt, and cilantro to the rice cooker bowl. Stir just to combine. Close the cover and reset for the regular/ Brown Rice cycle or let the regular/Brown Rice cycle complete.

3. When the machine switches to the Keep Warm cycle, let the rice steam for 15 minutes. Fluff the rice with a wooden or plastic rice paddle or wooden spoon. This rice will hold on Keep Warm for up to 1 hour. Serve hot.

roasted brown rice with gomasio

Beth's friend Mary Cantori roasts all her grains before cooking them to convert some of the starch into more usable food for the body. This is a technique for short-grain brown rice developed by the macrobiotic food gurus Lima and George Oshawa for their regimen of a fat-free diet based on the Zen

Buddhist philosophical principles of yin and yang, hot and cold, controlling the delivery of specific types of energy to the body. While this is a diet that has its roots in American counter-cuisine, it has found its way into the kitchens of health-conscious cooks and has become an alternative for people with life-threatening diseases who choose to heal themselves by focusing on food as medicine.

The finished rice is enticingly nutty and worth the extra step of roasting, which dramatically reduces its inherent starchiness. Serve with a sprinkling of *gomasio*, a sesame salt condiment very popular in Japanese cuisine. Look for Japanese sesame seeds; they are larger and more flavorful. We also like this with a pickled umeboshi plum or some pickled ginger for a bit of tang.

MACHINE: Medium (6-cup) rice cooker; fuzzy logic or on/off
CYCLE: Regular/Brown Rice
YIELD: Serves 3 to 4

GOMASIO
1/2 cup unhulled sesame seeds
2 teaspoons fine sea salt

1 cup short-grain brown rice
2 1/4 cups cold water

1. Make the *gomasio*. Place the sesame seeds in a dry skillet and cook over medium heat until lightly toasted, 2 to 3 minutes, shaking the pan occasionally. Transfer the seeds to a bowl and let cool. In a blender or using a mortar and pestle, combine the sesame seeds and salt and pulse to grind, or crush until just coarsely ground. Store the *gomasio* in a covered container at room temperature

for up to a week, though it is best made fresh.

2. Preheat the oven to 375°F.

3. Spread the rice out in a single layer on a baking sheet. Bake on the center rack until just toasty golden, 10 to 12 minutes, stirring the rice around the edges into the center.

4. Place the roasted rice in the rice cooker bowl. Add the water; swirl to combine. Close the cover and set for the regular/Brown Rice cycle.

5. When the machine switches to the Keep Warm cycle, let the rice steam for 10 minutes. Fluff the rice with a wooden or plastic rice paddle or wooden spoon. This rice will hold on Keep Warm for 1 to 2 hours. Serve hot, sprinkled with the *gomasio*.

brown rice with miso

Salty miso, a fermented soybean paste that is thick like peanut butter, adds a nice, healthy dimension to plain brown rice (a little dab will do ya, as it is quite strongly flavored). Miso is a traditional Japanese food and there are many types from which to choose, although sometimes finding the one to suit your palate is a challenge. There are the traditional misos, found in Japanese groceries, and unpasteurized misos, geared to health food devotees. The mildest misos are white and a creamy yellow-white, suitable for this recipe (the darker the color of the miso, from red to brown, the stronger the flavor). This rice is really good alongside simple steamed or sautéed vegetables. You can use long-, medium-, or short-grain brown rice in this recipe. Top with minced fresh Italian parsley, *mitsuba* (a Japanese herb found fresh in Asian markets), or green onion tops, and some cubed hot or cold tofu.

MACHINE: Medium (6-cup) rice cooker; fuzzy logic or on/off

CYCLE: Regular/Brown Rice

YIELD: Serves 3 to 4

1 1/2 tablespoons white or yellow miso
2 1/4 cups water or vegetable stock
One 1-inch piece fresh ginger, peeled
Juice of 1/2 small lemon (about 2 teaspoons)
1 cup brown rice

1. In a small bowl, mash the miso in 1/4 cup of the water to dissolve.

2. Place the dissolved miso, the remaining 2 cups water, the ginger, and lemon juice in the rice cooker bowl. Add the rice; swirl to combine. Close the cover and set for the regular/Brown Rice cycle.

3. When the machine switches to the Keep Warm cycle, let the rice steam for 15 minutes. Fluff the rice with a wooden or plastic rice paddle or wooden spoon. Remove and discard the ginger before serving. This rice will hold on Keep Warm for 1 to 2 hours. Serve hot.

japanese rice with chestnuts

Rice and steamed fresh chestnuts are a classic combination in Japanese cooking, with the chestnuts being treated more like a starchy vegetable than a nut. Fresh chestnuts are available throughout the fall in Japan and are a bit larger than their American counterparts, but our chestnuts are just as tasty in this rice. Known as *kuri gohan*, this recipe comes from food writer Hiroko Shimbo's book *The Japanese Kitchen* (Harvard Common Press, 2000); it is based on a dish she remembers eating as a child. *Oishii* (delicious)!

MACHINE: Medium (6-cup) rice cooker; fuzzy logic or on/off

CYCLE: Regular

YIELD: Serves 4

1 1/2 cups (2 rice cooker cups) Japanese-style medium- or short-grain white rice
1 3/4 cups water
20 to 25 chestnuts in their shells
1/2 teaspoon salt
1 tablespoon mirin (sweet rice wine)
2 tablespoons sake
2 tablespoons black sesame seeds
1/2 teaspoon fine sea salt

1. Wash the rice. Place the rice in a bowl (or use the bowl of your rice cooker) and fill the bowl about half-full with cold tap water. Swirl the rice in the water with your hand. Carefully pour off most of the water, holding one cupped hand under the

stream to catch any grains of rice that are carried away with the water. Holding the bowl steady with one hand, use the other to rub and squeeze the wet rice, turning the bowl as you go, so that all the rice is "scrubbed." The small amount of water in the bowl will turn chalky white. Now, run cold water into the bowl, give the rice a quick swish, and carefully drain off the water as before. Repeat the scrubbing and pouring-off process two more times. By the third time, the water you pour off will be nearly clear.

2. Place the rice in the rice cooker bowl. Add the water, close the cover, and let the rice soak for 30 minutes to 1 hour.

3. While the rice is soaking, peel the chestnuts. Place the whole chestnuts in their shells in a large bowl. Completely cover the chestnuts with boiling water. Let stand for 30 minutes, then drain in a colander. With a paring knife, peel off the brown shell and underlying thin brown skin. Cut each nut into 4 to 6 chunks.

4. Add the salt, mirin, and sake to the rice and its soaking water; swirl to combine. Arrange the raw chestnuts on top of the rice. Close the cover and set for the regular cycle.

5. While the rice is cooking, place the sesame seeds in a small dry skillet over medium-low heat. Shake the skillet to prevent burning and toast the seeds for 1 to 2 minutes. Transfer to a *suribachi* mortar and pestle and coarsely crush the seeds with the sea salt or pulse in a blender until just coarsely ground.

6. When the machine switches to the Keep Warm cycle, let the rice steam for 10 minutes. Gently but thoroughly stir the rice

with a plastic or wooden rice paddle or wooden spoon to distribute the steamed chestnuts. This rice will hold on Keep Warm for up to 1 hour. Serve hot, sprinkled with the sesame salt.

rice with three c's
(currants, coconut, and cashews)

We're always looking for something else to do with those luscious salted cashews besides snacking. This is a recipe from Beth's friend Julia Scannel. Be sure to use dried currants, not raisins, which are too big. Julia serves this with simple curries and roasted poultry.

MACHINE: Medium (6-cup) rice cooker; fuzzy logic or on/off
CYCLE: Regular
YIELD: Serves 3 to 4

1 cup white basmati rice
1 tablespoon unsalted butter
$1/4$ cup diced yellow onion
$1/4$ cup unsweetened shredded coconut
$1/4$ cup dried currants
$1/2$ teaspoon salt
$1 1/2$ cups water
$1/4$ cup salted roasted cashews, chopped

1. Place the rice in a fine strainer or a bowl. Rinse twice and drain twice. Cover the rice with more cold water and allow it to soak

Shelled nuts and seeds are often added to rice dishes, providing flavor along with naturally built-in nourishment. Nuts bring a unique character to rice dishes due to their high percentage of flavorful natural fat, which is released in the presence of heat. You can use raw nuts, toasted nuts, dry-roasted nuts, and nuts with or without salt, as desired. Favorite nuts include almonds, walnuts, and pine nuts. Chestnuts are used in Japanese and Italian rices, pistachios are used in Indian rices, and macadamia nuts are used in fusion recipes. Almonds and hazelnuts, unlike walnuts and pecans, have thin skins, which can be removed by blanching before using. Store all shelled nuts in the refrigerator for about nine months or in the freezer for no longer than one year, until the next year's new crop, but fresh is best.

To Toast Almonds, Pecans, Walnuts, and Pine Nuts

Toasting gives nuts a richer flavor and crisps the texture. Slivered or sliced nuts will toast much more quickly than pieces or halves.

■ *In a conventional oven:* Preheat the oven to 325°F. Place the nuts on an ungreased baking sheet on the center rack and toast for 10 to 15 minutes (depending on the size of the nuts), stirring once with a flat spatula. The nuts should be hot and very pale golden; if they get darker, the flavor will be destroyed and the nuts will taste burnt. Let cool to room temperature before using.

■ *In the microwave oven:* Place the nuts in a single layer on a shallow paper plate or double layer of paper towels. Toast the nuts on high power for 4 to 5 minutes per 1/2 cup, stirring every 1 to 2 minutes to prevent burning and facilitate even browning. This method toasts nuts very quickly, so watch carefully! Let cool to room temperature before using.

■ *On the stovetop:* When a recipe calls for 1/4 cup or less of toasted nuts, they can be toasted in a heavy skillet or sauté pan on the stovetop. Place whole or chopped nuts in a clean, dry skillet over medium-low heat. Stir constantly or shake the pan until the nuts are slightly colored and aromatic, 2 to 4 minutes. Remove from the pan to cool to room temperature before using.

To Blanch Almonds

Fill a medium-size saucepan three-quarters full of water and bring it to a boil. Add the whole shelled almonds and remove the pan from the heat. Let stand for 3 minutes, then rinse the nuts under cold running water. Squeeze the nut kernel out of its loosened brown layer of skin by holding the nut between your thumb and index finger. Let the nuts dry on a layer of paper towels for at least 2 hours or gently oven-dry on a baking sheet in a preheated 300°F. oven for 4 to 5 minutes.

To Skin and Oven-Dry Pistachio Nuts

Place the nuts in a heatproof bowl and cover with boiling water. Let the nuts stand for 1 minute, then drain. Turn the nuts out onto a dish towel and rub off the skins. Dry the nuts on a baking sheet in a preheated 300°F oven for about 8 minutes. Store in an airtight container in the freezer.

To Toast and Skin Hazelnuts or Filberts

These nuts have a tough, loose skin that is first removed by toasting. Preheat the oven to 350°F. Place the hazelnuts in one layer in a baking pan. Toast for 10 to 15 minutes, shaking the pan occasionally, until the nuts are lightly colored and the skins blister. Wrap the nuts in a dish towel and let them stand for 1 minute. Rub the nuts in a towel to remove the skins. Let cool to room temperature before using.

To Toast Macadamia Nuts

Macadamia nuts are most commonly available already salted. They are perfectly fine to use like this, just take care to adjust any other salt required in the recipe. If you want unsalted nuts, place the nuts in a mesh strainer and rinse with cold water. Drain on paper towels and proceed to toast as directed. Preheat the oven to 350°F. Place the nuts in one layer in a baking pan. Toast for about 7 minutes, shaking the pan occasionally, until the nuts are lightly colored. Macadamias burn easily, so take care not to overcook. Let cool to room temperature before using.

To Peel and Oven-Dry Chestnuts

While there are vacuum-packed cans of chestnuts in well-stocked grocery stores, the flavor of fresh chestnuts is a real treat in rice dishes. Chestnuts have the reputation of being the most time-consuming nut to peel, but the reward is apparent with the first bite. Place the whole chestnuts in their shells in a large bowl. Completely cover with boiling water. Let stand for 30 minutes, then drain in a colander. With a paring knife, peel off the brown shell and underlying thin brown skin. Cut the nut into the desired number of pieces. Use as is or oven-dry the pieces on a baking sheet in a preheated 300°F oven for 5 to 8 minutes, depending on the size of the pieces.

for 15 minutes and drain. Place the drained rice in the rice cooker bowl.

2. In a medium-size sauté pan, melt the butter over medium heat. Add the onion, and cook, stirring, until translucent and softened. Transfer the onion to the rice cooker bowl. Add the coconut to the sauté pan and toast over medium heat until it just begins to turn golden brown, stirring as needed. Add the coconut to the rice bowl, along with the currants, salt, and water; swirl to combine. Close the cover and set for the regular cycle.

3. When the machine switches to the Keep Warm cycle, let the rice steam for 15 minutes. Fluff the rice with a wooden or plastic rice paddle or wooden spoon. This rice will hold on Keep Warm for 2 to 3 hours.

4. When ready to serve, transfer the rice to a serving bowl and stir in the cashews. Serve immediately.

moroccan brown rice

As guests of the Oldways Food Preservation Society of Boston, a group of food writers and restaurateurs traveled en masse to Morocco a few years ago. The result has been an epiphany regarding North African cuisine, so influenced by the French and Arabs, with the food-loving public reaping the benefit of many excellent articles, travelogues, and exceptional recipes from the little-known land of Casablanca fame.

While couscous is the most prevalent starch in Moroccan cuisine, rice is also made.

Serve this slightly spiced rice with an array of plain, separately steamed vegetables—green beans, fava or lima beans, carrots, butternut squash, celery, zucchini—and some chickpeas. Preserved lemons are often available in Middle Eastern markets, or you can easily make your own (see page 71).

MACHINE: Medium (6-cup) rice cooker; fuzzy logic or on/off
CYCLE: Regular/Brown Rice
YIELD: Serves 4 to 5

1 1/2 cups aromatic long-grain brown rice, such as Texmati
2 3/4 cups water or vegetable stock
3/4 teaspoon salt
1/2 teaspoon freshly ground black pepper
1 teaspoon ground coriander
1/2 teaspoon ground cardamom
3 tablespoons unsalted butter, cut into pieces
1/4 cup minced preserved lemon, for garnish

1. Coat the rice cooker bowl with nonstick cooking spray or a film of vegetable oil. Place the rice in the rice bowl. Add the water, salt, pepper, coriander, and cardamom; swirl just to combine. Close the cover and set for the regular/Brown Rice cycle.

2. When the machine switches to the Keep Warm cycle, add the butter. Close the cover and let the rice steam for 10 minutes. Fluff the rice with a wooden or plastic rice paddle or wooden spoon. This rice will hold on Keep Warm for 2 hours. Serve hot, sprinkled with a bit of the preserved lemon.

PRESERVED LEMONS

Preserved lemons are made by soaking lemons in a brine solution made of lemon juice plus salt, sugar, or a combination of the two until the lemons turn pulpy and soft. They are used as a condiment or flavor accent in Moroccan cuisine. While they may sound exotic, one taste and people sure do get excited about preserved lemons! That's what our colleague Carolyn Jung at the *San Jose Mercury News* found when she wrote about making preserved lemons, an easy yet fascinating process. Carolyn had attended a class in Moroccan cooking taught by cookbook author Kitty Morse, stocked up on salt and Meyer lemons, and then found she was very nearly obsessed with watching the fruit change, day by day, into the tart, pulpy, and addictive preserved lemons. This can take a month or more, but you can speed up the process by chopping or slicing the lemons instead of just slitting them. Some cooks freeze the lemons for several hours first, or boil the filled jars, also to hasten the process. Many recipes say to rinse the salt off the lemons before using and to use only the peels. Carolyn disagrees, and so do we. We like the way preserved lemons add salt as well as a deeply lemony flavor to foods. Just finely chop the lemons and add to a dish (like our Moroccan Brown Rice) during cooking, or at the end. Or use the lemons uncooked, such as in vinaigrettes.

About 6 to 12 juicy lemons, preferably thin-skinned Meyers
Kosher salt
One 1-quart glass jar with a tight-fitting lid

1. Wash the lemons and dry them thoroughly. Using a clean dry knife, quarter the lemons, remove any seeds, and trim and discard the ends.

2. Sprinkle about 1 tablespoon of salt in the bottom of the jar. Layer the lemons in the jar, alternating with salt, adding 1 tablespoon of salt for each whole lemon. As you reach the top of the jar, press down on the lemons to cram as many pieces as possible into the jar. As you do this, the lemons will exude their juice. When the jar is tightly packed, the level of juice will have risen to or near the top of the jar. You want the jar to be truly full, so if need be, squeeze in some additional lemon juice. Seal the jar and gently shake it to mix the salt and juice. If you are having trouble submerging the lemons, fill the space at the top of the jar with a piece of crumpled plastic wrap.

3. Place the jar on a countertop out of direct sunlight and shake it gently every day or so. In the first few days, as the lemons begin to soften, they may pack down enough to allow you to add another lemon or two. Do so if you can. The lemons are done when they are truly mushy and the juice is syrupy. This will take a few weeks. Once you begin to use the lemons, store the jar in the refrigerator, where it will keep for several months.

basmati rice with corn and peas

This is a recipe from food writer and restaurateur Jesse Cool. For all her fancy gourmet cooking, this is one of her standbys for dinner at home. During the winter, Jesse uses organic frozen vegetables from Cascadian Farms. We like to use white corn, if it's available.

MACHINE: Medium (6-cup) rice cooker; fuzzy logic or on/off
CYCLE: Regular
YIELD: Serves 3 to 4

1 cup white basmati rice

1 1/2 cups water

1/2 teaspoon salt

2 tablespoons chopped fresh Italian
    parsley leaves

1 teaspoon paprika

1/2 cup finely chopped red onion

1/2 cup fresh or frozen English peas

1/2 cup fresh or frozen (and thawed) corn
    kernels

1. Place the rice in a fine strainer or bowl, rinse with cold water twice, and drain twice.
2. Coat the rice cooker bowl with nonstick cooking spray or a film of vegetable oil. Place the rice in the rice bowl. Add the remaining ingredients; stir just to combine. Cover and set for the regular cycle.
3. When the machine switches to the Keep Warm cycle, let the rice steam for 10 minutes. Fluff the rice with a wooden or plastic rice paddle or wooden spoon. This rice will hold on Keep Warm for up to 1 hour. Serve hot.

greek lemon and dill rice with feta

The Greeks have a culinary love affair with the mating of lemon and dill, two plants that have been used since antiquity (lemon trees were planted along the Tigris and Euphrates Valleys). Dill is native to the eastern Mediterranean and contains a flavor element called limonene, which is a natural flavor complement to lemon. In Greek cooking, you find this combination in everything from soups to meat dishes. Rice is no exception. The mint is an optional ingredient, but a traditional one. This dish is also good made with brown rice; if you use it, increase the amount of chicken stock to 2 2/3 cups.

MACHINE: Medium (6-cup) rice cooker; fuzzy logic or on/off
CYCLE: Regular
YIELD: Serves 3 to 4

1 1/2 cups long-grain white rice, such as
    basmati, Jasmati, Carolina, or jasmine

2 cups chicken stock

2 tablespoons olive oil

2 small white boiling onions, chopped

1/4 cup pine nuts

1/4 cup fresh lemon juice

1 tablespoon minced fresh dill or
    1 teaspoon dillweed

1½ teaspoons minced fresh mint leaves
or ½ teaspoon dried mint leaves,
crumbled

1 cup crumbled feta cheese

1 lemon, cut into 8 wedges

1. Coat the rice cooker bowl with nonstick cooking spray or a film of olive oil. Place the rice in the rice bowl. Add the stock; swirl to combine. Close the cover and set for the regular cycle.

2. When the machine switches to the Keep Warm cycle, let the rice steam for 10 minutes.

3. While the rice is steaming, in a small skillet, heat the olive oil over medium heat. Add the onions and cook, stirring, until translucent and softened, about 5 minutes. Add the pine nuts and cook, stirring constantly, until golden brown (it won't take long).

4. When the steaming period is finished, add the sautéed mixture to the rice bowl, along with the lemon juice, dill, and mint. Stir with a wooden or plastic rice paddle or wooden spoon to evenly distribute. Close the cover and let the rice steam for an additional 10 minutes on the Keep Warm cycle.

5. Serve the rice immediately, topped with some feta cheese and a lemon wedge on the side.

note: This rice will hold on Keep Warm for 1 to 2 hours, if necessary, but don't add the lemon juice, dill, and mint until 10 minutes before you plan to serve.

brown basmati almondine

(julie's "cheater's pilaf")

Brown basmati rice presented us with a bit of a challenge. Raw, it has a distinctly grassy odor. If you don't cook it for long enough, the grassy odor and flavor will linger. The trick is to cook it in plenty of water, which ensures that you will be rewarded with fluffy, aromatic grains and a delicate, almost nutty flavor. This elegant side dish is just right with a lightly seasoned baked fish or plain roasted chicken. No one will be able to identify the hint of allspice.

MACHINE: Small (4-cup) or medium (6-cup) rice cooker; fuzzy logic or on/off
CYCLE: Regular/Brown Rice
YIELD: Serves 3 to 4

¾ cup brown basmati rice

1¾ cups water

1 tablespoon ghee (clarified butter; page 117) or unsalted butter

3 tablespoons slivered almonds

¼ teaspoon salt

⅛ to ¼ teaspoon ground allspice, to taste

1. Place the rice in a fine strainer or bowl, rinse with cold water, rubbing it with your hands to remove any bits of dust; drain. Repeat.

2. Place the rice in the rice cooker bowl. Add the water; swirl to combine. Close the cover and set for the regular/Brown Rice cycle.

3. When the machine switches to the Keep Warm cycle, let the rice steam for 15 minutes.

4. While the rice is steaming, prepare the almonds. Melt the ghee in a small skillet over medium heat. Add the almonds and cook, stirring a few times, until golden brown, 2 to 3 minutes. Watch carefully; they burn easily. Set aside.

5. When the steaming period is finished, fluff the rice with a wooden or plastic rice paddle or wooden spoon. This rice will hold on Keep Warm for 3 to 4 hours.

6. Just before serving, add the almonds, salt, and allspice to the rice; stir to evenly distribute. Serve immediately.

matthew's rice

Matthew Bunson is a scholar and author of *The Wisdom Teachings of the Dalai Lama* (Dutton, 1997) and *Papal Wisdom, Words of Hope and Inspiration from Pope John Paul II* (Dutton, 1995). And he cooks rice in his ancient rice cooker. Serve his rice with roast lamb.

MACHINE: Small (4-cup) or medium (6-cup) rice cooker; fuzzy logic or on/off
CYCLE: Regular
YIELD: Serves 5 to 6

2 tablespoons unsalted butter
1/4 cup sliced carrot rounds
1 1/2 cups long-grain white rice or any
    flavorful favorite white rice
2 cups beef stock
1 tablespoon chopped fresh Italian parsley
    leaves

1 teaspoon dried thyme
1/4 cup frozen peas
1 tablespoon chopped almonds

1. Melt 1 tablespoon of the butter in a small skillet over medium heat. Add the carrots and cook, stirring occasionally, until they just begin to soften, 2 to 3 minutes.

2. Place the rice in the rice cooker bowl. Add the stock, parsley, thyme, peas, and sautéed carrots; swirl to combine. Close the cover and set for the regular cycle.

3. When the machine switches to the Keep Warm cycle, let the rice steam for 10 minutes. Fluff the rice with a wooden or plastic rice paddle or wooden spoon. This rice will hold on Keep Warm for 1 to 2 hours.

4. When ready to serve, add the remaining 1 tablespoon butter and the almonds; stir to evenly distribute. Serve immediately.

hunza rice

This dish combines basmati with dried apricots, the reputed fruit of longevity. In the summer, we like to sauté a chopped fresh apricot along with the onion and almonds. Hunza is the name of a tribe of people living in a remote valley of the Himalayas who are blessed with an exceptionally long and healthy life due to their vegetarian diet of unprocessed foods. Because of this, they have risen to mythical status.

MACHINE: Small (4-cup) or medium (6-cup) rice cooker; fuzzy logic or on/off
CYCLE: Regular/Brown Rice
YIELD: Serves 3 to 4

1 cup brown basmati rice

2 cups chicken or vegetable stock or water

¼ cup minced dried apricots

2 tablespoons ghee (clarified butter; page 117) or unsalted butter

¼ cup finely chopped red onion

¼ cup whole almonds, split in half lengthwise

1. Place the rice in a fine strainer or bowl; rinse with cold water, rubbing it with your hands to remove any bits of dust; drain. Repeat.

2. Place the rice in the rice cooker bowl. Add the stock and apricots; swirl to combine. Close the cover and set for the regular/Brown Rice cycle.

3. When the machine switches to the Keep Warm cycle, let the rice steam for 10 to 15 minutes.

4. While the rice is steaming, melt the ghee in a small skillet over medium heat. Add the red onion and cook, stirring a few times, until softened, about 5 minutes. Add the almonds and cook, stirring, until just golden, watching carefully that they don't burn. Remove from the heat and set aside.

5. When you are ready to serve, fluff the rice with a wooden or plastic rice paddle or wooden spoon. Add the sautéed onion mixture; stir to evenly distribute. This rice will hold on Keep Warm for 1 to 2 hours. Serve hot.

wehani rice with garden vegetables

The Lundberg family has been breeding and growing aromatic and organic rices for years in northern California. A favorite is the aromatic Wehani rice bred by the Lundbergs themselves. It packs such a wallop of flavor that it needs little embellishment. This recipe is from food and wine writer Lynn Alley, who leaves the rice cooking while she works in her garden. Then she tops it with young, fresh-picked veggies and a dusting of Parmesan. In the springtime, use peas, green onions, and fresh parsley from your garden, produce stand, or local farmer's market; in the summer, tiny baby zucchini, slender green beans, and strips of red or yellow pepper. And in the fall, try little florets of broccoli, purple potatoes, and baby carrots. Don't bother cutting up the small veggies, simply scrub and steam them whole. A little bit of experience will teach you when the rice is about 10 minutes away from being done; add the vegetables then.

MACHINE: Medium (6-cup) rice cooker; fuzzy logic or on/off

CYCLE: Regular/Brown Rice

YIELD: Serves 2 to 3

1 cup Wehani rice

1¾ cups plus 2 tablespoons water

1 tablespoon onion or mushroom food base (available in natural food stores; optional)

About 2 cups fresh vegetables (choice depending on the season)

3 tablespoons freshly grated Parmesan cheese

1. Place the rice in a fine strainer or bowl, rinse with cold water, and drain.
2. Place the rice in the rice cooker bowl. Add the water and food base, if using; stir briefly. Close the cover and set for the regular/Brown Rice cycle. About 10 minutes before the rice is finished cooking, arrange the vegetables on top of the rice

Sometimes you need an extra-large batch of rice for a special occasion—a holiday, a birthday party, an open house. Here are two recipes.

Rice with Fresh Greens

Here is steamed rice, just a little bit special, to serve with grilled fish and chicken. The combination of parsley, mint, and basil is very Italian and ever so good. Remember that, whenever cooking rice to the full capacity of the cooker bowl, the rice on the bottom will be a bit squishy, so a thorough but gentle mixing after the steaming period is imperative.

MACHINE: Large (10-cup) rice cooker; fuzzy logic or on/off
CYCLE: Regular
YIELD: Serves 20 to 24

6 cups long-grain white rice, such as basmati, Texmati, converted, or Carolina
7³/₄ cups water
5 tablespoons unsalted butter, cut into pieces
1¹/₄ tablespoons salt
¹/₂ cup chopped fresh Italian parsley leaves
¹/₂ cup chopped fresh mint leaves
¹/₂ cup chopped fresh basil leaves

1. Place the rice in a fine strainer or bowl, rinse with cold water 2 to 4 times, and drain.
2. Coat the rice cooker bowl with nonstick cooking spray or a film of vegetable oil. Place the rice in the rice bowl. Add the water, butter, and salt; swirl just to combine. Close the cover and set for the regular cycle.
3. When the machine switches to the Keep Warm cycle, let the rice steam for 15 minutes. Add the herbs to the rice bowl; stir with a wooden or plastic rice paddle or wooden spoon to evenly distribute. Close the cover and let the rice steam for 30 minutes. This rice will hold on Keep Warm for up to 2 hours. Serve hot.

to steam.

3. When the machine switches to the Keep Warm cycle, let the rice steam for 10 minutes.

4. To serve, divide the rice and vegetables into portions, or stir the vegetables into the rice, if desired. Sprinkle with the cheese and serve immediately.

Creamy Dill Rice

A simple but filling rice with herbs that can be served alongside roast turkey or ham. It is made creamy by the use of sour cream (reduced-fat, including nonfat, varieties are acceptable) stirred in at the very end just before serving.

MACHINE: Large (10-cup) rice cooker; fuzzy logic or on/off
CYCLE: Regular
YIELD: Serves 30

7^1/$_2$ cups long-grain white rice, such as basmati, Texmati, or Carolina
9^1/$_2$ cups chicken stock
6 tablespoons unsalted butter, cut into pieces
1 tablespoon salt
1 cup chopped fresh dill
^{1}/$_2$ cup minced fresh Italian parsley leaves
^{1}/$_4$ cup minced fresh tarragon leaves
3 cups sour cream
Freshly ground black pepper

1. Place the rice in a fine strainer or bowl, rinse with cold water 2 to 4 times, and drain.

2. Coat the rice cooker bowl with nonstick cooking spray or a film of vegetable oil. Place the rice in the rice bowl. Add the stock, butter, salt, dill, parsley, and tarragon; swirl just to combine. Close the cover and set for the regular cycle.

3. When the machine switches to the Keep Warm cycle, let the rice steam for 30 minutes. Fluff gently but thoroughly with a wooden or plastic rice paddle or wooden spoon. This rice will hold on Keep Warm for up to 2 hours.

4. When ready to serve, stir the sour cream to loosen it, then stir it into the hot rice. Serve immediately, passing the pepper grinder.

baby artichokes and arborio rice

In the Puglia area of Italy, rice is cooked "Spanish" style, that is, similar to paella. Called a *tiella*, after the round terra-cotta dish it is baked in, the rice is layered with vegetables. You can use other Italian medium-grain rices in this dish, such as the Argentinean-grown Carnaroli rice imported by Lotus Foods. We must admit we have substituted frozen artichoke hearts for the fresh when artichokes are out of season.

MACHINE: Medium (6-cup) or large (10-cup) rice cooker; fuzzy logic or on/off
CYCLE: Regular
YIELD: Serves 4

Juice of 1 lemon
8 baby artichokes of equal size
2 cups Arborio or other medium-grain (risotto-style) rice
1/4 cup (1/2 stick) unsalted butter, cut into 8 pieces
2 medium-size shallots, minced
1/4 cup minced fresh Italian parsley leaves
3 cups chicken stock
1/2 teaspoon salt
Freshly ground black pepper
3 tablespoons freshly grated Parmesan cheese, plus more for serving

1. Fill a large bowl with cold water and pour the lemon juice into it. Prepare the artichokes by bending the outer leaves back and snapping them off until only the yellow inside leaves remain. You will remove more leaves than you think you should; this is okay. How many you remove will depend on the size and tenderness of each artichoke. Cut 1/2 inch off the top of each artichoke with a sharp paring knife and trim the bottoms flat. Cut each in half lengthwise. Place the artichokes in the lemon water as you work to prevent discoloration.

2. Place the rice in a fine strainer or bowl, rinse with cold water twice, and drain twice.

3. Place the butter pieces evenly over the bottom of the rice cooker bowl. Sprinkle with the shallots, then cover with the rice, then the parsley. Arrange the artichokes on top, stem side slightly down, pressing into the rice. Pour the stock over the layered ingredients. Close the cover and set for the regular cycle.

4. When the machine switches to the Keep Warm cycle, stir in the salt, pepper to taste, and cheese. Close the cooker and let the rice steam for 10 minutes.

5. Serve immediately. Spoon the rice and vegetables onto serving plates and pass more cheese on the side.

polynesian tiki rice

From the exotic South Sea islands, this fruit-rich rice is a natural accompaniment to roast pork or chicken. The vegetables and fruit will be tossed in at the end of the cooking of the mild curried rice. Use fresh pineapple, if you can.

MACHINE: Medium (6-cup) rice cooker;
fuzzy logic or on/off

CYCLE: Regular

YIELD: Serves 3 to 4

1 cup long-grain white rice, such as
    basmati or Carolina
1¹/₂ cups water
1 tablespoon unsalted butter
¹/₄ teaspoon salt
¹/₄ teaspoon freshly ground black pepper
2 teaspoons mild curry powder
1 green onion, white part and a few
    inches of the green part, minced
¹/₂ cup finely chopped fresh pineapple or
    canned crushed pineapple in its own
    juice, drained
1 cup seedless green grapes
¹/₄ cup seeded and minced green bell
    pepper
1 cup diced cucumber, for garnish
1 lime, cut into 4 wedges

1. If using basmati, place the rice in a fine
strainer or bowl. Rinse with cold water and
drain. Repeat.

2. Coat the rice cooker bowl with nonstick
cooking spray or a film of vegetable oil.
Place the rice in the rice bowl. Add the
water, butter, salt, pepper, and curry
powder and stir a few times. Close the
cover and set for the regular cycle.

3. When the machine switches to the Keep
Warm cycle, sprinkle the green onion, pineapple, grapes, and green pepper on top of
the rice. Close the cover and let the rice
steam for 15 minutes. Stir the rice with a
wooden or plastic rice paddle or wooden
spoon to combine. Serve immediately,
sprinkled with the cucumber and with a
lime wedge on the side.

japanese three- mushroom rice

This lovely dish, from Naoko Boerger, a Tokyo
native who now lives in Palo Alto, California,
is perfect for autumn. It uses three very different types of mushrooms, shiitake, *shimeji*, and
oyster. The tiny *shimeji* mushrooms are sold in
100-gram clumps. If you can't find them, you
can use another variety of wild or domestic
mushroom. The tofu puff, which you can find
in the refrigerator case of Asian markets,
soaks up the mushroom flavor wonderfully,
but if you can't find it in your area, leave it
out. Naoko serves the rice with fried shrimp
coated with bread crumbs, and a green bean
salad with sesame dressing.

MACHINE: Medium (6-cup) rice cooker;
fuzzy logic or on/off

CYCLE: Regular

YIELD: Serves 6

3 cups (4 rice cooker cups) Japanese-style
    medium- or short-grain rice
1 large fresh shiitake mushroom or
    1 large or 2 small dried shiitake
    mushrooms
¹/₂ clump (50 grams) *shimeji* mushrooms
³/₄ cup oyster mushrooms
2 tablespoons plus 2 teaspoons soy
    sauce, plus more for serving
1 fried tofu puff (*abura age*; see note on
    page 85)
4 teaspoons sake
3 cups Dashi (page 349)

1. Wash the rice. Place the rice in a bowl (or use the bowl of your rice cooker) and fill the bowl about half-full with cold tap water. Swirl the rice in the water with your hand. Carefully pour off most of the water, holding one cupped hand under the stream to catch any grains of rice that are carried away with the water. Holding the bowl steady with one hand, use the other to rub and squeeze the wet rice, turning the bowl as you go, so that all the rice is "scrubbed." The small amount of water in the bowl will turn chalky white. Now, run cold water into the bowl, give the rice a quick swish, and carefully drain off the water as before. Repeat the scrubbing and pouring-off process two more times. By the third time, the water you pour off will be nearly clear.

2. Place the drained rice in the rice cooker bowl. Cover with a clean, wet tea towel and let the rice rest for 30 minutes

3. Set a kettle of water on to boil. Meanwhile, rinse the fresh shiitake mushroom, if using. If using the dried mushrooms, place in a small bowl, cover with water, partially cover with plastic wrap, and microwave on high for 2 minutes, or cover with warm water and let soak for 30 minutes. Drain, pat dry, and thinly slice.

4. Break apart the *shimeji* mushrooms; trim and discard the ends. Wipe gently with a damp tea towel or paper towel to clean. Gently brush or wipe any dirt from the oyster mushrooms, then slice them, trimming and discarding the ends. Put all the mushrooms in a medium-size bowl. Sprinkle the soy sauce over them and set aside.

5. Place the tofu puff in a colander in the sink and pour boiling water over it to re- move excess oil. Dry with a paper towel and cut into thin slices. Toss the tofu slices with the mushrooms and soy sauce.

6. Add the sake and dashi to the soaked rice. The dashi should not quite come up to the 4-cup level on the rice cooker bowl. (The mushrooms will contribute some moisture to the dish.) Add the mushroom mixture to the rice; stir to combine. Close the cover and set for the regular cycle.

7. When the machine switches to the Keep Warm cycle, let the rice steam for 15 minutes. Fluff with a wooden or plastic rice paddle or wooden spoon, mixing thoroughly but gently. This rice will hold on Keep Warm for 1 to 2 hours. Serve hot, with some soy sauce on the side, if desired.

mexican rice and beans

Rice and beans are partners in all ethnic cuisines—rice and lentils in India, sticky rice and red adzuki beans in Japan, black rice and beans in Cuba. Here, rice, beans, chile peppers, and tomatoes, staples in the Mexican kitchen, are combined for a very simple all-in-one meal. Serve with warm corn tortillas. If you have an avocado tree or can find avocado leaves in a Mexican market, give that option a try.

MACHINE: Medium (6-cup) rice cooker; fuzzy logic or on/off
CYCLE: Regular
YIELD: Serves 4

1 cup long-grain white rice

1 cup chicken stock

Pinch of salt

1 tablespoon olive oil, vegetable oil, or
  rendered chicken fat

1 large yellow onion, chopped

1 red bell pepper, halved, seeded, and
  sliced

1 jalapeño chile, seeded and minced

One 15-ounce can pinto beans, drained
  and rinsed

One 15-ounce can plum tomatoes
  (can be flavored with Mexican spices),
  with their juices

1 teaspoon crumbled dried oregano leaves
  or 1 small avocado leaf, toasted and
  crumbled

2 tablespoons capers, rinsed

Freshly ground black pepper

3 tablespoons chopped fresh cilantro
  leaves, for garnish

1/2 cup crème fraîche, *crema Mexicana*, or
  sour cream, for garnish

2/3 cup crumbled *queso fresco* (available in
  the dairy section in supermarkets) or
  feta cheese, for garnish

1. Coat the rice cooker bowl with nonstick cooking spray or a film of vegetable oil. Add the rice, stock, and salt; swirl to combine. Close the cover and set for the regular cycle.

2. While the rice is cooking, heat the olive oil in a large skillet over medium heat. Add the onion and bell pepper and cook, stirring, until softened, about 5 minutes. Open the cover of the rice cooker and add the jalapeño, onion-pepper mixture, pinto beans, tomatoes, oregano, capers, and a few grinds of black pepper; stir to combine. Close the cover and let the cycle complete.

3. When the machine switches to the Keep Warm cycle, let the rice steam for 10 minutes. Fluff the rice with a wooden or plastic rice paddle or wooden spoon. This rice will hold on Keep Warm for up to 1 hour.

4. Serve hot, garnished with the cilantro, crème fraîche, and crumbled cheese.

chinese sausage and rice

Food historian and cookbook author Barbara Grunes uses her rice cooker for her home meals. Her recipe for chewy medium-grain rice with spicy Chinese sausage and cilantro is good by itself or as a side dish to serve with other Asian-style foods. The sweet Chinese pork sausage is seasoned with sugar, salt, and wine (look for it in the refrigerator case in Asian markets). If you want to vary the flavor, use cooked Italian sausage and basil instead of the green onions, cilantro, and sesame seeds. The sausage gently flavors the rice as it cooks. Look for black sesame seeds in Asian markets. If you can't find them, use Japanese or regular white sesame seeds. The Japanese ones are more flavorful. This is a super-easy, satisfying dish.

MACHINE: Medium (6-cup) rice cooker;
fuzzy logic or on/off
CYCLE: Regular
YIELD: Serves 4

2 cups medium-grain white rice

1 cup Chinese sausage (*lop cheon*) thinly
   sliced on the diagonal

1/2 cup thinly sliced green onions, mostly
   green parts

2 3/4 cups water

1/4 cup chopped fresh cilantro leaves,
   for garnish

2 tablespoons black sesame seeds (*goma*),
   for garnish

1. Place the rice in a fine strainer or bowl, rinse with cold water twice, and drain twice.

2. Coat the rice cooker bowl with nonstick cooking spray or a film of vegetable oil. Place the rice, sausage, and green onions in the rice bowl. Add the water; stir just to combine. Close the cover and set for the regular cycle.

3. When the machine switches to the Keep Warm cycle, let the rice steam for 15 minutes. Fluff the rice with a wooden or plastic rice paddle or wooden spoon.

4. Serve immediately. Spoon the rice mixture into a deep serving bowl and sprinkle with the cilantro and then the sesame seeds.

super supper sausage and rice

Here is another super-simple, delicious meal. There are many brands of lowfat gourmet smoked sausages on the market; we use the locally produced Aidells (the smoked duck sausage and the smoked chicken and turkey with artichokes are also favorites). Laying the ingredients on top of the rice to steam is a Chinese technique developed when rice was cooked in a wok and the meat or vegetables cooked at the same time. If you double the recipe to feed four, adjust the proportions to 2 cups plus 2 tablespoons rice and 2 3/4 cups water.

MACHINE: Medium (6-cup) rice cooker;
fuzzy logic or on/off
CYCLE: Regular
YIELD: Serves 2

1 cup long-grain white rice

1 1/2 cups water

2 smoked chicken-apple sausages (about
   8 ounces total)

1. Place the rice in a fine strainer or bowl, rinse with cold water, and pour as much of the water off as you can, taking care to keep the rice in the bottom of the bowl.

2. Place the rice in the rice cooker bowl. Add the water; swirl to combine. Close the cover and set for the regular cycle. Set a timer for 15 minutes (or for 30 minutes if your rice cooker has a soaking period built in).

3. Cut the sausages into 1/2-inch-thick slices (slice completely through; you want separate pieces), leaving the sausage shape intact after slicing for easy transfer to the pot. When the timer sounds, open the cover and, holding the sausage at both ends, place the entire sausage on top of the rice, letting the slices fall open (sort of a fan design across the rice, but any way is okay). The sausages will cover the surface of the rice; press them slightly into the partially cooked rice. Close the cover and let the rice finish the cycle.

4. When the machine switches to the Keep Warm cycle, let the rice steam for 15 minutes. Serve immediately.

rainbow rice in a pot

This fantastic recipe is from talented food writer and TV chef Martin Yan. It is a lovely dish redolent of his love for and expertise in Chinese cuisine. Rainbow rice gets its evocative name from the array of colors that will be apparent when you serve this dish. Be sure to use a medium-grain rice; you want the slightly moist texture so it is easy to eat with chopsticks. We also like this with edamame instead of peas.

MACHINE: Medium (6-cup) rice cooker; fuzzy logic or on/off
CYCLE: Regular
YIELD: Serves 3 to 4

3 dried shiitake mushrooms
1¹/₂ cups medium-grain white rice
4 ounces boneless, skinless chicken breast, thinly sliced
2 tablespoons diced Smithfield ham
¹/₄ cup diced carrot
¹/₄ cup frozen peas
1¹/₄ cups water
1¹/₄ cups reduced-sodium chicken stock
2 tablespoons Shaoxing wine (available in Chinese markets) or dry sherry
1¹/₂ tablespoons soy sauce
¹/₂ teaspoon salt

1. Place the mushrooms in a small bowl, cover with hot water, and soak for 30 minutes. Or partially cover the bowl with plastic wrap and microwave on high for 2 minutes. Drain the mushrooms, remove the stems, and cut the caps into thin slices.
2. Place the rice in a fine strainer or bowl, rinse with cold water, and drain.
3. Coat the rice cooker bowl with nonstick cooking spray or a film of vegetable oil. Place the rice in the rice bowl. Add the remaining ingredients; stir just to combine. Close the cover and set for the regular cycle.
4. When the machine switches to the Keep Warm cycle, let the rice steam for 15 minutes. Serve immediately.

japanese rice with mushrooms and chicken

In Japan, there is an entire category of dishes called *takikomi gohan*, or ingredients cooked together with rice. One of the simplest is rice and peas, a combination that is a favorite in many parts of the world (*risi e bisi*, anyone?). Rice with chestnuts and rice with bamboo shoots are Japanese seasonal favorites: bamboo shoots in the spring and chestnuts in the fall. The category continues to grow today, as inventive cooks combine Eastern and Western ingredients with rice in new ways. With an electric rice cooker, *takikomi gohan* are easy, flavorful, and reliable one-dish meals—casseroles, essentially.

This recipe, from Julie's friend Atsuko Ishii, is a traditional-style *takikomi gohan*. It contains one ingredient that may be unfamiliar: *konnyaku*, sometimes translated as devil's-tongue jelly. As the name implies, it's gelatinous and gray in color. It has little flavor on its own but a nice, chewy texture, and it gains flavor during cooking. Made from yams, it is usually sold in small blocks in plastic pouches. It must be boiled briefly before using. The day Atsuko shopped for *konnyaku*, she found only *tama konnyaku*, or *konnyaku* shaped into little balls. We just sliced the balls and they worked out fine. *Konnyaku* is very low in calories and Atsuko says it's a favorite of dieters in Japan. Sweetened, it's a popular low-calorie dessert. If you can't find *konnyaku* in your local Asian market, just make the dish without it.

MACHINE: Medium (6-cup) rice cooker; fuzzy logic or on/off

CYCLE: Regular

YIELD: Serves 4 to 6

2 1/4 cups (3 rice cooker cups) Japanese-style short- or medium-grain rice

1/2 pound boneless, skinless chicken thighs

2 1/2 tablespoons soy sauce

4 medium-large dried shiitake mushrooms

1 medium-size carrot

About 4 ounces (125 grams) *konnyaku* (optional)

4 fried tofu puffs (*abura age*; see note on page 85; optional)

2 tablespoons sake

1 tablespoon mirin (sweet rice wine)

1/4 teaspoon salt

2 to 3 cups Sharon's Dashi (page 350) or 1/2 packet instant powdered dashi

1. Wash the rice. Place the rice in a bowl (or use the bowl of your rice cooker) and fill the bowl about half-full with cold tap water. Swirl the rice in the water with your hand. Carefully pour off most of the water, holding one cupped hand under the stream to catch any grains of rice that are carried away with the water. Holding the bowl steady with one hand, use the other to rub and squeeze the wet rice, turning the bowl as you go, so that all the rice is "scrubbed." The small amount of water in the bowl will turn chalky white. Now, run cold water into the bowl, give the rice a quick swish, and carefully drain off the water as before. Repeat the scrubbing and pouring-off process two more times. By the third time, the water you pour off will be nearly clear. Place the drained rice in the rice cooker bowl.

2. Trim any fat from the chicken and cut it into small bite-size pieces, about 3/4 inch square. Put the chicken in a small bowl with the soy sauce. Mix well, using your fingers to gently but firmly "massage" the soy sauce into the chicken. Spend at least 1 minute doing this. It is an important step that ensures that the chicken will not give off the objectionable odor that sometimes results when chicken is cooked in water. Leave the chicken marinating in the soy sauce.

3. Place the dried mushrooms in a microwave-safe dish just large enough to hold them in a single layer. Add water to the dish, 3/4 to 1 inch deep. Cover the dish tightly with plastic wrap and microwave it on high for 2 minutes. Remove from the microwave and allow it to cool. (Alternatively, you can soak the mushrooms in cold

water for several hours or in hot water for about 30 minutes.)

4. Slice the carrot into thin strips about 1½ inches long by ¼ inch wide, sort of like a fat julienne. Set aside.

5. Bring a small saucepan of water to a boil. While you are waiting for the water to boil, slice the *konnyaku* into pieces similar in shape to the carrot. If you are using *konnyaku* balls, slice them about ¼ inch thick. When the water boils, add the *konnyaku* and boil, uncovered, for 1 minute. Drain and set aside.

6. Rinse out the saucepan, refill it with water, and bring it to a boil again.

7. By now, the mushrooms should be cool enough to handle. Remove them from the liquid (reserving the liquid) and gently squeeze out any excess liquid. Cut off the stems and discard. Slice the mushrooms thinly and set aside.

8. When the water boils, add the tofu puffs and boil them for 1 to 2 minutes to remove any excess oil. Drain the puffs in a colander. When they are cool enough to handle, slice them in half crosswise, then stack the halves and cut into thin strips.

9. Add the sake, mirin, and salt to the rice in the rice cooker. Add most of the mushroom soaking liquid to the rice, pouring slowly and carefully and discarding the last bit, which always contains some grit from the mushrooms. If you are using the dashi powder, add it now, and then add water until the liquid reaches the 3-cup level on your rice cooker bowl. If you are using homemade dashi, add it until the liquid reaches the 3-cup level on your rice cooker bowl. Stir to combine. (Or use a U.S. measuring cup and combine the sake, mirin, salt, mushroom liquid, and dashi to equal 3 U.S. cups. Add the liquids to the bowl and stir to combine.)

10. Add the chicken, mushrooms, carrot, *konnyaku*, and tofu strips to the rice cooker. Stir gently but thoroughly to combine, but do not stir them down into the rice. Close the cover and set for the regular cycle.

11. When the machine switches to the Keep Warm cycle, let the rice steam for 15 minutes. Stir the rice thoroughly with a wooden or plastic rice paddle or wooden spoon to incorporate the chicken, tofu, and vegetables with the rice. Serve the rice immediately or hold on the Keep Warm cycle for up to 1 hour.

note: *Abura age*, or deep-fried tofu puffs, are sold fresh or frozen in Japanese markets or are available canned; fresh or frozen are preferred. If you buy fresh ones, you can keep them in the freezer so they'll be ready for *takikomi gohan*, *inari zushi*, or other uses. One variety of frozen puffs is already seasoned; this is best for *inari zushi*. For this recipe and other rice dishes, use the unseasoned variety.

indonesian rice bowl

From one of the Bay Area's favorite food writers, backyard gardeners, and seed purveyors, Renee Shepherd, comes this satisfying one-dish meal adapted from her book *Recipes from a Kitchen Garden* (Ten Speed, 1993). This is a great recipe to use up leftover chicken. The popular peanut sauce is one of the definitive tastes of the Southeast Asian and Thai cuisines. This simplified version of the *rijsttafel* table, a popular full-rice meal in Indonesia, looks incredibly festive served with all the condiments.

MACHINE: Medium (6-cup) rice cooker; fuzzy logic or on/off

CYCLE: Regular

YIELD: Serves 4

RICE

1 cup Thai jasmine rice

1 cup plus 2 tablespoons water

2¹/2 cups fresh or frozen petite peas (2 pounds fresh unshelled)

2¹/2 cups shredded poached chicken breast

¹/2 cup hot chicken stock

SAUCE

¹/3 cup creamy peanut butter

1 tablespoon dry sherry

2 tablespoons rice vinegar

2 teaspoons peeled and grated fresh ginger

¹/8 teaspoon cayenne pepper

¹/2 teaspoon sugar

1 clove garlic, minced

2 green onions, white parts only, minced (chop the green tops for garnish and reserve)

¹/2 cup chopped roasted peanuts, for garnish

CONDIMENTS

Separate small bowls of chutney, sliced bananas, raisins, unsweetened shredded coconut, minced fresh cilantro leaves, mandarin orange segments, chopped apples, plain yogurt

1. *Make the rice:* Coat the rice cooker bowl with nonstick cooking spray or a film of vegetable oil. Place the rice in the rice bowl. Add the water; swirl to combine. Close the cover and set for the regular cycle.

2. *Make the sauce:* In a medium-size saucepan, combine all the sauce ingredients. Cook over low heat, stirring a few times, until the mixture achieves a saucelike consistency. Cover and keep warm.

3. When the machine switches to the Keep Warm cycle, sprinkle the peas and chicken on top of the rice. Close the cover and let the rice steam for 20 minutes.

4. Transfer the rice mixture to a warmed serving platter with sloped sides. Pour the hot stock and peanut sauce over the rice. Stir gently to combine the peas and chicken with the stock and peanut sauce. Sprinkle with the green onion tops and peanuts. Serve immediately with a choice of condiments.

chicken donburi

Donburi is a Japanese dish that is served in a special oversized rice bowl of the same name. Once Beth discovered how much she loved Calrose and Tamaki Gold rices, she had to have a special simple little meal with which to eat them. Here is one of her best and fastest. If you use the chicken stock, you can add a small piece of kombu dried seaweed (cut an inch-square piece with kitchen shears), if you like. Mirin is a low-alcohol sweet cooking wine (of which there is also a non-alcohol version available) that you can find in the Asian food section of the supermarket.

MACHINE: Medium (6-cup) rice cooker; fuzzy logic or on/off
CYCLE: Regular
YIELD: Serves 3

2 dried shiitake mushrooms (optional)
1 1/2 cups (2 rice cooker cups) Japanese-style short- or medium-grain white rice (not Arborio or other risotto-style rice)
2 cups water (1 2/3 cups for short-grain rice)
Pinch of sea salt
2 cups Dashi (page 349) or chicken stock
3 tablespoons tamari soy sauce
3 tablespoons mirin (sweet rice wine) or 3 tablespoons sake and pinch of sugar
3 boneless, skinless chicken thighs, trimmed of fat and cut into 1-inch strips
6 to 8 ounces firm tofu, cut into cubes
Chopped green parts of green onions or minced fresh chives, for garnish
2 to 3 tablespoons toasted Japanese sesame seeds (page 145), for garnish

1. Place the mushrooms, if using, in a small bowl, cover with hot water, and soak for 30 minutes. Or partially cover the bowl with plastic wrap and microwave on high for 2 minutes. Drain the mushrooms, remove the stems, and cut the caps into thin slices.
2. Wash the rice. Place the rice in a bowl (or use the bowl of your rice cooker) and fill the bowl about half-full with cold tap water. Swirl the rice in the water with your hand. Carefully pour off most of the water, holding one cupped hand under the stream to catch any grains of rice that are carried away with the water. Holding the bowl steady with one hand, use the other to rub and squeeze the wet rice, turning the bowl as you go, so that all the rice is "scrubbed." The small amount of water in the bowl will turn chalky white. Now, run cold water into the bowl, give the rice a quick swish, and carefully drain off the water as before. Repeat the scrubbing and pouring-off process two more times. By the third time, the water you pour off will be nearly clear.

3. Place the rice in the rice cooker bowl. Add the water and salt; swirl to combine. Close the cover and let the rice soak for 30 minutes to 1 hour. When the soaking period is finished, set for the regular cycle.
4. When the machine switches to the Keep Warm cycle, let the rice steam for 15 minutes. Fluff the rice gently but thoroughly with a plastic or wooden rice paddle or wooden spoon. Close the cover and let the rice steam for another 10 to 15 minutes.
5. Meanwhile, poach the chicken. In a medium-size saucepan, combine the dashi, tamari, and mirin. Bring to a simmer over medium heat. Add the chicken and mushrooms, if using, and cook, partially covered, until the chicken is cooked through, 5 to 7 minutes. At the very end, toss in the tofu and let it heat for a minute or so.
6. When the rice has finished steaming, fluff it with the paddle or spoon again. Spoon the rice into individual bowls and top each with a portion of the chicken and tofu mixture. Ladle some of the poaching broth over the top and garnish with the greens and sesame seeds. Serve immediately.

paella sauté with saffron and spanish rice

Beth's dear friend and consummate food writer Rick Rodgers serves this dish to his own weekend guests. It has all the elements of a classic paella—rice, saffron, sausage, chicken, bell peppers—but is oh so much easier and so much quicker. It is adapted from his book, *On Rice* (Chronicle Books, 1997), and when we asked him what his favorite recipe was, this was it. We heartily agree.

MACHINE: Medium (6-cup) rice cooker; fuzzy logic or on/off
CYCLE: Regular
YIELD: Serves 4 to 5

2 cups medium-grain white rice or Valencia medium-grain rice (not Japanese style)
2²/₃ cups plus 2 tablespoons water
¹/₂ teaspoon salt
3 ounces Spanish chorizo or other smoked sausage, such as linguiça or andouille, cut into ¹/₄-inch dice
1¹/₂ pounds boneless, skinless chicken breasts, trimmed of fat and cut into 2-inch-long strips
2 tablespoons olive oil
1 shallot, minced
1 small red bell pepper, seeded and chopped
2 cloves garlic, minced
³/₄ cup frozen petite peas

1 teaspoon dried oregano or marjoram leaves, crumbled
¹/₄ teaspoon saffron threads, crumbled
1¹/₂ cups Fish Stock (page 348), or ³/₄ cup water and ³/₄ cup bottled clam juice
¹/₂ cup dry white wine
¹/₄ teaspoon red pepper flakes
2 teaspoons cornstarch
Pinch of salt
Hot pepper sauce
Chopped fresh Italian parsley leaves, for garnish

1. Coat the rice cooker bowl with nonstick cooking spray or a film of olive oil. Place the rice in the rice bowl. Add 2²/₃ cups of the water and the salt; swirl to combine. Close the cover and set for the regular cycle.
2. When the machine switches to the Keep Warm cycle, let the rice steam for 10 to 15 minutes. Fluff the rice with a plastic or wooden rice paddle or wooden spoon. The rice will hold on Keep Warm for up to 4 hours.
3. While the rice is cooking, in a 12-inch nonstick skillet cook the chorizo with the remaining 2 tablespoons water over medium-high heat, stirring, until the water evaporates and the sausage is browned, about 5 minutes. Using a slotted spoon, transfer the sausage to drain on a layer of paper towels. Add the chicken to the skillet; cook until cooked through, about 5 minutes, then transfer the chicken to the paper towels with the sausage.
4. Add the olive oil to the skillet along with the shallot, bell pepper, and garlic. Reduce the heat to medium-low and cover. Cook until tender, about 4 minutes. Stir in the peas, oregano, and saffron.

5. In a small bowl, combine the fish stock, wine, and pepper flakes. Whisk in the cornstarch until dissolved. Pour this mixture into the skillet and bring to a simmer. Return the sausage and chicken to the skillet. Cook until the sauce has thickened and is heated through, 1 to 2 minutes. Add the salt and hot pepper sauce to taste.

6. To serve, portion the rice into shallow soup bowls and top with the sauté and a bit of the sauce. Sprinkle with parsley and serve immediately.

madame soohoo's fish and rice

This is a home recipe from Elaine Corn and David SooHoo, owners of Bamboo Restaurant in Sacramento, California. "David's mother makes a marinated fish that cooks right on top of the rice in the cooker," said Elaine during one of our conversations about rice. She always uses Nishiki brand rice. "When my mother visits from Texas, she always carries back bags of Nishiki in her suitcase; they don't have it available down there," she adds. An excellent one-pot meal it is; perfect with a raw vegetable salad and steamed green beans or broccoli.

MACHINE: Medium (6-cup) rice cooker; fuzzy logic or on/off
CYCLE: Regular
YIELD: Serves 3 to 4

About 1 1/2 pounds fish fillets (red snapper, flounder, catfish, sole, or salmon)

MARINADE
2 teaspoons minced garlic or peeled and minced fresh ginger
3 green onions, sliced
1/4 cup chopped fresh cilantro leaves
1 tablespoon vegetable oil
3 tablespoons rice vinegar
2 tablespoons oyster sauce
2 tablespoons brandy or dry sherry
Pinch of sugar
1/4 teaspoon ground white pepper
1 1/2 tablespoons cornstarch
1/2 teaspoon Asian sesame oil

RICE
1 cup Japanese-style medium-grain white rice, such as Nishiki or Calrose
1 3/4 cups water

1. Break or slice the fish into 2-inch pieces. Place it in a shallow bowl or glass baking dish.

2. Make the marinade. In a small bowl, whisk the marinade ingredients together and pour over the fish. Marinate for 20 to 30 minutes at room temperature or cover with plastic wrap and refrigerate for up to 4 hours (not overnight; the fish will get mushy).

3. Wash the rice. Place the rice in a bowl (or use the bowl of your rice cooker) and fill the bowl about half-full with cold tap water. Swirl the rice in the water with your hand. Carefully pour off most of the water, holding one cupped hand under the stream to catch any grains of rice that are carried away with the water. Holding the bowl steady with one hand, use the other to rub and squeeze the wet rice, turning the bowl as you go, so that all the rice is "scrubbed." The small amount of water in the bowl will turn chalky white. Now, run cold water into the bowl, give the rice a quick swish, and carefully drain off the water as before. Repeat the scrubbing and pouring-off process two more times. By the third time, the water you pour off will be nearly clear.

4. Place the rice in the rice cooker bowl. Add the water; swirl to combine. Place the marinated fish pieces on top of the rice in the water; pour in any leftover marinade. Close the cover and set for the regular cycle.

5. When the machine switches to the Keep Warm cycle, let the rice steam for 5 minutes. Serve immediately.

salmon-stuffed japanese rice balls

Rice balls, called *onigiri*, are the sandwiches of Japan and a favorite portable food. They sport a variety of fillings, anything from tuna salad to an umeboshi plum. Tucked inside lunch boxes, briefcases, and backpacks, toted on picnics and car trips, rice balls are tasty, filling, nutritious, and cheap, and they hold up well for hours at room temperature. Flaked salted cooked salmon is perhaps the most popular filling. You can freeze salted uncooked salmon strips, individually wrapped. Then you can be ready to make *onigiri* anytime. There is no need to thaw the salmon strips before cooking them in the oven or microwave. Our thanks to Atsuko Ishii for this tip for busy cooks.

Salt is key to two parts of this recipe, so use a good-quality fine sea salt instead of the kind that comes in the box with the girl with the umbrella on the front. You can find Japanese sea salt in plastic bags in Asian markets, or use French sea salt or fine sea salt from the health food store or gourmet market. (If you're doubtful that it makes a difference, perform a side-by-side taste test. The mass-market salt is harsher.)

The Japanese technique of salting the salmon hours before cooking is used here. It flavors the fish and acts as a preservative and some say it diminishes any fishy taste. You can buy salmon already salted in Japanese markets, but it is certainly easy enough to do at home. Salt plays another important role in *onigiri*. Before shaping the balls of hot rice, you will rub a bit of salt on your wet hands. The salt will melt and gently flavor the rice. While you might be a bit awkward at first with the shaping, it is a skill that develops rapidly with practice. Have fun! Salmon balls are eaten at room temperature.

Sushi nori are the square sheets of thin seaweed used for wrapping sushi rolls. You can find them on the shelf in Asian markets, large supermarkets, or health food stores.

MACHINE: Medium (6-cup) rice cooker; fuzzy logic or on/off

CYCLE: Regular

YIELD: About 20 rice balls; serves 5 to 6

⅓ pound fresh salmon fillet, skin on

½ to ¾ teaspoon fine sea salt, plus extra for shaping

3 cups (4 rice cooker cups) Japanese-style short- or medium-grain rice

5 sheets sushi nori

1. At least 2 hours and up to 1 day before you want to make rice balls, salt the salmon. If your salmon is in a thick piece, cut it into pieces ½ to ¾ inch thick. Sprinkle the salt all over the cut sides of the salmon. Place the salmon in a container, cover tightly, and refrigerate until ready to use (or freeze; see headnote).

2. Preheat the oven to 375°F.

3. Wash the rice. Place the rice in a bowl (or use the bowl of your rice cooker) and fill the bowl about half-full with cold tap water. Swirl the rice in the water with your hand. Carefully pour off most of the water, holding one cupped hand under the stream to catch any grains of rice that are carried away with the water. Holding the bowl steady with one hand, use the other to rub and squeeze the wet rice, turning the bowl as you go, so that all the rice is "scrubbed." The small amount of water in the bowl will turn chalky white. Now, run cold water into the bowl, give the rice a quick swish, and carefully drain off the water as before. Repeat the scrubbing and pouring-off process two more times. By the third time, the water you pour off will be nearly clear.

4. Place the drained rice in the rice cooker bowl. Add water to the 4-cup mark on the rice cooker. Close the cover and set for the regular cycle.

5. While the rice cooks, prepare the salmon. Cover a small baking sheet with aluminum foil. Spray the foil with nonstick cooking spray. Arrange the salmon pieces on the foil. Bake the salmon for 5 to 6 minutes, turning the fish over and continuing to bake until it is just cooked through, about 5 minutes more, depending on the thickness of the fish. (Flake with a fork to check for doneness.) The fish should not brown.

6. When the fish is cooked, remove it from the foil and place on a plate. Remove and discard the skin and any bones. Using a fork or chopsticks, flake the salmon into very small pieces, not more than ½ inch long on a side. (Larger flakes might cause your rice balls to split open.)

7. When the machine switches to the Keep Warm cycle, let the rice steam for 15 minutes. Fluff the rice briefly with a wooden or plastic rice paddle or wooden spoon. Remove the bowl from the cooker and allow the rice to cool until it is just cool enough to easily handle, 3 to 4 minutes

8. Pour 1 tablespoon sea salt on a small plate. To shape the balls, wet your hands with cool water. Touch your index finger to the salt in the dish and rub your hands together to distribute the salt. Scoop a small handful of warm rice into your palm, ⅓ to ½ cup. (Only a bit of experience will tell you what a handful is for you; you need enough to make a nice-sized rice ball but not so much that you cannot shape it properly.) Make a dent in the center of the rice ball and fill the dent with 1 to 2 teaspoons of the salmon. Cup your hands and use them to bury the salmon and shape the rice into an oval, like an egg. You'll be holding the rice in one cupped hand and using the other one to smooth and turn the rice ball around. Use enough pressure so that the rice sticks together. When the rice ball is smooth and even, set it on a plate. Repeat with the remaining rice and salmon, remembering to wet and salt your hands after every 1 or 2 rice balls. You may have some salmon left over.

Rice balls can be eaten immediately or stored, covered tightly, at room temperature for several hours. Do not refrigerate; the rice will harden.

9. Just before serving or packing in a lunch box or picnic basket, add the nori wrap. Cut each sheet of nori into 4 thick strips. Wrap each rice ball in a nori sheet.

variations: Want to get fancy? Your *onigiri* can be shaped into triangles. Follow the instructions through step 7 for stuffing the rice with the salmon. Wet and salt your hands as described in step 8. Then scoop a smaller than usual handful of rice into your palm. Put 1 to 2 teaspoons of the salmon onto the rice, then top the salmon with a small dab of rice, 2 teaspoons or so. This makes it easier to bury the salmon. Press the rice around the salmon. To shape the stuffed rice into a triangle, fold the hand holding the rice in half, keeping your fingers together and straight. Use the fingers of your other hand to press the rice into an upright triangle shape. Rotate the rice and press again to shape. Continue rotating and pressing, balancing the triangle upright against the fleshy part of your hand right below your thumb. It's easier than it sounds!

bonito-stuffed rice balls: Instead of salmon, use katsuo flakes (those are the shavings of dried bonito that are used to make dashi), 1/2 cup or so, dampened with a bit of soy sauce. The larger bonito shavings are best for this, not the ones shredded as finely as angel hair pasta. (Don't use too much soy sauce or your rice balls will be brown instead of white.) Prepare the rice balls as directed, substituting the damp katsuo flakes for the fish.

tuna-stuffed rice balls: Make a simple tuna salad by combining a well-drained 6-ounce can of oil-packed tuna with 1 to 2 teaspoons mayonnaise and soy sauce to taste (start with 1/4 teaspoon or so). Stuff and wrap the rice balls as directed.

umeboshi-stuffed rice balls: Stuff the rice balls as directed with 1 small or half of a large umeboshi (pickled plum). These are sold in small jars in Asian markets. If you purchase umeboshi with their pits, take care when eating them. Wrap as directed.

the family of
PILAFS

A pilaf, so to speak, is as old as the hills. Invented in ancient Persia, it is derived from the Turkish word *pilau*, the method of preparing rice by first cooking it in meat fat or oil to enrich the flavor and keep the grains perfectly separated when cooked, then adding meat or poultry broth for steaming.

Rice, along with spices, incense, cloth, and jewels, was one of the basic commodities traded along the ancient sea route from Egypt down through the Red Sea and between the Arabian Peninsula and India. This maritime highway is known to have been in use by 2500 B.C.

An ancestor of the local wild grass called *nivara*, rice had been growing along the Indus River valley for about two thousand years when the first Near East sea traders began their merchant voyages to the ancient world's delta ports. The fertile, silt-rich area, perfect for the grain that needs so much water, runs along the western Indian border from the mountains of Tibet into the Arabian Sea, through the length of present-day Pakistan. It is one of the sites of rice's earliest cultivation, a populated area estimated at 500,000 square miles, and is the basis for India being one of the great rice centers of the world, along with China.

The great Indus River valley culture centered at the archaeological site of Mohenjo-Daro, one of six large cities as old and as sophisticated as the ancient civilization of Mesopotamia and the pyramid builders of Egypt. The inhabitants of Mohenjo-Daro ran their agricultural economy by nature's clock, the monsoon, which helped create an extensive natural irrigation system. At the time, the rice-growing area boasted a concentration of approximately one-quarter of the world's population, each person eating hundreds of pounds of rice per year. Soon rice became a delicious staple in the neighboring Persian Empire, which then introduced the art of rice cultivation to the Babylonians of the Euphrates Valley, the "cradle" of civilization.

Persian *pilaw* was a very popular dish, seasoned with anything from bits of lamb, venison, or ostrich, pistachios, and herbs to whole spices, raisins, dates, and figs. It was a favored stuffing for whole baby lamb or eggplant, a vegetable specialty that exists to this day. The hand-gathered stamens of the autumn crocus, saffron, have given us the favored combination of saffron with rice, a culinary masterpiece that has come up through the centuries into Iberian and Italian cooking as well.

Egypt was one of the first cuisines to use Persia's technique for cooking rice, and it spread quickly to Greece (Alexander the Great had brought rice back from his campaigns). Recipes for the fragrant *pilaffi* were recorded in the earliest Greek cookbook, *Gastrology*, by the poet Archestratus in 350 B.C. Greek cookbooks have recipes for *pilaffi* with everything from mussels to chicken, along with an extensive repertoire of delicious meatless renditions with simple vegetables or nuts, topped with mounds of fresh sheep or goat yogurt, to be served during the weeks of Lenten fasting. Rolls of stuffed grape leaves, *dolma*, are stuffed with lemon, dill, and mint-scented *pilaffi*.

India had a multitude of rice dishes already in its culinary repertoire by the time of Christ, dictated by the vegetarian diet outlined in the first Hindu Holy Book, the *Rig-Veda*. Centuries later, the Moghul Empire of Muslims from Turkey brought their recipe for *pilau* as they settled in the Ganges Valley. The dish called Sultan's rice immediately caught on in a world where beautiful cooking was a fashionable kingly pursuit. Made with one of the premium rices of the world—long-grain basmati grown in the Himalayan foothills—*pullao* became a dish fit for royal tables, state occasions, and major religious holidays, often concocted by the king or prince himself. Recipes evolved to include the multilayered *biryani*, one of the most complex and subtle variations of the pilaf family.

Persia—the site of today's Iran and sharing the western Indian border—was conquered by the Arabs in the seventh century, and the technique for *pilaw* moved with their foreign military campaigns across North Africa and into Spain and Mediterranean Europe. The Arabs planted rice along the way, wherever it would grow. *Pilaw* was so tasty that countries subject to any Arab influence quickly assimilated the simple recipe as their own, so there is a pilaf to be found from Greece and Egypt to Spain and Provence

The cuisines of eastern Europe, the Austrian Empire, and part of southern Russia, influenced by hundreds of years of Turkish occupation, all have pilaf. Known as *rys sumiany*, rice sautéed as for a roux until brown, pilaf was a favorite of the old Polish nobility and Hungarian peasants; they ate it alongside spit-roasted meats and game.

Provence is known for its delicious pilafs, although, surprisingly, rice dishes did not become a part of overall French cuisine until the late nineteenth century, after the French Revolution. This was due to the French love of bread as a staple carbohydrate. *Larousse Gastronomique*, the French bible of cooking, has a separate heading for pilaf and describes it as "the method of preparing rice originating in the East." French pilafs, *riz pilaf*, often have the addition of a bouquet garni, a fat bundle of aromatic herbs and parsley that is tied together, set into the liquid after sautéing the grains for flavor, and removed before serving. Favorite renditions include arranging the pilaf around cooked chicken livers or foie gras, or dotting it with slivers of truffle. Rice pilaf with toasted almonds is a traditional Provençal specialty.

The Spanish explorers brought pilaf to the New World along with the wonderful paella (*paella* is the Spanish word for pilaf). A full-meal pilaf with some combination of meat (there is a recipe that even includes frog's legs), fish, shellfish, rabbit, poultry, sausage, olives, and vegetables, paella is cooked in its own oversized (at least 12 inches in diameter) shallow iron or copper pan, a *paellera*. *Paella a la Valenciana* is described as a work of art, not just a dish of food.

After the conquest, Mexico had a steady supply of long-grain rice, imported from the Spanish-occupied Philippines (it was sometimes known as Java rice) to make their lusty pilaf, the *sopa seca*, the wonderful first course Mexican "dry soup" in which the rice is scorched by initially frying it with onions and sometimes tomatoes. Anyone traveling in Mexico for the first time and having ordered a bowl of soup, only to get a mound of burnished red-colored rice, has a fond memory of their first *sopa seca*.

In South America, the coastal lowlands of Colombia are perfect for growing rice. *Arroz con coco* is a pilaf with raisins using *titoté*, coconut oil rendered from fresh coconut milk, made for special occasions and served with turkey, ham, or locally caught grilled *pescado*—swordfish and talápia—and fried slices of plantain.

With the settling of the American colonies and slave labor, rice seed from Madagascar was planted in the Carolinas and Georgia. Thus named Carolina gold, the beautiful long-grain rice flourished. America had its own rice plantations and the rice grown there was some of the best in the world. African-American, Caribbean, New Orleans, and South Carolina cooks all devised variations of pilaf, often known as a perloo or pulao, with their own regional touches. An early edition of *Joy of Cooking* contains a recipe for Miss Emily's Perloo.

THE BASICS: PILAF IN THE RICE COOKER

You can sauté the rice right in the cooker bowl before adding the liquid. It will then finish cooking on the regular cycle just like plain rice.

1. Place the butter, in pieces, or oil in the rice cooker bowl. Set the bowl into the machine body. Plug it in.
2. Press the On switch to cook or set for the regular cycle. If your machine has a soaking period built in, use the Quick Cook cycle. Butter will melt in about 5 minutes or, if using oil, let it heat up for 5 minutes. Leave the cover open or closed while you are doing this.
3. Add the measured amount of rice to the hot butter or oil and stir with a wooden or plastic rice paddle or wooden spoon. Leave uncovered or cover, as you wish. Some on/off cookers won't heat without the cover on. The rice will gradually heat up and gently sizzle, releasing its natural fragrance. Stir occasionally. Cook for 10 to 15 minutes. You can sauté the rice for a short time, just until warm, or until it turns golden, according to your personal preference. Sautéeing the rice in the cooker like this will always take a bit longer than if you were doing it on the stovetop, but you won't have an extra pan to wash.
4. Add the liquid, salt, and any other ingredients as specified in the recipe. Close the cover and complete the cooking cycle. (If you used the Quick Cook cycle to sauté the rice, reset for the regular cycle.)
5. Let the cooked rice steam for 10 to 15 minutes on the Keep Warm cycle before serving. If the rice is too moist, leave it on the Keep Warm cycle longer, or reset for the regular cycle, set a timer for 10 minutes, and continue to steam until the desired consistency is achieved. Turn off the machine or unplug it to stop cooking.

Dishes such as hoppin' John (black-eyed peas and rice), Louisiana jambalaya, and Carolina red rice—filling, affordable peasant food at its finest, concocted to keep body and soul together—have become part of America's culinary heritage. The Italian risotto, really a stirred pilaf made from short-grain rice that is deliberately overcooked without a lid on the pan, has also been adopted as a favorite preparation in America.

We have provided an all-around selection of pilafs for preparation in your rice cooker. For the best results in the following recipes, we recommend using basmati, white Texmati, Jasmati, or Carolina and Texas long-grain rice, unless otherwise noted. If you like to use Uncle Ben's converted rice, be sure to increase the liquid by ⅓ to ½ cup per 1 cup of rice to compensate for that rice's longer cooking time.

r i z   a u   b e u r r e

This is an incredibly easy pilaf. The rice, which must be just plain old long-grain (not jasmine), is sautéed in butter before cooking. If you use converted rice, a Parisian home favorite, be sure to increase the amount of water. A bit more butter is stirred in at serving time and, *voilà*!

MACHINE: Medium (6-cup) rice cooker; fuzzy logic or on/off
CYCLE: Quick Cook and/or regular
YIELD: Serves 6 to 8

4½ tablespoons unsalted butter
2 cups long-grain white rice, such as Carolina or Texmati
2¾ cups water
1 teaspoon salt (¾ teaspoon if using salted butter)
Freshly ground black pepper (optional)
Soy sauce (optional)

1. Set the rice cooker for the Quick Cook or regular cycle. Place 2½ tablespoons of the butter in the rice bowl. When melted, add the rice. Cook, stirring a few times, until all the grains are evenly coated and hot, about 10 minutes. Add the water and salt; stir just to combine. Close the cover and reset for the regular cycle or let the regular cycle complete.
2. When the machine switches to the Keep Warm cycle, open the cover and dot the top of the rice with the remaining 2 tablespoons butter, cut into pieces. Close the cover and let the rice steam for 15 minutes. Fluff the rice with a wooden or plastic rice paddle or wooden spoon. This pilaf will hold on Keep Warm for 2 to 3 hours. Serve hot, passing the pepper grinder or a cruet of soy sauce.

q u i ' s   b a s m a t i   p i l a f

Qui was a Vedantic nun in the early 1960s when she learned the intricacies of cooking basmati rice, a favorite in the ashram kitchen, but unheard-of in American homes at the time. One of her special preparations when she comes to visit Beth is this rice served with Yellow Split Pea Soup with Fresh Lemon (page 215) poured over it and long pieces of curved butter-fried banana halves on the side. This is a delicious basic pilaf, one you will find yourself making often.

MACHINE: Medium (6-cup) rice cooker; fuzzy logic or on/off
CYCLE: Quick Cook and/or regular
YIELD: Serves 3

1 cup white basmati rice
2 tablespoons unsalted butter
1 1/2 cups water
1/4 teaspoon fine sea salt

1. Place the rice in a fine strainer or bowl, rinse with cold water two to four times, and drain. The water will be chalky and slightly foamy. Spread the wet rice out with your hands on a clean tea towel on the counter. Let the rice air-dry for at least 1 hour, until cooking time (optional).

2. Set the rice cooker for the Quick Cook or regular cycle. Place the butter in the rice bowl. When melted, add the rice. Cook, stirring a few times, until all the grains are evenly coated, just ever-so-slightly golden, and hot, 10 to 15 minutes. Add the water and salt; stir just to combine. Close the cover and reset for the regular cycle or let the regular cycle complete.

3. When the machine switches to the Keep Warm cycle, let the rice steam for 10 minutes. Fluff the rice with a wooden or plastic rice paddle or wooden spoon. This pilaf will hold on Keep Warm for 2 to 3 hours. Serve hot.

brown rice pilaf

Be sure to use long-grain brown rice in this recipe. We like to use organic, if possible, as the bran layers of brown rice can store the residue of any pesticides used in the growing. Keep your brown rice in the refrigerator, especially in the summer, as the good, nutritious oils can go rancid. We love to concoct the bouquet garni, especially nice if you have a small garden. If you don't, when you buy fresh herbs, air-dry some of the sprigs on a paper towel for a few days on the kitchen counter for later use in your herb bundles. The herbs and the olive oil cut the inherent sweetness of the rice perfectly.

MACHINE: Medium (6-cup) rice cooker; fuzzy logic or on/off
CYCLE: Quick Cook and/or regular/Brown Rice
YIELD: Serves 4

2 1/2 tablespoons extra virgin olive oil
1 cup long-grain brown rice
2 1/4 cups water
1/4 teaspoon salt

BOUQUET GARNI
Few sprigs fresh parsley
1 bay leaf
Few celery leaves
1 sprig fresh thyme, savory, marjoram, or rosemary

1. Set the rice cooker for the Quick Cook or regular/Brown Rice cycle. Place the olive oil in the rice bowl. When hot, add

the rice. Cook, stirring a few times, until all the grains are evenly coated and hot, about 10 minutes.

2. While the rice is cooking, assemble the bouquet garni. Tie the herbs into a bundle using a piece of chive or kitchen twine. Place the bouquet garni on top of the rice. Add the water and salt; stir just to combine. Close the cover and reset for the regular/Brown Rice cycle or let the regular/Brown Rice cycle complete.

3. When the machine switches to the Keep Warm cycle, remove the bouquet garni and discard it. Close the cover and let the rice steam for 10 minutes. Fluff the rice with a wooden or plastic rice paddle or wooden spoon. This pilaf will hold on Keep Warm for up to 2 hours. Serve hot.

riz au parmesan

Whenever we have plain rice and want to make it special, out comes the Parmesan cheese. Parmesan is a very hard cow's milk cheese, so it needs to be finely grated or shredded to eat. Good domestic Parmesan is made in the United States and is an acceptable substitute for the more complex flavored, and more expensive, imported Parmigiano-Reggiano. Palate dictates here. Beth likes to stir in some shredded mozzarella cheese at the end as well.

MACHINE: Medium (6-cup) rice cooker; fuzzy logic or on/off
CYCLE: Quick Cook and/or regular
YIELD: Serves 3 to 4

3 tablespoons unsalted butter
1/4 cup finely chopped onion
1/2 teaspoon minced garlic
1 cup long-grain white rice
1 2/3 cups chicken stock
Salt
Freshly ground black pepper
3 tablespoons freshly grated Parmesan or Asiago cheese

1. Set the rice cooker for the Quick Cook or regular cycle. Place 2 tablespoons of the butter in the rice bowl. When melted, add the onion and garlic. Cook, stirring a few times, until softened, about 2 minutes. Add the rice and cook, stirring a few times, until all the grains are evenly coated and hot, about 10 minutes. Add the stock and salt and pepper to taste; stir just to combine. Close the cover and reset for the regular cycle or let the regular cycle complete.

2. When the machine switches to the Keep Warm cycle, let the rice steam for 10 minutes. Fluff the rice with a wooden or plastic rice paddle or wooden spoon. This pilaf will hold on Keep Warm for up to 1 hour.

3. When ready to serve, stir in the remaining 1 tablespoon butter and the cheese. Serve immediately.

indian yellow rice

Turmeric is a rhizome, like ginger, and is grown in tropical areas, including India, the Philippines, Indonesia, and Taiwan. No surprise, it is used for its pungent flavor and dark yellow color in the cuisines of those regions.

It is essential to some Indian spice blends, but is able to stand on its own in this simple aromatic rice that is perfect served with stir-fried vegetables.

MACHINE: Medium (6-cup) rice cooker; fuzzy logic or on/off
CYCLE: Quick Cook and/or regular
YIELD: Serves 6 to 8

1 tablespoon olive oil
2 tablespoons unsalted butter
2 cups white basmati rice
2 teaspoons turmeric
2$^{1}/_{2}$ cups chicken stock
$^{1}/_{2}$ teaspoon salt

1. Set the rice cooker for the Quick Cook or regular cycle. Place the oil and butter in the rice bowl. When melted, add the rice and turmeric. Cook, stirring a few times, until the rice is shiny and hot, about 10 minutes. Add the stock and salt; stir just to combine. Close the cover and reset for the regular cycle or let the regular cycle complete.
2. When the machine switches to the Keep Warm cycle, let the rice steam for 10 minutes. Fluff with a wooden or plastic rice paddle or wooden spoon. This pilaf will hold on Keep Warm for 1 to 2 hours. Serve hot.

orange rice pilaf

For the holidays, orange rice pilaf is good with roast turkey, capon, partridge, duck, or goose. The orange flavor ends up being quite subtle.

Since citrus tends to harden the rice grain during cooking, it is best to keep the proportions small so that the dish cooks properly.

MACHINE: Medium (6-cup) rice cooker; fuzzy logic or on/off
CYCLE: Quick Cook and/or regular
YIELD: Serves 4

1 tablespoon olive oil
2 tablespoons unsalted butter or rendered
    duck fat
2 tablespoons minced shallots
$^{1}/_{4}$ cup minced celery, with some leaves
1 cup long-grain white rice
1$^{1}/_{4}$ cups chicken stock
$^{1}/_{2}$ cup orange juice
$^{1}/_{2}$ teaspoon salt
Pinch of dried thyme
Grated zest of 1 orange

1. Set the rice cooker for the Quick Cook or regular cycle. Place the oil and butter in the rice bowl. When melted, add the shallots and celery. Cook, stirring a few times, until softened, about 2 minutes. Add the rice and cook, stirring a few times, until all the grains are evenly coated and hot, about 10 minutes. Add the stock, orange juice, salt, thyme, and zest; stir just to combine. Close the cover and reset for the regular cycle or let the regular cycle complete.
2. When the machine switches to the Keep Warm cycle, let the rice steam for 10 minutes. Fluff with a wooden or plastic rice paddle or wooden spoon. This pilaf will hold on Keep Warm for up to 1 hour. Serve hot.

vintner's rice

Vintner's rice, *boros rizs*, is a variation on a Hungarian recipe for pilaf from food entrepreneur George Lang. Rice pilaf was another food, like coffee and *langós* flatbread, left over from the Turkish military occupation. It has the addition of some dry white wine, such as a Chardonnay or Chablis, along with the broth.

MACHINE: Medium (6-cup) rice cooker; fuzzy logic or on/off
CYCLE: Quick Cook and/or regular
YIELD: Serves 3 to 4

2 tablespoons unsalted butter
1 small white onion, coarsely grated
Dash of ground white pepper
1 cup long-grain white rice
3 thin lemon slices
$1/2$ bay leaf
$1^1/4$ cups chicken stock
$1/2$ cup dry white wine
$1/3$ teaspoon salt

1. Set the rice cooker for the Quick Cook or regular cycle. Place the butter in the rice bowl. When melted, add the onion and cook, stirring a few times, until softened, about 2 minutes. Sprinkle with the pepper. Add the rice and cook, stirring a few times, until all the grains are evenly coated and hot, about 10 minutes. Place the lemon slices and bay leaf on top of the rice. Add the stock, wine, and salt; stir just to combine. Close the cover and reset for the regular cycle or let the regular cycle complete. 2. When the machine switches to the Keep Warm cycle, let the rice steam for 10 minutes. Fluff with a wooden or plastic rice paddle or wooden spoon. Remove the bay leaf. This pilaf will hold on Keep Warm for up to 1 hour. Serve hot.

tomato-rice pilaf

It is a long-forgotten food fact that the culinary artist Escoffier, the king of chefs and the chef of kings, invented the canned tomato in 1895 while he worked at his London Savoy restaurant kitchen. Tomato pilaf made with canned tomatoes, called *riz et tomate* in France, is good with roast beef and veal. It is similar to a favorite dish made in the Greek Peloponnesus, *spanakorizo*, where it can have fresh spinach or sautéed leeks added in and cooked lightly with the rice. If you like pilaf with a bit more zing, add a few shots of your favorite south-of-the-border hot sauce or Tabasco sauce with the cooking broth. Serve topped with cold sour cream and minced fresh chives, or crumbled feta or goat cheese.

MACHINE: Medium (6-cup) rice cooker; fuzzy logic or on/off
CYCLE: Quick Cook and/or regular
YIELD: Serves 6

3 tablespoons unsalted butter
2 cups long-grain white rice
2 cups or one 14-ounce can chopped tomatoes, with their juices
$1^1/4$ cups chicken stock or water
$3/4$ teaspoon salt

1. Set the rice cooker for the Quick Cook or regular cycle. Place the butter in the rice

bowl. When melted, add the rice. Cook, stirring a few times, until all the grains are evenly coated and hot, about 10 minutes. Add the tomatoes, stock, and salt; stir just to combine. Close the cover and reset for the regular cycle or let the regular cycle complete.

2. When the machine switches to the Keep Warm cycle, let the rice steam for 10 minutes. Fluff with a wooden or plastic rice paddle or wooden spoon. This pilaf will hold on Keep Warm for 1 to 2 hours. Serve hot.

rice pilaf with fresh peas

Rice has a natural affinity for peas. Food writer Bert Greene once remarked that fresh peas in the pod will eventually be as rare and as expensive as truffles. With due respect, this wonderful recipe should be made exclusively when fresh peas hit the market; frozen peas just will not taste the same. This recipe is made with two different rices, to give the pilaf a firmer texture than if it was made with all medium-grain rice, which is stickier.

MACHINE: Medium (6-cup) rice cooker; fuzzy logic or on/off

CYCLE: Quick Cook and/or regular

YIELD: Serves 3 to 4

1 tablespoon unsalted butter

1 tablespoon minced shallots

2 tablespoons minced celery

1 1/2 cups chicken stock

1 cup fresh peas

1/2 teaspoon salt

1/2 cup long-grain white rice

1/2 cup Italian Arborio or California medium-grain rice

1. Set the rice cooker for the Quick Cook or regular cycle. Place the butter in the rice bowl. When melted, add the shallots and celery. Cook, stirring a few times, until softened, about 2 minutes. Add the stock, peas, salt, and rices; stir just to combine. Close the cover and reset for the regular cycle or let the regular cycle complete.

2. When the machine switches to the Keep Warm cycle, let the rice steam for 10 minutes. Fluff with a wooden or plastic rice paddle or wooden spoon. This pilaf will hold on Keep Warm for up to 1 hour. Serve hot.

carrot basmati pilaf

The distinctly orange root of the carrot has been a common ingredient in both Eastern and Western kitchens for centuries. It has been a cultivated vegetable for 2,000 years. This Indian-style rice is slightly sweet and ends up looking like it is studded with vibrant jewels, with the bits of carrot strewn throughout. Serve with simple roasted meats.

MACHINE: Medium (6-cup) rice cooker; fuzzy logic or on/off

CYCLE: Quick Cook and/or regular

YIELD: Serves 4

1 1/2 tablespoons unsalted butter or ghee
   (clarified butter; page 117)
3 tablespoons minced shallots
1 cup white basmati rice
2 to 3 carrots, cut into thin strips or very
   coarsely grated
1 1/2 cups chicken stock
1/4 teaspoon ground cardamom
Pinch of red pepper flakes
Grated zest of 1 small orange
1/2 teaspoon honey
1/8 teaspoon salt

1. Set the rice cooker for the Quick Cook
or regular cycle. Place the butter in the rice
bowl. When melted, add the shallots. Cook,
stirring a few times, until softened, about
2 minutes. Add the rice and carrots and
cook, stirring a few times, until all the
grains are evenly coated and hot and the
carrots have softened slightly, about 10
minutes. Add the stock, cardamom, red
pepper flakes, orange zest, honey, and salt;
stir just to combine. Close the cover and
reset for the regular cycle or let the regular
cycle complete.
2. When the machine switches to the Keep
Warm cycle, let the rice steam for 15 minutes. Fluff the rice with a wooden or plastic rice paddle or wooden spoon. This pilaf
will hold on Keep Warm for up to 1 hour.
Serve hot.

french pilaf

Once the French decided they liked rice, they
adopted the method of sautéing the rice first
with shallots—one of the stalwart members
of the onion family but less assertive than
onions and garlic—then braising the rice in
a rich broth. The result is sophisticated and
heartwarming food at its best, characteristic
of French cuisine in general. This is an all-
purpose pilaf and this recipe can easily be
cut in half for two people, with some leftovers
to reheat the next day.

MACHINE: Medium (6-cup) rice cooker;
fuzzy logic or on/off
CYCLE: Quick Cook and/or regular
YIELD: Serves 6 to 7

1/4 cup (1/2 stick) unsalted butter
1/2 cup chopped shallots
2 cups long-grain white rice
3 1/4 cups chicken stock
1/2 teaspoon salt

1. Set the rice cooker for the Quick Cook
or regular cycle. Place the butter in the rice
bowl. When melted, add the shallots. Cook,
stirring a few times, until softened, about 2
minutes. Add the rice and cook, stirring a
few times, until all the grains are evenly
coated and hot, about 10 minutes. Add the
stock and salt; stir just to combine. Close
the cover and reset for the regular cycle or
let the regular cycle complete.
2. When the machine switches to the Keep
Warm cycle, let the rice steam for 10 minutes. Fluff the rice with a wooden or plastic rice paddle or wooden spoon. This pilaf
will hold on Keep Warm for 1 to 2 hours.
Serve hot.

riz persillé

Parsley, *persil*, is a Mediterranean herb that is cultivated literally all over the world and is a favored seasoning in many cuisines. Appealing to the palate, it is also appealing to the sense of smell, mildly refreshing without being overassertive. We prefer the Italian flat-leaf parsley, as it lacks the fibrous nature of curly-leaf parsley. Rice with parsley is good with all sorts of roasted meats and poultry. If you have an orange tree in the backyard, go ahead and grate a bit of the zest into the rice at the end when adding the butter and parsley.

MACHINE: Medium (6-cup) rice cooker; fuzzy logic or on/off
CYCLE: Quick Cook and/or regular
YIELD: Serves 3 to 4

2¹/₂ tablespoons unsalted butter
2 tablespoons finely chopped shallots or onion
1 cup long-grain white rice
1³/₄ cups water
Pinch of salt
Splash of Tabasco sauce
2 to 3 tablespoons chopped fresh Italian parsley leaves, to your taste

1. Set the rice cooker for the Quick Cook or regular cycle. Place 2 tablespoons of the butter in the rice bowl. When melted, add the shallots. Cook, stirring a few times, until softened, about 2 minutes. Add the rice and cook, stirring a few times, until all the grains are evenly coated and hot, about 10 minutes. Add the water, salt, and Tabasco; stir just to combine. Close the cover and reset for the regular cycle or let the regular cycle complete.

2. When the machine switches to the Keep Warm cycle, stir in the parsley and the remaining ½ tablespoon butter using a plastic or wooden rice paddle or wooden spoon. Close the cover and let the rice steam for 10 minutes. Fluff the rice with the rice paddle or spoon. This pilaf will hold on Keep Warm for up to 1 hour. Serve hot.

rice pilaf with fresh herbs

If you like to cook, sooner or later you will experiment with growing your own herb garden, whether in a corner of the yard or in pots. In lieu of this, head on down to the supermarket or farmer's market, where an astounding array of nice fresh herbs in little bundles awaits your impulse to cook this rice. Summer or winter, beef stock or chicken stock, each time you make this rice, it will taste just a little bit different. If you find a favorite combination, be sure to jot it down in the margins so that you are able to re-create it at a moment's notice.

MACHINE: Medium (6-cup) rice cooker; fuzzy logic or on/off
CYCLE: Quick Cook and/or regular
YIELD: Serves 3 to 4

2 tablespoons olive oil
¹/₄ cup diced shallots
1 cup long-grain white rice
1³/₄ cups chicken, beef, fish, or vegetable stock

¹/₄ teaspoon salt

¹/₄ cup minced mixed fresh herb leaves
(any combination of tarragon, dill,
chives, Italian parsley, thyme, savory,
oregano, marjoram, chervil, and
watercress)

1 large clove garlic, peeled

1. Set the rice cooker for the Quick Cook or regular cycle. Place the oil in the rice bowl. When hot, add the shallots. Cook, stirring a few times, until softened, about 2 minutes. Add the rice and cook, stirring a few times, until the rice turns opaque, about 5 minutes. Add the stock, salt, and herbs; stir just to combine. Place the garlic clove in the center of the rice, close the cover, and reset for the regular cycle or let the regular cycle complete.

2. When the machine switches to the Keep Warm cycle, remove and discard the garlic. Close the cover and let the rice steam for 10 minutes. Fluff the rice with a wooden or plastic rice paddle or wooden spoon. This pilaf will hold on Keep Warm for up to 1 hour. Serve hot.

arroz negro

From a recipe in Jacquie McMahan's self-published book, *Healthy Mexican*, comes what we consider the original dirty rice. It uses left-over black bean liquid, slightly viscous and protein rich. As Jacquie describes it, be prepared for a delicious surprise. Use the liquid from cooking black turtle beans (with an extra cup of water added to the cooking pot) or the liquid drained from canned beans, thinned with a bit of water, although, as usual, home-made is best.

MACHINE: Medium (6-cup) rice cooker;
fuzzy logic or on/off
CYCLE: Quick Cook and/or regular
YIELD: Serves 4

1 tablespoon olive oil

¹/₄ cup finely chopped onion

1 large clove garlic, minced

1 cup long-grain white rice

2 tablespoons tomato paste

1³/₄ cups black bean liquid

3 tablespoons cooked black beans

¹/₂ teaspoon salt

1. Set the rice cooker for the Quick Cook or regular cycle. Place the oil in the rice bowl. When hot, add the onion and garlic. Cook, stirring a few times, until softened, about 2 minutes. Add the rice and cook, stirring a few times, until it turns ever-so-slightly golden, about 10 minutes. Add the tomato paste, black bean liquid, beans, and salt; stir just to combine. Close the cover and reset for the regular cycle or let the regular cycle complete.

2. When the machine switches to the Keep Warm cycle, let the rice steam for 10 minutes. Fluff the rice with a wooden or plastic rice paddle or wooden spoon. This pilaf will hold on Keep Warm for up to 1 hour. Serve hot.

green pilaf with baby spinach and endive

The baby spinach that is available now in supermarkets is tender and sweet—and nice and clean. Belgian endive is a small, tightly packed head of pale, elongated leaves with green tips; it has a slightly bitter quality. if you can't find it, use watercress, with the stems removed. Gently cooked at the end of the cycle, the greens make a bright-colored, fresh-tasting pilaf.

MACHINE: Medium (6-cup) rice cooker; fuzzy logic or on/off
CYCLE: Quick Cook and/or regular
YIELD: Serves 3 to 4

3 tablespoons unsalted butter
1 cup long-grain white rice
1³/4 cups chicken or vegetable stock
¹/2 teaspoon salt
²/3 cup packed chopped spinach leaves
¹/4 cup chopped endive
3 tablespoons chopped fresh Italian
    parsley leaves
Extra virgin olive oil

1. Set the rice cooker for the Quick Cook or regular cycle. Place the butter in the rice bowl. When melted, add the rice. Cook, stirring a few times, until all the grains are evenly coated and hot, about 10 minutes. Add the stock and salt; stir just to combine. Close the cover and reset for the regular cycle or let the regular cycle complete.

2. About 10 minutes before the rice finishes cooking, arrange the spinach, endive, and parsley on top of the rice to steam.
3. When the machine switches to the Keep Warm cycle, stir the greens into the rice using a plastic or wooden rice paddle or wooden spoon. Close the cover and let the rice steam for 10 minutes. Fluff the rice with the rice paddle or wooden spoon. Serve immediately, drizzled with a bit of the olive oil.

riz à l'indienne

We don't know anyone who doesn't like the colorful, flavorful array of Indian food. The basis of the aromatic kitchen is spice blends, or masalas, selected and ground fresh for every dish. In the West, we have curry powder, a shortcut that evokes but does not equal real Indian spicing. Curry powder contains a blend of nine standard ingredients: turmeric, ginger, cardamom, coriander, cumin, nutmeg, cloves, black pepper, and cinnamon. This is a nice pilaf to serve with the simplest of roast poultry preparations and egg dishes.

MACHINE: Medium (6-cup) rice cooker; fuzzy logic or on/off
CYCLE: Quick Cook and/or regular
YIELD: Serves 3 to 4

2 tablespoons unsalted butter
2 tablespoons finely chopped shallots
1 cup long-grain white rice
1 tablespoon mild or hot curry powder
²/3 cup peeled, cored, and chopped apple

1³/₄ cups chicken stock

2 tablespoons chopped fresh Italian
   parsley leaves

Pinch of salt

1 small bay leaf

1. Set the rice cooker for the Quick Cook or regular cycle. Place the butter in the rice bowl. When melted, add the shallots. Cook, stirring a few times, until softened, about 2 minutes. Add the rice and curry powder and cook, stirring a few times, until all the grains are evenly coated and hot, about 10 minutes. You will be able to smell the curry. Stir in the apple. Add the stock, parsley, and salt; stir just to combine, then tuck in the bay leaf. Close the cover and reset for the regular cycle or let the regular cycle complete.

2. When the machine switches to the Keep Warm cycle, let the rice steam for 10 minutes. Fluff the rice with a wooden or plastic rice paddle or wooden spoon. Remove the bay leaf. This pilaf will hold on Keep Warm for up to 1 hour. Serve hot.

brown butter apricot and pine nut pilaf

"Oh phooey, an extra step!" you say when you read through this recipe. But we assure you that taking the time to sauté the nuts and letting the butter get a bit brown will make a big difference in the final flavor. This pilaf, dotted with scrumptious dried apricots, is positively addictive and a real favorite.

MACHINE: Medium (6-cup) rice cooker;
fuzzy logic or on/off

CYCLE: Quick Cook and/or regular

YIELD: Serves 4

1 tablespoon walnut or vegetable oil

3 tablespoons unsalted butter

¹/₄ cup diced shallots

1 cup long-grain white rice

1³/₄ cups chicken stock

¹/₄ teaspoon salt

¹/₄ cup pine nuts

¹/₂ cup chopped dried apricots

1. Set the rice cooker for the Quick Cook or regular cycle. Place the oil and 1 tablespoon of the butter in the rice bowl. When the butter is melted, add the shallots. Cook, stirring a few times, until softened, about 2 minutes. Add the rice and cook, stirring a few times, until it turns opaque, about 5 minutes. Add the stock and salt; stir just to combine. Close the cover and reset for the regular cycle or let the regular cycle complete.

2. While the rice is cooking, melt the remaining 2 tablespoons butter in a small sauté pan. Add the pine nuts and cook over medium heat, stirring constantly, until evenly browned. The butter should be richly browned but not burnt. Set aside.

3. When the machine switches to the Keep Warm cycle, add the pine nuts in their butter and the apricots. Close the cover and let the rice steam for 10 minutes. Fluff the rice with a wooden or plastic rice paddle or wooden spoon. Serve immediately.

note: If need be, this pilaf will hold on Keep Warm for 1 to 2 hours, but do not add the pine nuts and apricots until 10 minutes before serving.

riz oriental

Riz Oriental is a favorite in the Provence region of France. It takes its name from the faraway countries of the Orient, but also from the dictionary definition of *oriental*, namely, something of superior value or the method of cooking rice from the East. Everything goes in the cooker at once, the way we like it.

MACHINE: Medium (6-cup) rice cooker; fuzzy logic or on/off
CYCLE: Quick Cook and/or regular
YIELD: Serves 4

2 tablespoons unsalted butter
3 heaping tablespoons finely chopped
  shallots or onion
1 cup long-grain white rice
1³/₄ cups chicken stock
¹/₄ teaspoon salt
1 tablespoon dried currants or golden
  raisins
¹/₄ cup slivered blanched almonds

1. Set the rice cooker for the Quick Cook or regular cycle. Place the butter in the rice bowl. When melted, add the shallots. Cook, stirring a few times, until softened, about 2 minutes. Add the rice and cook, stirring a few times, until it turns opaque, about 5 minutes. Add the stock, salt, currants, and almonds; stir just to combine. Close the cover and reset for the regular cycle or let the regular cycle complete.
2. When the machine switches to the Keep Warm cycle, let the rice steam for 10 minutes. Fluff the rice with a wooden or plastic rice paddle or wooden spoon. This pilaf will hold on Keep Warm for 1 to 2 hours. Serve hot.

mexican rice

Tomato-based Spanish rice, *arroz a la Mexicana*, is a real standard in every Mexican home or restaurant kitchen. There are as many recipes as there are cooks, so Beth went to Jacquie McMahan for advice. "Always fresh tomato," she canted, "and not too much." She uses pure ground New Mexico chile for a kick; in lieu of that, you can use a mixed chili powder, which also includes cumin and a few other spices. In central Mexico, this rice would be served with a topping of finely diced potato, carrot, and peas that have been tossed in a bit of vinegar and oil.

MACHINE: Medium (6-cup) rice cooker; fuzzy logic or on/off
CYCLE: Quick Cook and/or regular
YIELD: Serves 4

1 tablespoon olive oil
¹/₃ cup finely chopped onion
1 teaspoon minced garlic
1 cup long-grain white rice, such as
  Texmati or Uncle Ben's converted
¹/₂ cup peeled and chopped fresh tomato
1³/₄ cups water (2 cups for Uncle Ben's)
2 teaspoons pure ground chile or chili
  powder (we use Grandma's)
¹/₂ teaspoon salt

1. Set the rice cooker for the Quick Cook or regular cycle. Place the oil in the rice bowl. When hot, add the onion and garlic. Cook, stirring a few times, until softened, about 2 minutes. Add the rice and cook, stirring a few times, until it turns ever-so-slightly golden, about 10 minutes. Add the tomato and sauté a bit longer. Add the water, chile,

and salt; stir just to combine. Close the cover and reset for the regular cycle or let the regular cycle complete.

2. When the machine switches to the Keep Warm cycle, let the rice steam for 10 minutes. Fluff the rice with a wooden or plastic rice paddle or wooden spoon. This pilaf will hold on Keep Warm for 1 to 2 hours. Serve hot.

rice and vermicelli pilaf

The combination of rice and thin pasta in a pilaf has pure Middle Eastern roots and is the prototype for the commercial Rice-A-Roni mix. The secret is not to use too much pasta; just crumble some angel hair, vermicelli, or one little nest of pasta called a *fideo*. Beth's friend graphic designer Cindy Lee still uses Rice-A-Roni in a pinch, a recipe she learned from her mother. "Well, you will laugh," said Cindy when Beth asked her how she makes it. "You basically use either the family box or the regular box of Rice-A-Roni, dump the rice into the rice cooker bowl, and do not use the flavoring packet at all. Then, as my mom always taught me, add enough water up to your thumb knuckle; it should be about 1/2 inch of water above the rice."

MACHINE: Medium (6-cup) rice cooker; fuzzy logic or on/off

CYCLE: Quick Cook and/or regular

YIELD: Serves 4

1 tablespoon unsalted butter

1 tablespoon olive oil or bacon drippings

1 cup long-grain white rice

1/4 cup vermicelli or 1 *fideo* broken into 1- to 2-inch pieces

13/4 cups chicken or beef stock

1 teaspoon onion-flavored Mrs. Dash seasoning

1/4 teaspoon salt (optional)

Freshly ground black pepper

1. Set the rice cooker for the Quick Cook or regular cycle. Place the butter and olive oil in the rice bowl. When the butter is melted, add the rice and pasta pieces. Cook, stirring a few times, until the pasta turns golden brown, about 10 minutes. Add the stock, Mrs. Dash, salt, if using, and a few grinds of pepper; stir just to combine. Close the cover and reset for the regular cycle or let the regular cycle complete. At the end of the cycle, the liquid should all be absorbed and the pasta tender.

2. When the machine switches to the Keep Warm cycle, let the rice steam for 15 minutes. Fluff the rice with a wooden or plastic rice paddle or wooden spoon. This pilaf will hold on Keep Warm for 1 to 2 hours. Serve hot.

classic sopa seca

Mexico's *sopas secas*—literally dry soups—are soft and comforting rice or pasta dishes, sometimes served as a first course, sometimes alongside the entree. You'll notice that more liquid is called for in these recipes than in many other rice recipes. Generally speaking, broth is preferred over water. Also, the rice is always sautéed in oil before the liquid and flavorings are added. This technique produces a savory rice that is moist but not mushy. We've included a rainbow here—red (*rojo*), green (*verde*), and yellow (*amarillo*).

MACHINE: Medium (6-cup) rice cooker; fuzzy logic or on/off
CYCLE: Quick Cook and/or regular
YIELD: Serves 4

3 tablespoons vegetable oil

1 cup long-grain white rice

1/2 cup diced onion

1/4 cup seeded and diced red or green bell pepper

1/2 cup diced carrot

One 14.5-ounce can chicken broth, 2 1/4 cups homemade chicken stock plus 3/4 teaspoon salt, or 2 1/4 cups water plus 3/4 teaspoon salt

Half of a 6-ounce can tomato paste (5 1/2 tablespoons)

1/4 teaspoon freshly ground black pepper

2 to 3 cloves garlic, minced

1/4 cup minced fresh Italian parsley leaves

1/2 cup frozen peas

1. Set the rice cooker for the Quick Cook or regular cycle. Place the oil in the rice bowl. When the oil is hot, add the rice. Cook, stirring, until the rice turns opaque, about 1 minute. Add the onion, bell pepper, and carrot and cook, covered, until the vegetables soften and the rice begins to brown, about 15 minutes.

2. Meanwhile, pour the broth into a 4-cup glass measuring cup and add water to equal 2 1/4 cups. (Or place the homemade stock or water in a measuring cup.) Add the tomato paste and stir to dissolve completely. Add the black pepper. Add the broth mixture to the rice. Add the garlic and parsley; stir just to combine. Close the cover and reset for the regular cycle or let the regular cycle complete.

3. When the machine switches to the Keep Warm cycle, sprinkle the peas on top of the rice. Close the cover and let the rice steam for 10 minutes. Fluff the rice with a wooden or plastic rice paddle or wooden spoon. This dish will hold on Keep Warm for up to 1 hour. Serve hot.

variation: To make enough *sopa seca* to serve 8, use a large (10-cup) rice cooker and double everything except the liquid and oil. For 2 cups rice, use 1/4 cup oil and 4 cups broth, water, or a combination of the two.

arroz verde

Mexican cooks use their electric blenders frequently, for sauces, moles, and, here, to pulverize herbs and spinach in a flash. *Verde* means "green" in Spanish. Don't be intimidated by the amount of herbs called for; their flavor mellows substantially during cooking and creates a dish that's perfect alongside grilled chicken or fish, or under a spicy stew.

MACHINE: Medium (6-cup) rice cooker; fuzzy logic or on/off
CYCLE: Quick Cook and/or regular
YIELD: Serves 4

2 cloves garlic, peeled

1/2 cup packed fresh Italian parsley leaves and small stems

1/2 cup packed fresh cilantro leaves and small stems

1 cup packed spinach leaves

2 cups chicken or vegetable stock

2 tablespoons vegetable oil

1/2 cup finely chopped onion

1 cup long-grain white rice

1/4 teaspoon freshly ground black pepper, or to taste

Salt, if needed (omit if using canned broth)

1. Combine the garlic, parsley, cilantro, spinach, and 1 cup of the stock in a blender and process until smooth. Set aside.

2. Set the rice cooker for the Quick Cook or regular cycle. Place the oil in the rice bowl. When the oil is hot, add the onion. Cook, stirring a few times, until soft but not brown, about 5 minutes. Add the rice, stirring a few times, until all the grains are evenly coated and hot, about 10 minutes. Close the cover and allow the rice to cook, stirring a few times, until it smells toasty and begins to brown, about 5 minutes.

3. Add the herb and spinach puree, remaining 1¼ cups stock, the pepper, and salt to taste, if using. Stir well with a plastic or wooden rice paddle or wooden spoon. Close the cover and reset for the regular cycle or let the regular cycle complete.

4. When the machine switches to the Keep Warm cycle, let the rice steam for 10 minutes. Stir well to incorporate the puree. This pilaf will hold on Keep Warm for up to 1 hour. Serve hot.

arroz amarillo
(caribbean yellow rice)

This makes a pretty accompaniment for many meat and poultry dishes, and is also lovely for soaking up the juices from highly flavored baked fish dishes. Achiote paste is found in Latin markets (see page 123); it is sold in small, plastic-wrapped bricks.

MACHINE: Medium (6-cup) rice cooker; fuzzy logic or on/off

CYCLE: Quick Cook and/or regular

YIELD: Serves 4

2 tablespoons vegetable oil

1 cup long-grain white rice

1/2 medium-size yellow onion, finely chopped

1 teaspoon achiote paste, 1/4 teaspoon Bijol seasoning, or 1/2 teaspoon turmeric

1 2/3 cups water or light chicken stock

1 clove garlic, minced

1/2 teaspoon salt, if using unsalted chicken stock

2 tablespoons chopped fresh cilantro leaves (optional)

1. Set the rice cooker for the Quick Cook or regular cycle. Add the oil to the rice cooker bowl. When the oil is hot, stir in the rice and onion, close the cover, and cook, stirring occasionally, until the rice is opaque and the onion has begun to soften, about 5 minutes.

2. Meanwhile, dissolve the achiote paste in the water, breaking it up with your fingers and stirring with a spoon. Be careful, it can stain. (Or stir the Bijol or turmeric into the water.)

3. Add the dissolved achiote to the rice along with the garlic and salt, if using. Close the cover and reset for the regular cycle or let the regular cycle complete.

4. When the machine switches to the Keep Warm cycle, stir in the cilantro, if using. Close the cover and let the rice steam for 10 minutes. Fluff the rice with a wooden or plastic rice paddle or wooden spoon. This pilaf will hold on Keep Warm for 1 to 2 hours. Serve hot.

thai curried rice

This is a complex, spicy rice pilaf: it has spices, a bit of coconut milk, lime juice, soy sauce, ginger, raisins, almonds, and green onions. These recipe proportions are designed for American jasmine rice; if you use imported Thai jasmine rice, decrease the total liquid (some stock and some coconut milk) by ¹/₃ cup. Serve with grilled or sautéed fish and poultry.

MACHINE: Medium (6-cup) rice cooker; fuzzy logic or on/off
CYCLE: Quick Cook and/or regular
YIELD: Serves 4

3 tablespoons unsalted butter
1 tablespoon peeled and minced fresh ginger

1 cup domestic jasmine rice
1 tablespoon mild or hot curry powder
1 cup plus 2 tablespoons chicken stock
¹/₃ cup canned unsweetened coconut milk (can be light)
2 tablespoons soy sauce
2 tablespoons fresh lime juice
Grated zest of 1 small lime
1 teaspoon Chinese hot chile sauce
Pinch of salt
¹/₃ cup dark raisins, dried tart cherries, or dried currants
¹/₃ cup slivered blanched almonds
¹/₂ cup minced green onions, both white and green parts

1. Preheat the oven to 325°F.

2. Set the rice cooker for the Quick Cook or regular cycle. Place the butter in the rice cooker bowl. When melted, add the ginger and rice. Cook, stirring a few times, until the grains are evenly coated and hot, about 10 minutes. Add the curry powder and stir.

3. Meanwhile, in a large measuring cup, combine the stock, coconut milk, soy sauce, lime juice and zest, chile sauce, and salt. Add the stock mixture and raisins to the rice; stir just to combine. Close the cover and reset for the regular cycle or let the regular cycle complete.

4. While the rice is cooking, place the almonds on a baking sheet and bake until lightly toasted, about 6 minutes. Remove from the baking sheet and let cool to room temperature.

5. When the machine switches to the Keep Warm cycle, sprinkle the rice with the toasted almonds and green onions. Close the cover and let the rice steam for 15 minutes. Fluff the rice with a wooden or plastic rice paddle or wooden spoon. Serve immediately.

note: This pilaf can be held for 1 to 2 hours on Keep Warm; however, do not add the almonds and green onions to the rice until 15 minutes before serving.

aromatic kalijira rice pilaw

Pilaw or pilaf, as this rice-based dish is known in some parts of the world, is made in different ways in different regions of India. A rice reserved for special occasions, *pilaw* is served with a generous sprinkling of almonds and raisins on top. But even without the embellishment, this *pilaw* is a pleasant change from boiled rice. This is a traditional northern Indian method of preparation, courtesy of Lotus Foods.

MACHINE: Medium (6-cup) rice cooker; fuzzy logic or on/off
CYCLE: Quick Cook and/or regular
YIELD: Serves 4

RICE
2 cups Kalijira rice
1 tablespoon vegetable oil or ghee
   (clarified butter; page 117)
2 small white boiling onions, finely
   chopped
2 1/2 cups water
1/4 teaspoon turmeric

3 cloves
3 green cardamom pods
One 4-inch cinnamon stick
1 teaspoon salt

GARNISH (OPTIONAL)
1 tablespoon vegetable oil or ghee
2 tablespoons slivered blanched almonds
2 tablespoons raisins

1. Place the rice in a fine strainer or bowl and rinse with cold water, rubbing the rice with your hands to remove any bits of dust; drain.
2. Set the rice cooker for the Quick Cook or regular cycle. Place the oil in the rice cooker bowl. When the oil is hot, add the onions. Cook, stirring a few times, until softened, about 2 minutes. Add the rice and cook, stirring a few times, until the rice turns opaque, about 5 minutes. Add the water, spices, and salt; stir just to combine. Close the cover and reset for the regular cycle or let the regular cycle complete.
3. Make the garnish, if using. Heat the oil in a small skillet over medium heat. Add the almonds and sauté until they are golden brown, about 3 minutes. Remove the almonds with a slotted spoon and drain on a paper towel. Add the raisins to the same oil and sauté until they puff up, in about 1 minute or less. Remove the raisins with a slotted spoon and drain with the almonds.
4. When the machine switches to the Keep Warm cycle, let the rice steam for 10 minutes. Fluff the rice with a wooden or plastic rice paddle or wooden spoon. This pilaf will hold on Keep Warm for 1 to 2 hours. Serve hot, topped with the almond-raisin garnish, if using.

fruited pilaf

Fruited pilaf is pretty enough for a party and a smashing foil for grilled lamb chops. This pilaf combines an Indian spice blend called garam masala with dried cranberries—an Old World tradition with a New World flourish.

MACHINE: Medium (6-cup) or large (10-cup) rice cooker; fuzzy logic or on/off
CYCLE: Quick Cook and/or regular
YIELD: Serves 8

3 cups white basmati rice
1/4 cup ghee (clarified butter; page 117) or unsalted butter
2 teaspoons garam masala (see box)
1 teaspoon salt
3 tablespoons dried currants
1/4 cup chopped dried apricots
1/4 cup dried cranberries
4 cups water
1/4 teaspoon saffron threads (optional)
2 tablespoons pine nuts

GARAM MASALA

The blending of spices, as opposed to using a solitary herb or spice, is characteristic of Indian cuisine. A garam masala, or melange of "hot spices," is the essence of this custom and it is said that one must be a good *masalchi*, a fearless blender of spices, before one can become a good Indian chef. The art of the blending involves grinding or pounding (in a mortar and pestle) a combination of roasted or sun-dried spices.

There are almost as many formulas for this Indian spice blend as there are families in India. Some are chile hot, others more aromatic. The proportions even change with the seasons. You can buy garam masala in jars or boxes, but if you make it yourself, it will be fresher and more fragrant. Beth used to work at India Joze, a restaurant in Santa Cruz that specialized in cooking from all sorts of cuisines. Every day the backup chefs, who all had their own coffee grinders just for spices by their cooking stations, prepared their garam masala spice blends right before making a particular dish. You could hear the whir of the grinders as they cooked!

Green cardamom pods are easily found at an Indian market or any store that sells spices in bulk, as so many natural food stores do. Nutmegs are easier to split than they appear. Just place one on a cutting board and rap it with the bottom of a heavy skillet, or split it with a sharp, heavy knife or cleaver, keeping your fingers well out of the way.

Here is a mild aromatic formula we like; adjust the proportions to suit yourself.

1. Place the rice in a fine strainer or bowl, rinse with cold water, and drain.

2. Set the rice cooker for the Quick Cook or regular cycle. Add the ghee to the rice bowl. When melted, add the garam masala and salt. Cook, stirring, until the spices are fragrant, 1 to 2 minutes. Add the drained rice; stir well to combine. Cook, stirring a few times, until the rice is shiny, fragrant, and transparent, about 5 minutes more. Add the currants, apricots, and cranberries; stir well to combine. Cook for 1 to 2 minutes more. Add the water. Crumble the saffron threads, if using, into the water.

Close the cover and reset for the regular cycle or let the regular cycle complete.

3. While the rice is cooking, toast the pine nuts in a small, dry skillet over medium heat until golden, watching carefully so they do not burn. Set aside to cool.

4. When the machine switches to the Keep Warm cycle, let the rice steam for 10 to 15 minutes. Fluff the rice well with a plastic or wooden rice paddle or wooden spoon. It will hold on Keep Warm for 1 to 2 hours.

5. When ready to serve, spoon the pilaf into a dish, sprinkle it with the toasted pine nuts, and serve immediately.

YIELD: About 2 tablespoons

1 tablespoon green cardamom pods
One 2-inch cinnamon stick
1 teaspoon cumin seeds
1/2 teaspoon black peppercorns
10 cloves
1 teaspoon coriander seeds
About 1/4 of a whole nutmeg

1. Remove the seeds from the cardamom pods. You can gently smash the pods against a cutting board with the bottom of a drinking glass or use a rolling pin to crush them on a sheet of waxed paper. Then pick out and discard the outer pods, reserving the small, round seeds. Place the cardamom seeds and the rest of the spices in a small, dry skillet.

2. Place the skillet over medium heat and toast the spices until they are fragrant, 3 to 5 minutes. Shake the skillet periodically or stir with a wooden spoon, so the spices don't burn. Transfer the toasted spices to a small plate to cool. (If they remain in the hot skillet, even off the heat, they are liable to burn.)

3. When the spices are cool, grind them to a powder in a blender or a clean coffee grinder. You can store the garam masala in a tightly capped glass jar, but it is best fresh.

lamb biryani

Biryanis are the deliciously complex layered rice dishes of India. In this rendition, the layers of saffron-streaked rice conceal tender pieces of boneless lamb cooked in a spicy yogurt marinade. Creating a *biryani* is a three-step process. First, the rice and filling ingredients are each cooked separately. Then the dish is assembled and cooked again. This final step is usually done in a tightly sealed dish set in the oven (or sometimes on top of the stove). We found that a rice cooker set on the Keep Warm cycle accomplishes the final cooking beautifully, and with one less pot to clean. But for a more authentic, or more dramatic, presentation, the dish can be assembled in a pretty casserole, covered very tightly with aluminum foil and the lid, and baked for about 30 minutes at 250°F. (If your rice cooker doesn't have a Keep Warm cycle, you will have to finish it in the oven.) Rose water is available in Indian, Middle Eastern, and gourmet markets.

MACHINE: Large (10-cup) rice cooker; fuzzy logic or on/off
CYCLE: Regular
YIELD: Serves 6 to 8

MARINADE AND LAMB

1 medium-size onion, quartered
4 cloves garlic, peeled
One 1¹/₂-inch piece fresh ginger, peeled
1 jalapeño chile, halved and seeded
2 cups plain yogurt (don't use nonfat)
1 tablespoon ground coriander
2 pounds boneless lamb, trimmed of fat and cut into ³/₄-inch cubes

2 tablespoons ghee (clarified butter; page 117)
¹/₂ teaspoon salt
¹/₄ teaspoon freshly ground black pepper

FILLING

2 tablespoons ghee
2 medium-size onions, halved and thinly sliced
2 tablespoons slivered blanched almonds
2 tablespoons dried currants

RICE

3 cups white basmati rice
5 green cardamom pods
One 4-inch cinnamon stick
2 tablespoons ghee
2 tablespoons rose water
3¹/₂ cups water
1 teaspoon salt
¹/₂ cup milk
¹/₂ teaspoon saffron threads

1. *Make the marinade:* Place the onion, garlic, ginger, and jalapeño in a food processor. Pulse 10 to 20 times, until everything is finely chopped. Add the yogurt and coriander; pulse until well mixed. Place the lamb cubes in a large bowl. Pour the marinade over the lamb and stir to combine. Cover and marinate for 1 to 2 hours in the refrigerator.

2. Meanwhile, rinse the rice in a bowl, let it soak for 15 minutes, drain well, and allow to dry, spread out on a clean tea towel.

3. *Make the filling:* In a large sauté pan, heat the ghee over medium-high heat. Cook the sliced onions until they begin to brown, about 10 minutes. Add the almonds and currants; continue to cook,

Ghee is clarified butter, a fat used extensively in Indian cookery and known for its especially delicious flavor. It is cooked long enough for the milk solids to separate from the melted butter; it develops a deliciously nutty aroma and a beautiful golden hue. Ghee contains no oxidized cholesterol or hydrogenated fat, so it is good for special diets, and it has a very high smoking point (unlike plain butter, the solids of which burn quickly), so it is good for cooking. Ghee keeps well (it can be kept at room temperature but lasts for weeks in the refrigerator), so you might want to make a larger amount so you'll have it on hand.

To make enough ghee for this recipe, cut 1/2 cup (1 stick) unsalted butter into quarters. Heat slowly in a small, heavy saucepan set on the lowest heat; do not stir. Allow the butter to simmer gently for about 20 minutes. (If you are making a larger amount, it will take longer.) It will smell nutty and the milk solids, which will settle on the bottom of the pan, will start to turn golden brown. The transparent butter will float on the top; this is the ghee (known as *desi ghee* in India). Strain the butter through a tea strainer or cheesecloth into another container without disturbing the sediment. Store ghee in a covered container in the refrigerator; it will solidify.

stirring occasionally, until they are well browned but not burnt, about 5 minutes more. Remove the onion mixture from the pan and drain on a double layer of paper towels.

4. In the same pan, heat the 2 tablespoons ghee over medium-high heat. Using a slotted spoon, remove the lamb from the marinade and place in the skillet. Reserve the marinade. Cook the lamb, stirring occasionally, until the mixture is browned and almost dry, about 15 minutes.

5. While the lamb is cooking, make the rice. Place the rice in the rice cooker bowl along with the cardamom pods, cinnamon stick, ghee, and rose water; stir to combine. Close the cover and set the rice cooker for the regular cycle. Cook until the rice is fragrant and translucent, about 5 minutes. Add the water and salt, stir to combine, and let the cycle complete.

6. Warm the milk in the microwave or in a small saucepan on the stove. Add the saffron threads, stir to combine, and set aside.

7. Add the reserved marinade to the lamb in the skillet; stir to combine. Season with the 1/2 teaspoon salt and 1/4 teaspoon pepper. When the marinade comes to a boil, cover the skillet and cook over the lowest heat possible until the lamb is tender and the marinade has almost cooked away, checking the liquid level occasionally, about 15 to 20 minutes. Remove the skillet from the heat if the mixture appears to be in danger of burning.

8. When the machine switches to the Keep Warm cycle, let the rice steam for 10 to 15 minutes. Fluff the rice with a wooden or

plastic rice paddle or wooden spoon. Scoop out about half of the rice into a medium-size bowl. Smooth the rice remaining in the rice cooker into an even layer. Sprinkle about half of the saffron milk over the rice in the rice cooker. Layer the lamb on top of the rice, arranging it in a smooth layer. Layer the onion filling on top of the lamb. (If desired, reserve a small amount of the onion mixture for garnish.) Top with the remaining rice, smoothing it with a rice paddle or wooden spoon. Sprinkle the rice with the remaining saffron milk. Close the cover and continue to steam on the Keep Warm cycle for 30 to 45 minutes.

9. Serve the *biryani* immediately. It can be served directly from the rice cooker bowl, or for a more elegant presentation, invert the rice cooker bowl onto a large platter with raised sides. Carefully remove the bowl and garnish, if desired, with the reserved onion filling.

zucchini and mung dal

This is a small-batch, very traditional dal recipe (double or triple the recipe, if necessary, and use a 10-cup rice cooker) using split mung, also known as yellow dal, known for being the most digestible of all the beans (see page 119). While Indian food has a reputation for being hot because of the spices, dishes can be quite delicately flavored as well. This mild dal would be the Indian equivalent of chicken soup, as it has healing, nurturing qualities.

The important technique to master is initially heating the spices in oil. Leave the rice cooker cover open and listen until you hear the seeds start to pop or jump up in the bowl. You must immediately add the rest of the ingredients to stop the spices from overcooking or browning. If this does happen, just turn off the cooker, wipe out the oil and spices, discard, and start over, rather than ruin the flavor of an entire pot of soup. Buy black mustard seeds at a natural food store or Indian grocery; you will need them for both the dal and the rice. Asafoetida is available at Indian markets. Serve with whole wheat chapatis or tortilla flatbread, heated on a griddle, and a green salad.

MACHINE: Medium (6-cup) rice cooker; fuzzy logic or on/off
CYCLE: Quick Cook and/or Regular
YIELD: Serves 4

1 1/4 cups split mung dal
1 1/2 tablespoons sunflower or sesame oil or ghee (clarified butter; page 117)
1/2 teaspoon black mustard seeds
1/2 teaspoon turmeric
1/4 teaspoon mild curry powder
1/8 teaspoon asafoetida (optional)
1 teaspoon peeled and minced fresh ginger
1/4 green chile pepper, seeded and minced, or 2 heaping tablespoons hot salsa
Juice of 1 large fresh lime (at least 2 tablespoons)
4 1/2 cups water
1 teaspoon fine sea salt, or more to taste
1/2 teaspoon ground coriander
2 cups zucchini cut into 1/2-inch cubes

1 recipe Simple Indian Rice (page 120)

Freshly ground black pepper

1¼ cups cold yogurt or sour cream, plain or with 1 teaspoon peeled and grated fresh ginger stirred in, for serving (optional)

1. Place the dal in a deep bowl, cover with cold water, and soak for 2 hours at room temperature. Drain well.

2. Set the rice cooker for the Quick Cook or regular cycle. Place the oil in the rice bowl. When hot, add the mustard seeds. With the cover open, cook until the seeds just begin to pop, no longer. Immediately add the turmeric, curry powder, asafoetida (if using), ginger, chile, lime juice, drained dal, and water (take care, in case of splattering). Close the cover and reset for the regular cycle or let cook for 45 minutes, until the dal is soft.

3. Add the salt, coriander, and zucchini. Adjust the consistency with some more water if you want a thin dal. Close the cover and cook for 15 minutes longer.

4. To serve, spoon the Simple Indian Rice into bowls and sprinkle with some black pepper to taste, then top with the dal and cold plain or ginger yogurt, if desired. Dal can be made the day ahead and reheated.

WHAT IS DAL?

Dal, or *dahl*, are dried peas and beans that have been part of the Indian cuisine since ancient times. Dals are available whole, split, or ground into flour, and to find a good assortment of them you must shop at an Indian grocery. Not only is dal the name of the dried bean, it is what the cooked dish is called as well. While Americans are familiar with split pea soup or lentil soup, the repertoire of dals is staggering: thick or thin soups, sauces, stews, pancakes, even desserts. Our favorite dals are soups, Zucchini and Mung Dal (opposite) and Yellow Split Pea Soup with Fresh Lemon (page 215) included here.

Dal soups are seasoned with ginger, to aid digestion, and a fried spice blend known as *chaunk*, enhancing the flavor considerably. Some dals are prepared with garlic or onions, but traditional dals do not contain these, or any member of the onion family, in the manner of the ancient Hindu culinary laws that have been practiced for 5,000 years.

The most popular dal for soup is the diminutive pale green or yellow mung or *moong* dal, whole or split without skins. Green or yellow split peas (*matar dal*), golden lentils (*toovar dal*), or *urad dal*, also known as black gram, can be substituted, but will taste slightly different and have a different texture and color. Dals are traditionally served with fresh white Indian rices.

Dal should be rinsed with cold water and sorted before soaking. We always make simple dals with split dals; they take less time to cook. While split mung dal generally takes about an hour to cook, remember that the hardness or softness of the water and the age of the dal affect cooking times, so don't worry if you need to cook your dal an extra 15 to 30 minutes.

simple indian rice

MACHINE: Medium (6 cup) rice cooker; fuzzy logic or on/off
CYCLE: Quick Cook and/or regular
YIELD: Serves 4

2 teaspoons sunflower or sesame oil
$1/2$ teaspoon black mustard seeds
$1/2$ teaspoon cumin seeds
1 cup white basmati rice
$1^{1}/2$ cups water
1 teaspoon fresh lime juice
$1/4$ teaspoon fine sea salt
Freshly ground black pepper

1. Set the rice cooker for the Quick Cook or regular cycle. Place the oil in the rice bowl. When hot, add the mustard and cumin seeds. With the cover open, cook until the seeds just begin to pop, no longer. Immediately add the rice, water, lime juice, and salt; stir just to combine. Close the cover and reset for the regular cycle or let the regular cycle complete.
2. When the machine switches to the Keep Warm cycle, let the rice steam for 10 minutes. Fluff the rice with a wooden or plastic rice paddle or wooden spoon, and add pepper to taste. This rice will hold on Keep Warm for up to 2 hours.

rice cooker paella

You will need a large (10-cup) rice cooker to prepare paella for 8; halve the recipe for medium (6-cup) machines. Don't be tempted to make this without the saffron; it is essential. You can order it (rather) reasonably from Penzeys, the spice merchants. This paella, born in Julie's kitchen, is a great dish for entertaining.

MACHINE: Large (10-cup) rice cooker; fuzzy logic or on/off
CYCLE: Quick Cook and/or regular
YIELD: Serves 8

$1/4$ cup extra virgin olive oil
2 boneless, skinless chicken thighs, trimmed of fat and cut into $3/4$-inch pieces
1 medium-size onion, chopped
2 cloves garlic, peeled
1 medium-size red bell pepper, seeded and cut into strips, the strips halved crosswise
1 cup seeded and chopped fresh tomatoes
2 ounces fully cooked smoked garlicky sausage (Spanish chorizo is traditional), sliced $1/3$ inch thick
4 calamari (squid), cleaned, bodies cut into $1/3$-inch-wide rings, and each set of tentacles halved (about $1/3$ cup total)
3 cups Arborio, Valencia, or other medium-grain white rice (not Japanese style)
5 cups water
2 teaspoons salt
$1/2$ teaspoon freshly ground black pepper

1/2 teaspoon saffron threads

1 cup fresh green beans, ends trimmed, cut into 1 1/2-inch lengths

1/2 cup small scallops

8 medium-size or large shrimp, shelled (tails left on) and deveined

1/2 cup frozen peas

8 small clams, washed in cold water to remove sand

1. In a small nonstick skillet, heat 1 tablespoon of the olive oil over medium-high heat. When hot, add the chicken and cook, stirring, until just cooked through, 5 to 7 minutes. Remove the skillet from the heat. 2. Set the rice cooker for the Quick Cook or regular cycle. Add the remaining 3 tablespoons olive oil to the rice bowl. When hot, add the onion. Cook, stirring a few times, until softened, about 2 minutes. Add the garlic, bell pepper, and tomatoes, stir to combine, and close the cover. Cook, stirring a few times, until the tomatoes break down and the bell pepper softens, about 10 minutes. Add the sausage, calamari, rice, chicken, water, salt, and black pepper; stir to combine. A pinch at a time, crumble the saffron threads into the rice bowl. Close the cover and reset for the regular cycle or let the regular cycle complete. When the liquid boils (open the cooker occasionally to check, if yours doesn't have a glass lid), add the green beans, stir quickly to combine, and close again.

PAELLA

Paella is Spain's grandest and best-known rice dish, and variations of it turn up today in the places that were once part of the Spanish empire—the yellow-hued *arroz con pollo* of Puerto Rico, Cuba, and Mexico; yellow rice, chicken, and seafood in the Philippines; the *arroz amarillo* (yellow rice) of Mexico's Yucatán. All of these share a family tree with paella.

What is a "true" paella? To a cook in Valencia, where paella was invented, it would be a dish of short-grain rice colored yellow with saffron and flavored with meat or seafood, but not both. (Snails—land snails—are one traditional element of the meat rendition.) This is charmingly illustrated in the classic Time-Life cookbook *The Cooking of Spain and Portugal* with a series of photos showing a family picnicking in a park in Valencia: assembling their rabbit paella on the spot, cooking it over an open fire, and, in the last frame, consuming it. The grand mixed paella, frequently including chicken, sausage, and several kinds of seafood, found in Barcelona and elsewhere in Catalonia, is the version that was exported to the United States.

Of course, it's a kind of heresy to cook paella in the rice cooker. Paella has its own special pan, which resembles a very shallow, flat-bottomed wok. Paella is cooked over an open fire, or on the stove, but certainly not in a deep pot in an electric appliance! So, we cheerfully admit that our paella is not the real thing. But it looks gorgeous and tastes terrific, and that's enough for us.

3. When the machine switches to the Keep Warm cycle, be ready to act quickly. Open the cover, toss in the scallops, and quickly stir them into the rice mixture. Place the shrimp around the border of the rice bowl, pressing them partway into the rice, so that their tails stick up. Sprinkle the peas over the entire surface of the rice. Nestle the clams about halfway into the rice, hinged sides down. Close the cover and let the paella steam until the clams open and the shrimp turn pink, about 15 minutes. Serve the paella immediately.

note: If the clams do not open, perhaps there is not enough heat remaining in the rice cooker. Take them out and put them in a medium-size saucepan with about 1 inch of water. Cover the pot and bring the water to a boil. The clams should open in a few minutes. Throw out any that do not.

vegetable paella

Here is an unorthodox, vegetarian, and much simplified version of the elaborate Spanish paella. It is an excellent side dish or vegetarian entrée.

MACHINE: Medium (6-cup) or large (10-cup) rice cooker; fuzzy logic or on/off
CYCLE: Quick Cook and/or regular
YIELD: Serves 4

1/4 cup olive oil
1 small dried red chile, broken
1/2 cup diced onion

1/2 medium-size red bell pepper, halved, seeded, and sliced
1/2 medium-size green bell pepper, halved, seeded, and sliced
2 cloves garlic, minced
1 teaspoon fresh oregano leaves, crushed between your fingers
1 teaspoon sweet or hot paprika
1 medium-size zucchini, cut into 1/2-inch cubes
2 large ripe tomatoes, peeled, seeded, and coarsely chopped
1 1/4 cups Arborio, Valencia, or other medium-grain white rice (not Japanese style)
1 3/4 cups vegetable or chicken stock
Few saffron threads, crushed
1 teaspoon salt
Freshly ground black pepper
1/2 cup fresh or frozen petite peas

1. Set the rice cooker for the Quick Cook or regular cycle. Place the oil in the rice bowl. When hot, add the chile, onion, and bell peppers. Cook, stirring a few times, until softened, about 10 minutes. Add the garlic, oregano, paprika, zucchini, and tomatoes. Close the cover and cook for 5 minutes. Stir in the rice, stock, and saffron. Add the salt and black pepper to taste; stir just to combine. Close the cover and reset for the regular cycle or let the regular cycle complete.
2. When the machine switches to the Keep Warm cycle, scatter the peas on top of the rice mixture. Close the cover and let the rice steam for 15 minutes. Fluff the rice with a wooden or plastic rice paddle or wooden spoon. This paella will hold on Keep Warm for up to 1 hour. Serve hot.

arroz
con pollo

There is no best recipe for *arroz con pollo*, or chicken with rice. Some feature yellow-tinted rice, some red, and, in some versions, the rice is not colored at all. Some are spicy with hot chiles; others are mild. Green olives and capers make their piquant appearance in many versions, especially those from Cuba or Puerto Rico. Some cooks use long-grain rice; others choose regular medium-grain or a risotto-type rice. Wine and beer are popular flavorings. Some versions of this dish are quite rich, with chicken skin, plenty of oil, and even bits of ham added. Ours is a deep yellowish red, accented with red bell pepper bits and bright green peas. Because we use skinless chicken and are careful with the oil, it's relatively low in fat. The spicing is warm, not hot. We chose long-grain rice for its texture.

The yellow color comes not from saffron but achiote paste (*pasta de achiote* in Spanish). This is sold in a small brick form and is made from annatto seeds, which contribute a deep yellow color, as well as other spices. Achiote paste is available in Latin markets. The blocks we found were 3.5 ounces; we use about a quarter of one for this recipe. You cut or break off as much achiote paste as you need, then wrap the rest up airtight. If you can't find achiote paste, you can try to find Bijol, a yellow coloring and seasoning that comes in a small red shaker. It contains annatto as well as food coloring. You don't need much Bijol, maybe 1/2 teaspoon; add it when you add the liquid. If you are lucky enough to encounter annatto seeds themselves (try an Indian market if your local Latin market doesn't carry

them), you can make a brilliant yellow annatto oil by frying the seeds in a bit of vegetable or olive oil, then straining out the seeds. Use the oil to make the dish, and your rice will turn a lovely color without the use of artificial colorings. Or simply color the rice with turmeric, adding 1 teaspoon along with the liquid.

MACHINE: Large (10-cup) rice cooker; fuzzy logic or on/off
CYCLE: Quick Cook and/or regular
YIELD: Serves 4

4 skinless, boneless chicken thighs,
    trimmed of fat
Juice of 1 large or 2 small limes
Salt
Freshly ground black pepper
2 tablespoons olive or vegetable oil
1 medium-size onion, chopped
3 cloves garlic, minced
2 medium-size red bell peppers, seeded
    and cut into 1/2-inch square pieces
2 cups long-grain white rice
1/2 teaspoon ground cumin
1 cup lukewarm water, plus more water as
    needed
About 1 tablespoon achiote paste
    (use less, 1 to 2 teaspoons, if you don't
    want a warmly spicy dish)
1/2 cup chopped fresh cilantro leaves
1 cup seeded and chopped fresh tomatoes
    (or use canned, reserving their juices)
One 12-ounce bottle medium- or
    light-bodied beer
1 cup frozen peas

1. Cut each chicken thigh in two. Place the chicken pieces on a plate and season them with half the lime juice and salt and pepper to taste. Let the chicken marinate for about 15 minutes.

2. In a heavy medium-size nonstick skillet, heat 1 tablespoon of the oil over high heat. When hot, brown the chicken pieces on both sides until golden, about 5 minutes per side. As they are browned, transfer them to a clean plate and set aside.

3. Set the rice cooker for the Quick Cook or regular cycle. Heat the remaining 1 tablespoon oil in the rice cooker bowl. When hot, add the onion and garlic and stir to combine. Cook until the onion begins to soften, about 2 minutes. Do not allow the garlic to burn. Add the bell peppers; stir to combine. Add the rice and cumin; stir to combine and cook, stirring occasionally, until the rice is opaque, about 10 minutes.

4. Meanwhile, put the water in a 2-cup glass measuring cup. Add the remaining lime juice and the achiote paste, breaking up the achiote paste with your fingers as you add it (it can stain fabric, so take care). Stir to dissolve the achiote.

5. Add the cilantro and tomatoes to the rice cooker, along with 1 teaspoon salt and ½ teaspoon black pepper. Add the beer and achiote water. You'll need about ¾ cup additional liquid. If you have reserved tomato juices from the canned tomatoes, measure it, adding water to reach the ¾-cup level. If not, add an additional ¾ cup water. Stir well to combine the ingredients. Add the chicken, along with any juices that have accumulated on the plate. Push the chicken pieces down into the rice. Close the cover and reset for the regular cycle or let the regular cycle complete.

6. When the machine switches to the Keep Warm cycle, quickly open the cover and sprinkle the peas on top. Close the cover and let the rice steam for 10 to 15 minutes. Gently fluff the rice with a wooden or plastic rice paddle or wooden spoon and stir to incorporate the peas. Serve immediately.

RISOTTO

Risotto is part of the triumvirate of soul-satisfying Italian starches, along with polenta and pasta. It is described in literature as "gilded grains of gold," in reference to risotto alla milanese, where the cooked rice is bathed in a pale golden sheen of saffron. It is traditionally exclusively a first course dish, a *primi piatti*, not an accompaniment like American rice, except when paired with osso bucco. Risotto is a unique type of rice dish with its very own consistency, which is likened to a sauce. Pearl-colored Arborio, the most well-known Italian rice for risotto, has a lot of surface starch, so the rice becomes creamy during cooking, almost like a savory rice pudding. Think of it cooking like pasta: tender on the outside and a hint of resistance on the inside. The center remains *al dente*, a very different culinary experience if you have never had it before; you might think your rice is not quite cooked.

Arborio medium-grain *japonica* rice was planted in the Po River valley around Lombardy (its capital is Milan) and Piedmont during the thirteenth century by the Sforza brothers, Visconti dukes of Milan, with seeds from the Benedictine rice crops flourishing at Montecassino. For years it was exported in little canvas sacks, but small plastic bags are now the norm. The top quality rice will be labeled *Arborio fino* or *superfino*, a sign that the kernel is the biggest, a standard established in 1931. Lesser grades are labeled *fino*, *semifino*, and *commune*, and are fine to use in soups. A 500-gram bag, a little over a pound, yields about two cups of raw rice.

If you love risotto, you will be pleasantly surprised that there is an entire little family of regionally grown Italian medium-grain rices that include Carnaroli and Vialone nano along with the Arborio. Carnaroli is grown alongside Arborio in Piedmont and Lombardy, those regions having the largest canal-irrigated rice paddies in all of present-day Italy. The newest hybrid of Italian Carnaroli is just starting to be exported from Argentina (where the Italians planted it early in the twentieth century to cater to the tastes of the Italian immigrants to South America) and is considered equal, even superior, to Arborio. In Venice and Verona, Vialone nano (the rice of choice grown outside Venice and Mantova since the 1600s) is cooked until *all'onde*, or "wavy," which is a bit looser texture than the other risotto recipes.

"There is not a huge difference between the texture and mouthfeel of the three Italian medium-grain rices," says Mediterranean food expert and writer Joyce Goldstein. "They behave and taste the same. You can use the rices interchangeably in risotto recipes. The big difference is the region in which they are grown and the length of the grain. There is even a fourth risotto rice, a miniature, called Baldo." Vialone nano is an impressive offering by chefs, but Arborio is easily available. Try all three and make your decision about which one you like the best.

American rice growers are onto developing their own strains of Arborio, the seed stock of which is available from the Rice Research Station seed bank at Biggs, California. Lundberg rice of California has a domestic California Arborio on the market that they have been developing for 10 years. RiceSelect has Texas Arborio (called risotto rice), and there is another domestic called CalRiso. All can be substituted cup for cup for their imported Italian cousins, making lovely, less expensive risottos, although gourmets insist the Italian rices make the most authentic risottos. Similar grains such as quinoa, quick-cooking barley, millet, and bulgur, which cook in a similar manner as rice, can all be substituted for the rice in a risotto.

Risotto is known as a time-consuming rice dish to make because you need to stir it constantly and add the boiling stock in small portions for about half an hour. It is deliberately overcooked and braised uncovered. In the fancy fuzzy logic cooker, you can make really fabulous risotto on the Porridge cycle, which allows it to be braised at a gentle, steady low boil/high simmer. If all you have is the basic kind of rice cooker, you can make a risotto that is almost as good, but you'll have to watch the time closely, and the consistency will not be quite as sublime. It is a great dish for everyday eating and, once you find out how easy it is to make, you will perhaps make it as often as regular pilaf or plain steamed rice.

To make risotto, use a light stock, like chicken, duck, or veal (see The Basics: Homemade Stocks, page 341), and about three to four times the volume of the rice. You don't have to fuss about the exact amount. You may use less liquid than for stovetop risottos because there is less evaporation with the cover closed. You just add all the stock at once (with no preheating of the stock) and only stir a few times. Butter is the traditional cooking fat for sautéing the onion, but these days a bit of olive oil is added, and maybe some pancetta. The bit of butter at the end of cooking is also traditional, but optional.

We found that risotto made with 1 cup of rice cooks in about 20 to 25 minutes in an on/off rice cooker. Note that you will have to set a timer if you are using an on/off cooker. The Porridge cycle on the fuzzy logic machines will time automatically. To serve six to eight people as a first course or three to four as a luncheon main dish, do not use more than 2 cups rice in the medium (6-cup) or large (10-cup) rice cookers, as it is just hard to work with. If you need more risotto, it is best to use two rice cookers at the same time.

Risotto is best served immediately (it thickens dramatically as it stands at room temperature), but in a pinch, it will hold on the Keep Warm cycle for up to an hour. When serving, a warm shallow soup bowl is nice, and a soup spoon, but correct etiquette calls for a fork. Of course, the Italians are sticklers for the right cheese: Parmigiano-Reggiano. Buy imported, even just a little bit, if you can. You can use Pecorino Romano sheep's milk cheese, even Asiago, in place of the Parmesan (it is quite a bit stronger), or a combination of two, if you like.

There are three distinct steps to making risotto: cooking the onion and rice, adding the stock and other ingredients, and adding the butter and cheese to finish, known as "creaming." Note that Arborio rice is never washed; you want all the starch to make the creamy dish just right.

1. Risotto must be made by first sautéing chopped onion in butter (or half butter and half olive oil), then sautéing the rice in the hot fat. You can sauté the onion and rice right in the rice cooker bowl before adding the liquid; then it will just finish cooking on the Porridge or regular cycle. If you have a non-stick rice cooker bowl, you can use a bit less fat.

Place the butter, in pieces, in the rice cooker bowl. Set the bowl into the machine body. Plug in. Set the rice cooker to start the Porridge or regular cycle (use the Quick Cook cycle if your regular cycle has a built-in soaking period). The butter will melt in 1 to 2 minutes. Leave the cover open or off (some cookers will shut off if the cover is left off). Add the chopped onion, leeks, or shallots; cook until soft and any liquid they exude has evaporated, stirring a few times. Add wine, if using, and cook to burn off the alcohol, a minute or two. Add the measured amount of rice to the hot fat and stir with a wooden or plastic rice paddle or wooden spoon. The rice will gradually heat up and gently sizzle. Stir occasionally, and gently, with the wooden spoon or rice paddle. Give the rice a full 3 to 5 minutes to cook and coat the grains, just like for a pilaf. This precooks the outer coating of the rice to keep the grains separate and release their amylopectin, while slowly absorbing and cooking in the aromatic stock later on.

2. Add the stock and any other ingredients as specified in the recipe. Stir a few times. Close the cover and reset for the Porridge cycle, if your machine has it, or the regular cycle. While cooking, open the cooker once or twice and stir gently, but this is optional. If you are using an on/off cooker or one without a Porridge cycle, set a timer for 20 minutes to time the cooking.

3. At the end of the Porridge cycle or when the timer sounds, turn off the machine or unplug it to stop cooking. If the risotto is too thick, add $1/4$ to $1/2$ cup stock; if it is too soupy, allow it to cook longer, checking at 5-minute intervals. When the rice is *al dente* and the texture is like that of oatmeal, it is ready. Stir the risotto a few times, adding the butter and cheese, if using. Serve immediately in shallow soup bowls with more Parmesan cheese for sprinkling (use as much as you like) and the pepper grinder. If you're not ready to serve, you can hold the risotto on the Keep Warm cycle for up to an hour, stirring in the butter and cheese right before serving.

Use the following chart to help adapt your own risotto recipes to the rice cooker.

SERVES	RICE (in U.S. cups)	STOCK Small (4-cup) Rice Cooker	Medium (6-cup) Rice Cooker	Large (10-cup) Rice Cooker	COOKING TIME On/off machines	Fuzzy logic machines
2	1/2 cup	2 cups*	2 cups*	2¼ cups	20 to 25 minutes	1 Porridge cycle
4	1 cup		2¾ cups	3 cups	20 to 28 minutes	1 Porridge cycle
8	2 cups		5 cups	5 cups	25 to 35 minutes	1 Porridge cycle

*For fuzzy logic rice cookers, use only 1½ cups of stock.

risotto milanese

Risotto Milanese, or risotto with saffron, is the national dish of the Lombardy region of Italy. It has been made there since the late eighteenth century as a special first course washed down with red wine. Use saffron threads here, as powdered saffron is really a lot more potent; you want a faint saffron flavor, not overpowering. It is traditionally served as a starchy side dish to osso bucco (braised veal shanks) and *carbonata* (Milanese beef stew).

MACHINE: Medium (6-cup) or large (10-cup) rice cooker; fuzzy logic or on/off
CYCLE: Quick Cook and/or regular or Porridge
YIELD: Serves 4 to 5

3 cups chicken stock, or one 14.5-ounce can chicken broth plus water to equal 3 cups
Pinch of saffron threads
1 tablespoon olive oil
1 tablespoon unsalted butter
³/₄ cup finely chopped yellow onion
¹/₄ cup dry white wine

1 cup plus 2 tablespoons medium-grain risotto rice (*superfino* Arborio, Carnaroli, or Vialone nano)

TO FINISH
1 tablespoon unsalted butter
¹/₄ cup freshly grated Parmesan cheese, plus more for serving
Salt

1. In a small saucepan or using the microwave, heat 1 cup of the stock and crush the saffron into it; let stand for 15 minutes.
2. Set the rice cooker for the Quick Cook or regular cycle. Place the olive oil and butter in the rice cooker bowl. When the butter melts, add the onion. Cook, stirring a few times until softened, about 2 minutes. Stir in the wine and cook for 1 minute. Add the rice and stir occasionally until the grains are transparent except for a white spot on each, 3 to 5 minutes. Stir in the saffron stock and remaining chicken stock. Close the cover and reset for the Porridge cycle, or for the regular cycle and set a timer for 20 minutes.
3. When the machine switches to the Keep Warm cycle or the timer sounds, stir the rice with a wooden or plastic rice paddle or wooden spoon. The risotto should be only

a bit liquid and the rice should be *al dente*, tender with just a touch of tooth resistance. If needed, cook for a few minutes longer. This risotto will hold on Keep Warm for up to 1 hour.

4. When ready to serve, add the butter. Close the cover for a minute to let the butter melt. Stir in the cheese and salt to taste. Serve immediately.

butternut squash risotto

This risotto is heavier on the vegetables (the winter squash and the onion) than is traditional, but it is a favorite autumn and winter variation. Use less squash if you like, but we feel the extra contributes a lovely flavor and color along with a nutritional boost. We also use half stock and half water in order not to overwhelm the delicate squash flavor. You can add some diced zucchini as well; it is a good flavor combination. We like the unconventional addition of lime juice; it brightens the flavor of the squash.

MACHINE: Medium (6-cup) or large (10-cup) rice cooker; fuzzy logic or on/off
CYCLE: Quick Cook and/or regular or Porridge
YIELD: Serves 4 to 5

2 tablespoons olive oil
2 tablespoons unsalted butter
$2/3$ cup finely chopped yellow onion
1 cup plus 2 tablespoons medium-grain risotto rice (*superfino* Arborio, Carnaroli, or Vialone nano)
$1^3/4$ to 2 cups peeled and seeded butternut squash cut into $1/2$-inch cubes
$1^1/2$ cups water
$1^1/2$ cups chicken, veal, or vegetable stock

TO FINISH
2 teaspoons unsalted butter
2 tablespoons fresh lime juice
$1/4$ cup minced fresh Italian parsley leaves
$1/4$ cup freshly grated Parmesan cheese, plus more for serving
Salt

1. Set the rice cooker for the Quick Cook or regular cycle. Place the olive oil and butter in the rice cooker bowl. When the butter melts, add the onion. Cook, stirring a few times, until softened, about 2 minutes. Add the rice and stir with a wooden or plastic rice paddle or wooden spoon to coat the grains with the hot butter. Cook, stirring a few times, until the grains of rice are transparent except for a white spot on each, 3 to 5 minutes. Add the squash, water, and stock; stir to combine. Close the cover and reset for the Porridge cycle, or for the regular cycle and set a timer for 20 minutes.

2. When the machine switches to the Keep Warm cycle or the timer sounds, stir the risotto. It should be only a bit liquid, and the rice should be *al dente*, tender with just a touch of tooth resistance. If needed, cook for a few minutes longer. This risotto will hold on Keep Warm for up to 1 hour.

3. When ready to serve, add the butter. Close the cover for a minute to let the butter melt. Stir in the lime juice, parsley, cheese, and salt to taste. Serve immediately.

dried mushroom risotto

The Italians have a great love for dried mushrooms and, to our advantage, most supermarkets are catching on and offering this once gourmet treasure of flavor. If you like cream of mushroom soup, you will love this risotto, known as *risotto con funghi secchi*. Choose porcini, the Italian favorite, or another type of dried mushroom like morels, chanterelles, or shiitakes. Or try a blend; we found one called Melissa's Exotic Mushroom Medley that contains porcini, chanterelle, shiitake, and oyster mushrooms.

MACHINE: Medium (6-cup) or large (10-cup) rice cooker; fuzzy logic or on/off
CYCLE: Quick Cook and/or regular or Porridge
YIELD: Serves 4 to 5

$\frac{1}{2}$ ounce dried mushrooms
$1\frac{3}{4}$ cups hottest possible tap water
About $1\frac{1}{2}$ cups beef, chicken, or
    vegetable stock
1 tablespoon olive oil
1 tablespoon unsalted butter
$\frac{1}{2}$ cup minced onion
$\frac{1}{4}$ cup dry white wine
1 cup plus 2 tablespoons medium-grain
    risotto rice (*superfino* Arborio, Carnaroli,
    or Vialone nano)

TO FINISH
2 teaspoons unsalted butter, or more,
    if desired
2 tablespoons chopped fresh Italian
    parsley leaves

$\frac{1}{4}$ cup freshly grated Parmesan cheese,
    plus more for serving
Freshly ground black pepper
Salt

1. Place the mushrooms in a small bowl and add the hot water. Let stand for an hour or longer. (Or combine the mushrooms and water in a microwave-safe container, cover tightly with plastic wrap, and microwave on high for 5 minutes. Let cool to room temperature.) When the mushrooms are soft, remove them from the liquid, squeezing gently to extract as much liquid as possible. Slice the mushrooms into pieces about $\frac{1}{4}$ x 1 inch, discarding any tough stems. The exact size is not important, but if you cut them too small, their flavor will not be as intense. Carefully pour the mushroom soaking liquid into a measuring cup, leaving any grit behind. (If the mushrooms were especially gritty, you may want to pour the liquid through a coffee filter–lined strainer, but in general this is not necessary.) Add the stock to the mushroom soaking liquid to equal 3 cups.
2. Set the rice cooker for the Quick Cook or regular cycle. Place the olive oil and butter in the rice cooker bowl. When the butter melts, add the onion. Cook, stirring a few times, until softened, about 2 minutes. Stir in the wine and cook for 1 to 2 minutes. Add the rice and stir until the grains are evenly coated and hot. Cook, stirring occasionally, until the grains are transparent except for a white spot on each, 3 to 5 minutes. Add the stock mixture and mushrooms to the rice; stir to combine. Close the cover and reset for the Porridge cycle, or for the regular cycle and set a timer for 20 minutes.

3. When the machine switches to the Keep Warm cycle or the timer sounds, open the cover and stir with a wooden or plastic rice paddle or wooden spoon. The risotto should be only a bit liquid and the rice should be *al dente*, tender with just a touch of tooth resistance. If needed, cook for a few minutes longer. This risotto will hold on Keep Warm for up to 1 hour.

4. When ready to serve, add the butter. Close the cover for a minute to let the butter melt. Stir in the parsley, cheese, a few grinds of pepper, and salt to taste. Serve immediately.

asparagus and mushroom risotto

This is the risotto Beth (and her mother) make *every* time they make risotto. The asparagus and mushrooms cook with the rice, so it is sort of a primavera (spring vegetable) stew. Asparagus risotto is one of the most popular variations after the saffron version. Vary this by substituting green beans, fresh peas, or zucchini for the asparagus, or combining any of them with it. This risotto is nice finished off with 2 tablespoons of heavy cream, if you happen to have any hanging around in the fridge.

MACHINE: Medium (6-cup) or large (10-cup) rice cooker; fuzzy logic or on/off
CYCLE: Quick Cook and/or regular or Porridge
YIELD: Serves 4 to 6

³/₄ pound fresh asparagus

1¹/₂ tablespoons olive oil

1¹/₂ tablespoons unsalted butter

2 tablespoons minced shallots

1 cup plus 2 tablespoons medium-grain risotto rice (*superfino* Arborio, Carnaroli, or Vialone nano)

2 ounces fresh mushrooms, sliced

3 cups chicken stock, or one 14.5-ounce can chicken broth plus water to equal 3 cups

TO FINISH

2 teaspoons unsalted butter

¹/₃ cup freshly grated Parmesan cheese, plus more for serving

Salt

1. Snap off the ends of the asparagus stalks and discard. If the remaining stalks are thick, peel with a vegetable peeler. Cut the spears on the diagonal into 2-inch pieces.

2. Set the rice cooker for the Quick Cook or regular cycle. Place the olive oil and butter in the rice cooker bowl. When the butter melts, add the shallots. Cook, stirring a few times, until softened, about 2 minutes. Add the rice and stir until the grains are evenly coated and hot. Cook, stirring occasionally, until the grains are transparent except for a white spot on each, 3 to 5 minutes. Add the mushrooms and asparagus, stirring for a minute or two. Add the stock; stir to combine. Close the cover and reset for the Porridge cycle, or for the regular cycle and set a timer for 20 minutes.

3. When the machine switches to the Keep Warm cycle or the timer sounds, stir the risotto with a wooden or plastic rice paddle or wooden spoon. The risotto should be only a bit liquid, and the rice should be *al dente*, tender with just a touch of tooth resistance. If needed, cook for a few minutes longer. This risotto will hold on Keep Warm for an hour or so.

4. When ready to serve, add the butter. Close the cover for a minute or so to allow the butter to melt. Stir in the cheese and salt to taste. Serve immediately.

prawn risotto with seasonal vegetables

Look on a map and it is easy to see that Italy is a country with plenty of coastline bordering on the Mediterranean, *Mare Nostrum* to the ancients. Seafood is reflected in every type of Italian recipe and anything from smoked and fresh salmon, clams, mussels, and scallops, to fresh tuna are included in delicious risottos. Prawn risotto is probably the most popular shellfish risotto and can be made with either fresh raw or frozen prawns. You can use either a fish or chicken stock (the flavor will be slightly different with each). Please note that seafood risottos are never served with cheese; just plain.

MACHINE: Medium (6-cup) or large (10-cup) rice cooker; fuzzy logic or on/off
CYCLE: Quick Cook and/or regular or Porridge
YIELD: Serves 3 to 4

1/2 cup water
1/2 cup dry white wine
1 bay leaf
12 ounces medium-size prawns, shelled, deveined, and each cut into 2 or 3 pieces
2 tablespoons olive oil
1/4 cup finely chopped shallots
1 small clove garlic, minced
1 cup diced zucchini, asparagus pieces, or fresh peas, or 3 cups baby spinach
1 cup medium-grain risotto rice (*superfino* Arborio, Carnaroli, or Vialone nano)
About 2 cups chicken or fish stock
Salt
Freshly ground black pepper

1. In the rice cooker bowl (or in a shallow pan on the stovetop if you want to get the rice started), combine the water, wine, and bay leaf. Close the cover and set for the Quick Cook or regular cycle. When the liquid comes to a boil, add the prawns and cook, uncovered, until they turn pink and are opaque in the center, about 2 minutes, stirring occasionally. If you are using frozen cooked prawns, just immerse them in the boiling liquid for 15 seconds. With a slotted spoon, transfer the prawns to a plate and set aside. Pour the remaining liquid into a measuring cup and discard the bay leaf. Wipe out and dry the rice cooker bowl.

2. Set the rice cooker for the Quick Cook or regular cycle. Add the oil and, when hot, stir in the shallots and garlic. Cook, stirring a few times, until soft but not browned, 2 to 3 minutes. Add the vegetables and cook briefly to take off the raw edge, another few minutes. When the vegetables have softened, add the rice and stir to coat the grains with oil. Cook, stirring occasionally, until the grains of rice are transparent except for a white spot on each, 3 to 5 minutes. Add the reserved prawn liquid and stock to equal 3 cups; stir to combine. Reset for the Porridge cycle, or for the regular cycle and set a timer for 20 minutes.

3. When the machine switches to the Keep Warm cycle or the timer sounds, stir in the prawns. Close the cover and let steam for 5 minutes. The risotto should be only a bit liquid and the rice should be *al dente*, tender with just a touch of tooth resistance. If needed, cook for a few minutes longer. This risotto will hold on Keep Warm for up to 20 minutes. Serve immediately, with salt and pepper to taste.

italian sausage risotto

This hearty winter risotto focuses its flavor on the spicy sausage, another Italian favorite. This recipe is a most basic method and can be made with vegetables instead of the sausage; substitute one to two diced roasted red or yellow bell peppers for the sausage. Note that this recipe is slightly larger than the others; it feeds six.

MACHINE: Medium (6-cup) or large (10-cup) rice cooker; fuzzy logic or on/off
CYCLE: Quick Cook and/or regular or Porridge
YIELD: Serves 6 to 8

³/₄ pound fennel or sweet Italian sausage, cut into ¹/₂-inch-thick slices
2 tablespoons water

2 tablespoons olive oil
2 tablespoons unsalted butter
¹/₄ cup finely chopped yellow onion
¹/₂ cup dry white wine
2 cups medium-grain risotto rice (*superfino* Arborio, Carnaroli, or Vialone nano)
5 cups chicken stock, or two 14.5-ounce cans chicken broth plus water to equal 5 cups)

TO FINISH
2 tablespoons chopped fresh Italian parsley leaves
¹/₂ cup freshly grated Parmesan cheese, plus more for serving
Salt
Freshly ground black pepper

1. In a small skillet, combine the sausage and water. Cover and cook over medium-low heat until browned and heated through, about 5 minutes. Remove with a slotted spoon and drain on a double layer of paper towels.

2. Set the rice cooker for the Quick Cook or regular cycle. Place the olive oil and butter in the rice cooker bowl. When the butter melts, add the onion. Cook, stirring a few times, until softened, about 2 minutes. Add the sausage and cook for a few minutes to heat it. Add the wine and cook until reduced, 1 to 2 minutes. Add the rice and stir to coat the grains with the hot butter. Cook, stirring occasionally, until the grains of rice are transparent except for a white spot on each, 3 to 5 minutes. Add the stock; stir to combine. Close the cover and reset for the Porridge cycle, or for the regular cycle and set a timer for 25 minutes.

3. When the machine switches to the Keep Warm cycle or the timer sounds, stir the risotto with a wooden or plastic rice paddle or wooden spoon. The risotto should be only a bit liquid and the rice should be *al dente*, tender with just a touch of tooth resistance. If needed, cook for a few minutes longer. This risotto will hold on Keep Warm for an hour or so.

4. When ready to serve, stir in the parsley and cheese, season with salt and pepper to taste, and serve immediately.

risi e bisi

Rice and peas is a beloved comfort food in Italy. It's not technically a risotto because when it's made in the conventional manner on the stovetop, the broth is added at once, not ladleful by ladleful as with risotto. In the rice cooker, of course, the method is the same as for risotto. You can make it with fresh or frozen peas. Fresh peas should be added at the beginning of the cooking time, unless they are very young and tender; add frozen peas at the end.

MACHINE: Medium (6-cup) or large (10-cup) rice cooker; fuzzy logic or on/off
CYCLE: Quick Cook and/or regular or Porridge
YIELD: Serves 4 to 5

1 tablespoon olive oil
1 tablespoon unsalted butter
1/2 cup minced shallots or mild onion
1/2 cup minced celery
2 tablespoons dry white wine
1 cup plus 2 tablespoons medium-grain risotto rice (*superfino* Arborio, Carnaroli, or Vialone nano)
3 cups chicken, meat, or vegetable stock
1 1/2 cups fresh or frozen peas

TO FINISH
2 teaspoons unsalted butter
2 tablespoons heavy cream
1/4 cup freshly grated Parmesan cheese, plus more for serving
Salt

1. Set the rice cooker for the Quick Cook or regular cycle. Place the olive oil and butter in the rice cooker bowl. When the butter melts, add the shallots and celery. Cook, stirring a few times, until the shallots are softened but not browned, 2 to 3 minutes. Add the wine and cook for a couple of minutes. Add the rice and stir to coat the grains with the hot butter. Cook, stirring occasionally, until the grains of rice are transparent except for a white spot on each, 3 to 5 minutes. Add the stock and peas, if you are using fresh, mature peas; stir to combine. Close the cover and reset for the Porridge cycle, or for the regular cycle and set a timer for 20 minutes.

2. When the machine switches to the Keep Warm cycle or the timer sounds, stir the rice with a wooden or plastic rice paddle or wooden spoon. The rice should be only a bit liquid and the rice should be *al dente*, tender with just a touch of tooth resistance. If needed, cook for a few minutes longer. This rice will hold on the Keep Warm cycle for up to 1 hour.

3. When you are ready to serve, add the peas, if you are using frozen or very tender fresh ones; stir just to combine. Add the butter and close the cover for 2 to 3 minutes to allow it to melt and the peas to heat through. Stir in the cream, cheese, and salt to taste. Serve immediately.

BOIL YOUR ITALIAN RICE LIKE SPAGHETTI

There is a method for cooking rice, not only medium-grain rice, but long-grain rice as well (the French love rice cooked like this), in a pot of vigorously boiling water until al dente, then draining it. If you have Arborio rice around and don't want to make risotto, this is the way you can cook it and have an instant side dish. It is as delicious as it is simple. Serve with butter and freshly grated cheese, or with some homemade marinara sauce or Fondutta (page 237) over the top. The on/off rice cooker is perfect for making this rice since it boils water vigorously. You can also make this with half the amount of rice and water in a medium (6-cup) on/off cooker.

Boiled Italian Rice

MACHINE: Large (10-cup) rice cooker: on/off only
CYCLE: Regular
YIELD: Serves 3 to 4

2¹/₂ quarts water
Pinch of salt
1¹/₄ cups medium-grain risotto rice (*superfino* Arborio, Carnaroli, or Vialone nano)
¹/₂ to ³/₄ cup freshly grated or shredded Parmesan cheese, to your taste, plus more for serving
2 to 3 tablespoons unsalted butter, to your taste
Freshly ground black pepper

1. Place the water and salt in the rice cooker bowl (we fill to the 6- to 7-cup line on the inside of the bowl). Set for the regular cycle and bring the water to a rolling boil, 5 to 7 minutes.
2. Add the rice in a steady stream, stirring with a wooden spoon. Bring the water back to a boil and set a timer for 18 minutes. Boil the rice the entire time, uncovered. When the timer sounds, check the rice; you want it tender with a bit of bite, just like spaghetti. Cook for a few minutes longer, if necessary, until the desired texture is reached.
3. Turn off the cooker by unplugging it. Using oven mitts, carefully remove the full rice bowl from the machine. Drain the rice through a fine strainer into the sink, then pour the rice into a medium-size serving bowl. Immediately stir in the cheese and butter. Serve hot with more cheese and black pepper on the side.

SUSHI

Japanese home cooks make sushi often, but not the little fish-topped rice logs, called *nigiri* sushi, that are perhaps the most common sushi bar offerings. The word *sushi*, in fact, refers not to fish but to the vinegar-dressed rice that is the basis for a wide variety of sushi dishes. *Nigiri* sushi is deemed too hard to make at home. The sushi chef's special training is required for almost every step of the process—shaping the rice just so, cutting the fish properly, and so on. Home cooks have their own versions of sushi. Japanese home cooks prepare:

■ **Maki sushi**—seaweed-wrapped rolls that are sliced to expose the carefully arranged fillings inside.

■ **Hand rolls**—the sushi rice is spread on a piece of seaweed, topped with fillings (you can use the fillings detailed below under the *maki* section), and casually rolled up in an ice-cream cone shape to be eaten out of hand.

■ **Inari zushi**—the rice is stuffed into hollow little "pockets" made from fried tofu. This is great lunch box and picnic food.

■ **Chirashi sushi**—like a rice salad, a sort of sushi in a bowl.

A NOTE ABOUT STORAGE

Some sushi, especially that containing raw fish, is eaten soon after it is made. But other types of sushi, especially *inari zushi* or the Osaka-style *chirashi* sushi on page 146, can be made hours ahead. Store in an airtight container at *cool* room temperature. Don't refrigerate unless absolutely necessary; the rice will harden.

Many sushi recipes call for the use of raw fish. You would be crazy to go to the supermarket, casually buy a piece of fish from the case, and go home and slice it up raw for sushi. Only the freshest, cleanest (and we're speaking microscopically here), best quality fish that has been meticulously monitored at every step in the supply chain is deemed suitable to be eaten raw. If you are lucky enough to live in an area with a good Japanese market or to have some Japanese friends who like to make sushi, no problem. Go to the market and ask for sushi-quality fish, or ask your friends where you should buy it. Maybe your local sushi bar will sell you some. It will be expensive, but you don't need very much. Always eat raw fish the day it is purchased. If sushi-quality fish is not available in your town, content yourself with the many kinds of sushi that do not involve raw fish. You can make a huge and delicious array of dishes with cooked fish and seafood, vegetables, and eggs.

sushi rice

For any form of sushi, the first step is the rice, which your rice cooker will allow you to prepare perfectly. Many rice cookers made for the Japanese market have a special Sushi cycle. Even if your cooker doesn't have this cycle, you can use it to make great sushi rice.

This is a basic recipe for rice cooker sushi rice. The amount of the vinegar dressing—and the manner in which it is seasoned with salt and sugar—is subject to both regional and personal variation. Sushi rice is said to be made saltier in the Tokyo area, sweeter near Osaka. Individual cooks vary the sugar and salt to suit their own tastes. The type of rice you use is very important; it will be labeled "short-grain" or "medium-grain" and you want a Japanese-style medium-grain rice, not a risotto or Carolina medium-grain rice. An excellent, but somewhat expensive, brand is Tamaki Gold from Williams Rice Milling

Company of Williams, California. Other favorites that are good, and likely to be slightly cheaper, are Kokuho Rose and Nishiki. If you can't find them, look for rice labeled "new variety" or "sushi rice." Calrose is okay if you can't find anything else.

It is traditional to use a wooden bowl to mix your sushi rice because the wood absorbs excess moisture. This mixing tub is called a *han giri*, and it looks like half of a very flat wine barrel. It is made of a wood from the paulownia tree and banded with copper strips. *Han giri* are expensive, but new ones are easily available in Japanese hardware stores or large Asian markets. You can also use any large wooden bowl that isn't oily and doesn't smell like salad dressing. If you don't have a wooden bowl that is pristine, a medium-large plastic, metal, or glass bowl works fine.

You will also need something to blow cool air on the rice while you mix it. A hand fan or a folded-up newspaper is okay in a pinch, but many Japanese home cooks just aim an electric fan at the bowl. One friend uses a hair dryer set on "cool." That delivers a nicely focused stream of air and is especially good if you have a friend there to hold it steady. (A blow dryer or a hand fan is tricky to juggle by yourself.)

MACHINE: Medium (6-cup) rice cooker; fuzzy logic or on/off
CYCLE: Regular or Sushi
YIELD: 5 1/2 cups loosely packed rice

2 1/4 cups (3 rice cooker cups) high-quality Japanese-style short- or medium-grain rice

About 2 1/4 cups water

2 tablespoons sake

1/4 cup rice vinegar

1 1/2 to 2 tablespoons sugar, to your taste

1 teaspoon salt

1. Wash the rice thoroughly. Place the rice in the rice cooker bowl and fill the bowl about half-full with cold tap water. Swirl the rice in the water with your hand. Carefully pour off most of the water, holding one cupped hand under the stream to catch any grains of rice carried away with the water. Holding the bowl steady with one hand, use the other to rub and squeeze the wet rice, turning the bowl as you go so that all the rice is "scrubbed." (One friend calls this giving the rice a massage, and you definitely do want to use some muscle power.) The small amount of water in the bowl will turn chalky white. Now, run cold water into the bowl, give the rice a quick swish, and carefully drain off the water as before. Repeat the scrubbing and pouring-off process twice more. By the third time, the water you pour off will be nearly clear.

2. Add the cooking water. Some cooks like to use bottled water; do this if you are not crazy about the taste of your tap water. (Note that you are using slightly less water than the regular 3-cup level marker on your cooker bowl; the exact amount depends on how much water remains in your washed and drained rice.) Let the rice soak in the rice cooker bowl for 30 minutes if your machine has a built-in soak period, 45 minutes if it doesn't.

3. Add the sake to the rice. Close the cover and set for the regular or Sushi cycle.

4. While the rice is cooking, prepare the vinegar mixture. In a small saucepan, combine the vinegar, sugar, and salt. Simmer over medium heat, stirring occasionally, just until the salt and sugar melt. Or you can heat the vinegar mixture in a microwave oven. Remove from the heat and allow to cool to room temperature.

5. While the rice is cooking, lay out the following items around your workspace. When the rice is done, you will have to act quickly, so everything should be assembled and available within arm's reach.

■ a clean dishcloth or cloth napkin, rinsed in cool water and wrung out

■ a *han giri*, a clean bowl, wooden (if it is pristine), plastic, metal, or glass (if your bowl is wooden, rinse it out with cool water to prevent the rice from sticking)

■ the plastic rice spatula that came with your cooker, rinsed in cool water

■ your vinegar mixture, at room temperature

■ an electric fan, a hair dryer with a "cool" setting, a hand fan, or a folded newspaper

6. When the machine switches to the Keep Warm cycle, let the rice steam for 15 minutes. Then use the spatula to scoop all the rice into the bowl. Holding the spatula in one hand (with the curved back side facing up) over the rice and the pan with the vinegar mixture in the other, slowly pour the vinegar over the spatula, letting it run off and fall lightly onto the rice. Move the spatula around the bowl as you pour. The net effect will be to sprinkle the vinegar as evenly as possible over the surface of the rice. Gently nestle the damp cloth over the rice, covering it completely and bunching up the cloth against the side of the bowl. Wait 2 minutes.

7. Mix and cool the rice. You want rice that is shiny, body temperature or a bit cooler, mostly dry, and fairly sticky. The grains should be distinct, not mashed. Force-cooling the rice keeps it from absorbing the vinegar and getting too sticky.

Aim the electric fan at the rice in the bowl (or get your hair dryer or hand fan ready), but don't turn it on yet. Mix the rice with the spatula, holding the spatula vertically and using it like a knife, gently and repeatedly cutting through and lifting sections of rice. (If you stirred the rice in the traditional manner, you would quickly make rice mush.) Rotate the bowl so that all of the rice gets mixed. After 1 minute of mixing, turn the fan to low or medium speed (or begin to use the hair dryer or to fan the rice by hand). Continue "cutting," lifting, fanning, and turning the bowl until the rice is shiny and about body temperature (feel it with your palm). The rice is now ready to use.

If you are not ready to assemble your sushi, just set the spatula on top of the rice and re-cover the rice with the towel. The rice can wait, covered with the towel, for about an hour or so.

maki sushi

Maki are seaweed-wrapped rolls of rice with something tasty centered inside. The rolls are sliced to expose a cross section of the fillings, which range from the extremely simple, like cucumber strips, to the inventive, like California rolls, the crab, avocado, sesame, and cucumber combination that indeed was created in the United States. *Maki* sushi is typically made in three thicknesses; medium (about 1 1/2 inches across) is the easiest to handle. You can be as creative as you want, but remember that anything used to stuff *maki* sushi should be soft. Raw cucumber is okay, but carrot strips should be cooked.

The only piece of special equipment you will need is a *maki-su*, the little bamboo-and-string mat used to support the seaweed while you roll it around the rice and fillings (it looks like a miniature window shade). These cost only a few dollars and are easy to find in Asian markets, import stores like Cost Plus, cookware shops, or health food stores. (Or substitute a piece of heavy-duty aluminum foil.) The dried seaweed wrappers, *yaki sushi nori*, wasabi, and ginger are all sold in Asian markets, health food stores, and gourmet markets.

Here we provide general directions for making *maki* sushi, followed by a selection of common, easy-to-prepare fillings.

1 recipe Sushi Rice (page 139)

6 sheets *yaki sushi nori* (roasted seaweed sheets)

Desired fillings (see below)

Soy sauce, ready-to-eat wasabi (sold in a plastic tube or as a powder that you mix with water to make the paste), and slices of pickled ginger, for serving

1. Arrange around your work surface for assembly:

- the sushi rice in its cloth-covered bowl
- the sheets of nori
- your fillings
- a bamboo rolling mat for forming the rolls, or a 9 x 10-inch sheet of heavy-duty aluminum foil
- 2 forks
- a clean, damp dishcloth

SOME FILLINGS FOR MAKI SUSHI

- **Cucumber:** Japanese cucumbers are small, slender, and less watery than the American or even the long English ones. If you can't find Japanese cucumbers, the English variety is a good substitute. To cut them for sushi: Cut the unpeeled cucumber on the diagonal into slices about 1/4 inch thick, forming long ovals. Stack the ovals and cut into thin matchsticks. If you use English cucumbers, you may want to let the pieces wait for you on a double layer of paper towels so that any extra moisture is absorbed.

- **Radish sprouts:** These long white sprouts topped by delicate green leaves make a tasty, slightly spicy addition to sushi rolls. To use, trim away the roots, then wash the sprouts by swishing them gently in a bowl of cold water. Let dry on a double layer of paper towels.

- **Broiled eel (unagi kabayaki):** *Unagi kabayaki* is eel that has been steamed, broiled, and seasoned with a slightly thick, slightly sweet sauce. This procedure is considered to be beyond the scope of most home cooks, but fortunately, you can buy already prepared *unagi* frozen or canned. To use frozen *unagi*, place the unopened package in a pot of boiling water that is large enough to hold it. Boil the package for 10 minutes, covered, then remove from the water. When the package is cool enough to handle, cut it open and remove the eel. To slice for sushi, cut the eel crosswise into pieces 2 to 3 inches wide. Then cut each piece lengthwise into thin strips (about 1/3 inch wide). It is okay to eat the skin. Eel and cucumber (use plenty of each) is a classic sushi combination called *unakyu.* (You can eat any leftover eel with plain rice as a simple *donburi.*)

- **Shiitake mushrooms:** Dried shiitake mushrooms are softened by soaking in water, then seasoned by simmering in a small amount of flavorful liquid. They are a very tasty and popular sushi filling. To prepare 8 medium-size dried shiitake mushrooms: Place the mushrooms in a small bowl; add water to just cover. Let the mushrooms soak until softened, 2 to 4 hours at room temperature. (If you are short

- a sharp chef's knife
- a plastic or wooden cutting board
- a small saucer of rice vinegar (may be needed to seal the rolls)
- a serving platter (a cake plate or small square platter works nicely)
- condiments in serving bowls

2. Arrange the rolling mat in front of you, with the pieces of bamboo running horizontally (parallel to the edge of the work surface). Place a piece of nori on the mat, with the smoother side down.

3. Uncover the rice and use the spatula to section the rice into 6 parts. Scoop out one section and place it on the bottom half of the sheet of nori. Re-cover the remaining rice to keep it from drying out. Hold a fork in each hand, tines down, rounded side up. Use the forks like garden rakes to spread out the rice as evenly as possible over the on time, soak in hot water for 1 hour, or cover the bowl of mushrooms and water tightly with plastic wrap and microwave for 2 minutes on high. Allow to cool before proceeding.) Squeeze any liquid from the mushrooms, reserving it. Cut the tough stems from the mushrooms and slice the mushrooms into matchsticks. Slowly pour the mushroom soaking liquid into a small saucepan, being careful to leave any grit behind in the bowl. To the saucepan add about 2 tablespoons each sake, mirin (sweet rice wine), and soy sauce. Add $1/4$ teaspoon salt and, if desired, $1/2$ teaspoon chicken bouillon granules (or $1/2$ cube). Add the mushrooms and cook over medium-high heat until most of the liquid is absorbed. Remove the mushrooms from any remaining liquid.

If you want to use fresh shiitakes for sushi, skip the soaking step and season by cooking them with sake, mirin, and soy sauce as above, adding a bit of Dashi (page 349), if needed.

- **Scrambled eggs:** Finely crumbled, seasoned scrambled eggs are popular as a rice topping as well as a sushi filling. They are a lot easier to make than the thin Japanese omelets. Beat 2 eggs in a bowl with $1/2$ teaspoon potato starch (also called potato starch flour; do not use regular potato flour! If you don't have an Asian market in your town, you can find potato starch with the kosher foods in large supermarkets), $1/2$ teaspoon water, 2 rounded teaspoons sugar, $1/2$ teaspoon salt, and 2 drops soy sauce. Coat an 8-inch skillet with nonstick cooking spray. Place the skillet over high heat. When it is hot, add the egg mixture and cook, stirring with chopsticks or a spatula to break up the egg into firm but tender fine crumbles. Let cool before using.

- **Raw tuna:** If you can buy sushi-quality tuna in your town, by all means go ahead! It makes simple and delicious *maki*. Just cut the tuna into strips the thickness of a pencil. You can add radish sprouts if desired. One-half pound of tuna will fill 6 rolls very generously.

bottom two-thirds of the nori. Don't leave any margins; spread the rice all the way to the edges. About 1 inch up from the bottom, use the side of a fork to push aside some of the rice and make a sort of depression or trough where the filling will go. The trough should extend all the way across the nori. Don't expose the nori, though; you want your filling to be enclosed in a layer of rice.

4. Lay the desired filling in the trough. It is okay to mound it rather high. You will compress it as you complete the roll. (You will quickly learn how much filling to use to produce a roll that is neither skimpy nor bulging.)

5. Slide the nori to the edge of the mat closest to you. Lifting the mat, not the nori, begin the roll by bringing the strip of rice closest to you to meet the strip of rice on the other side of the filling. Squeeze the mat gently but firmly, moving your hands along the entire length of the mat, to create a nice, even log shape. Now complete the roll, stopping every so often to gently squeeze the mat and shape the roll. At the end, give a final squeeze, hard enough to firm and seal the roll but not so hard that the filling oozes out the ends. If the nori doesn't seal, dip your finger in vinegar and wet the edge of the nori.

Set the finished roll aside and continue filling and rolling the remaining 5 sheets of nori.

6. When all the rolls are finished, cut each into 6 pieces. You will make the cleanest cuts if you use a wet knife, wipe it with the damp towel after every cut, and cut with a back-and-forth sawing motion instead of pressing down. Arrange the rolls cut side

up on the serving platter. Serve with the soy sauce, wasabi, and pickled ginger.

california rolls

YIELD: 3 rolls; serves 2 to 4

$1/4$ pound cooked crabmeat, picked over for shells and cartilage

1 to 4 teaspoons Chinese (hot) mustard, to your taste

1 to 4 teaspoons mayonnaise, to your taste

1 medium-size avocado (Hass is best)

1 to 2 Japanese cucumbers or part of a long English one

$1/2$ recipe Sushi Rice (page 139)

3 sheets *yaki sushi nori* (toasted seaweed sheets)

Toasted Japanese sesame seeds (see Note)

Soy sauce and wasabi paste, for serving

1. Using two forks or your fingers, finely shred the crabmeat. Mix the crabmeat with a dab of Chinese mustard and enough mayonnaise to hold the crab together; start with 1 or 2 teaspoons. Add more mustard if you want a spicier flavor.

2. To prepare the avocado, cut it in half the long way, working your knife around the pit. Remove the pit and use a knife to score the avocado into slices about $1/3$-inch thick. Don't cut all the way through the skin. Use a large soup spoon to scoop the slices right out of the avocado shell.

If the avocado is large, you may wish to halve the slices lengthwise. Prepare the cucumbers as described on page 142.

3. For each California *maki*, spread the rice on the nori as described on pages 143–144. In the trough, layer the crab salad, cucumber, and avocado strips. Sprinkle the rice generously with the sesame seeds. Roll up carefully and cut each *maki* into 6 pieces, wiping the knife with a damp towel between cuts.

4. Serve with soy sauce and wasabi paste for dipping.

note: Toasted Japanese sesame seeds are light tan and sold in a shaker jar in Japanese markets; they are larger and more flavorful than ordinary sesame seeds and have already been toasted; toast them again in a small skillet to enhance the flavor.

variation: Shrimp-filled California rolls were the stars of the sushi platter at a Japanese restaurant in the shrimp-fishing town of Mazatlán, Mexico. Substitute 1/4 pound poached shrimp, shelled and finely chopped, for the crabmeat.

inari zushi

These stuffed tofu pockets are great picnic or lunch box sushi; they travel well and are neat and easy to eat. Despite their exotic look, they are not difficult to make. You buy the tofu pockets packaged and ready to go in Asian markets. Look for packages marked "fried bean curd" or "seasoned fried bean curd" (*ajitsuke inari age*). Shirakiku is one brand.

Inari zushi can be starkly simple; vinegared sushi rice is a delicious filling on its own. You can add toasted sesame seeds, cooked egg, bits of vegetables like seasoned shiitake mushrooms or blanched grated carrot, or cooked fish. Whatever ingredients you mix with the rice should be soft and diced, shredded, or minced very finely. If you keep the tofu pockets on hand in the freezer, you can pull out a few whenever you make *maki* or hand roll sushi; finely chop your leftover fillings, mix with vinegared rice, and stuff a few *inari zushi*. If you are short on time, you can just add a package of the prepared vegetable mix called *gomoku sushi no moto* to freshly cooked hot rice. (This product typically is sold in cans or plastic pouches.) These vegetable mixes include the vinegar; you just mix them into the hot rice while fanning to cool.

When you shop for tofu pockets, you are likely to see three styles. One (*ajitsuke inari age*), sold frozen in a plastic boil-in bag, is already seasoned and ready to use after thawing or boiling for about 10 minutes in a covered pot of boiling water. A second kind is canned; it is the easiest to use but not as tasty as frozen or fresh *age*. The third style is fresh, *abura age*. It is sold in plastic bags at Asian markets and, please note, it is not seasoned.

6 fresh or canned *abura age*
Boiling water
2 cups dashi (page 349)
1/4 cup soy sauce
1/4 cup mirin (sweet rice wine)
1/4 cup sugar
1/2 recipe Sushi Rice (page 139), mixed with additional filling ingredients (see above) as desired

1. To use canned or fresh *abura age*, open the bag or can and place the desired number of pouches in a large bowl or a colander in the sink. Pour boiling water over the pouches to remove excess oil. (Or blanch them for a minute or two in a pot of boiling water.)

2. Slice each pouch in half crosswise and gently open it up with your fingers, as you would open a pita half. Then season by simmering in a small pot with Dashi (page 349), soy sauce, mirin, and sugar. Continue simmering the tofu pouches for 20 to 30 minutes more, covered with a sheet of parchment paper, a saucer, the lid to a slightly smaller pan, or an *otoshi buta* (a flat wooden drop lid designed to keep simmering items submerged and yet allow some steam to escape; they are sold in Japanese markets or hardware stores).

3. To stuff, drain, then let the tofu pouches cool until you can handle them. Gently use your fingers to open one, being careful not to tear it. (Again, this is somewhat like opening a pita.) Fill with sushi rice. For the neatest looking *inari zushi* and to lessen the chance of ripping the pouch, shape the rice into a small oval first. Place about 3 tablespoons of your rice stuffing on a square of plastic wrap. Bring the ends of the plastic wrap tightly together and use your fingers to gently but firmly shape the rice into an oval. Remove the plastic and carefully insert the rice into the tofu pouch. (You can also shape the rice balls by hand, dampening your hands first with vinegar water.)

chirashi sushi
(osaka style)

In Tokyo, *chirashi* sushi is like unconstructed *nigiri* or *maki* sushi, except the ingredients are layered in a bowl. It is typically made with slices of raw fish, vegetables, and other ingredients, beautifully arranged on a bed of rice. In Osaka, though, *chirashi* sushi is a more casual dish, somewhat akin to a rice salad. Sometimes called *barazushi* or *maze gohan* (mixed rice), it is frequently made at home or for parties with friends and family. Like a potato salad, it is subject to the cook's skill, tastes, and whims, and the ingredients can vary enormously. Here is the way Julie's colleague Sharon Noguchi makes it. Sharon is a terrific cook whose family came to San Francisco from the Osaka area about a hundred years ago. Sharon notes that it's considered lucky to make *chirashi* sushi with an odd number of ingredients: five or seven, usually. She uses seven.

The vinegar dressing Sharon uses is much sweeter and more abundant than that used in the *maki* sushi recipe on page 141, which we learned from a Tokyo-born cook. Sharon's seasoned shiitake mushrooms, too, are sweeter and much less salty. If you like the Osaka-style sushi rice, by all means use these vinegar dressing proportions to make rice for *maki* sushi, hand rolls or *inari zushi*.

MACHINE: Medium (6-cup) or large (10-cup) rice cooker; fuzzy logic or on/off
CYCLE: Regular or Sushi
YIELD: Serves 10 to 12

RICE

4¹/₈ cups (5¹/₂ rice cooker cups) high-
   quality sushi rice
About 4¹/₈ cups water
³/₄ cup rice vinegar
³/₄ cup sugar
1 teaspoon salt

INGREDIENT LAYERS

Kampyo (dried gourd strips; page 148)
Grated Carrots (page 148)
Seasoned Shiitake Mushrooms (page 148)
Peas (page 149) or snow peas
Japanese Omelet (page 150)
1 teaspoon to 3 to 4 tablespoons red
   pickled ginger strips (*beni shoga*), to
   your taste
About ¹/₄ ounce shredded nori (*kizami
   nori*) (about 1 loosely packed cup)

1. *Make the rice:* Wash it as directed for
Sushi Rice (page 139). Place the rice in the
rice cooker bowl. If your machine has a
Sushi cycle, add the amount of water
directed. If not, add the water so that
it's under the 5-cup water line in the rice
bowl (about 4⅛ cups). Soak the rice for
about 30 minutes. Set for the regular or
Sushi cycle.

2. In a small saucepan, combine the vinegar,
sugar, and salt and heat on the stove or in a
microwave oven just until the sugar and salt
melt. Let the mixture cool. (If you're short
on time, cool quickly by placing the container in a larger bowl of ice water.)

3. When the rice is ready, prepare it as
described in steps 6 and 7 for Sushi Rice.
Cover it with a clean, damp towel and
leave at room temperature until you are
ready to proceed.

4. Uncover your prepared rice and add the
prepared *kampyo*, mushrooms, and carrots.
Mix well with a dampened rice spatula,
holding the spatula vertically and using the
same cutting and lifting motions you did to
mix the rice and vinegar.

5. Arrange the rice in a large serving bowl.
Smooth the top without smashing the rice.
Top the rice with the peas in a single layer,
then with the omelet strips. Arrange a few
red pickled ginger strips decoratively on
top of the omelet strips or just make a
little pile in the center.

6. Just before serving (you don't want it to
get soggy), sprinkle on the nori strips. If
you can't find *kizami nori*, buy *ajitsuke nori*
(seasoned) in strips and use scissors to cut
the strips into fine shreds.

   Chirashi sushi can be made several
hours ahead of time. If you are making
chirashi sushi 2 hours or less before you
intend to serve it, complete the dish up
through the ginger topping and let it rest,
tightly covered, at cool room temperature.
Add the nori just before serving.

   If you must make *chirashi* sushi 2 to
about 8 hours ahead, complete the recipe
up through adding the peas. Store the
chirashi sushi tightly covered at room
temperature. An oversize plastic container
with a snap-on lid is perfect for this—
authentic Tupperware will preserve it
best. Refrigerate the omelet strips, tightly
covered. When you are ready to serve,
finish assembling the dish, adding the nori
at the very last minute.

kampyo (dried gourd strips)

These are white strips of a dried gourd; the long strands look like fettuccine. They must be soaked with salt to soften, then cooked and seasoned before use. They may look strange, and they're a bit of work to prepare, but they are moist, sweet, and delicious. You can find *kampyo* in plastic packets on the shelf in Asian markets.

About 1 ounce *kampyo*

4 teaspoons salt

1 cup plus 2 tablespoons water

2 tablespoons sugar

2 to 3 tablespoons soy sauce, to your taste

¼ cup Sharon's Dashi (page 350)

1 tablespoon sake

1. Place the *kampyo* in a bowl with the salt and 2 tablespoons of the water. Knead it with your hands for a few minutes, rubbing the salt into the strips. Add the remaining 1 cup of water and let soak for 20 minutes.
2. Massage the softened *kampyo* strips with your fingers, smoothing out any that are curled up. Drain the salted water from the bowl, add fresh cool water to the bowl, and massage the *kampyo* underwater to remove as much salt as possible. Drain and rinse again.
3. Place the *kampyo* in a small saucepan with the sugar, soy sauce, dashi, and sake. Bring to a boil, then reduce the heat to a simmer. Cover the *kampyo* (not the pan) with a circle of parchment paper cut just a bit smaller than the diameter of the pan; a small saucer; the lid to a slightly smaller pan; or an *otoshi buta*, a flat wooden drop lid designed to keep simmering items submerged and yet allow some steam to escape. (They are sold in several sizes in Japanese markets or hardware stores.) Let the *kampyo* cook about 15 minutes, stirring occasionally, until most of the liquid is absorbed. The *kampyo* will be shiny and amber-colored. It should be tender, not rubbery; if it's not tender, cook it longer. Drain.
4. When the *kampyo* is cool enough to work with, line up the strands on a cutting board, and dice.

grated carrots

1 large or 2 medium-size carrots

1½ cups Sharon's Dashi (page 350)

¼ teaspoon salt

1. Peel and grate the carrots.
2. Bring the dashi and salt to a boil in a small saucepan. Add the carrots. When the liquid returns to a boil, immediately drain the carrots and run cold water over them to stop the cooking.

seasoned shiitake mushrooms

6 large dried shiitake mushrooms

½ cup Sharon's Dashi (page 350)

⅓ cup soy sauce

¼ cup sugar

3 tablespoons sake

Toasted Sesame Seeds

Iri gomi are readily available in Asian groceries and convenient to have around for sprinkling on anything, even plain rice. They are pan-toasted for this dish, even though they are already toasted, as toasting them again enhances the flavor considerably. This is an alternative topping instead of the *kampyo*.

^{1}/4 cup Japanese toasted sesame seeds (*iri gomi*)

Place the sesame seeds in a small, dry skillet over medium heat and shake the pan until evenly toasted, 2 to 3 minutes.

Kamaboko (Japanese Fish Cakes)

Kamaboko are steamed fish cakes, often with the distinctive pink-dyed edges. They are sold fully cooked and can be found in the refrigerator section of Asian markets. This is an alternative topping instead of the *kampyo*. Cut half a *kamaboko* into thin strips.

1. Place the mushrooms in a small bowl; add warm water to just cover. Let the mushrooms soak until softened, 2 to 4 hours at room temperature. (If you are short on time, soak in hot water for 1 hour, or cover the bowl of mushrooms and water tightly with plastic wrap and microwave for 2 minutes on high. Allow to cool before proceeding.)

2. Drain and cut the mushrooms into ⅛-inch-wide strips, or as thinly as possible, discarding the stems.

3. Combine the dashi, soy sauce, sugar, and sake in a small saucepan over medium-high heat. When the mixture boils, add the mushroom slices and stir. Reduce the heat to a simmer. Cover the mushrooms (not the pan) with a circle of parchment paper cut just a bit smaller than the diameter of the pan, a small saucer, the lid to a slightly smaller pan, or an *otoshi buta*, a flat wooden drop lid designed to keep simmering items submerged and yet allow some steam to escape. (They are sold in several sizes in Japanese markets or hardware stores.) Let the mushrooms simmer slowly for about 20 minutes. Most of the liquid will be absorbed or evaporated and the mushrooms will have turned a caramel color. Drain any remaining liquid.

peas

1½ cups Sharon's Dashi (page 350)
1 teaspoon salt
One 12-ounce package frozen petite peas

Bring the dashi and salt to a boil in a medium-size saucepan. Add the peas and cook briefly, about 1 minute, just until thawed and separate. Drain the peas and cool quickly under cold running water.

snow peas: Substitute 2 cups snow peas, trimmed of tough strings and sliced on the diagonal into ¼-inch-wide strips.

japanese omelet

2 large or extra-large eggs
1 teaspoon sugar
1 tablespoon mirin (sweet rice wine) or
   sake (for a less sweet omelet)
Pinch of salt
1 teaspoon mild vegetable oil

1. Lightly beat the eggs in a small bowl with the sugar, mirin, and salt.
2. Coat a 10-inch nonstick skillet with the oil. Heat the skillet over low heat. Pour in the egg mixture, cover the skillet, and cook, undisturbed, until the egg is set but not browned, about 2 minutes, or longer, if needed.
3. Flip the omelet out of the pan and onto a cutting board. (If the omelet is cooked through, it should pop right out.) A perfect omelet will be all yellow, with no browned spots.
4. When the omelet is cool enough to handle, cut into 2-inch-wide strips. Stack the strips and slice into thin slivers.

the whole-grain
COOKER

There is a saying that good things come in small packages. Well, when it comes to grains, including rice, that is an understatement. They come in diminutive packages, ready to contribute to your health and well-being like no other food. The cereal grasses—wheat, maize (corn), rye, millet, buckwheat, barley, and rice—are the building blocks of civilization, for with their domestication begins the history of the world and enough dependable, high-powered fuel food to feed it.

The history of grains reaches far back into the ancient, unwritten past, with humans gathering the fruits of wild grasses for food. The great cultures of antiquity grew up from the prehistoric times around cereal grain–growing areas, referred to as hearths of domestication, giving rise to the many scholarly debates about when and why our ancestors turned from being hunters and gatherers to settled agriculturalists. Surprisingly, the invention of agriculture arose independently in very diverse locales at the same time. All practical implications aside, there can be no generalizations on the complex factors that brought primitive humans to tilling the earth and domesticating principal grain crops. It is even postulated that the deliberate planting of seeds of native wild grasses was an act that had magico-religious motives. Simply speaking, life as we know it would certainly be impossible without cereal grains.

Early civilized life is mostly chronicled from the fecund environments in easily cultivated areas such as the rich river valleys of the Tigris and Euphrates, the Lower and Upper Nile in Egypt and Abyssinia, the Yang-shao in China, and the Indus in India. Based on archaeological evidence and plant genetics, by the time Egypt and Sumer on the Euphrates River were fledgling civilizations, wheat and barley were long considered the staff of life in Europe and the Middle East, rice was the central grain of southern China and India, and maize and quinoa flourished in the tropics of Meso-America and South America.

Grains have been tireless travelers, spreading around the globe overland by horseback and camelback, over and through the air by the winds and in the beaks of birds, by sea clipper, and in the carefully guarded pockets and pouches of wanderers on foot. From pots cooked over open fires and woodstoves to our plug-in rice cooker, you can safely consider these grains as a gift to us from these ancient cultures. Amazingly enough, they have been cooked in the exact same manner for all time. Only the cooking vessel has evolved.

Just as you cook rice in your rice cooker, you can cook whole grains. You use exactly the same technique, which is to press the regular/Brown Rice cycle button. The machine does the rest. Be prepared for different aromas and very different textures; each whole grain has a character unto itself. Terms such as "groat" and "berry" are references to the hulled whole grain. If the bran layer on the grain is especially tough, a soak may be in order to help with the cooking. If you end up with whole grains that are too wet, just drain off the excess water as if you were cooking on the stovetop. If your grains are too dry, drizzle them with another ¼ cup water and continue cooking or leave on the Keep Warm cycle. As with rice, if you turn off the machine and leave the lid closed, the inherent warmth of the environment will keep your grains warm for an hour.

basic pearled barley

While most of the barley grown in this country goes to brewing beer, you can still find pearled barley on most supermarket shelves. It is called pearled barley since, when cooked, it looks just like little pearl seeds. A favorite in soups because of its comforting digestive quality, pearled barley is a nice alternative to rice, works well in a grain and rice combination, and can be cooked like risotto. Barley is also great in salads or stuffed peppers. Pearled barley is hulled, so it is very white, needs no soaking, and cooks in under an hour. It is *not* the same as what is sold as "Quick Barley," which is pre-cooked and dried, and cooks up very mushy. You want barley to be chewy.

MACHINE: Medium (6-cup) rice cooker; fuzzy logic or on/off
CYCLE: Regular/Brown Rice
YIELD: About 3 cups; serves 4

1 cup pearled barley
2 cups plus 2 tablespoons water
Pinch of salt

1. Place the barley in the rice cooker bowl. Add the water and salt; swirl to combine. Close the cover and set for the regular/Brown Rice cycle.
2. When the machine switches to the Keep Warm cycle, let the barley steam for 15 minutes. If there is water left over, drain it off; if it is too dry, drizzle with hot water, 1 tablespoon at a time, and let steam until the barley has the right texture. Fluff with a wooden or plastic rice paddle or wooden spoon, and let the barley cool in the bowl or serve hot. It will hold on Keep Warm for up to 1 hour.

basic brown barley

Whole-grain hulled barley looks like the brown rice of barley; only its outer layer has been removed. It is also marketed as pot barley. Brown barley takes more water than pearled barley, usually calling for an overnight soak. There are strains of barley on the market called hull-less under the name of Nu-Barley; there is Black Buffalo (yes, it is black) and Bronze Nugget (golden), both from Western Trails—use these with this recipe. You can use brown barley just like pearled barley, but it is chewier and more nutritious. Cooked barley can be left at room temperature all day, so that it stays soft when you reheat it.

MACHINE: Medium (6-cup) rice cooker; fuzzy logic or on/off

CYCLE: Regular/Brown Rice

YIELD: About 3 cups; serves 4

1 cup whole-grain hulled barley
2 1/2 cups water
Pinch of salt
1 tablespoon unsalted butter, margarine, or olive oil

1. Place the barley in the rice cooker bowl and add the water; let soak in the machine for 1 hour. Add the salt and butter; swirl to combine. Close the cover and set for the regular/Brown Rice cycle.

2. When the machine switches to the Keep Warm cycle, let the barley steam for 15 minutes. Fluff with a wooden or plastic rice paddle or wooden spoon, and let the barley cool in the bowl or serve hot. It will hold on Keep Warm for up to 1 hour.

four-grain pilaf

Barley, wild rice, short-grain brown rice, and wheat berries all cook in the same amount of time. Here they are combined with some aromatics to make a delicious winter side dish.

MACHINE: Medium (6-cup) rice cooker; fuzzy logic or on/off

CYCLE: Regular/Brown Rice

YIELD: Serves 4

1/4 cup pearled barley
1/4 cup wild rice

1/4 cup short-grain brown rice
1/4 cup wheat berries
2 1/4 cups vegetable stock
2 thin slices red onion
1/2 teaspoon chopped fresh thyme leaves or 1/4 teaspoon dried thyme
1/4 teaspoon salt
Pinch of freshly grated nutmeg
Extra virgin olive oil

1. Place the barley, rices, and wheat berries in the rice cooker bowl and add the stock; let soak in the machine for 30 minutes. Add the onion, thyme, salt, and nutmeg; swirl to combine. Close the cover and set for the regular/Brown Rice cycle.

2. When the machine switches to the Keep Warm cycle, let the grains steam for 15 minutes. Fluff the grains with a wooden or plastic rice paddle or wooden spoon. This dish will hold on Keep Warm for up to 1 hour. Serve hot, garnished with a drizzle of olive oil.

japanese barley and rice

Cooking barley with some brown rice in a miso broth is an incredibly satisfying way to eat your grains. This would be the style of a homemade rice dish in some country hamlet in the mountains of Japan. It is distinctive and pleasing. Serve with a raw salad of leafy greens vinaigrette and broiled chicken breasts.

MACHINE: Medium (6-cup) rice cooker;
fuzzy logic or on/off
CYCLE: Regular/Brown Rice
YIELD: Serves 4 to 6

1 cup pearled barley
2¼ cups warm water
3 tablespoons white miso
⅓ cup short-grain brown rice
3 tablespoons sesame seeds, toasted
   (page 67), for garnish
Pickled ginger, cold cubed tofu, and
   minced green onion, for garnish

1. Place the barley in the rice cooker bowl and cover with hot water; let soak in the machine for 1 hour. Drain the barley and return it to the rice cooker.
2. In a small bowl, combine ½ cup of the water with the miso; whisk to break up the miso. Add the miso water to the drained barley along with the remaining 1¾ cups water and the rice; swirl to combine. Close the cover and set for the regular/Brown Rice cycle.
3. When the machine switches to the Keep Warm cycle, let the grains steam for 10 minutes. Fluff the grains with a wooden or plastic rice paddle or wooden spoon. This dish will hold on Keep Warm for up to 1 hour.
4. Serve hot, garnished with a sprinkling of sesame seeds and a few strips of pickled ginger, tofu, and green onion.

basic
couscous

The Berbers of North Africa have a granular semolina cereal called couscous, which is steamed in a special two-part steaming pot called a *coucousière*. We fell in love with couscous years ago, when this staple starch of Morocco began to appear regularly in supermarkets. Almost all of the couscous available in the United States is an instant refined variety, whether or not it says so on the box or bin, although health food stores often carry whole wheat couscous. Couscous is quick and easy to prepare in the rice cooker. It is a go-with-anything side dish, a bed for spicy stews, and a wonderful change from pasta or rice in hearty salads. Couscous can be prepared with apple juice and cinnamon for a sweeter breakfast-style dish.

MACHINE: Medium (6-cup) rice cooker;
fuzzy logic or on/off
CYCLE: Regular
YIELD: About 2 cups; serves 2

1 cup couscous, refined or whole wheat
1 cup water
2 tablespoons unsalted butter or olive oil
¼ teaspoon salt

1. Place the couscous, water, butter, and salt in the rice cooker bowl; swirl to combine. Close the cover and set for the regular cycle.
2. When the machine switches to the Keep Warm cycle, let the couscous steam for 5 minutes. Fluff the grains with a wooden or plastic rice paddle or wooden spoon. This

couscous will hold on Keep Warm for up to 1 hour. Serve hot.

prune couscous

Couscous is easy to dress up. Here we made an herbed dried fruit version. While you might think this combination of fruit, herbs, and nuts unusual, this is a traditional Turkish-style treatment of the grain. It goes well with roasted poultry.

MACHINE: Medium (6-cup) rice cooker; fuzzy logic or on/off
CYCLE: Quick Cook and/or regular
YIELD: Serves 4

2 tablespoons unsalted butter
$1/2$ cup sliced almonds
1 medium-size yellow onion, chopped
1 cup diced pitted prunes, preferably moist-pack
$2/3$ cup chicken stock
$1/2$ cup unsweetened prune juice
2 teaspoons dried mixed herb blend, such as Italian seasoning
1 cup couscous, refined or whole wheat
3 green onions, white parts and an inch of the green parts, chopped, for garnish

1. Set the rice cooker for the Quick Cook or regular cycle. Place the butter in the rice bowl. When melted, add the almonds and yellow onion. Cook, stirring a few times, until the onion and nuts are soft and just starting to brown, about 5 minutes. Add

the prunes, stock, prune juice, herb blend, and couscous; swirl to combine. Close the cover and reset for the regular cycle or let the regular cycle complete.

2. When the machine switches to the Keep Warm cycle, let the couscous steam for 5 minutes. Fluff with a plastic or wooden rice paddle or wooden spoon. This couscous will hold on Keep Warm for up to 1 hour.

3. Mound the couscous on a serving platter, garnish with the green onions, and serve hot or warm.

zucchini couscous

Another quick and filling couscous to whip up for dinner. Chickpeas have a natural affinity for couscous; wait until you taste them together.

MACHINE: Medium (6-cup) rice cooker; fuzzy logic or on/off
CYCLE: Quick Cook and/or regular
YIELD: Serves 4

2 tablespoons olive oil
$1 1/2$ pounds zucchini, cut into $1/2$-inch cubes
$1/2$ teapoon ground cumin
1 cup water
1 cup couscous, refined or whole wheat
1 cup canned chickpeas, drained and rinsed

1. Set the machine for the Quick Cook or regular cycle. Place the oil in the rice bowl. When hot, add the zucchini and cumin.

Cook, stirring a few times, just to take the raw edge off of the cumin, about 2 minutes. Add the water, couscous, and chickpeas; swirl to combine. Close the cover and reset for the regular cycle or let the regular cycle complete.

2. When the machine switches to the Keep Warm cycle, let the couscous steam for 5 minutes. Fluff with a wooden or plastic rice paddle or wooden spoon. This couscous will hold on Keep Warm for up to 1 hour. Serve hot.

ABOUT COUSCOUS

Although couscous is the national dish of northern African countries like Tunisia and Morocco, it is considered an ethnic grain in the United States. To food professionals, couscous is known as the grain with an identity crisis; it is considered both a pasta and a grain, depending on the ingredients. Attributed to the nomadic Berbers, who have been eating couscous for over 2,000 years, the staple starch found its place in Moorish cuisine. It is traditionally served before the dessert course on a shallow serving platter with stewed meat and vegetables on top, extra meat or poultry broth, and harissa, the fiery Tunisian hot sauce, on the side.

Couscous is made from semolina flour, the flour ground from durum wheat that is used to make premium Italian pastas, thus the association with pasta. If barley or millet flour and grits are used instead of the semolina, couscous instantly becomes a grain, but the semolina version is far more common.

Couscous can be made by hand and is a specialty in cooking classes in North African cuisine, such as the ones given by Paula Wolfert. She claims that making homemade couscous is easier than making pasta or even bread. Fine semolina flour is combined with coarse semolina, water, salt, and olive oil in a shallow wooden or earthenware bowl until the water is absorbed and the mixture sticks together. Using your open fingers and palm, and rhythmically mixing in one direction only, the mixture is deftly "rolled" to form granules called the couscous "beads." The beads are pressed through three sieves of varying sizes to create the small, uniform bits of couscous. The smallest are *s'ffa* and are very tiny indeed, but couscous comes in a variety of sizes. This fresh couscous is ready to be cooked. If the couscous is to be stored, it is oven- or sun-dried.

Our commercial brands of couscous, usually a medium-size granule that has been pre-steamed and labeled "instant," are made by using the vats and chutes of modern production methods; it will swell during cooking to about twice its dry size.

israeli couscous with orange

Israeli couscous is larger than regular couscous, and the little pasta bits are perfectly round. It is a type of couscous growing in popularity in the United States, and no wonder. It is tender, with a slightly toasty taste, and it takes happily to almost any kind of herb or seasoning. It cooks up beautifully in the rice cooker. The brand we found is Osem, which is imported from Israel. This savory dish is positively addicting.

MACHINE: Medium (6-cup) rice cooker; fuzzy logic or on/off
CYCLE: Quick Cook and/or regular
YIELD: Serves 4

1 tablespoon extra virgin olive oil
1 medium-size shallot, minced
1 cup Israeli couscous
2 cups chicken stock
1/2 teaspoon salt, if unsalted stock
   is used
1/2 teaspoon grated orange zest
2 tablespoons finely chopped fresh Italian
   parsley leaves

1. Set the rice cooker for the Quick Cook or regular cycle. Place the oil in the rice bowl. When hot, add the shallot, and let soften in the oil, 1 to 2 minutes. Stir in the couscous and cook until aromatic and lightly browned, 2 to 3 minutes. Add the stock and salt, if needed. Close the cover and reset for the regular cycle or let the regular cycle complete.

2. When the machine switches to the Keep Warm cycle, let the couscous steam for 10 minutes. Open the cover and add the orange zest and parsley. Fluff with a wooden or plastic rice paddle or wooden spoon to loosen the grains and blend in the zest and parsley. This couscous will hold on Keep Warm for up to 1 hour. Serve hot or warm.

israeli couscous with orange and olives: Omit the parsley. Stir in 2 tablespoons sliced pitted Kalamata olives with the orange zest.

israeli couscous with orange and almonds: Omit the parsley. Stir in 2 tablespoons toasted slivered almonds with the orange zest.

israeli couscous with mushrooms: Omit orange zest. Increase the oil to 2 tablespoons. Sauté 1/2 cup sliced fresh mushrooms along with the shallot.

basic farro

Our agent, Martha Casselman, sent Beth a bag of farro imported from Italy by Bartolini, with the label "Farro Semiperlato," which looked just like regular wheat berries. What should we do with them, we wondered? Farro is a different strain of wheat than the one that gives us plain wheat berries; the grains are larger and redder. It is descended from emmer, one of the earliest wheats in the Middle East, and the grain of choice in ancient Egypt and the highlands of Abyssinia, at the source of the Nile. This was the wheat the Egyptians were using when they discovered wild yeasts and made their first breads; it was the wheat the Romans ate. Over time, emmer evolved naturally into durum wheat, the same large-grained, amber-colored grain we use today ground into flour for pasta.

At the same time, showing up in the Bronze Age in alpine southern Germany and Switzerland, was spelt, a natural mating of the same durum with the Egyptian pedigree and another early common wild European grasslike weed. A pure European grain that never grew east of Iran, spelt is a bread wheat. That means it has lots of protein, or gluten. The French word for spelt, *epeautre*, means "sticky hull." Spelt, known as *farro* in northern Italy and *Dinkel* in Germany, Switzerland, and Austria, is the delicious wheat that was grown and eaten during the Middle Ages. Now an heirloom grain, farro may seem old-fashioned, but it is still grown in areas along the Rhine and Danube Rivers, and has found an escalating market with travelers from America who have visited these areas and had a taste. Farro is a softer wheat than regular wheat berries, so it cooks faster, needs less water, and is more digestible. Use it exactly like regular wheat berries. These same proportions can be used for another ancient wheat berry, kamut.

MACHINE: Medium (6-cup) rice cooker; fuzzy logic or on/off
CYCLE: Regular/Brown Rice
YIELD: About 2 cups; serves 3 to 4

1 cup farro
1 1/2 cups water
1 tablespoon olive oil
Pinch of salt

1. Place the farro in a dry skillet over medium-high heat. Toast, stirring constantly, until the grains pop and deepen in color, about 4 minutes.

2. Place the toasted farro and water in the rice cooker bowl and cover with the water; let soak in the machine for 1 hour. Add the oil and salt; swirl to combine. Close the cover and set for the regular/Brown Rice cycle.

3. When the machine switches to the Keep Warm cycle, let the farro steam for 10 minutes. Fluff with a wooden or plastic rice paddle or wooden spoon. This farro will hold on Keep Warm for up to 1 hour. Serve hot.

farro with shiitakes

The rich, meaty flavor and texture of fresh shiitake mushrooms is a great foil to the chewy whole-grain Italian spelt. Serve with roast chicken or beef dishes.

MACHINE: Medium (6-cup) rice cooker; fuzzy logic or on/off
CYCLE: Quick Cook and/or regular
YIELD: Serves 3 to 4

2 tablespoons unsalted butter
1 large or 2 small shallots, finely chopped
6 ounces (2 medium-large) fresh shiitake mushrooms, stems removed and caps chopped
1 cup farro
1 1/2 cups water
Pinch of salt
Freshly ground black pepper
Small sprig fresh savory, marjoram, or oregano

1. Set the rice cooker for the Quick Cook or regular cycle. Place the butter in the rice bowl. When melted, add the shallots and stir to coat with the butter. Add the mushrooms and close the cover. Let the shallots and mushrooms cook, stirring occasionally, until completely soft, about 7 minutes.

2. Open the cover, add the farro, and stir to combine. Continue to cook, stirring occasionally, until the farro smells toasty, about 3 minutes. Add the water, salt, pepper to taste, and herb sprig. Close the cover and reset for the regular cycle or let the regular cycle complete.

3. When the machine switches to the Keep Warm cycle, remove the herb sprig and let the farro steam for 10 minutes. Fluff with a wooden or plastic rice paddle or wooden spoon. This farro will hold on Keep Warm for 1 hour. Serve hot.

basic buckwheat groats

Unroasted buckwheat groats, also called white buckwheat, have a much milder flavor than the roasted kasha. You can immediately tell them apart—the toasted groats (another name for kasha) are russet colored. Kasha is a very old and traditional cereal grain in the Russian hinterlands; the word *kasha* can also mean "meal." The Russians feel about kasha the way the Japanese feel about rice. While normally coated with egg to keep the grains separate, this version is from natural foods writer Rebecca Wood and has no egg. Buckwheat is an acquired taste to the uninitiated. Use fresh groats; we mail-order them from Birkett Mills in New York (see page 351). If you use the delicious Japanese heirloom miniature buckwheat called *soba gome*, follow this recipe but reduce the liquid by 1/2 cup and omit the sunflower seeds or nuts.

MACHINE: Medium (6-cup) rice cooker; fuzzy logic or on/off
CYCLE: Regular/Brown Rice
YIELD: About 2 1/2 cups; serves 3 to 4

1 cup unroasted white buckwheat groats
2 cups water or chicken stock
1 tablespoon unsalted butter or walnut oil
Pinch of salt, if unsalted sunflower seeds are used
1/2 cup shelled sunflower seeds or walnuts, toasted (page 68)

1. Place the groats in a dry skillet over medium-high heat. Toast, stirring constantly, until the color deepens a few shades, about 4 minutes. You can toast groats light or dark, to your own preference.

2. Place the groats in the rice cooker bowl. Add the water, butter, salt, if using, and sunflower seeds; swirl to combine. Close the cover and set for the regular/Brown Rice cycle.

3. When the machine switches to the Keep Warm cycle, let the groats steam for 15 minutes. Fluff the grains with a wooden or plastic rice paddle or wooden spoon. These groats will hold on Keep Warm for up to 1 hour. Serve hot.

kasha varnishkes

This is a very basic recipe for an old Jewish favorite, the nutritious and nutty roasted buckwheat called kasha mixed with tiny egg pasta bows. Cooked conventionally, the pasta must be prepared separately. But the gentle action of the rice cooker allows the pasta to cook perfectly perched right on top of the kasha.

MACHINE: Large (10-cup) rice cooker; fuzzy logic or on/off
CYCLE: Quick Cook and/or regular/Brown Rice
YIELD: Serves 6 to 8

3 large eggs
1 teaspoon salt
$1/8$ teaspoon freshly ground black pepper
$1^1/2$ cups whole kasha (roasted buckwheat)
2 tablespoons unsalted butter
1 medium-size yellow onion, chopped
4 cups water
$3/4$ cup tiny egg pasta bows

1. Beat the eggs in a medium-size bowl with $1/2$ teaspoon of the salt and the pepper. Add the kasha and stir to coat with egg. Set aside at room temperature for 10 to 15 minutes to air-dry.
2. Set the rice cooker for the Quick Cook or regular/Brown Rice cycle. Place the butter in the rice cooker bowl. When melted, add the onion, stir to coat with the butter, and close the cover. Cook, stirring occasionally, until the onion is completely soft, about 10 minutes.
3. Open the cover and add the kasha. Stir to combine and continue to cook, stirring a few times, until the kasha appears dry and smells toasty, about 5 minutes. Add the water and remaining $1/2$ teaspoon salt; stir to combine. Carefully sprinkle the pasta bows on top of the kasha, spreading them out as evenly as possible over the surface. Close the cover and reset for the regular/Brown Rice cycle or let the regular/Brown Rice cycle complete (or let it cook for about 30 minutes, until the kasha is puffed and tender and the pasta is cooked through).
4. When the machine switches to the Keep Warm cycle, let the kasha steam for 5 to 10 minutes. Stir gently with a wooden or plastic rice paddle or wooden spoon to combine the kasha and pasta. This dish will hold on Keep Warm for up to 1 hour. Serve hot.

kasha varnishkes with mushrooms: Add 1 cup (or more) thinly sliced fresh mushrooms to cook along with the onion.

basic millet

Millet has a fluffy texture, is very easy to digest, and has a very sweet, delicate, almost imperceptible nutty flavor. It can become bitter and sticky when steamed raw, so here it is first dry-toasted before steaming, turning a bright golden color. Food writer Elizabeth Schneider describes the flavor of millet as having "a hint of cashew and corn." Native to China, millet was being gathered around 7000 B.C. in Japan. Reflecting the importance that millet has maintained over the centuries, there is a beautiful family crest design of a foxtail millet plant in a book of Japanese textile emblems that adorned battlefield identification banners and court kimonos in the Middle Ages. The Stone Age Lake Dwellers, in what is now Switzerland, had wild millet. It is still the grain of choice in Central Asia, Africa, and India, while virtually unknown as a cereal grain in America. As an alternative to rice, cook up some millet. Toss it with some chopped fresh cilantro or basil leaves right before serving.

MACHINE: Medium (6-cup) rice cooker; fuzzy logic or on/off
CYCLE: Regular/Brown Rice
YIELD: About 3½ cups; serves 4 to 5

1 cup whole millet
1³/₄ cups water or chicken stock
1 tablespoon unsalted butter or margarine
Pinch of salt

1. Place the millet in a dry skillet over medium-high heat. Toast, stirring constantly, until the color deepens a few shades and the grains pop, about 4 minutes. Immediately place the hot millet in a deep bowl, fill with cold water, and swirl with your fingers. Drain in a fine strainer.
2. Place the millet in the rice cooker bowl. Add the water, butter, and salt; swirl to combine. Close the cover and set for the regular/Brown Rice cycle.
3. When the machine switches to the Keep Warm cycle, let the millet steam for 10 minutes. Fluff the grains with a wooden or plastic rice paddle or wooden spoon. This millet will hold on Keep Warm for up to 1 hour. Serve hot.

basic quinoa

In Quechua—the language of one of the main native Andean peoples and descendants of the Incas—the word *quinoa*, like so many other grains, poetically translates to "mother grain." Quinoa was a staple grain of equal importance to maize, and was considered a source of strength and endurance for working in the thin mountain air of the altiplano. After the Spanish conquest, quinoa crops were destroyed and the grain was virtually lost to the world until it appeared in the United States through the work of visionary horticulturalist Luther Burbank. The "forgotten cereal of the ancients," as he dubbed it, did not catch on as the food source he predicted. It is now imported from Bolivia by the Quinoa Corporation under the name Ancient Harvest Quinoa.

The grains are coated with a resiny natural pesticide and preservative compound, saponin, which is bitter and soapy flavored. The grain needs to be rinsed well before cooking. The seed is a round, flat disc with a very mild flavor that has a gentle tangy aftertaste. Quinoa turns translucent and fluffy when cooked. A hoop-like bran layer surrounds each grain, and it looks like a half-moon-shaped crescent or curly tail in the pot with the grain after cooking (a sure sign it is cooked enough). Quinoa is very light and extremely digestible, with a surprising crunch despite its tiny size. If left to rest after steaming on the Keep Warm cycle, the grains will swell a bit more. You can add tamari soy sauce, minced fresh herbs, garam masala, or cumin to the cooking water to vary the flavor.

Try this exotic grain; we think you will be pleasantly surprised by how much you like it.

MACHINE: Medium (6-cup) rice cooker; fuzzy logic or on/off
CYCLE: Regular/Brown Rice
YIELD: About 3 cups; serves 4 to 6

1½ cups imported quinoa
2 cups water or chicken stock
¼ teaspoon salt

1. Place the quinoa in a deep bowl, fill with cold water, and rub between your fingers. Drain in a fine strainer. Rinse two or three times, until the foam disappears.
2. Place the quinoa in the rice cooker bowl. Add the water and salt; swirl to combine. Close the cover and set for the regular/Brown Rice cycle.
3. When the machine switches to the Keep Warm cycle, let the quinoa steam for 10 minutes. Fluff with a wooden or plastic rice paddle or wooden spoon. This quinoa will hold on Keep Warm for up to 1 hour. Serve hot or let cool to room temperature and chill.

orange dessert quinoa

Quinoa is fantastic cooked in fruit juice. This recipe was adapted from the food writer who first brought quinoa to the attention of the grain-loving public 20 years ago, Rebecca

Wood. This is good drizzled with a bit of organic heavy cream.

MACHINE: Medium (6-cup) rice cooker; fuzzy logic or on/off
CYCLE: Regular/Brown Rice
YIELD: Serves 4 to 6

1½ cups imported quinoa
2 cups orange juice or passion fruit–orange juice combination
1 tablespoon firmly packed brown sugar
1 tablespoon unsalted butter
Pinch of salt
3 tablespoons chopped nuts, such as macadamia nuts, almonds, or pecans, toasted (page 68)

1. Place the quinoa in a deep bowl, fill with cold water, and rub between your fingers. Drain in a fine strainer. Rinse two or three times, until the foam disappears.
2. Place the quinoa in the rice cooker bowl. Add the juice, brown sugar, butter, and salt; swirl to combine. Close the cover and set for the regular/Brown Rice cycle.
3. When the machine switches to the Keep Warm cycle, let the quinoa steam for 10 minutes. Fluff with a wooden or plastic rice paddle or wooden spoon and stir in the nuts. Serve immediately.

basic rye berries

Rye has a characteristically bitter-strong, earthy-grassy flavor, usually with a pleasant sour aftertaste. Whole-grain rye berries are the whole kernels and are used in pilafs like rice or wheat berries, in salads, or for a breakfast cereal. Whole-grain rye is known for flourishing in cold countries with rocky, acid soil and, for that reason, rye has been a flour of choice for centuries in Scandinavia, Germany, Poland, and Russia; it is grown up to the Arctic Circle and mountain areas above 14,000 feet, which is highly unusual for a grain!

Because the grain is so soft and does not have a hull as tough as wheat, it is traditionally "parched" or roasted to bring out the best flavor. Food writer Bernard Clayton describes rye berries as having "a look like suntanned oatmeal" after cooking.

MACHINE: Medium (6-cup) rice cooker; fuzzy logic or on/off
CYCLE: Regular/Brown Rice
YIELD: About 3 cups; serves 4

1 cup rye berries
2 cups hot water
1 tablespoon vegetable or olive oil
Pinch of salt

1. Place the rye berries in a dry skillet over medium-high heat. Toast, stirring constantly, until the grains pop and deepen in color, about 4 minutes.
2. Place the toasted rye berries and water in the rice cooker bowl; let soak in the machine for 1 hour. Add the oil and salt; swirl to combine. Close the cover and set for the regular/Brown Rice cycle.
3. When the machine switches to the Keep Warm cycle, let the rye berries steam for 15 minutes. Fluff with a wooden or plastic rice paddle or wooden spoon. The rye berries will hold on Keep Warm for up to 1 hour. Serve hot.

mary's rice and rye pilaf

This recipe came from Beth's friend Mary Cantori, who is an inventive and intuitive cook. She never writes her recipes down, but luckily Beth did when Mary told her the details of this wonderful pilaf served with Thanksgiving turkey at Yosemite one year.

MACHINE: Medium (6-cup) rice cooker; fuzzy logic or on/off
CYCLE: Regular/Brown Rice
YIELD: Serves 6

1 cup rye berries
2 tablespoons olive oil
1/2 cup chopped yellow onion
1/2 cup chopped celery
1/2 cup coarsely shredded carrot
1 3/4 cups chicken stock
Pinch of salt
1/2 cup chopped pitted prunes, preferably moist-pack
1 1/2 cups cooked long-grain brown rice (page 52)
3 tablespoons chopped fresh Italian parsley leaves, for garnish

1. Place the rye berries in a dry skillet over medium-high heat. Toast, stirring constantly, until the grains pop and deepen in color, about 4 minutes.

2. Place the toasted rye berries and hot water to cover in the rice cooker bowl; let soak in the machine for 1 hour.

3. While the rye is soaking, heat the oil in a medium-size skillet over medium-high heat. Add the onion, celery, and carrot and cook, stirring, until softened, 2 to 3 minutes. Set aside.

4. Drain the rye berries and return them to the rice cooker bowl. Add the stock, salt, sautéed vegetables, and prunes; swirl to combine. Close the cover and set for the regular/Brown Rice cycle.

5. When the machine switches to the Keep Warm cycle, open the cover and stir in the cooked rice. Close the cover and let the grains steam for 15 minutes. Fluff with a wooden or plastic rice paddle or wooden spoon. Serve the pilaf immediately, sprinkled with the parsley.

basic wheat berries

Wheat berries, whole-grain wheat with all its natural bran and germ intact, are well known to health-food enthusiasts and people who grind their own flour. Sadly, wheat berries are little known to many other well-versed cooks. We use so many wheat products, from whole wheat flour and commercial cereals to farina and bulgur, but wheat berries are still rarely used. But one taste of a simple wheat berry salad with orange zest and red onion in a plain Dijon vinaigrette, and you will be hooked. Wheat berries have a chewy texture and lovely sweet aroma and flavor. They are good in casseroles, in soups used like rice or barley, as part of a grain stuffing, in pilafs, and as the base for salads or even sprinkled over them. They make a natural pairing with rice. Wheat berries have the best aroma when they are cooking in the rice cooker; they fill the kitchen with a perfect grain-sweet scent. The berries really need the presoak to soften the outer layers.

MACHINE: Medium (6-cup) rice cooker; fuzzy logic or on/off
CYCLE: Regular/Brown Rice
YIELD: About 3 cups; serves 4

1 cup wheat berries
2 cups water
Pinch of salt

1. Place the wheat berries in a dry skillet over medium-high heat. Toast, stirring constantly, until the grains pop and deepen in color, about 4 minutes. (This step is optional, but many cooks like this flavor a bit better than the untoasted grain.)

2. Place the wheat berries in the rice cooker bowl and cover with hot water; let soak in the machine for 1 hour. Drain the wheat berries and return them to the rice bowl. Add the water and salt; swirl to combine. Close the cover and set for the regular/Brown Rice cycle.

3. When the machine switches to the Keep Warm cycle, let the wheat berries steam for 15 minutes. Fluff with a wooden or plastic rice paddle or wooden spoon. The wheat

berries will hold on Keep Warm for up to 1 hour. Serve hot.

wheat berry and wild rice pilaf

The combination of wheat berries and wild rice has been heartily embraced by the priests of spa cuisine. The inherent low calories and pure source of concentrated vitamins and minerals make the most delicious grain combinations. The wheat berries and wild rice both cook in the same amount of time. Serve with roasted meats.

MACHINE: Medium (6-cup) rice cooker; fuzzy logic or on/off
CYCLE: Regular/Brown Rice
YIELD: Serves 6

1/2 cup wheat berries
1/2 cup wild rice
2 1/4 cups chicken stock
2 tablespoons olive oil
1 tablespoon unsalted butter
1/2 cup chopped yellow onion
1/2 pound fresh mushrooms, sliced
Pinch of salt
1 tablespoon white Worcestershire sauce

1. Place the wheat berries and wild rice in the rice cooker bowl and add the stock. In a large skillet, heat the olive oil and butter together over medium-high heat. Add the onion and mushrooms and cook, stirring, until very brown, about 15 minutes. Add the vegetables to the grains along with the salt and Worcestershire; swirl to combine. Close the cover and set for the regular/Brown Rice cycle.

2. When the machine switches to the Keep Warm cycle, let the pilaf steam for 10 to 15 minutes. Fluff with a wooden or plastic rice paddle or a wooden spoon. This pilaf will hold on Keep Warm for up to 1 hour. Serve hot.

basic bulgur cracked wheat

Cracked wheat is the whole, raw wheat berry that has been broken into pieces, while bulgur cracked wheat is made from whole wheat berries that have been hulled, steamed, and kiln-dried before cracking. We have found that plain cracked wheat is virtually impossible to find, but bulgur cracked wheat, a favorite in the popular tabboulé salad, is available in every supermarket. It is available in three grades, fine, medium, and coarse (known as grade C), with the supermarket variety being medium unless otherwise labeled.

Since the wheat berries have already been steamed, the cooking process is considerably shorter than for raw grains. The box gives instructions for simply soaking with boiling water, but cooking in the rice cooker makes for an even better, more tender grain. The rice cooker will automatically take into account the slight variables in cooking times among the different grades, so cooking is no fuss, and what emerges is a wonderful alternative to rice. Plain cooked bulgur has one of the most appealing flavors of all grains but is rarely served as a side dish. We have changed all that with this simple recipe.

MACHINE: Medium (6-cup) rice cooker; fuzzy logic or on/off
CYCLE: Regular/Brown Rice
YIELD: About 2 cups; serves 3 to 4

1 cup bulgur cracked wheat
1³/₄ cups water
Pinch of salt
1 tablespoon olive oil

1. Coat the rice cooker bowl with nonstick vegetable spray. Place the bulgur cracked wheat in the rice bowl. Add the water, salt, and olive oil; swirl to combine. Close the cover and set for the regular/Brown Rice cycle.

2. When the machine switches to the Keep Warm cycle, let the bulgur steam for 5 to 10 minutes. Fluff with a wooden or plastic rice paddle or wooden spoon. This bulgur will hold on Keep Warm for 1 to 2 hours. Serve hot.

bulgur wheat pilaf

Bulgur can be cooked using a number of techniques, as for a risotto, with plenty of liquid and, as for a pilaf, with the grain initially cooked in some fat before adding the cooking liquid. Be sure to use just plain old bulgur, not one of the seasoned pilaf mixes. You want to use a medium or coarse grade for pilafs, and a coarse grade for risottos.

MACHINE: Medium (6-cup) rice cooker; fuzzy logic or on/off
CYCLE: Quick Cook and/or regular/Brown Rice
YIELD: Serves 6

2 tablespoons unsalted butter or chicken fat
2 small white boiling onions, minced
2 cups bulgur cracked wheat
3¹/₄ cups water or chicken stock
Pinch of salt, if needed

1. Set the rice cooker for the Quick Cook and/or regular/Brown Rice cycle. Place the butter in the rice bowl. When melted, add the onions and cook, stirring, until softened, 3 minutes. Add the bulgur and stir to coat and thoroughly heat the grains. Add the water and salt; stir just to combine. Close the cover and reset for the regular/Brown Rice cycle or let the regular/Brown Rice cycle complete.

2. When the machine switches to the Keep Warm cycle, let the pilaf steam for 15 minutes. Fluff with a wooden or plastic rice paddle or wooden spoon. This pilaf will hold on Keep Warm for up to 1 hour. Serve hot.

basic wild rice

All wild rice, our native North American grass, is sold with the bran on the kernel (like brown rice) and this gives it its black appearance; the water it cooks in will always be dark because of the rich bran layer. In California today, wild rice is mechanically farmed and harvested and then parched (a type of parboiling), which gives it a strong flavor. Labels will usually tell you if the rice is hand-harvested or cultivated, but the color will tell you immediately how it was grown: hand-harvested rice is distinctly matte (as opposed to shiny) in a range of colors from a ruddy red-brown, deep chocolate, and tan to a subtle gray-green, and paddy rice is very shiny sable black. Since the outer bran coat is very tough, it is scratched, or scarified, so that water is more easily absorbed. The more scarifying, the lighter or more variegated the grain and, hence, the shorter the cooking time.

Wild rice is available in bulk grain bins and small boxes in a growing number of supermarkets, natural food stores, and gourmet food shops in a variety of grades. Select wild rice contains short and broken grains; it is good for puddings. Extra-fancy wild rice has uniform, medium-size grains about 1/2 inch long graded equally in color and is the most commonly available wild rice. Giant wild rice (known as long-grain) has grains about an inch in length (or longer) and is considered the premium grade. The cooking times for these grades are different because of the size of the grains, but that is not a problem when cooked in the rice cooker. All the grades taste the same.

Each brand of wild rice has its own particular taste, so if you have experienced a brand that was too husky or bitter for your palate, experiment with others, or use it in combination with other rices for a milder taste. Wild rice has a smoky, rich, nutty flavor, much like a strong herbal, woodsy tea; the darker the rice, the stronger the flavor.

This method of cooking the rice in a bit more than twice its volume of liquid is known as the Ojibway method, after a tribe of Native Americans who use the grain as a staple in their diet. The grain will swell and split slightly down the side, and some will curl like a butterfly. Do not rinse wild rice. While cooking, the liquid will look cloudy gray and sometimes have some foam. This is okay; it is part of the grain (the foam is the dusty by-product of the scarifying process). Wild rice is done when each kernel is swollen and cracked down the side. If a kernel has turned back, it has overcooked, although it is not unusual to have a percentage of these in every pot due to uneven cooking; we love the mixture of soft and chewier grains.

MACHINE: Medium (6-cup) rice cooker; fuzzy logic or on/off
CYCLE: Regular/Brown Rice
YIELD: About 3 cups; serves 4

3/4 cup wild rice
2 cups water, stock, or a combination of stock and dry white wine
1/4 teaspoon salt, or to taste

1. Place the rice in the rice cooker bowl. Add the water and salt; swirl to combine. Close the cover and set for the regular/Brown Rice cycle.
2. When the machine switches to the Keep Warm cycle, open the cover and stir to dissipate the heat to prevent overcooking. Close the cover and let the rice steam for 15 to 20 minutes. This rice will hold on Keep Warm for up to 1 hour. Serve hot, or cool to room temperature and chill.

wild rice with dried cherries and scallions

The following three recipes feature wild rice and are designed to be served as side dishes. You can mix some cooked long-grain white or brown rice with the cooked wild rice to tone down the earthy flavor, if you so desire.

MACHINE: Medium (6-cup) rice cooker; fuzzy logic or on/off
CYCLE: Regular/Brown Rice
YIELD: Serves 4 to 6

1 cup wild rice
2 1/2 cups chicken stock
4 scallions, white parts and a few inches of the green parts, minced
2 tablespoons chopped fresh cilantro leaves
1 cup dried tart cherries
1/3 teaspoon seeded and minced fresh jalapeño chile (optional)

1. Coat the rice cooker bowl with nonstick cooking spray or a film of vegetable oil. Place the rice in the rice bowl. Add the stock; swirl to combine. Close the cover and set for the regular/Brown Rice cycle.
2. When the machine switches to the Keep Warm cycle, open the cover and stir to dissipate the heat to prevent overcooking. Scatter the onions, cilantro, cherries, and jalapeño, if using, over the top of the rice. Close the cover and let the rice steam for 15 minutes. Stir with a wooden or plastic rice paddle or wooden spoon to combine the ingredients. This rice will hold on Keep Warm for up to 1 hour. Serve hot.

wild rice and bulgur with leeks and toasted almonds

Once we discovered the extra-delicious property of bulgur, it ended up being added to all sorts of grains. Here wild rice and bulgur are cooked together with leeks and almonds, a winning, very French, culinary mating.

MACHINE: Medium (6-cup) rice cooker; fuzzy logic or on/off
CYCLE: Quick Cook and/or regular/Brown Rice
YIELD: Serves 8

1/4 cup (1/2 stick) unsalted butter
5 small leeks, white parts only, washed well and thinly sliced
1 1/2 cups wild rice
3 1/3 cups chicken stock
1/4 teaspoon salt
1/2 cup bulgur cracked wheat
1 cup boiling water
1/2 cup slivered blanched almonds

1. Set the rice cooker for the Quick Cook or regular/Brown Rice cycle. Place the

butter in the rice cooker bowl. When melted, add the leeks and cook, stirring a few times, until softened, about 3 minutes. Add the rice, stock, and salt; stir just to combine. Close the cover and reset for the regular/Brown Rice cycle or let the regular/Brown Rice cycle complete.

2. Meanwhile, in a small bowl, cover the bulgur with the boiling water. Let stand on the counter to soften while the rice is cooking.

3. Preheat the oven to 325°F.

4. Place the almonds on a baking sheet and toast until just golden, 5 to 7 minutes. Remove from the sheet and set aside.

5. When the machine switches to the Keep Warm cycle, drain the bulgur, pressing to remove any excess liquid. Open the cover and stir in the almonds and bulgur, using a wooden or plastic rice paddle or wooden spoon. Close the cover and let the grains steam for 15 minutes. This dish will hold on Keep Warm for up to 1 hour. Serve hot.

wild rice with fennel and dried cranberries

This recipe has the wild rice cooked in a combination of chicken stock and cranberry juice. A great addition to Thanksgiving dinner!

MACHINE: Medium (6-cup) rice cooker; fuzzy logic or on/off
CYCLE: Regular/Brown Rice
YIELD: Serves 4

1 cup plus 2 tablespoons wild rice
2 cups plus 2 tablespoons chicken stock
2/3 cup reduced-sugar or unsweetened cranberry juice cocktail or unsweetened cranberry juice
3 tablespoons dried cranberries
2 tablespoons unsalted butter
1 shallot, chopped
1 small bulb fennel, stalks and greens discarded, bulb chopped (about 1 1/4 cups)
Salt
Freshly ground black pepper

1. Place the rice in the rice cooker bowl. Add the stock and cranberry juice; stir a few times to combine. Close the cover and set for the regular/Brown Rice cycle.

2. When the machine switches to the Keep Warm cycle, add the cranberries, close the cover, and let the rice steam for 15 minutes.

3. While the rice is steaming, melt the butter in a medium-size sauté pan over medium heat. Add the shallot and fennel and cook, stirring, until tender, 5 to 8 minutes. Season to taste with salt and pepper. When the rice has finished steaming, stir the fennel mixture into the rice. Adjust the seasonings again and serve hot.

polenta, grits, and
HOMINY

Polenta, grits, and hominy have one thing in common: they are all products made from corn. All have the delicate sweet flavor that is distinctly "corny," but each is made quite differently.

Is there any home gardener who has not tried his or her hand at a few rows of corn? The familiar tassel coming out the top of the ear, tightly covered by the husk which protects the multiple kernels that are developing in rows on the inner cob—it is a vegetable as familiar as a child's nursery rhyme. This is known as field corn and the pleasure of corn on the cob is an American summer ritual. When this soft, juicy corn is allowed to mature and dry on the stalk, the sugar turns to starch. This is the corn that is made into myriad corn products, including polenta, grits, and hominy.

Corn is one of the oldest cultivated grains, and a New World plant that reached Europe and beyond only because of the Columbus maritime exploration teams. In 1496 Columbus brought the first corn plants from the Caribbean islands back to Spain. Within 200 years, Indian corn would take its place as one of the three most important cereals around the world, from Mexico to China.

The Italians were the first Europeans to plant cornfields, in Crete. Enough of the new grain was grown to supply the entire Mediterranean Basin. The Near East became a golden field of maize and it was referred to as Turkish corn. Wherever the Ottoman army traveled, they left behind this grain that had become a staple in their traveling outdoor army kitchens. Corn became commonplace from the Euphrates River valley and Africa to Hungary and the Balkans.

Remember that, with all these corn products, if they are stone-ground and contain the germ and bran, they are highly perishable. Store cornmeal in the freezer for 6 to 12 months. Degerminated meals can be kept in the cupboard, tightly covered, indefinitely.

POLENTA

"Just as our greatest architectural surprise in Italy was to find St. Francis' first church was a log cabin (at Assisi), so were we amazed to discover that the Italians do even more delicious and interesting things with cornmeal than you can find in the (American) deep south" was how an early edition of *Joy of Cooking* introduced its readers to polenta cornmeal mush.

In the 1600s, an Italian farmer was asked to cultivate some of the seed plants of this Turkish corn for Romanian royalty so they could cook it up into a porridge, one that was usually made from millet. The result was a bright yellow-orange variety of flint corn, with its hard shell that looks translucent like a piece of amber—still cultivated today in northern Italy specifically for polenta. It is a dish still made in neighboring Romania as *mamaliga* and *puliszka* in Hungary. While you can most certainly make polenta with a medium or coarse grind of regular yellow cornmeal, it will not be authentic unless you get the strain of cornmeal specifically milled for polenta.

Polenta is a ground cornmeal that is degermed and it comes in a coarse or fine grind, regular or instant (traditionalists scoff at this last, since it is cooked, then dehydrated, but many cooks swear it has its own place in the kitchen, such as for frying). Toss a fistful of coarse cornmeal into boiling water, cook and stir with plenty of muscle for an hour, and you have polenta, a creamy gruel that can be eaten like oatmeal or poured out onto a plate in a thick layer, cooled, and cut into cubes to put into soup or pan-fried. It is a food that is so humble that it was once considered a staple peasant food with lower status than bread, but, of course, food so simple in the hands of a good cook ends up ingeniously versatile. While polenta today is usually made exclusively from corn, polenta is a regional dish that can be made from any number of grains—eastern Europe and Russia make their polenta mush from fine buckwheat groats; Polish cooks use farina; northern Italians also use millet.

Polenta has a long shelf life and can be kept in a canister in the cupboard, but keep it in the freezer if you buy it in bulk and plan to use it over a year. If you want authentic polenta, you must buy an imported brand, but there are also some domestic polentas available in natural food stores, so you can take your pick. It comes in yellow or white versions, with the yellow having the more robust flavor and the white, a specialty of Venice served in place of rice or pasta, more subtle and delicate. Our specialty grocery stocks a brand called Moretti, which comes in unique flavorful varieties: Lampo (instant), Taragna (with buckwheat meal or flour, a specialty of the Valtellina Valley in northern Italy), Friulana (from Italian white corn), and Integrale (with wheat germ), a testament to the many different ways the Italians can dress up cornmeal mush.

While authentic polenta has instructions for constantly stirring over low heat to prevent lumping, it can be made in the rice cooker with great success, without the laborious stirring. For the smoothest polenta, use the Porridge cycle. Polenta can be made in the on/off machine, but it is not as smooth, and you must not overload the cooker or it will boil over. On the regular cycle, you must stir two or three times during the cooking and stir thoroughly when the cycle completes. The closed environment of the rice cooker prevents a top crust from forming, but it does concentrate the flavor of the salt, so the amount of salt used is less than you would normally use if you were cooking polenta in an open saucepan. You can make your polenta soft (more water), to serve immediately out of the cooker in a mound with butter and cheese. Or you can make a stiffer (less water) polenta, to pour into a glass pan to cool, then turn out in a firm block and cut into pieces with a wet knife to grill or fry in a nonstick skillet with some olive oil as a side dish, or to be layered in a casserole like lasagne. Polenta works well with any sauce that is good on pasta—a light fresh tomato sauce or a rich ragu with meatballs, or topped with a meat stew. Cut polenta with a small cookie cutter and bake it with a topping of Gorgonzola, another native foodstuff of Lombardy, and you have a nice, filling appetizer. Soft polenta can be made ahead and held on the Keep Warm cycle for hours. To simplify cleanup, fill the rice cooker bowl with cold water and soak for 10 minutes before washing.

italian polenta

Italian polenta, the darling of all teachers of Italian cuisine, is labeled *farina di granoturco* on the package, the Italian name of corn since the time of Columbus. It was often made in a traditional copper polenta pot, replete with a special wooden stirring stick, that was handed down within rural families. This is a really nice, fluffy polenta that is foolproof. It uses two full cycles of the Porridge cycle. It thickens considerably during the second cycle and even spits a few times during the cooking. You can double the recipe in a large 10-cup machine. Serve with the Parmesan and a pat of garlic butter for a lovely treat, or sprinkled with grated Fontina cheese.

MACHINE: Medium (6-cup) rice cooker; fuzzy logic (preferred) or on/off
CYCLE: Porridge or regular
YIELD: Serves 4

4 cups water
1 cup coarse-grain yellow polenta
$1/2$ teaspoon salt
Freshly ground black pepper
$1/4$ cup ($1/2$ stick) unsalted butter, or more to taste
$2/3$ cup freshly grated Parmesan cheese (optional)

1. Place the water in the rice cooker bowl. Add the polenta and salt; stir for 15 seconds with a wooden spoon or wooden or plastic rice paddle. Close the cover and set for the Porridge or regular cycle. A few

SMALL-PORTION POLENTA

Sometimes you want just a little bit of hot polenta mush with butter and Parmesan or Asiago cheese to serve as a side dish. This is the perfect recipe.

MACHINE: Small (4-cup) rice cooker; fuzzy logic (preferred) or on/off
CYCLE: Porridge or regular
YIELD: Serves 1 to 2

3 tablespoons coarse-grain yellow polenta
1 cup water
$1/4$ teaspoon salt
Freshly ground black pepper
2 teaspoons unsalted butter

1. Place the polenta, water, and salt in the rice cooker bowl; stir to combine. Close the cover and set for the Porridge or regular cycle.
2. At the end of the Porridge cycle, reset for a second Porridge cycle. At the end of the second Porridge cycle, or when the regular cycle completes, open the cover and add a couple of grinds of black pepper and the butter. Stir quickly, close the cover, and allow the polenta to rest at least until the butter melts. This polenta can be held on Keep Warm for up to 2 hours. Stir before serving.

times during the cooking, open the cover, stir for 15 seconds, then close the cover.

2. At the end of the Porridge cycle, reset for a second Porridge cycle; the polenta needs two full cycles to lose its raw, grainy texture. At the end of the second Porridge cycle, or when the regular cycle completes, taste the polenta and make sure the desired consistency has been reached. Stir in the butter and cheese, if using (if you are chilling the polenta for frying or grilling, or using it under seafood, like grilled pesto prawns, the cheese is not necessary).

3. This polenta will hold on Keep Warm for up to 1 hour, if necessary. Add a bit more hot water if it gets too stiff. Stir before serving.

french polenta

The French also make cornmeal mush, which was originally brought to their country by the armies of the king of Spain in the Middle Ages. Made in all regions of France, the most famous polenta preparation is Savoy mush, and French polenta can sport toppings and additions like roasted game, stewed prunes, cheese, a variety of meat and vegetable sauces, meat pan juices, and truffles, and sometimes is an addition to soup.

MACHINE: Medium (6-cup) or large (10-cup) rice cooker; fuzzy logic (preferred) or on/off
CYCLE: Porridge or regular
YIELD: Serves 6

2 cups coarse-grain yellow polenta
3 cups water
3 cups chicken stock or milk
Salt
Freshly ground black pepper
Freshly grated nutmeg
6 ounces goat cheese, crumbled,
    for garnish

1. Place the polenta and water in the rice cooker bowl; stir for 15 seconds with a wooden spoon or wooden or plastic rice paddle. Add the stock and salt, pepper, and nutmeg to taste. Close the cover and set for the Porridge or regular cycle. About every 20 minutes, open and stir for 15 seconds, then close the cooker.

2. At the end of the Porridge cycle, reset for a second Porridge cycle; the polenta needs two full cycles to lose its raw, grainy texture. At the end of the second Porridge cycle, or when the regular cycle completes, taste the polenta to make sure the desired consistency has been reached. This polenta will hold on Keep Warm for up to 1 hour.

3. When ready to serve, spoon onto serving plates and sprinkle with the goat cheese.

gorgonzola polenta

Gorgonzola and polenta are a culinary team like spaghetti and Parmesan cheese. They just go together; maybe it is because they are both native to the area around Milan. Use a young Gorgonzola, aged under six months, so it is creamy and mild. It will melt into the mush, giving it a sophisticated flavor. Serve as a side dish alongside roast meats. Some people like to top the hot polenta with a dab of pesto and some chopped cherry tomatoes seasoned with salt, pepper, and a tablespoon of olive oil.

MACHINE: Medium (6-cup) rice cooker; fuzzy logic (preferred) or on/off
CYCLE: Quick Cook and/or regular or Porridge
YIELD: Serves 6

¹/₄ cup (¹/₂ stick) unsalted butter
1 small white onion (you can use a boiling onion), finely chopped
1 cup chicken stock
1 cup milk
³/₄ cup coarse-grain yellow polenta
5 ounces Gorgonzola cheese
¹/₂ cup heavy cream
¹/₂ teaspoon freshly grated nutmeg
2 teaspoons salt
Freshly ground black pepper
2 tablespoons shredded Parmesan cheese (optional), for garnish

1. Set the rice cooker for the Quick Cook or regular cycle. Place the butter in the rice cooker bowl. When melted, add the onion and cook, stirring a few times, until soft, about 8 minutes. Add the stock, milk, and polenta; whisk to combine. Close the cover and reset for the Porridge or regular cycle. A few times during the cooking, open the cover and stir the polenta for 15 seconds, then close the cover.

2. Coat 6 cups of a standard muffin tin with butter-flavored nonstick cooking spray or grease them with butter.

3. At the end of the second Porridge cycle, or when the regular cycle completes, stir in the cheese, cream, nutmeg, salt, and black pepper to taste. Using a plastic soup ladle, divide the polenta among the 6 muffin cups, filling to the brim. Let come to room temperature. At this point, you can cover with plastic and refrigerate overnight.

4. Preheat the oven to 400° F. Brush a small earthenware roasting pan with olive oil.

5. Remove the polenta from the muffin tin and place in the roasting pan (not touching each other). Sprinkle the Parmesan cheese on top, if using. Bake until hot, 15 to 20 minutes. Serve immediately, using a metal spatula to remove the polenta from the pan.

villa floriani grilled polenta with sausages

Beth's dear friend Rosmarie Finger worked for years on an estate called Villa Floriani in Portola Valley, California. Every summer there would be a charity celebrity tennis match on the grounds for the Peninsula Volunteers of Northern California, with a fantastic buffet luncheon for three hundred. Beth was lucky to be invited to a number of these functions and enjoyed the excellent food, prepared by a different chef each year. One year this dish was the main offering and it has become a favorite for summer entertaining. The original recipe is from Northwest food writer and chef Joan Deccio Wickham, who designed the menu that year. The recipe is immortalized in her Italian cookbook *The Sporting Gourmet Cookbook* (The Sporting House, 1983).

MACHINE: Medium (6-cup) or large (10-cup) rice cooker; fuzzy logic (preferred) or on/off
CYCLE: Porridge or regular
YIELD: Serves 6

4 cups chicken stock
1²/₃ cups coarse-grain yellow polenta
2 small yellow onions, chopped
2 tablespoons fruity olive oil
8 ounces Parmesan cheese, freshly
  grated, plus more for serving
1/8 teaspoon ground white pepper
6 tablespoons (³/₄ stick) unsalted butter,
  cut into pieces
Tomato Coulis (page 178)
6 medium-size Italian sausages, grilled

1. Place 2 cups of the stock in the rice cooker bowl and add the polenta. Stir for 15 seconds with a wooden spoon or wooden or plastic rice paddle; set aside.
2. In a medium-size sauté pan, combine the onions and olive oil. Cook over medium-high heat, stirring a few times, until the onions are transparent, about 5 minutes.

Add the remaining 2 cups stock and bring to a boil. Slowly pour the stock mixture into the rice bowl and stir briefly.
3. Close the cover and set the rice cooker for the Porridge or regular cycle. A few times during the cooking, open the cover and stir for 15 seconds, then close the cover.
4. When the machines switches to the Keep Warm cycle or the regular cycle ends, taste the polenta to make sure the desired consistency has been reached. Add the cheese, pepper, and butter, stirring until well blended.
5. Coat two 9 x 5-inch loaf pans with olive oil. Pour the hot polenta into the pans, filling each about three-fourths full. If you are planning to serve the dish that evening, set aside, covered with plastic wrap, to firm up. Otherwise, cover and refrigerate the polenta overnight.
6. Prepare a grill. *For an outdoor charcoal or wood chip fire:* When the coals are covered with gray ash, throw a few herb sprigs (like rosemary, if you have some) on top of the coals for extra aroma while grilling. *For a gas grill with two burners:* Preheat one burner on high, leaving the other side open for the sausages. *For a single-burner gas grill:* Preheat on high, then lower the flame while grilling the second side of the polenta. Spray the clean grill grate with an olive oil cooking spray and place it 4 inches above the fire.
7. Turn the polenta loaf out onto a cutting board and cut into 1-inch-thick slices. Place the slices on the grill and cook, turning once, until golden brown on both sides. Serve with more grated Parmesan, a ladleful of the coulis, and the grilled sausages.

tomato coulis

This is an excellent all-purpose tomato-herb sauce that is as good hot as it is cold. Use it as a topping for quiche, pizza, sautéed meats, or vegetables.

YIELD: 3 cups

1/4 cup fruity olive oil

1/2 cup chopped shallots

2 to 3 cloves garlic, crushed

One 28-ounce can crushed tomatoes, with their juices

2 tablespoons dry white wine

1/2 cup chopped fresh Italian parsley leaves

10 fresh basil leaves, chopped

Pinch *each* of fresh or dried thyme, oregano, and marjoram leaves

Salt

Freshly ground black pepper

1. In a large sauté pan, combine 3 tablespoons of the olive oil, the shallots, and garlic. Cook over medium-high heat, stirring a few times, until the shallots are softened, about 5 minutes. Add the tomatoes, wine, and herbs. Bring to a boil and reduce the heat to low. Simmer, uncovered, for 30 minutes, stirring a few times. Season with salt and pepper to taste.

2. Pour the sauce into a jar and cover with the remaining 1 tablespoon olive oil. Let cool to room temperature. The sauce will keep in the refrigerator for 2 days and in the freezer for up to 1 month.

GRITS

If you have ever traveled in the southern United States, you know about grits. A puddle of hot grits, sometimes called hominy grits (even though they are not from ground hominy at all), is served in every café for breakfast with a pat of butter, syrup, or redeye gravy. Grits are just the coarsest grind of plain old cornmeal, ground from white or yellow corn that is grown in the South, then simmered in water or milk and ending up not quite as smooth as polenta. If the grits are stone-ground, there will be black bits of bran and germ speckled throughout, and they are mighty tasty. These may be labeled "old-fashioned" (see facing box). When you prepare grits, first cover them with water and let the husks rise to the top, then drain and proceed with the recipe. If the grits are degerminated, they will be a uniform color, and come in instant and quick-cooking varieties, which are both chemically enriched. They have different cooking times, with the stone-ground taking by far the longest; the regular cycle handles this automatically when you vary the amount of liquid. Grits are a snap in the fuzzy logic rice cooker using the Porridge cycle. While grits normally need a proportion of 1 cup grits to 4 cups water to soften properly, the closed environment of the rice cooker prevents a lot of water evaporation, so the ratio drops slightly.

Crushed kernels of dried corn with the consistency of coarse sand and a shiny luminescence rather like that of seashells is the best description of grits. They are made from either white or yellow corn, although they both taste quite similar despite the difference in color. Yellow grits look a lot like polenta but are coarser, and polenta is cleaned of all flour and milling dust; you can't substitute one for the other. Instant grits is a degerminated cereal with its bran and germ sifted out. Out goes the character and taste as well.

When you get a bag of old-fashioned grits, they might be labeled "speckled" on the bag. The black speckles in the yellow are the sign of stone-ground grits, residue from the black base of each kernel. White grits, traditional in the Carolinas, are often flecked with yellow. Some cooks (like us) aren't bothered by the earthy look of the flecks, while others skim the grits after covering them with water before cooking.

Stone-ground grits can be mail-ordered from southern mills that have been grinding grits since before the Civil War (see Online and Mail-Order Resources, page 351), as well as some new mills that know a good thing when they taste it. You know the food world is getting wise when *The New York Times* describes grits as "good alone, with other foods, godly." Southern cooks have never paid any attention to fashion; they have been in the know for generations.

traditional grits

If you live outside the southern part of the United States, the only grits you will find in the supermarket will be instant or quick cooking. Luckily, there are excellent mail-order sources for fresh ground grits, including the Old Mill of Guilford in Oak Ridge, North Carolina (910-643-4783), and War Eagle Mill in Rogers, Arkansas (501-789-5343). Fresh ground grits are speckled from the bits of grain left over from the milling, so be sure to cover them first with water and let the husks rise to the top, then drain and proceed from the beginning of the recipe. If you want to use quick-cooking grits, just cook for one cycle in the rice cooker and they will still be very good.

MACHINE: Medium (6-cup) rice cooker; fuzzy logic (preferred) or on/off
CYCLE: Porridge or regular
YIELD: Serves 4

1 cup coarse stone-ground grits
3 cups water
1/2 teaspoon salt
3 tablespoons unsalted butter
Ground white pepper

1. If you'd like to remove the husks, combine the grits and some cold tap water in a bowl or use the rice cooker bowl; the husks will rise to the top and can be skimmed off. Drain the grits.
2. Place the grits, water, and salt in the rice cooker bowl; stir for 15 seconds with a wooden spoon or wooden or plastic rice

paddle. Close the cover and set for the Porridge or regular cycle. A few times during the cooking, open the cover and stir for 15 seconds, then close the cover.

3. At the end of the Porridge cycle, reset for a second Porridge cycle, giving the grits two full cycles to reach the optimum consistency.

4. At the end of the second Porridge cycle, or when the regular cycle completes, stir in the butter, season to taste with pepper, and serve hot. These grits will hold on Keep Warm for up to 2 hours.

creamy traditional grits: Replace 1 cup of the water with 1 cup whole milk and omit the white pepper. Good served with pure maple syrup and chopped crisp bacon.

traditional grits with cheddar: Add 1 cup coarsely shredded mild or sharp cheddar cheese 10 minutes before the end of cooking. Stir to distribute evenly.

traditional grits with hominy: Add one 16-ounce can whole hominy, drained, rinsed, and coarsely chopped, 15 minutes into the second Porridge cycle or when the water comes to a boil in the regular cycle.

fried grits

You can't get a more traditional southern breakfast than one with a slice of hot fried grits. This is a great way to use up any left-over grits, but if you are having a few hungry folks in the morning, fried grits, a rasher of bacon, an egg over easy, juice, and hot coffee are a welcome treat.

MACHINE: Medium (6-cup) rice cooker; fuzzy logic (preferred) or on/off
CYCLE: **Porridge or regular**
YIELD: Serves 6

1 1/2 cups coarse stone-ground grits
4 cups water
1/2 teaspoon salt
1/4 cup unsalted butter, margarine, or
    bacon drippings, for frying
Pure maple syrup, for serving

1. Combine the grits and some cold tap water in a bowl or use the rice cooker bowl; the husks will rise to the top. Drain through a mesh strainer.

2. Place the grits, water, and salt in the rice cooker bowl; stir for 15 seconds with a wooden spoon or wooden or plastic rice paddle. Close the cover and set for the Porridge or regular cycle. A few times during the cooking, open the cover and stir for 15 seconds, then close the cover.

3. When the machine switches to the Keep Warm cycle or the regular cycle ends, pour the grits into a greased 9 x 5-inch loaf pan, filling it up to the top. Cover with plastic wrap and refrigerate overnight.

4. The next morning, turn the loaf of grits out of the pan onto a cutting board. With a sharp chef's knife, cut into 1/2-inch-thick slices. Heat a cast-iron or other heavy large skillet over medium-high heat. Place a knob (about 1 1/2 tablespoons) of the butter in the pan to melt. Lay the grits slices in the pan and cook until brown, about 8 minutes on each side, turning once. Add more butter for each new batch, as needed. Remove from the pan with a metal spatula to a serving plate. Serve with the maple syrup.

creamy old-fashioned grits

Adding a small amount of cream at the end of cooking makes these grits that little bit more special for a breakfast side dish with eggs or as a hot cereal.

MACHINE: Medium (6-cup) rice cooker; fuzzy logic (preferred) or on/off
CYCLE: Porridge or regular
YIELD: Serves 4

1 cup coarse stone-ground grits
3 cups water
1/2 teaspoon salt
2 tablespoons unsalted butter
1/4 cup heavy cream

1. Combine the grits and some cold tap water in a bowl or use the rice cooker bowl; the husks will rise to the top. Drain through a mesh strainer.
2. Place the grits, water, salt, and 1 tablespoon of the butter in the rice cooker bowl; stir for 15 seconds with a wooden spoon or wooden or plastic rice paddle. Close the cover and set for the Porridge or regular cycle. A few times during the cooking, open the cover and stir for 15 seconds, then close the cover.
3. At the end of the Porridge cycle, reset for a second Porridge cycle, giving the grits two full cycles to reach the optimum consistency.
4. At the end of the second Porridge cycle, or when the regular cycle completes, open the cover and stir in the remaining 1 tablespoon butter and the cream. Stir quickly, close the cover, and allow the grits to rest at least until the butter melts, about 10 minutes. These grits will hold on Keep Warm for up to 1 hour. Stir before serving.

pumpkin grits

Grits have become a fashionable side dish outside the South, so finally there are creative recipes floating around. Here mashed pumpkin puree, fresh if you can manage it, is added and you have a nice accompaniment to roast pork, turkey, duck, or chicken.

MACHINE: Medium (6-cup) rice cooker; fuzzy logic (preferred) or on/off
CYCLE: Porridge or regular
YIELD: Serves 4

2/3 cup coarse stone-ground grits
1 1/2 cups water
1 cup whole milk
1 teaspoon salt
1 cup cooked mashed pumpkin or other winter squash, such as blue Hubbard or butternut
Freshly ground black pepper
1/4 cup (1/2 stick) unsalted butter
1/2 cup (4 ounces) grated cheddar cheese

1. Combine the grits and some cold tap water in a bowl or use the rice cooker bowl; the husks will rise to the top. Drain through a mesh strainer.

2. Place the grits, water, milk, and salt in the rice cooker bowl; stir for 15 seconds with a wooden spoon or wooden or plastic rice paddle. Add the pumpkin and a few grinds of pepper and stir again. Close the cover and set for the Porridge or regular cycle. A few times during the cooking, open the cover, stir for 15 seconds, then close the cover.

3. At the end of the Porridge cycle, reset for a second Porridge cycle and cook until the grits reach the optimum consistency, thick like breakfast porridge.

4. When the right consistency is achieved or the regular cycle ends, stir in the butter and cheese. Stir quickly, close the cover, and allow the grits to rest at least until the butter melts, about 5 minutes, and up to 1 hour, if desired.

shrimp and grits

Beth's Aunt Joan lives in Florence, South Carolina, the heart of grits country. Shrimp and grits is real southern coastal Atlantic country food, but can now be found served at lots of southern parties and in restaurants. Here is an authentic recipe, just the way they like it in the Carolinas, which we made with Old-Fashioned Stone-Ground Speckle Yellow Grits from Blackwell Mills (decorated with a line drawing of a smiling pig in a neckerchief holding a corncob with the saying "Pig Out") that Aunt Joan sent Beth. The original recipe calls for the grits to be cooked for three hours, so run the grits through a third Porridge cycle, if you wish, for a softer consistency.

MACHINE: Medium (6-cup) or large (10-cup) rice cooker; fuzzy logic (preferred) or on/off
CYCLE: Porridge or regular
YIELD: Serves 6

2 cups coarse stone-ground grits
6 cups water
1 teaspoon salt
$^1/_2$ cup (1 stick) unsalted butter or margarine
$^1/_4$ cup olive oil
$^1/_4$ teaspoon Texas Pete hot sauce or Tabasco sauce
1 bay leaf
1 teaspoon pressed garlic
3 tablespoons fresh lemon juice
1 teaspoon minced fresh Italian parsley leaves
1 teaspoon minced fresh chives
$^1/_2$ teaspoon dried tarragon
$^1/_2$ teaspoon dried chervil
$^1/_2$ teaspoon freshly ground black pepper
2 tablespoons Worcestershire sauce
1 pound miniature shrimp (90/110 count), shelled and deveined (you can buy these already shelled; look for P&Ds)
Chopped fresh Italian parsley leaves, for garnish
Chopped fresh chives, for garnish

1. Combine the grits and some cold tap water in a bowl or use the rice cooker bowl; the husks will rise to the top. Drain through a mesh strainer.

2. Place the grits, water, and salt in the rice cooker bowl; stir for 15 seconds with a wooden spoon or wooden or plastic rice paddle. Close the cover and set for the Porridge or regular cycle. A few times during the cooking, open the cover and stir for 15 seconds, then close the cover.

3. At the end of the Porridge cycle, reset for a second Porridge cycle and cook until the grits reach the desired consistency, thick like breakfast porridge. When the right consistency is achieved or the regular cycle ends, hold on Keep Warm until the shrimp is ready.

4. Fifteen minutes before the grits are done, melt the butter in a large sauté pan over medium-high heat. Add the olive oil, hot sauce, bay leaf, garlic, lemon juice, minced parsley, minced chives, tarragon, chervil, pepper, and Worcestershire, bring to a simmer over medium heat, and add the shrimp. Cook, stirring, until the shrimp turn bright pink on both sides, 2 to 3 minutes.

5. Spoon the hot grits into a large serving bowl. Immediately spoon the shrimp over the grits and drizzle with the sauce from the pan. Sprinkle with the chopped parsley and chives and serve hot.

HOMINY

The premier gift from Native Americans to the colonists, hominy is dried whole corn kernels that are cooked in a solution of ashes or slaked lime in water to loosen the hulls. Hominy became a staple food for generations in the Appalachian backwoods, bayous of the Louisiana delta, and rural Deep South, made with wood ashes. While Mexican-Americans remember the large pot of beans always cooking on the back of the stove all day, southerners have the same memory about a pot of hominy.

Today commercial hominy is made by boiling the corn in a solution of sodium hydroxide, which acts the same way as the organic alkali ash bath. The germ and hulls are washed off, leaving a plump, soft kernel the size of a chickpea that is chewy in texture and earthy in flavor, as well as easy to digest. Also known by its Spanish name, *posole*, in the Latin community or the Indian name of *nixtamal* in the southwest United States, hominy is now chic peasant food. It is available dried, fresh or frozen ready-to-eat (both must be reconstituted), and canned.

fresh hominy

Fresh or partially cooked frozen whole hominy needs to be cooked before using. Fresh is usually available in the meat department of supermarkets, especially around the holidays. Do not add any salt while cooking, or the kernels will never soften properly. You can use fresh hominy instead of canned in soups and stews. If you happen to use dried hominy, you will need to double the amount of water and double the cooking time. You can double this recipe in the large-capacity rice cooker.

MACHINE: Medium (6-cup) or large (10-cup) rice cooker; fuzzy logic or on/off
CYCLE: Regular
YIELD: About 4 cups

1 pound fresh or frozen hominy, thawed overnight in the refrigerator

1. Place the hominy in the rice cooker bowl and cover with 2 inches of cold water.

Close the cover and set for the regular cycle. Cook until it is tender and the kernels burst open, but are still slightly firm to the bite, 1 hour or more.

2. Remove the bowl from the rice cooker, drain off most of the liquid by pouring through a colander, and let cool to room temperature. Store in the refrigerator, covered, for up to 2 days.

posole nuevo

Posole, the spicy New Mexican stew that is based on hominy, is usually a long-simmered dish made with pork or beef. This version is quicker and lighter, yet just as hearty and comforting. Because canned hominy is already cooked, this posole can be ready to eat in less than an hour. The carrots and chayote are not traditional. Two chiles make a slightly spicy version; add more than four at your own risk. Serve in bowls with crusty bread or rolls.

MACHINE: Large (10-cup) rice cooker; fuzzy logic or on/off
CYCLE: Regular
YIELD: Serves 8

Two 30-ounce cans white hominy or 4 to 5 cups Fresh Hominy (page 183)
2 to 4 large dried New Mexico chiles
1 pound skinless, boneless chicken thighs, trimmed of fat, and cut into bite-size pieces
3 cups chicken stock
2 cups water
1 medium-size onion, sliced
3 cloves garlic, chopped
1 teaspoon dried oregano leaves, crumbled
2 to 3 carrots, to your taste, sliced
1 medium-size chayote squash, peeled, seeded, and cut into bite-size pieces
$1/4$ cup fresh lime juice
1 teaspoon salt, or more to taste, if needed (depending on saltiness of stock)

1. Coat the rice cooker bowl with nonstick cooking spray. Place the hominy in a colander and rinse with cool water; allow to drain.

2. Meanwhile, rinse the chiles with cool water if they appear dusty. Pull off the stems and shake out most of the seeds.

3. Place the chiles, hominy, chicken pieces, stock, water, onion, garlic, and oregano in the rice cooker bowl. Close the cover, set for the regular cycle, and set a timer for 40 minutes.

4. When the liquid comes to a boil (open the cooker to check if yours doesn't have a glass lid), add the carrots and chayote. When the timer sounds, the chicken should be cooked through and the vegetables tender. Add the lime juice and salt. Remove the chile pods and discard, or slit open and scrape out the red pulp and return it to the pot, discarding the skins. This dish will hold on Keep Warm for up to 1 hour. Serve hot.

hot breakfast cereals and PORRIDGES

Breakfast cereals happen to be the way the majority of people eat whole grains. When grains are cooked in water or milk, they become a porridge, a food that has sustained humans since the first wild grains were gathered. Hot cooked grains are traditional fare the world over. Who could have predicted the long nutritious future of a group of Seventh-Day Adventists who in 1877 touted a vegetarian diet and opened a sanitarium based on the principles of evangelist and whole foods advocate Sylvester Graham? Developing a breakfast cereal of wheat, oats, and cornmeal baked into biscuits and then ground up, Dr. John Harvey Kellogg made the first roughage-rich granola, a name later adopted in the health food–conscious 1960s (mixed and served at the first Woodstock music festival) for a sweetened combination of roasted rolled grains, nuts, and seeds.

Kellogg later cooked grains of wheat and rolled them flat, making the first rolled cereals. Steam-injected puffing guns made whole grains porous and were introduced at the 1904 St. Louis World's Fair. The highly original Minnesota food eccentrics were off and running with the cereal boom. Americans fell in love with cereal and the demand has not diminished to this day. Unfortunately, the ever-growing line of commercial cereals are laced with preservatives and lots of refined sugar products tailored to the tastes of we're not sure whom.

Recipes for robust, luscious, or austere mixed grain cereals abound and, whether served hot or cold, offer a tasty way to feed your body in the morning. Making your own cereal blends or using leftover cooked grains such as rice is a perfect place to practice improvisation with a dash of kitchen creativity.

The Porridge cycle in the fuzzy logic machines does a beautiful job of cooking a wide variety of whole grains into breakfast porridges. Most of your own special slow-cooked breakfast cereals can be on the table after you finish dressing.

The secret to making excellent porridges is to use very fresh whole-grain cereals, such as rolled oats and bran. Be sure to get residue-free organically-grown whole grains every chance you get for the maximum health benefit. Commercial brands like Arrowhead Mills' Bear Mush is an excellent alternative to processed farina, and McCann's imported quick-cooking Irish oats are rolled from whole oats. Look for real old-fashioned rolled oats (as well as barley and wheat flakes) rather than the quick-cooking varieties. We also love old-fashioned hot cereals like Maltex and Wheatena. And although the long-cooking rough-cut steel-cut oats—chopped groats known as Irish-cut or Scotch-cut—can be intimidating to cook properly on the stove, they are easy to cook into a creamy cereal with no fuss in the rice cooker. Cracked grain cereal combinations—usually a blend such as cracked wheat, rye, oats, barley, millet, flaxseed, and corn—cook up as beautifully as oatmeal with the slow cooking of a rice cooker.

A key to how cereals will cook is to look at how they were processed. If processed minimally, as is the case for cracked grains, they will need more water (because they must absorb more to soften) and longer cooking times. Processed grains, such as rolled flakes, are first steamed, then passed through rollers to flatten. Some require as little as half the amount of water as cracked grains to cook, and they become a smoother mush. Sometimes, though, they absorb a lot of liquid and you end up with a dry mixture, like rice; just add some more water and cook a bit longer. Make a note on the package for the next time. Toasted flakes, as in granola, absorb less water than the raw flakes. Thick-cut flakes will absorb more water than thinner ones. Whole grains, with their bran and germ intact, cook more slowly and take more water than grains that have been hulled and degermed, the difference, for example, between brown and white rice. Previously cooked grains require the least amount of extra liquid and will break down very quickly.

As with the cooking of all grains, we all have a way we like our cereal cooked: smooth and loose so it is a homogeneous mush, with milk, or a bit stiff, so that the milk is a moat and can be cut into with a spoon. Open the cover and check the consistency of the cereal; give a stir with your wooden or plastic rice paddle. If it looks too stiff, simply add another ¼ to ½ cup of water or milk. If it looks too loose, either set for a second Porridge cycle to continue the cooking (it won't hurt the mush one bit) or hold the cereal on the Keep Warm cycle for up to two hours before serving. Hot cereals hold perfectly on the Keep Warm cycle.

How to serve your porridge is entirely a matter of personal preference. Dried or fresh fruit can be used as a topping or an ingredient to be cooked with the cereal. If refined sweeteners such as brown sugar are not in your diet, cereals can be made with pure maple syrup, date sugar, or honey. Create a moat of milk, half-and-half, rice milk, soy milk, or oat milk around your hot cereal. Whatever your choice, it's good morning to you!

hot oatmeal and rice

We consider this porridge an oatmeal inspiration. It is Beth's liberal adaptation of a Marie Simmons recipe from her wonderful book *Rice: The Amazing Grain* (Henry Holt and Company, 1991). You can use any leftover white or brown rice, long- or short-grain. An excellent grain combination and a breakfast favorite.

MACHINE: Medium (6-cup) rice cooker; fuzzy logic only
CYCLE: **Porridge**
YIELD: Serves 2

1 cup rolled (old-fashioned) oats (not quick-cooking)
1 cup cooked white or brown rice
2 tablespoons oat bran
2 1/4 cups water
Cold milk or soy milk
Pure maple syrup or honey
3 tablespoons toasted wheat germ

1. Place the oats, rice, oat bran, and water in the rice cooker bowl; stir gently to combine. Close the cover and set for the Porridge cycle.
2. At the end of the cycle, the cereal will be thick and will hold on Keep Warm for 1 to 2 hours. Spoon into bowls and serve hot, topped with milk, a drizzle of maple syrup or honey, and wheat germ.

wheatena

High-fiber Wheatena, a combination of wheat grits, wheat bran, and wheat germ, is a robust toasted wheat cereal that has been on the supermarket shelves for decades. Normal stovetop cooking is recommended at about five minutes, way too short, we think, to soften it properly; the coarse grain really tastes best when it has been slow-cooked. We use more water to get a smooth, thick porridge. Simple and delicious, Wheatena just needs some cold milk poured over it.

MACHINE: Medium (6-cup) rice cooker; fuzzy logic only
CYCLE: **Porridge**
YIELD: Serves 2

1 cup Wheatena
2 1/3 cups water
Pinch of fine sea salt

1. Place the Wheatena, water, and salt in the rice cooker bowl; stir gently to combine. Close the cover and set for the Porridge cycle.
2. At the end of the cycle, the cereal will be thick and will hold on Keep Warm for 1 to 2 hours. Spoon into bowls and serve hot.

hot oatmeal with grape-nuts

We love Grape-Nuts, but, well, sometimes they are just too hard on the teeth to eat cold. So, inspired by food writer Barbara Grunes, we put them in with oatmeal and ended up with a nice oat and wheat breakfast cereal.

MACHINE: Medium (6-cup) rice cooker; fuzzy logic only
CYCLE: Porridge
YIELD: Serves 3 to 4

1¼ cups steel-cut oats
¼ cup Grape-Nuts cereal
2¾ cups water
Pinch of fine sea salt
½ teaspoon ground cinnamon or cardamom
Cold milk and brown sugar, for serving

1. Coat the rice cooker bowl with butter-flavored nonstick cooking spray. Place the oats, Grape-Nuts, water, salt, and spice in the rice bowl; stir gently to combine. Close the cover and set for the Porridge cycle.
2. At the end of the cycle, the cereal will be thick and will hold on Keep Warm for 1 to 2 hours. Spoon into bowls and serve hot, with a moat of milk and brown sugar.

hot fruited oatmeal

As you can surmise, just like the Scots, we love oatmeal in its many guises. It is the most heartwarming and nutritious of grains. This is the perfect place to use old-fashioned rolled oats (the ones that take longer to cook and are chewier) or thick-cut rolled oats (there is a brand packaged by The Silver Palate), rather than the quick-cooking variety, as the rice cooker lets them cook nice and slow with some fresh fruit.

MACHINE: Medium (6-cup) rice cooker; fuzzy logic only
CYCLE: Porridge
YIELD: Serves 4

2 cups rolled (old-fashioned) oats (not quick-cooking) or Four-Grain Flakes (page 196)
2 cups milk or buttermilk, plus more for serving, if desired
2 cups water
¼ teaspoon fine sea salt
2 apples or pears, peeled, cored, and chopped, or 4 fresh apricots, pitted and chopped
¼ cup slivered almonds, chopped walnuts, or shelled sunflower seeds

1. Place the oats, milk, water, salt, and fruit in the rice cooker bowl. Close the cover and set for the Porridge cycle.
2. At the end of the cycle, stir in the nuts. Let the oatmeal steam on Keep Warm for 5 minutes. This cereal will hold on Keep Warm for up to 1 hour. Spoon into bowls and serve hot, with more milk, if desired.

Rolled oats are comfort food and have been gracing the morning table throughout the Western world for centuries. Food writer Elizabeth Schneider aptly describes the flavor of "lusciously rich oats" as "a cross between wheat and brown rice—with no trace of stickiness." The flattened little flakes with the pale brown seam down the center have had a revival in some new diets, since the compounds in oats have been found to lower serum blood cholesterol. It seems like everyone is eating oatmeal these days, both in summer and winter.

Rolled oats are one of the easiest, and most familiar, grains to find on a supermarket shelf in the breakfast cereal section. Commercial oats—such as Quaker Oats, and McCann's Irish Oatmeal (which is unbelievably sweet and delicate) in a fetching green-and-gold box or can—are very easy to find in supermarkets in both regular and quick-cooking varieties. Natural food stores carry organic brands that will amaze you with their texture and nutty flavor, such as The Silver Palate thick-cut rolled oats. Our local dairy and grain specialty grocery carries a large barrel filled with delicious fresh rolled oats from Grain Millers in Washington State.

Since oats are rich in antioxidant fats, they have an indefinite shelf life; you can keep them in your kitchen cupboard for a year in a closed container.

Oat groats are whole hulled oats still containing the bran and germ. Prepare these as you would cooked rice, or eat as a rugged hot breakfast cereal.

Steel-cut oats are groat kernels cut into two or three uniform chunks by steel bits and are used for making breakfast porridge. Scotch-cut, Irish-cut oats, or Irish oats, are the same size as steel-cut oats and are cut by stone buhrs; they make a creamier porridge than the bits cut by the steel bits. Finely ground, this style of oats is similar in texture to polenta after a long, slow cooking.

Rolled oats, "old-fashioned oats" to the Quaker Oats people and thick-cut "oatflakes" in Britain, are crushed and pressed from whole hulled and steamed oat groats by mechanical rollers into uniform flakes. They come in a variety of thicknesses, from medium to thick, to make the familiar slick and rich oatmeal breakfast cereal. Of the three types of rolled oats, these take the longest time to cook properly.

Quick-cooking rolled oats are made from groats that have been cut into small pieces, then thinly rolled and slightly toasted during rolling so that they cook really fast. We are passionate about the imported McCann's Quick-Cooking Irish Oatmeal, which is made from whole-grain groats.

Instant oats, which are different than quick-cooking oats, are cut groats that have been rolled, precooked, dried, and mixed with sugar, flavoring agents, salt, and wheat germ. These become a very different ingredient than just rolled oats, so do not use them in slow-cook porridge recipes.

breakfast barley

Barley flakes seem like a cereal relegated to the aisles of the health food store, but in early history barley was as central to the human diet as rice. When wheat became the dominant grain, barley became more of a specialty grain. It has a sweet, nurturing flavor as a porridge; it makes a good alternative to oatmeal, especially nice for children. Please note that barley does not break down and dissolve into a traditional mush like oatmeal; the grains will be very soft, but stay distinct.

MACHINE: Medium (6-cup) rice cooker; fuzzy logic only
CYCLE: Porridge
YIELD: Serves 2

1 cup barley flakes or Four-Grain Flakes (page 196)
2¹/₄ cups water
2 tablespoons firmly packed light brown sugar
1 teaspoon apple pie spice or ground cinnamon
Pinch of fine sea salt
Cold milk or soy milk, for serving

1. Place the barley, water, brown sugar, spice, and salt in the rice cooker bowl; stir gently to combine. Close the cover and set for the Porridge cycle.
2. At the end of the cycle, the cereal will be thick; let it steam on Keep Warm for 10 minutes. This cereal will hold on Keep Warm for 1 to 2 hours. Spoon into bowls and serve hot, with milk.

granola oatmeal

Granola, which is primarily lightly baked rolled oats, is excellent served as a hot cereal. Use your favorite brand of granola or one of our mixtures in the Custom Cereal Blends section (page 196). We favor one packaged by Cafe Fanny in Berkeley—it is sumptuous—but one of the lowfat versions will also work.

MACHINE: Medium (6-cup) rice cooker; fuzzy logic only
CYCLE: Porridge
YIELD: Serves 4

1 cup rolled (old-fashioned) oats (not quick-cooking)
³/₄ cup granola, store-bought or home-made (page 197)
1 tablespoon millet meal or farina
2¹/₂ cups water
8 dried apple rings
Pure maple syrup and cold milk, for serving

1. Place the oats, granola, millet meal, and water in the rice cooker bowl; stir to combine. Lay the apple rings on top of the cereal mixture. Close the cover and set for the Porridge cycle.
2. At the end of the cycle, the cereal will be thick; let it steam on Keep Warm for 10 minutes. This cereal will hold on Keep Warm for 1 to 2 hours. Spoon into bowls and place 2 apple rings on each. Drizzle with maple syrup and serve with milk.

old-fashioned steel-cut oatmeal

Steel-cut oats are much chewier than regular rolled oats and the cooking time is considerably longer, but the rice cooker is perfect for cooking the hearty, old-fashioned grain, especially after an overnight soak. If you like your oatmeal creamy, substitute 1 cup of milk for 1 cup of the water.

MACHINE: Medium (6-cup) rice cooker; fuzzy logic only
CYCLE: Porridge
YIELD: Serves 3

1¼ cups steel-cut oats
3 cups cold water
Pinch of sea salt
Pure maple syrup and cold milk, for serving

1. The night before serving, place the oats, water, and salt in a lidded bowl or the rice cooker bowl. Cover and set aside at room temperature until morning.
2. In the morning, pour the mixture with its liquid into the rice cooker bowl, if necessary; stir gently to combine. Close the cover and set for the Porridge cycle. At the end of the cycle, the cereal will be thick and will hold on Keep Warm for 1 to 2 hours.
3. Spoon into bowls and serve hot, with a drizzle of maple syrup and the milk.

creamy breakfast oatmeal

Oats have a reputation for contributing to health similar to a homeopathic cure. Oats and milk are said to ward off the worst of chills, as well as making a great poultice-like mask for the face. With maple syrup and sweet dried dates, plain old oatmeal is a morning feast that raises its status above that of a humble grain. Note that this recipe calls for steel-cut oats rather than rolled oats, making an exceptionally creamy porridge.

MACHINE: Medium (6-cup) rice cooker; fuzzy logic only
CYCLE: Porridge
YIELD: Serves 2

⅔ cup steel-cut oats
1¾ cups milk mixed with 1 teaspoon pure vanilla extract, or 1¾ cups vanilla soy milk
1¼ teaspoons ground cinnamon
Pinch of fine sea salt
2 tablespoons pure maple syrup
¼ cup chopped dates

1. Place the oats, vanilla milk, cinnamon, salt, and maple syrup in the rice cooker bowl; stir gently to combine. Sprinkle with the dates. Close the cover and set for the Porridge cycle.
2. At the end of the cycle, the cereal will be thick and will hold on Keep Warm for up to 1 hour. Spoon into bowls and serve hot.

hot apple granola

This hearty grain and fruit blend cooks up into a flavorful and sustaining breakfast cereal.

MACHINE: Medium (6-cup) rice cooker; fuzzy logic only
CYCLE: Porridge
YIELD: Serves 2

1 cup Apple Granola (page 196)
2¹/₂ cups water
Pinch of fine sea salt
Cold milk or soy milk, for serving

1. Place the granola, water, and salt in the rice cooker bowl; stir gently to combine. Close the cover and set for the Porridge cycle.
2. At the end of the cycle, the cereal will be thick and will hold on Keep Warm for 1 to 2 hours. Spoon into bowls and serve hot, with a moat of milk.

mixed grain porridge

This porridge, with almost more grains than you can count, is anything but dull. The farina and couscous give texture and an extra dimension of flavor.

MACHINE: Medium (6-cup) rice cooker; fuzzy logic only
CYCLE: Porridge
YIELD: Serves 3 to 4

¹/₂ cup Apple Granola (page 196) or store-bought cracked seven-grain cereal
¹/₂ cup quick-cooking Irish oats (McCann's)
¹/₄ cup farina (such as Cream of Wheat or Arrowhead Mills' Bear Mush)
¹/₄ cup barley grits (Arrowhead Mills) or couscous
2 tablespoons millet meal
Pinch of fine sea salt
3¹/₄ cups water
Cold milk and brown sugar, for serving

1. Place the granola, grains, salt, and water in the rice cooker bowl; stir gently to combine. Close the cover and set for the Porridge cycle.
2. At the end of the cycle, the cereal will be thick and will hold on Keep Warm for 1 to 2 hours. Spoon into bowls and serve hot, with the milk and a bit of brown sugar.

hot cornmeal mush

Adapted from one of our favorite food writers, Deborah Madison, this is old-fashioned corn-meal mush laced with vanilla. Look for Cook's Cookie vanilla at the supermarket; it is a combination of Bourbon and Tahitian vanilla beans and has a distinctly floral quality you will find positively addicting. It sweetens the mush, so to speak.

MACHINE: Medium (6-cup) rice cooker; fuzzy logic only
CYCLE: Porridge
YIELD: Serves 3 to 4

1¼ cups stone-ground fine- or medium-grind yellow cornmeal
4 cups water
1 tablespoon unsalted butter
2½ teaspoons pure vanilla extract
½ teaspoon fine sea salt
Cold milk and brown sugar, for serving

1. Place the cornmeal, water, butter, vanilla, and salt in the rice cooker bowl; stir gently to combine. Close the cover and set for the Porridge cycle.
2. At the end of the cycle, if the mush looks too thick, stir in more water in ¼-cup increments and let steam on the Keep Warm cycle. Stir every 15 to 20 minutes to avoid lumping. This cereal will hold on Keep Warm for 1 to 2 hours. Spoon into bowls and serve hot, with the milk and brown sugar.

sweet breakfast grits with fresh fruit

When you see the word *grits*, it is easy to assume it means cracked hominy grits made from cornmeal, but in reality *grits* can refer to any coarsely cracked grain, including millet, corn, oats, or barley. Grits can be in a fine, medium, or coarse grind; the finer the grind, the faster it cooks. Here old-fashioned grits ground from corn are cooked in milk and are perfect for the breakfast table. The stone-ground grits will have much more flavor than the quick-cooking variety, but we give both here due to availability.

MACHINE: Medium (6-cup) rice cooker; fuzzy logic only
CYCLE: Porridge
YIELD: Serves 3

¾ cup stone-ground or quick-cooking yellow or white grits
2½ cups milk
3 to 4 tablespoons honey
½ teaspoon fine sea salt
Hulled and sliced fresh strawberries, blackberries, blueberries, or peeled, pitted, and sliced peaches, sprinkled with a teaspoon or two of sugar, for topping

1. Place the grits, milk, honey, and salt in the rice cooker bowl; stir gently to combine. Close the cover and set for the Porridge cycle.

2. At the end of the cycle, the cereal will be thick and creamy, and will hold on Keep Warm for 1 to 2 hours. Spoon into bowls and serve hot, topped with the fruit.

morning
rice pudding

In a conversation with California rancho cooking expert Jacquie McMahan, the talk turned to *arroz de crema*, rice pudding, a favorite in Mexican cuisine. Jacquie remembered leftover rice being cooked in milk for breakfast. Her version did not have the egg, so you can leave it out, if you wish. This dish works perfectly in the rice cooker on the Porridge cycle.

MACHINE: Medium (6-cup) rice cooker; fuzzy logic only

CYCLE: **Porridge**

YIELD: Serves 3 to 4

3 cups cooked white or brown rice

3¹/₂ cups milk

1 large egg, beaten (optional)

2 tablespoons firmly packed dark brown sugar

¹/₄ cup chopped dried apricots or golden raisins

¹/₄ teaspoon ground cinnamon

3 or 4 small pats unsalted butter, for serving

Freshly grated nutmeg, for sprinkling

1. Place the rice, milk, egg (if using), sugar, dried fruit, and cinnamon in the rice

cooker bowl; stir gently to combine. Close the cover and set for the Porridge cycle.

2. At the end of the cycle, the cereal will be thick and creamy. Serve immediately. Spoon into bowls and top with a small pat of butter and a few gratings of nutmeg.

maple-
cinnamon
rice pudding

This is a creamy breakfast rice pudding that is perfectly addictive. It can also be made with long-grain brown rice, but the white rice is the creamiest and most nurturing. Serve with pure maple syrup or sliced or chopped fresh or canned fruit, such as bananas, berries, or peaches.

MACHINE: Medium (6-cup) rice cooker; fuzzy logic only

CYCLE: **Porridge**

YIELD: Serves 3 to 4

2 cups cooked white rice

2¹/₂ cups milk

¹/₄ cup heavy cream or milk

¹/₄ cup pure maple syrup

¹/₄ cup dried tart cherries, dried cranberries, or raisins

¹/₃ teaspoon ground cinnamon

Pinch of freshly grated nutmeg

Pinch of fine sea salt

1. The night before serving, combine the rice, milk, cream, maple syrup, dried fruit, spices, and salt in a bowl. Cover and refrigerate until morning.

2. In the morning, coat the rice cooker bowl with butter-flavored nonstick cooking spray. Pour the soaked rice mixture into the rice bowl; stir gently to combine. Close the cover and set for the Porridge cycle.

3. At the end of the cycle, the cereal will be thick and creamy; let it steam on Keep Warm for 10 minutes. Spoon into bowls and serve immediately.

CUSTOM CEREAL BLENDS

Given a jar of old-fashioned granola as a gift, we learned to appreciate the subtle art of impeccable ingredients streamlined to an individual palate. Homemade granola quickly became a pantry staple and a favorite ingredient in hot cereals along with oats, or just eaten cold with milk. You can store your mixtures in quart or half-gallon spring-top jars (they look nice on the counter) or plastic buckets with airtight lids for inside the cupboard. Beyond breakfast cereals, use your custom cereal blend as an ingredient in yeast breads, as a streusel topping for coffee cakes, in muffins, or in a crumb pie crust.

apple granola

This is a cracked grain blend we use to make a great hot morning cereal. All the grains are readily available at natural food stores.

YIELD: About 5 cups (ten 1-cup cooked servings)

1 cup steel-cut oats

1 cup cracked wheat

1 cup cracked rye

1 cup barley grits

1/2 cup Cream of Buckwheat cereal

1 cup minced dried apple

3/4 cup dried tart cherries, dried cranberries, or dried currants

2 teaspoons ground cinnamon

In a large bowl, combine all the ingredients; mix well. Store in a covered container or plastic bag at room temperature.

four-grain flakes

YIELD: About 5 cups (ten 1-cup cooked servings)

1 cup rolled (old-fashioned) oats (not quick-cooking)

1 cup wheat flakes

1 cup rye flakes

1 cup barley flakes

1 cup minced dried apple

1 tablespoon apple pie spice

In a large bowl, combine all the ingredients; mix well. Store in a covered container or plastic bag at room temperature.

your own old-fashioned granola

This is Beth's friend Dan Snow's famous granola. He got the recipe from a friend he met at a pottery workshop, who brought it to a potluck buffet. The group all ate big bowls doused with cold milk for dessert. After that, it was often a welcome and coveted gift in an old wide-mouth peanut butter jar. Luckily, Beth got the recipe from him, handwritten and stuck to the side of the kitchen shelf with a thumbtack, and is now giving it to you. The secret to making excellent granola is to use very fresh, high-quality rolled oats and brans. This recipe makes a big batch, so store it in an airtight plastic container or jars.

YIELD: About 14 cups

DRY INGREDIENTS

6 cups (1 pound) rolled (old-fashioned) oats (not quick-cooking)
$1^{1}/_{2}$ cups shelled sunflower seeds
1 cup ($^{1}/_{4}$ pound) wheat bran
1 cup ($^{1}/_{4}$ pound) wheat germ
1 cup ($^{1}/_{4}$ pound) oat bran
1 cup instant nonfat dry milk
1 cup almonds or other nuts, chopped or slivered
1 cup unsweetened shredded coconut
$^{1}/_{3}$ cup sesame seeds
1 tablespoon ground cinnamon

WET INGREDIENTS

1 cup mild honey
1 cup cold-pressed canola oil
1 tablespoon pure vanilla extract
1 teaspoon pure almond extract

$1^{1}/_{2}$ cups raisins, dried currants, or dried cherries
$1^{1}/_{4}$ cups dried apricots or other favorite dried fruit, such as figs, chopped

1. Preheat the oven to 250°F. Line 2 large baking sheets with aluminum foil or parchment paper. Set aside.
2. In a large bowl, combine all the dry ingredients and stir well. In a medium-size bowl, combine the wet ingredients and beat with a small whisk. Combine the wet and dry ingredients; stir until evenly moistened.
3. Spread the mixture evenly over the baking sheets. Bake on the center rack, stirring every 20 to 25 minutes with a spatula for even toasting, until pale golden and dry, about 1 hour. When done, the granola will slide off the spatula and be a very light color. Do not let it brown, as the granola continues to cook while cooling and will become too strongly flavored.
4. While hot, stir the raisins and apricots into the granola on the baking sheets and place the sheets on wire racks to cool completely. The mixture will become crisp as it cools. Transfer to a tightly covered container and store in the refrigerator indefinitely.

triple-oat granola with dried cranberries

This is a dark amber, deep-flavored, lowfat cereal. It is as good hot as it is cold.

YIELD: About 9 cups

DRY INGREDIENTS

3 cups (1/2 pound) rolled (old-fashioned) oats (not quick-cooking)

3 cups (1/2 pound) quick-cooking Irish oats

1 cup shelled sunflower seeds

1/2 cup oat bran

WET INGREDIENTS

1/2 cup mild honey

1/2 cup pure maple syrup

3/4 cup water

1/4 cup firmly packed light brown sugar

1/4 cup cold-pressed canola oil

1 cup (1/4 pound) honey-toasted wheat germ

1 1/2 cups dried cranberries

1. Preheat the oven to 325°F. Line 2 large baking sheets with aluminum foil or parchment paper. Set aside.

2. In a large bowl, combine all the dry ingredients and mix well. In a small saucepan, combine all the wet ingredients and bring to a gentle boil. Pour the hot mixture over the grains and stir well.

3. Spread the granola evenly over the baking sheets (you will have to bake this in batches). Bake on the center rack, stirring every 10 minutes, until evenly golden in color, about 30 minutes.

4. While hot, stir the wheat germ and cranberries into the granola on the baking sheets and place the sheets on wire racks to cool completely. Transfer to a tightly covered container and store in the refrigerator indefinitely.

RICE PORRIDGE

The Porridge cycle on your rice cooker was invented for a food that many in the United States have never even heard of, much less eaten: rice porridge, a staple in much of Asia. It's served for breakfast, for snacks, and as an easy-to-digest and restorative food for the sick, whether they are seriously ill or just dealing with a passing case of the blahs. Called *okai* or *okayu* by the Japanese and *shi-fan*, *congee* (the second syllable is pronounced the same as in "gee whiz"), or *jook* (pronounced juk) by the Chinese, rice porridge takes myriad forms. At its most basic, it is simply rice cooked in lots of water until it forms an oatmeal-like mass. It can be served absolutely plain, a shimmering, pure white bowl of creamy comfort. Even the salt is optional. From there, the symphony of creativity begins.

A Japanese cook may pour a splash of green tea over the rice, or nestle one of the tart pickled plums called umeboshi into the porridge, or top the bowl with something savory: seasoned shiitake mushrooms (page 202), homemade or purchased pickled or preserved vegetables such as cucumber, daikon, eggplant, or Napa cabbage (page

200), some thin shreds of the crisp seaweed nori (cut a sheet designed for wrapping sushi with a pair of sharp scissors), or some other tidbit from the pantry or the fridge. Another type of Japanese-style rice porridge, called *zosui*, is made with leftover rice (page 317).

A few slices of green onion are almost always scattered atop Chinese-style rice porridge. A Chinese cook of Mandarin heritage might set out a small array of toppings for plain porridge, anything from shreds of dried pork (called pork sung, it's sold in plastic tubs in Asian markets) to pungent pickled or preserved vegetables (you'll find a huge variety of these in jars in Asian markets) to the startlingly colored but absolutely delicious preserved eggs. To serve preserved eggs, peel as with hard-boiled eggs by cracking the shell all over by rolling gently on the counter. Remove the shell to reveal the black jelly-like "white." Rinse the egg under cool running water and dry it. Slice the egg into wedges or chop it. Stir the egg into fresh porridge. One egg is enough for at least two people.

Cantonese-style porridge is often prepared with broth rather than water and frequently features savory ingredients cooked along with the rice. Pork with pieces of preserved egg is the type most commonly served at dim sum restaurants. One Cantonese restaurant near our homes has five porridges on their regular menu, featuring everything from aromatic and deeply flavorful roast duck to delicate seafood. We've included just one recipe here (page 202).

The rice cooker Porridge cycle makes perfect rice porridge, yet, because the feature is relatively new (it debuted in the fuzzy logic machines), even experienced rice cooker owners may never have tried it. "It is just the way I always make it on the stove," one friend exclaimed in pleased amazement when we asked her to evaluate rice cooker porridge. As always, we recommend starting out with the proportions of water and rice recommended by the manufacturer of your rice cooker. If you like the consistency thinner, try using a bit less rice; if you like it thicker, use a bit less water. Write down the proportions you like best, but be sure not to use more water than the maximum amount of water recommended by the manufacturer for your particular machine. And be careful not to accidentally program your machine for the regular cycle. Either error will lead to a boil over. And try to eat rice porridge right after making it. As it stands on the Keep Warm cycle, it will thicken and grow starchy. Please note: These rice porridges *cannot* be made in the on/off machines.

What kind of rice should be used for porridge? Japanese-style short- or medium-grain white rice is the most common choice; it produces a smooth porridge that almost glistens. Long-grain white rice yields a somewhat rougher porridge. Sticky rice porridge is a bit chewier. Some cooks use a blend of two or all three. A tablespoon or two of sticky rice, if you have it, is a nice addition; just put it into your measuring cup before you fill it with short-, medium- or long-grain rice.

We have included some recipes here, but you should feel free to experiment. Just don't add too much of any other ingredient: The rice should be the star.

plain rice porridge

Like saltine crackers and flat 7-Up, plain porridge is renowned as a get-well food in Asian and Asian-American families. Or dress it up by stirring in flavorful extras, such as Quick Pickled Cabbage (recipe follows), but Beth likes it just plain.

MACHINE: Medium (6-cup) rice cooker; fuzzy logic only
CYCLE: Porridge
YIELD: Serves 2 to 4

¾ cup (1 rice cooker cup) Japanese-style short- or medium-grain rice
4½ cups water
Salt (optional)

1. Wash the rice. Place the rice in a bowl (or use the bowl of your rice cooker) and fill the bowl about half-full with cold tap water. Swirl the rice in the water with your hand. Carefully pour off most of the water, holding one cupped hand under the stream to catch any grains of rice that are carried away with the water. Holding the bowl steady with one hand, use the other to rub and squeeze the wet rice, turning the bowl as you go, so that all the rice is "scrubbed." The small amount of water in the bowl will turn chalky white. Now, run cold water into the bowl, give the rice a quick swish, and carefully drain off the water as before. Repeat the scrubbing and pouring-off process two more times. By the third time, the water you pour off will be nearly clear.

2. Place the drained rice and water in the rice cooker bowl; stir gently to combine. Close the cover and set for the Porridge cycle.

3. When the machine switches to the Keep Warm cycle, stir the porridge with a wooden or plastic rice paddle or wooden spoon. Serve immediately, ladling the porridge into small bowls. Add salt to taste, if desired.

quick pickled cabbage

These one-day Japanese pickles are called *asa zuke*, or morning pickles, because they are easily made in the morning and served for that night's dinner. They are a slightly crunchy accompaniment to plain porridge or to other dishes. This recipe makes enough pickles to eat with one recipe of Plain Rice Porridge.

2 cups Napa cabbage cut into ½-inch-wide strips
1¼ teaspoons sea salt

1. In a glass or other nonreactive bowl, mix together the cabbage strips and salt. Weight down the cabbage by placing a small plate inside the bowl. Top the plate with one or two 1-pound cans of food or other items weighing about 2 pounds. After about 15 minutes, remove the weights and stir the cabbage again. Return the weights and let the pickles sit for at least 6 hours at room temperature in a spot out of direct sunlight.

2. When you are ready to serve the pickles, drain them. If they are too salty for your taste, rinse them lightly in cool water.

quick pickled cucumbers: Substitute 2 cups cucumber cut into spears about 3 inches long for the cabbage, and use only 1/2 teaspoon salt. If you are using American or other seedy cucumbers, scoop out and discard the seeds. Japanese cucumbers or other cukes with tender skins do not need to be peeled; if you are using American cucumbers, peel the skin entirely, or peel most of it away so that only thin strips remain.

rice and sweet potato porridge

Sweet potatoes are a wintertime fixture in Japan, where they are sold by vendors on the street. This recipe for an almost-plain porridge livened up with tender sweet potatoes comes from Julie's friend Sharon Noguchi. If you are ailing, you'd want to eat this plain. If you're not, you might like it with a sprinkle of toasted Japanese sesame seeds or green onion, or a drizzle of sesame oil.

MACHINE: Medium (6-cup) rice cooker; fuzzy logic only
CYCLE: Porridge
YIELD: Serves 2 to 4

3/4 cup (1 rice cooker cup) Japanese-style short- or medium-grain white rice

1 cup peeled and chopped sweet potato (chop the pieces about 3/4 inch on a side; you will need about 1 small sweet potato)
5 cups water
Salt (optional)

1. Wash the rice. Place the rice in a bowl (or use the bowl of your rice cooker) and fill the bowl about half-full with cold tap water. Swirl the rice in the water with your hand. Carefully pour off most of the water, holding one cupped hand under the stream to catch any grains of rice that are carried away with the water. Holding the bowl steady with one hand, use the other to rub and squeeze the wet rice, turning the bowl as you go, so that all the rice is "scrubbed." The small amount of water in the bowl will turn chalky white. Now, run cold water into the bowl, give the rice a quick swish, and carefully drain off the water as before. Repeat the scrubbing and pouring-off process two more times. By the third time, the water you pour off will be nearly clear.

2. Place the drained rice, sweet potato, and water in the rice cooker bowl. Close the cover and set for the Porridge cycle.

3. When the machine switches to the Keep Warm cycle, stir the porridge with a wooden or plastic rice paddle or wooden spoon. Serve immediately, ladling the porridge into small bowls. Add salt to taste, if desired.

savory rice porridge with shiitake and preserved egg

This is our interpretation of a Cantonese-style rice porridge. If you don't like preserved egg, by all means leave it out.

MACHINE: Medium (6-cup) rice cooker; fuzzy logic only
CYCLE: Porridge
YIELD: Serves 2 to 4

4 medium-size dried shiitake mushrooms

3/4 cup (1 rice cooker cup) Japanese-style short- or medium-grain rice

5 cups chicken stock

1 medium-size carrot, diced

1/4 cup shrimp, cooked or raw, shelled and deveined

1/4 cup frozen peas

1 preserved egg (optional), peeled, rinsed, and cut into 8 to 12 wedges, the largest wedges halved

Salt and ground white pepper, if unseasoned stock is used

1 green onion, white and tender green parts, sliced, for garnish

1. Place the mushrooms in a small bowl, cover with hot water, and soak for 30 minutes. Or partially cover the bowl with plastic wrap and microwave on high for 2 minutes. Drain the mushrooms, remove the stems, and cut the caps into thin slices.

2. Wash the rice. Place the rice in a bowl (or use the bowl of your rice cooker) and fill the bowl about half-full with cold tap water. Swirl the rice in the water with your hand. Carefully pour off most of the water, holding one cupped hand under the stream to catch any grains of rice that are carried away with the water. Holding the bowl steady with one hand, use the other to rub and squeeze the wet rice, turning the bowl as you go, so that all the rice is "scrubbed." The small amount of water in the bowl will turn chalky white. Now, run cold water into the bowl, give the rice a quick swish, and carefully drain off the water as before. Repeat the scrubbing and pouring-off process two more times. By the third time, the water you pour off will be nearly clear.

3. Place the mushrooms, rice, stock, and carrot in the rice cooker bowl. Close the cover and set for the Porridge cycle.

4. About 5 minutes before the cycle completes, open the cover and scatter the shrimp and peas over the porridge. (The time will vary according to manufacturer; experience will tell you how long the Porridge cycle is on your rice cooker, or on some models, there is a digital count-down for the final few minutes.) Close the cover and let the cycle complete.

5. Just before serving, add the preserved egg, if using, and season with salt and pepper, if needed; stir to combine. Serve the porridge immediately, topped with the green onion.

thanksgiving jook

There's a Thanksgiving joke in many Asian-American families that goes something like this: "Forget the turkey. We don't even like turkey. We only have turkey so that we can make *jook* afterward." And, even though it's a joke, there's no question that turkey *jook* is terrific, a substantial yet healthful meal-in-a-bowl that tastes especially good after an overindulgent holiday dinner. In fact, you don't really have to wait for Thanksgiving. Julie's friend Grace Liu suggests making it any time a big party leaves you with a turkey or duck carcass, a big ham bone, or some other left-over that is just too good to throw away.

MACHINE: Medium (6-cup) rice cooker; fuzzy logic only
CYCLE: Porridge
YIELD: Serves 4 to 6

STOCK

1 medium-size turkey carcass
About 12 cups water
1 small onion, quartered
One 1-inch piece fresh ginger, cut into 4 pieces and each piece lightly crushed

RICE

3/4 cup (1 rice cooker cup) Japanese-style short- or medium-grain white rice
2 cups shredded Napa cabbage
1 cup diced carrot (about 2 medium-size carrots)
Some or all of the following, for topping: sliced green onions, chopped fresh cilantro leaves, peeled and grated fresh ginger, sesame oil, a few drops of soy sauce, salt

1. Make the stock. Put the carcass into a soup pot, breaking or cutting it into 2 to 4 pieces if necessary to fit. Add the water, using more if necessary so that all or most of the carcass is submerged. Add the onion and ginger. Bring the water to a boil over high heat, cover the pot, and let the stock simmer for 2 hours, until the meat is falling away from the bones. If you are not making *jook* right away, let the stock cool, uncovered, then cover the pot and refrigerate it for several hours or overnight.

2. When you are ready to make the *jook*, skim off any fat from the surface of the stock. Strain the stock. Dice or shred 1 cup of the turkey meat and reserve it. Discard the rest of the meat. Discard the turkey bones and skin, onion, and ginger.

3. Wash the rice. Place the rice in a bowl (or use the bowl of your rice cooker) and fill the bowl about half-full with cold tap water. Swirl the rice in the water with your hand. Carefully pour off most of the water, holding one cupped hand under the stream to catch any grains of rice that are carried away with the water. Holding the bowl steady with one hand, use the other to rub and squeeze the wet rice, turning the bowl as you go, so that all the rice is "scrubbed." The small amount of water in the bowl will turn chalky white. Now, run cold water into the bowl, give the rice a quick swish, and carefully drain off the water as before. Repeat the scrubbing and pouring-off process two more times. By the third time, the water you pour off will be nearly clear..

4. Place the drained rice in the rice cooker bowl. Add 4½ cups of the stock, or use a combination of stock and water if there is not enough stock. Add the cabbage and

carrot. Close the cover and set for the Porridge cycle.

5. When the machine switches to the Keep Warm cycle, stir in the diced turkey; let the *jook* steam for 10 minutes. Serve immediately, with any or all of the toppings.

beans and
LEGUMES

One of the best ways to consume complex carbohydrates, fiber, and vegetable protein in a low-calorie, no-cholesterol package is with beans and legumes. Along with cereal grains, beans are part of our earliest culinary roots, reaching back over 8,000 years. Easily dried for preservation purposes, beans were eaten extensively during long sea voyages and winter months when fresh food was at a premium. They pack a lot of protein into a little package. They are as much a staple today, and for good reason: They are a very versatile food. Beans are notoriously economical: 1 pound of dried beans (approximately $2^{1}/_{3}$ cups) will yield about 5 cups of cooked beans. They tend to show up mostly on winter menus, although that is fast changing; there is nothing quite like a cold cabernet vinegar and olive oil vinaigrette–marinated white bean salad in the summer!

In every cuisine, in every climate, there are delicious and excitingly flavored bean dishes: Indian dal, Mexican refried pinto beans, Middle Eastern chickpea falafels, Cuban black beans, Southwest chili, the New England maple-infused baked beans, Italian *pasta e fagioli*, even the beloved British baked beans on toast. The lima, native to Guatemala and called *haba* in Spanish, was found in archaeological digs of Incan tombs, making it one of the oldest cultivated vegetables (limas were exported from Peru during the California gold rush to feed the miners). Lentils—the oldest cultivated Old World legume and a nonmeat staple for European Catholics during Lent—come in a variety of sizes and colors, from the red lentil (a favorite in India) to the lovely, diminutive French green lentil, *lentilles vertes*, imported from the lentil capital of the world, Le Puy, and great in salads. And what would cassoulet be without navy beans along with the sweet Italian sausage and confit of duck?

Heirloom seed growers dote on many old varieties of beans that were enjoyed long ago. Beautiful, delicately flavored Christmas limas, black runner beans, Swedish bush beans, and appaloosas end up alongside commonplace red kidney beans, pinto beans, and black-eyed peas. The fava bean, an Old World bean that was as prevalent in early Rome as it was in colonial American home gardens centuries later, is the darling of the restaurant scene.

The term *bean* refers not only to regular beans, but to other legumes and peas as well. Beans can be consumed in both the fresh and dried forms. The fully mature ones are never eaten raw, as they are completely indigestible uncooked. Once you embrace the world of beans, you will be amazed at the vast variety available and the wide range of flavors and textures. And, of course there is a veritable cornucopia of shapes, colors, and sizes! During the summer months you may also come across fresh beans—always called fresh shell beans—in the produce section of the supermarket or your farmer's market. Fresh beans will always cook much faster than dried beans and need no soaking. Many discriminating cooks use only organically grown dried beans since they claim that they taste better.

While canned beans are convenient, home-cooked beans have a completely different texture. Cooking beans takes time, not effort, and the electric rice cooker does a great job in lieu of cooking them in a pan atop the stove, where the risk of sticking and scorching is ever present. The rice cooker acts like a slow cooker; simmering the contents rather than boiling it makes for a more tender bean that will hold its natural shape. And there's no stirring! Since beans should always be completely covered with

THE BASICS: SOAKING BEANS

All beans except for lentils and split peas need to be presoaked before cooking, although if you're using the lentils for a salad or side dish, soak them in cold water for 1 hour before cooking and they will retain their distinct shape. Presoaking will improve the taste and digestibility of beans, as well as decrease the cooking time; the technique was originally invented to conserve fuel. We find the quick-soak method to be the most efficient, but you can use the overnight method if you prefer. Buy beans that are smooth and whole, as lots of cracked, broken beans and shriveled skins mean the beans are old and will take a long time to soften and cook.

Before soaking, pour the beans into a shallow bowl and pick over by hand to remove any visible organic debris, small rocks, or damaged beans. Pour the beans into a colander and clean thoroughly by rinsing under cold running water.

Quick-Soak Method

For every 2 cups of beans (1 pound), use 6 to 8 cups of hot water. Place the beans and water in a medium-size or large stockpot and bring to a rapid boil over high heat (or use your rice cooker). Boil for 3 minutes and remove from the heat. Cover and let the beans soak for 1 to 1½ hours, depending on the size of the bean. Discard any damaged beans, drain well, and rinse. The beans are now ready to be cooked plain or added to a recipe.

Overnight-Soak Method

For every 2 cups of beans (1 pound), use 6 to 8 cups of cold water. Place the beans and water in a medium-size or large stockpot or bowl (or use your rice cooker). Cover and let the beans soak for 8 hours to overnight, depending on the size of the bean. Discard any damaged beans, drain well, and rinse. The beans are now ready to be cooked plain or added to a recipe.

water during the extended cooking time, the rice cooker environment conveniently provides a minimal amount of evaporation, just like the *olla*, the traditional earthenware bean pot of the Americas. As with all the rice cooker functions, cleanup is a snap.

Beans can be cooked alone and then used as an ingredient in other dishes, or you can add onions, garlic, celery, herbs, and salt during the last half hour of cooking and have a ready-to-eat entrée. Since the rice cooker is also conducive to making soups, split peas and lentils can easily be made into yummy slow-cooked potages and chilis. One of our favorite ways to eat freshly cooked beans is simply to drizzle them with a fruity extra virgin olive oil and a squeeze of fresh lemon juice, sprinkle over some coarse sea salt and freshly ground black pepper, and serve them in a shallow soup bowl with an oversized spoon, with fresh tomatoes and some fresh country bread or fresh flour tortillas on the side to sop up all the thick juices in the bottom of the bowl.

HOW TO COOK BEANS

1. Place the beans in the rice cooker bowl and cover with the amount of water specified in the Cooking Beans chart (page 209). Some cooks like to add a bay leaf, a leaf or two of fresh sage, or a teaspoon of epazote (an herb found in Latin markets) to help break down the natural starches while cooking. Please, no salt or acid ingredients (tomatoes or wine) at this time, as they toughen and shrivel the beans, as well as increase the cooking time; salt will inhibit cooking.

2. Set the rice cooker for the regular cycle in the fuzzy logic or on/off machine. The rice cooker will bring the water to a boil, then stay at a rolling high simmer. You will set a timer for the amount of time specified in the recipe. When the timer sounds, check the beans; you want them to be tender, yet a bit firm at the same time. Don't worry if you need as much as an hour longer than the cooking time specified. You want enough liquid to keep the beans submerged the entire cooking time, turning into that wonderful thick, velvety sauce. If you have to replenish the water at any time, be sure to add boiling water.

3. When the beans are tender, turn off the rice cooker and carefully open the cover. Carefully remove the rice cooker pan with oven mitts. Add the salt and any other seasonings. If you add wine or sherry, cook for a few minutes longer to let the alcohol cook off and set the flavor.

4. Now the beans are ready to eat (go ahead and dip some fresh bread or flour tortillas into the pot), to be refrigerated, or to be used as an ingredient in another recipe. Let cool to room temperature, then store in a covered container for up to five days or freeze for up to six months. Beans tend to improve in flavor a day or so after cooking.

COOKING TIMES

While beans are often categorized by whether they were first grown in the Old or New World, I like how chef and food doyenne Madeleine Kamman denotes them: by color.

The white varieties include garbanzos (also called chickpeas or cecis), small plump navy beans, soldier beans, plain white beans (known as haricots), Great Northern beans, black-eyed peas, and butter beans. White beans take the longest time to cook.

The rose-pink to red-black varieties include red kidney beans, small pink (a small kidney) and red beans, black or turtle beans, black runner beans, pinto beans (nicknamed the Mexican strawberry because of their mottled coloring) and its hybrids like rattlesnake and appaloosa beans, and cranberry beans, the traditional New England bean used in succotash.

The green varieties include all types of large and baby limas and flageolets. The lighter the color of the bean, the more delicate the flavor; the darker the bean, the sweeter, more robust, and earthier its taste.

The following chart is based on using 1 cup of dried beans or legumes with at least 3 inches of water to cover in the rice cooker. Beans can also be cooked in chicken or vegetable stock, which tastes especially nice if the beans will be eaten as a side dish. If the beans are to be used in another dish, such as chili or a cassoulet, you will cook them al dente rather than totally soft because they will be cooked further. It is important to remember that the beans should always be completely covered with water

Cooking Beans

TYPE OF BEAN	AMOUNT OF WATER	COOKING TIME
Adzuki	3 cups	45 to 60 minutes
Black beans	3 to 4 cups	75 to 90 minutes
Black-eyed peas	3 to 4 cups	1 to $1^1/_4$ hours
Cranberry beans	3 to 4 cups	$1^1/_2$ hours
Fava beans	3 cups	$1^1/_2$ to 2 hours
Flageolets	3 to 4 cups	$1^1/_4$ to $1^1/_2$ hours
Garbanzos	4 cups	2 hours
Kidney beans	3 to 4 cups	1 to $1^1/_4$ hours
Lentils		
Brown	2 to 3 cups	40 to 50 minutes
Green	2 to 3 cups	30 to 40 minutes
Petite French	3 cups	30 to 40 minutes
Red	2 to 3 cups	30 to 40 minutes
Limas		
Baby	2 to 3 cups	1 to $1^1/_2$ hours
Butter bean	3 to 4 cups	$1^1/_4$ to $1^1/_2$ hours
Christmas	3 to 4 cups	2 hours
Large	2 to 3 cups	$1^1/_2$ hours
Mung beans	3 to 4 cups	1 to $1^1/_2$ hours
Painted desert beans	3 to 4 cups	1 to $1^1/_2$ hours
Pink beans	3 cups	1 to $1^1/_2$ hours
Pinto beans	3 to 4 cups	$1^1/_2$ to 2 hours
Soybeans	4 cups	3 to 4 hours
Split peas, green and yellow	2 cups	45 to 60 minutes
White beans		
Baby white beans	3 to 4 cups	1 to $1^1/_4$ hours
Cannellini/white kidney	3 to 4 cups	$1^1/_4$ to $1^1/_2$ hours
Great Northern	4 cups	2 to 3 hours
Navy beans	4 cups	$1^1/_4$ to $1^1/_2$ hours
Soldier beans	3 to 4 cups	$1^1/_4$ to $1^1/_2$ hours
Whole peas	4 cups	$1^1/_2$ to 2 hours

throughout the entire cooking time, because the cooker cooks at a high simmer and some evaporation is expected. Beans are done when tender and most of the cooking liquid has been absorbed.

You can use a medium-size rice cooker for this measurement or a large rice cooker and double the proportions. If you have a small rice cooker, cook only ½ cup of beans at a time. Be sure the total amount of ingredients does not exceed the limitations of your rice cooker's capacity. These times are meant as guidelines, as variables such as hard or soft water, the mineral composition of the soil where the beans were grown, and the age of the beans can affect cooking times, sometimes significantly. Remember that beans and legumes always take slightly longer to cook at higher altitudes.

petite french green lentils

Serve these delightful lentils, known as *lentilles du Puy*, as a side dish with roasted or broiled meats and poultry. They are especially delicious as a bed for Cornish game hens or pheasant during the winter holidays. While this lentil is a special import from France, there is now a domestic grown variety that is every bit as good.

MACHINE: Medium (6-cup) rice cooker; fuzzy logic or on/off
CYCLE: Regular
YIELD: 2 cups; serves 4

1 cup dried petite French green lentils, rinsed
2 cups chicken or vegetable stock
3 tablespoons unsalted butter
Salt
Freshly ground black pepper

1. Place the lentils and stock in the rice cooker bowl. Close the cover, set for the regular cycle, and set a timer for 40 minutes. **2.** At the end of cooking, the liquid will all be absorbed. When the machine switches to the Keep Warm cycle or the timer sounds, remove the bowl from the rice cooker and stir in the butter and salt and pepper to taste. Serve immediately.

hummus

Hummus is a mashed puree of chickpeas, garlic, olive oil, and lemon that is immensely popular in the Middle East. People who love it always make it from scratch, cooking their own chickpeas. It can be served as a dip or thinned and served as a sauce for foods such as falafel. Some people like their hummus really garlicky, others like it milder. If you like it with garlic, be prepared to eat it within two days for the best flavor.

To serve, make a depression in the top of the hummus and drizzle with olive oil until it runs down the sides and pools in the side of the dish. Place spears of romaine lettuce all around for dipping. Give each person a whole fresh pita bread to tear and scoop up this dip.

MACHINE: Medium (6-cup) or large (10-cup) rice cooker; on/off or fuzzy logic
CYCLE: Regular
YIELD: 3 cups; serves 12 as an appetizer

1 cup dried chickpeas, picked over, rinsed, soaked in water to cover (overnight or quick-soak method), and drained
Salt
2 to 3 cloves garlic, or more to taste, peeled
¹/₄ to ¹/₃ cup fresh lemon juice
¹/₃ cup sesame paste (tahini)
¹/₄ cup extra virgin olive oil
Pinch of cayenne pepper

1. Place the chickpeas in the rice cooker bowl and cover with 3 inches of water. Close the cover, set for the regular cycle, and set a timer for 1½ hours. During the last half hour of cooking, season with salt to taste.

2. When the timer sounds, test the beans for doneness. Drain the beans, reserving the liquid.

3. In a food processor, finely chop the garlic. Add the warm chickpeas and pulse to mash them. Add the lemon juice, sesame paste, olive oil, and cayenne and, while the machine is running, slowly add ⅓ cup of the reserved cooking liquid through the feed tube until you get a fluffy, smooth consistency. Taste and adjust the flavors.

4. Transfer to a serving bowl and serve immediately, or refrigerate, covered, until ready to serve.

frijoles negros

Black beans, also known as turtle beans, are the cornerstone of Central and South American soul food, just like the pinto bean is in Mexican cooking. Once a specialty item, we now see black beans in every supermarket. They have an appealing, rather addictive, natural flavor and are easy to digest. If you like a smoky edge to your black beans, add two canned chipotle chiles. I like to float a few tablespoons of olive oil on top of the cooked beans before serving.

MACHINE: Medium (6-cup) or large (10-cup) rice cooker; fuzzy logic or on/off
CYCLE: Regular
YIELD: About 4 cups; serves 8

1 pound (about 2 cups) dried black beans, picked over, rinsed, soaked in water to cover (overnight or quick-soak method), and drained
1 medium-size yellow onion, finely chopped
1 medium-size green or red bell pepper, seeded and finely chopped
1 or 2 fresh jalapeño chiles, seeded and minced
¹/₂ teaspoon ground cumin
1 bay leaf
¹/₂ cup tomato sauce or salsa
2 quarts water
1 tablespoon red wine vinegar
Salt

1. Place the beans, onion, bell pepper, jalapeño, cumin, bay leaf, tomato sauce or salsa, and water in the rice cooker bowl. Close the cover, set for the regular cycle, and set a timer for 1½ hours.

2. When the timer sounds, you will have plenty of liquid with the cooked beans. Taste the beans for doneness. Remove the bay leaf. Stir in the vinegar, season with salt to taste, and serve immediately.

italian white beans

The large oval white kidney bean, also called cannellini, is a favorite home-cooked bean. It has a delicate, sweet flavor and cooks up nice and firm. These beans are a great side dish for fish and meats.

MACHINE: Medium (6-cup) or large (10-cup) rice cooker; fuzzy logic or on/off
CYCLE: Regular
YIELD: About 3 cups; serves 6

¼ cup olive oil
1 medium-size yellow onion, cut into 8 wedges
1 large piece prosciutto rind or 1 small smoked ham hock
1 large carrot, cut into thick slices
2 stalks celery, with leaves, cut into chunks
1 cup dried cannellini beans, picked over, rinsed, soaked in water to cover (overnight or quick-soak method), and drained
3 cups chicken stock
2 bay leaves

Pinch of dried thyme
Salt
Freshly ground black pepper

1. Place the olive oil, onion, and meat in the rice cooker bowl. Set the rice cooker for the regular or Quick Cook cycle and cook for about 15 minutes, stirring a few times. Add the carrot and celery and cook for another 10 minutes to soften slightly, stirring a few times.

2. Add the beans, then add the chicken stock and herbs; stir to combine. Close the cover, reset for the regular cycle, and set a timer for 1¼ to 1½ hours.

3. When the timer sounds, remove the meat and bay leaves and taste for doneness. Season the beans with salt and pepper to taste and serve immediately.

jacquie's rancho beans

Frijoles—beans, refried beans, or leftover beans—are mainstays of old California rancho cooking. This is the real thing from food writer Jacquie McMahan, who grew up on a Bay Area rancho, or Spanish land grant. You never add any special flavorings and every meal offers them, especially barbecues and family holidays. Traditionally cooked in an earthenware bean pot called a *cazuela*, the rice cooker mimics its lovely slow-cooked quality that makes great beans. You will need a cast-iron skillet (10- to 12-inch is perfect) or other nice, heavy skillet to finish cooking the beans.

MACHINE: Large (10-cup) rice cooker;
fuzzy logic or on/off

CYCLE: Regular

YIELD: Serves 6

1 pound (about 2 cups) dried pink or pinto
   beans, picked over, rinsed, soaked for 4
   hours in water to cover (or use quick-
   soak method), and drained

6 cups water

1 medium-size yellow onion, finely
   chopped

3 cloves garlic, chopped

1 heaping teaspoon chili powder

1 teaspoon salt

1 teaspoon freshly ground black pepper

2 to 3 tablespoons canola or olive oil

1. Place the beans in the rice cooker bowl and cover with the water. Add the onion, garlic, and chili powder. Close the cover, set for the regular cycle, and set a timer for 1½ hours. Add the salt and pepper during the last half hour of cooking.

2. Heat the oil in a large cast-iron or other heavy metal skillet over medium heat. Ladle in 1 cup of the beans and about ¼ cup of their liquid. Simmer over medium to medium-high heat to evaporate the liquid, mashing the beans with the back of an oversized metal spoon. When the mixture is very thick, add another cup of beans and ¼ cup liquid, cooking and mashing. Continue until you have mashed all of the beans and used up at least half of the cooking liquid (reserve the excess so you can add some later if the beans are too thick).

3. Reduce the heat to low and simmer the beans until thick, but not as thick as refried beans, about 20 minutes. Serve immediately or let cool to room temperature and refrigerate, covered. The beans will thicken further as they cool.

refried beans: To make refried beans, heat 1 tablespoon vegetable or canola oil over medium heat in a medium-size heavy skillet and add 2 cups of the cold rancho beans. Let cook until they sizzle around the edges. Sprinkle with cheese and serve.

sesame and tamari soybeans

Anyone familiar with Tassajara Hot Springs and Ed Brown's wonderful cookbooks might already be a fan of these tahini-glazed hot soybeans. Soybeans come in a few colors, but the buff yellow is the most familiar. They are the strongest flavored bean, so they are not served very often unless you know your diners, although roasted soybeans are tasty as a garnish like toasted nuts. A vegetarian delight and nice side dish for lamb, beef, or tofu.

MACHINE: Medium (6-cup) or large (10-cup) rice cooker; fuzzy logic or on/off

CYCLE: Regular

YIELD: Serves 4

1 cup dried soybeans, picked over, rinsed, soaked in water to cover (overnight or quick-soak method), and drained

4 cups water

³/₄ cup sesame paste (tahini)

3 to 4 tablespoons tamari (a thick, strong soy sauce), to your taste

Freshly ground black pepper

1. Place the soybeans in the rice cooker bowl and cover with the water. Close the cover, set for the regular cycle, and set a timer for 2½ hours.

2. When the timer sounds, test the beans for doneness; if still firm, cook for an additional 20 to 30 minutes. Drain off any excess cooking liquid into a measuring cup.

3. In a small bowl, thin the sesame paste with some of the hot cooking liquid and add the tamari. Pour this mixture over the hot beans and toss until evenly coated, using a wooden or plastic rice paddle or wooden spoon. Adjust the consistency with some more cooking liquid if the beans seem too dry.

4. Serve hot, with tamari and a pepper mill for seasoning to taste.

hearty split pea soup with turkey sausage

This is a great lunchtime food. Hearty, nutritious, and low in fat, it packs a garlic punch yet is mild enough for children to enjoy. We developed the recipe when spring garlic was in season. Spring, or immature, garlic is just beginning to divide into cloves; rinse it, peel away any discolorations on the outer layer, and chop it. There are no papery skins to discard. If you can't find the mild spring garlic, use regular garlic, the freshest you can find.

MACHINE: Large (10-cup) rice cooker; fuzzy logic or on/off
CYCLE: Regular
YIELD: Serves 6

2 cups dried green split peas, picked over and rinsed

6 cups water (7 cups, if you like a thin soup)

¹/₂ pound turkey kielbasa, split lengthwise and cut into ¹/₄-inch-thick slices

1 medium-size yellow onion, chopped

1 head spring garlic or 6 cloves regular garlic, chopped

2 medium-size carrots, halved lengthwise and cut into ¹/₄-inch-thick slices

2 large stalks celery, chopped

1¹/₂ teaspoons salt, or more to taste

¹/₄ teaspoon freshly ground black pepper

About 2 teaspoons chopped fresh thyme leaves or ¹/₂ teaspoon dried thyme

1 bay leaf

1. Place all the ingredients in the rice cooker bowl. Close the cover, set for the regular cycle, and set a timer for 1 hour.

2. When the timer sounds, check the peas for doneness; they should be very soft. Taste the soup for seasoning, adding more salt and pepper, if needed. Remove the bay leaf before serving.

yellow split pea soup with fresh lemon

Beth has been making some version of this soup, originally from the first edition of *The Tassajara Recipe Book* (Shambala, 1985), since she got the book. Beth's dear friend Qui, who made lots of Indian-style food when she cooked in an ashram in the early 1960s, showed Beth how to cook basmati rice and make a spicy dal to top it. This soup is a simplified version of the dal. It is especially easy if you have two rice cookers so you can make the soup and rice at the same time; otherwise, just reheat either the rice or soup. Everyone asks for this recipe.

MACHINE: Large (10-cup) rice cooker; fuzzy logic or on/off
CYCLE: Quick Cook and/or regular
YIELD: Serves 6

2 tablespoons unsalted butter
1 tablespoon olive oil
1 medium-size yellow onion, chopped
1 clove garlic, chopped
1 medium-size carrot, halved lengthwise
    and diced
2 large stalks celery, chopped
2 teaspoons ground cumin
2 cups dried yellow split peas, picked over
    and rinsed
6 cups water
1 bay leaf
Grated zest and juice of 1 large or 2 small
    lemons
1 1/2 teaspoons salt, or more to taste
1/4 teaspoon freshly ground black pepper
1 recipe Basmati Rice (page 38)
1/4 cup fresh Italian parsley leaves and
    1/4 cup fresh cilantro leaves, chopped
    together, for garnish

1. Set the rice cooker for the Quick Cook or regular cycle. Place the butter, olive oil, and onion in the rice cooker bowl. Cook, stirring a few times, until the onion softens, about 10 minutes. Add the garlic, carrot, celery, and cumin and cook until soft, another 5 to 10 minutes. Add the split peas, water, and bay leaf. Close the cover, set for the regular cycle, and set a timer for 1 hour.
2. When the timer sounds, stir in the lemon zest and juice, salt, and pepper. Close the cover and cook for 10 minutes longer. Remove the bay leaf.
3. Serve the soup in bowls with the rice, and sprinkle with the chopped parsley and cilantro.

old-fashioned black bean soup

Whereas black bean chili is a stick-to-your-ribs thick bean stew, the delightful black bean soup is quite a bit thinner in consistency but every bit as soul satisfying. This is a soup that is made in the southern part of the United States, so it has a bit of bacon in it. Of course, you can leave it out and use additional vegetable oil. Black beans have a black skin, but after cooking the inside is sweet and creamy. This soup is so good you often just cannot stop with one bowlful. This is our favorite recipe, adapted from food doyenne and cooking teacher Charlotte Coombe, one she made for our local bakery café when they offered a daily hot soup to serve with their fresh bread.

MACHINE: Large (10-cup) rice cooker; on/off or fuzzy logic
CYCLE: Quick Cook and/or regular
YIELD: Serves 8

8 ounces (about 6 slices) bacon, chopped
2 tablespoons vegetable oil
2 tablespoons olive oil
2 medium-size yellow onions, chopped
2 to 3 cloves garlic, minced
1 cup chopped celery, with some leaves
2 teaspoons ground cumin
1 teaspoon dried marjoram or savory
    leaves, crumbled
6 cups chicken stock
1 bay leaf

1 pound dried black turtle beans, picked over, rinsed, soaked in water to cover (overnight or quick-soak method), soaking water reserved
2 teaspoons salt, or more to taste
1/4 teaspoon freshly ground black pepper, or to taste
3/4 cup dry sherry (optional)
Crumbled goat cheese or sour cream, for garnish

1. Place the bacon, oils, and onions in the rice cooker bowl. Set for the Quick Cook or regular cycle and cook until the bacon is just browned and the onions are soft, about 15 minutes. Add the garlic and cook, stirring, for 1 to 2 minutes.
2. Add the celery, cumin, marjoram, chicken stock, and bay leaf; cook for 5 to 10 minutes. Add the beans and their soaking liquid. Close the cover, set for the regular cycle, and set a timer for 1½ hours.
3. When the timer sounds, add the salt, pepper, and sherry, if using. Close the cover and cook for 20 minutes longer.
4. Remove the bay leaf. Puree in batches in a food processor or with a handheld immersion blender. Taste the soup, adding more salt and pepper, if needed. Serve hot, topped with crumbled goat cheese or a dollop of sour cream.

turkey chili with baby white beans

Now this is a recipe that calls for canned beans for convenience. It is ready in about 1¹/₂ hours and has been deemed the best version yet.

MACHINE: Large (10-cup) rice cooker; on/off or fuzzy logic
CYCLE: Quick Cook and/or regular
YIELD: Serves 8

2 tablespoons olive oil
2 medium-size yellow onions, chopped
1¹/₂ teaspoons dried marjoram
1¹/₂ teaspoons ground cumin
1¹/₂ pounds lean ground dark turkey meat
3 tablespoons chili powder
1 bay leaf
1 tablespoon unsweetened cocoa powder
1¹/₂ teaspoons salt, or to taste
¹/₄ teaspoon ground cinnamon
One 28-ounce can whole tomatoes, with their juices
3 cups beef stock
One 8-ounce can tomato sauce
Three 15-ounce cans small white beans, rinsed and drained

GARNISH
Chopped red onion
Chopped fresh cilantro leaves
Grated Monterey Jack cheese
Sour cream

1. Place the olive oil and onions in the rice cooker bowl. Set for the Quick Cook or regular cycle. Cook, stirring a few times, until the onions are soft, about 10 minutes. Add the marjoram and cumin and cook for another 1 minute. Add the turkey and cook, stirring, until the meat is no longer pink, 10 to 15 minutes. Stir in the chili powder, bay leaf, cocoa, salt, cinnamon, and tomatoes. Break up the tomatoes with the plastic rice paddle. Stir in the stock and tomato sauce. Close the cover, reset for the regular cycle, and set a timer for 1 hour.
2. When the timer sounds, add the beans and stir to evenly distribute, using a plastic rice paddle or wooden spoon. Close the cover and cook for another 20 to 30 minutes.
3. Serve the chili in bowls with the accompaniments nearby for diners to garnish their own.

vegetarian black bean chili

After trying scores of vegetarian chilis, including those made with black-eyed peas, cracked wheat, or soybeans, we've decided that black bean chili is just the very best. Rich, dark, and flavorful, this recipe is easy to make and even more of a delight to devour. We were introduced to this version in the 1980s at Greens Restaurant in San Francisco, where you can buy it to go at the bakery and sit outside on one of the docks to eat it with some fresh herb bread.

MACHINE: Large (10-cup) rice cooker; fuzzy logic or on/off
CYCLE: Regular
YIELD: Serves 6 to 8

2 cups (1 pound) dried black turtle beans,
  picked over, rinsed, soaked in water to
  cover (overnight or quick-soak method),
  and drained

1 bay leaf

1¹/₂ tablespoons dried marjoram or
  savory

1 tablespoon cumin seeds

1 tablespoon hot paprika

¹/₂ teaspoon cayenne pepper

2 tablespoons chili powder

3 tablespoons olive oil

3 medium-size yellow onions, chopped

3 cloves garlic, chopped

One 28-ounce can chopped tomatoes, with
  their juices

1¹/₂ teaspoons chopped canned chipotle
  chiles in adobo sauce

1 teaspoon salt, or to taste

¹/₄ cup chopped fresh cilantro leaves

1 to 2 tablespoons rice vinegar or
  champagne vinegar

GARNISH

Grated Muenster cheese

Sour cream or crème fraîche

6 to 8 sprigs fresh cilantro
  (optional)

1. Place the beans in the rice cooker bowl with the bay leaf and cover with 3 inches of water. Close the cover, set for the regular cycle, and set a timer for 45 minutes.

2. Heat a large cast-iron or other heavy metal skillet. Add the marjoram and cumin seeds, shaking the pan to lightly toast them. Add the paprika, cayenne, and chili powder at the end and just warm them. Pour this mixture into a mortar to grind the herb into a coarse powder.

3. Heat the oil in the skillet over medium heat. Add the onions and garlic and cook, stirring, until softened, about 5 minutes. Add the toasted spices, tomatoes, chipotles, and salt and stir to combine. Simmer, uncovered, for 20 minutes.

4. When the timer sounds, add the tomato mixture to the beans and stir well with a wooden or plastic rice paddle or wooden spoon. Close the cover, reset for the regular cycle, and simmer until the beans are nice and soft, 1¼ to 1½ hours. Test for doneness; the beans should be tender. Stir in the cilantro and vinegar.

5. Serve the chili in bowls, layering the cheese on the bottom and the sour cream on top, with a sprig of cilantro, if you like.

Next to cooking rice, steaming vegetables is the best type of cooking done in the on/off rice cookers. And there are never enough new ways to serve vegetables. Well-cooked (and we don't mean overcooked) vegetables are considered good eating no matter where you go. Steaming has long been acknowledged as the best method for cooking vegetables, as it preserves the natural color, texture, flavor, and nutrients in them. And there is no draining to contend with. The golden rule for most vegetables is not to overcook them, but also be sure not to undercook the harder ones such as winter squashes, and potatoes.

Most models of on/off rice cookers, no matter what size, come equipped with a perforated metal steamer tray that fits into the top of the rice cooker bowl. Other models, usually large 10-cup machines, can come with a double set of plastic steamer baskets that look just like the bamboo steamer baskets that fit over a wok. This means you can either start your rice, then fill the steamer tray with vegetables and let them cook while the rice finishes its cycle, or fill the rice bowl with a few inches of water and just steam the vegetables over boiling water. Vegetables can be served hot from the cooker, or chilled and served cold later in the day, perfect for summer dining. Vegetables cook most evenly in a large cooker; if they are piled up, the steam cannot reach the center. Unfortunately, the fuzzy logic rice cookers are *not* designed for steaming.

STEAMING IN THE RICE COOKER

Steaming, cooking with moist heat, is probably the oldest type of cooking. It is possible that it predates fire, which makes it the cooking method of choice in a cold world. Along with being cooked on hot sunbaked rocks, foods could be cooked over hot springs or steamed in pits. The ancient cuisines of the Asian continent all use steaming as a primary cooking method, since firewood was often in short supply and regular enclosed ovens were rare.

Rice, and many of its accompanying foods, were cooked in this manner and steaming is still a popular cooking method to this day. Carefully steamed vegetables are known for their color, texture, and flavor, far superior to methods like boiling and blanching. The tender outcome is the result of the food being exposed to gentle moist heat rather than intense dry heat. In the rice cooker, food can be steamed in a steamer basket or tray over boiling water or over rice while it is cooking in the rice cooker bowl below it.

The Chinese steamer basket has been in use for approximately 3,000 years; archaeologists have unearthed stoneware steamers in the Yunnan province to prove it. Around the eighth century, steamers were first made of thin strips of cypress, an evergreen wood noted for its ability to retain its shape as it absorbs water.

The steamer basket was later made from bamboo, a tree-like plant found in tropical and semitropical regions, which also has nonwarping properties. The round, multitiered woven and slatted bamboo design with a tight-fitting, solid woven cover, and bottoms that fit tightly into one another (in sets of twos and threes) is a classic design still in use today. It sets over a wok or soup kettle that is one to two inches wider than the base of the steamer and the food never touches the boiling water below. The evaporating hot water, building up in the cooking vessel to create moist steam, does all the work. In addition to the bamboo steamer, there is also the aluminum Chinese steamer, which has a chimney through the center, distributing the steam heat quickly through the multitude of tiers, and French gourmet shops boast tin-lined copper versions of the same. Italian stainless steel steamers are popular, as are ones made of Calphalon and enamel.

Ingenious rice cooker manufacturers have made a large 10-cup, 10-inch-diameter model, fitted with a double tier of plastic steaming baskets, specifically designed to mimic the two-tiered bamboo steamer with a thermostatically controlled heating element. A set of heat-resistant plastic steamer baskets set snugly set into the rice cooker bowl and there is a tempered glass cover, for easy viewing of the food while it cooks. The diameter of the basket is 9 inches, a size that makes cooking for one or eight a snap. Alternatively, you can steam in any of the on/off rice cookers using your own set of bamboo steamers set on top, as long as they fit properly.

Most of the models of on/off machines we tested came with a perforated metal steamer tray that fits into the top of the rice cooker bowl (this type of tray would not fit properly in a machine with a hinged cover). One model came with a small steamer plate that looks like a baking rack and fits into the bottom of the bowl. In lieu of the tray, you can use the folding metal or plastic expanding basket insert easily available in supermarkets and cookware stores; just set it in the bottom of the cooker on the round steamer plate to protect the bottom of the rice bowl. This is perfect for steaming vegetables for one or two people. While the basket setup is best used with a liner such as greaseproof cooking parchment, cabbage, chard, or corn husks to prevent the food from sticking, a heatproof shallow baking dish or Pyrex pie plate can also be set inside the basket if it has no center post. The metal or plastic steamer tray can be used with a simple coating of nonstick cooking spray or lined.

We use our steamer equipment not only for making little meals and steaming vegetables, but for tamales, dim sum, and dolmas, all of which are cooked with steam. For dessert, the rice cooker makes remarkably easy and delicious cup-custards and the best steamed puddings.

■ Be sure you distinguish the difference among the three types of steamer equipment that may have come with your machine (some machines come with no steaming equipment, others with one or more of the following): One is a round metal trivet, called a steamer plate, that sits in the bottom of the rice cooker; this is for holding heat-resistant plates and pudding molds. The second is a steamer tray that fits into the top of on/off machines with a separate lid. This tray is good for steaming vegetables, a heat-resistant plate, and individual custard cups, but you will probably need to steam in batches. The third is a set of heat-resistant stacked plastic steamer baskets. The recipes that follow are specific about what type of equipment is best to use.

■ Use good-quality ingredients in perfect condition. Tainted vegetables and other foods get worse tasting, as steam accentuates the natural flavors. Use lean meats, such as chicken, and fish, which do not need lengthy cooking times. Use fully thawed food.

■ Make sure the cover fits tightly. If it doesn't, the steam and built-up pressure from the moist heat will escape and the food will not cook properly.

■ Place very hot water in the rice cooker bowl, then turn on the cooker. Our cookers efficiently heat to a low boil and start filling with steam after about 10 minutes.

■ Place the food baskets over very hot to boiling water and *then* start the cooking time. If you place the food over the water, then turn the cooker on and have to wait for the water to heat up, the food will not start cooking immediately and that will change the cooking time.

■ Baskets and steamer plates need to be coated with nonstick cooking spray or lined with greaseproof cooking parchment, a layer of cheesecloth, whole cabbage or chard leaves, or corn husks to prevent the food from sticking or dripping.

■ Arrange the food in the steamer basket in a single layer, and leave space between the bottom of the next basket or lid, for proper circulation of the steam during cooking.

■ Do not allow the boiling water in the cooking bowl to touch the food or you will not have enough room for the steam to build up. The baskets should be at least 3 inches above the liquid; never fill the bowl more than two-thirds full of liquid. In the large cooker, we fill to the 4- or 5-cup line, which is about one-third full. With the cover on tight, you will lose about 1 to $1^1/2$ inches of water per half hour through evaporation.

- Be certain that the liquid level is maintained during the cooking time. If the liquid evaporates, fill with more *boiling* water to maintain the cooking temperature.

- Make certain the foods—meat, fish, vegetables, tofu, noodles, cold rice—are of a similar size so they will cook in the same amount of time.

- Food from the upper basket will often drip below, so line the basket or place stronger-tasting foods on the lower level. Allow for at least an extra 5 minutes of cooking time for the upper basket since it is farther away from the source of the steam.

- Check the cooked food for doneness. If it is not completely cooked through or to your liking, no matter what the time on the recipe says, continue to cook and check at 10-minute intervals until the desired degree of doneness is achieved.

Here is a guide on how to prepare vegetables for the steamer basket and some recipes to help you get inspired. Remember that produce is seasonal, so your daily melange of vegetables will vary. Cooks usually choose a variety of vegetables from different groupings to balance color, taste, nutrition, and texture. Try a new vegetable once in a while, like steamed fresh water chestnuts with butter or white eggplant drizzled with a spicy oil. You can steam only one vegetable at a time, or two or more at the same time, mixing and matching with what you have.

HOW TO STEAM VEGETABLES

1. Fill the rice cooker bowl about one-quarter full with tap water (use less water if steaming only soft vegetables that cook quickly, and a bit more water if a longer steaming time is required, as for winter squash). If you start with hot water, it will come to a boil faster. Carefully place the bowl in the machine body, taking care that the bowl is set in properly and level. Position the cooker on the counter away from low cupboards and walls.

2. Close the cover and set for the regular cycle. The water will boil in 5 to 10 minutes.

3. Prepare the steamer tray or baskets by coating with nonstick cooking spray or lining with a single layer of cooking parchment, cheesecloth, whole cabbage or chard leaves, or corn husks to prevent the food from sticking or dripping. Arrange the vegetables in the perforated metal steamer tray that sets into the top of the cooker, or in the single or double tier of the plastic steamer basket set. Distribute the vegetables in a single layer and leave a bit of room in various places for the steam to circulate. If steaming two or more vegetables at one time, place the harder vegetables, such as carrots, around the outside, and the more tender, such as green beans, in the center. Or place the tender vegetables in the top basket and the harder vegetables in the bottom basket.

4. When the water comes to a boil, remove the cover and place the tray or baskets on top of the cooker. Quickly replace the cover. Consult the timing guide in the next section and set a manual timer for the appropriate time. The rice cooker will stay at a rolling boil throughout the cooking time. The unit will automatically switch to the Keep Warm cycle or Off should the water evaporate entirely. The water evaporates 1 to 1½ inches every 25 to 30 minutes if covered for the entire cooking time.

5. When the timer sounds, remove the cover (away from yourself and keeping your arms away from the top of the cooker to prevent burns) and check the vegetables for doneness by piercing them with the tip of a small knife. Rearrange, if necessary, re-cover, and steam until done. Carefully remove the cover and unplug the unit to completely turn it off. The unit can also be switched to Keep Warm if the vegetables need to sit a while until serving. (They will continue to cook, however, and there *must* be some water in the bowl.)

6. Using tongs, remove the vegetables from the steamer tray or remove the baskets by their handles. Place the vegetables on a serving platter or dinner plates. Remove the tray from the unit, if necessary. Let the water cool in the bowl before carefully lifting and pouring it down the drain or in the garden.

GUIDE TO THE VEGETABLE FAMILIES AND COOKING TIMES

The following list of vegetables is grouped by like characteristics, giving simple instructions for preparation and a timing guide for steaming. Cooking times are approximate, varying with quantity, size of pieces, and how much you fill the baskets. Be adventurous: rinse, pare, and trim as needed, then cut into wedges, quarters, julienne, diagonal or straight slices, thick or thin, dice—just keep the pieces uniform in size for even steaming. If you are cutting a lot of vegetables, the food processor or a mandoline can help with slicing, fat dice, and julienne. Remember, denser vegetables, such as roots and tubers, and winter squash, will take longer to cook than, say, beans and pods. Mix and match your vegetable combinations, then serve plain, or with a flavored oil, compound butter, or sauce (see pages 241–244 for some ideas). If you are serving the vegetables with a dip, you will steam them for only a few minutes, just until the raw flavor disappears, so the vegetable is still crispy. One to one and a half pounds of a vegetable like zucchini or green beans will serve four people as a side dish; if you need to trim the vegetable, like broccoli or asparagus, you will need two to three pounds for the same number of people. A bunch of greens will feed two to four people.

Stalks and Leafy Greens
Timing: Steam stalks until crisp-tender, 6 to 14 minutes. Steam greens until wilted, 4 to 7 minutes.

■ Asparagus: Trim or snap off the thick end of the stalk and peel the rest of the stalk if it is thick and you prefer it that way. Leave the stalk whole or cut it on the diagonal into pieces. Serve loose or "tie" the stalks in bundles with a green onion or chive green before steaming.

■ Celery: Trim the ends and cut the stalk into chunks.

■ Fennel bulb: Trim away the stalks and fronds and trim the root end. Cut into halves or quarters.

■ Swiss chard, spinach, bok choy, arugula, beet greens, collard greens, dandelion greens, broccoli rabe, mustard greens, kale, sorrel, Belgian endive (left whole), radicchio, fiddlehead ferns, watercress, grape leaves.

Beans, Pods, and Seeds

Timing: Steam until crisp-tender, 4 to 6 minutes for young green beans, sprouts, and snow peas; 9 to 15 minutes for older beans. Steam corn on the cob for 10 to 15 minutes, depending on the size and age.

■ Butter beans, fava beans, and lima beans: Remove from the shell.

■ Corn on the cob: Shuck and steam whole or broken into pieces.

■ Edamame (fresh soybeans in the pod): Thaw, if frozen, and leave whole.

■ Green beans, haricots verts, Chinese long beans, and wax beans: Trim away the ends and any tough strings. Leave whole or cut into pieces.

■ Green peas: Remove the peas from their shells.

■ Mung bean sprouts: No prep required.

■ Okra: Trim the stem end and steam sliced or whole.

■ Snow peas and sugar snap peas: Remove the string from the stem end.

Vegetables That Are Fruits

Timing: Steam until crisp-tender or warmed through, 12 to 15 minutes.

■ Bell peppers (green, red, yellow, orange): Cut in half and remove the stem, seeds, and white ribs. Steam sliced, in strips, or cut into chunks.

■ Japanese or baby eggplant: Leave the skin on; remove the stem end and cut in half or quarters.

■ Mild chile peppers (Anaheim, Big Jim, poblano): Cut a lid around the stem and remove the seeds and ribs from the inside.

■ Tomatillos: Remove the papery coating and cut in half or quarter.

■ Tomatoes: Cut in half or leave whole.

Cabbage Family and Onions

Timing: Steam until tender, 8 to 17 minutes.

■ Broccoli and cauliflower: Trim off the thick end of the stalk. Break the head into equal-size florets. For broccoli, peel the stalks and cut into matchstick-size pieces.

■ Brussels sprouts: Leave whole or cut in half or quarters.

■ Cabbage (green, red, Napa, or Savoy): Cut off the stem end and quarter or coarsely shred.

■ Leeks and green onions: Wash thoroughly, cut off the roots and green tops, and split the white bulb in half. For leeks, wash again, checking between the layers for dirt and grit.

■ Red onions, white boiling onions, baby pearl onions: Cut off both ends and peel off the papery outer layers. Leave whole or quarter.

Summer Squashes

Timing: Steam until crisp-tender, 6 to 12 minutes.

■ Cucumber: Trim ends, peel or not, and seed, if necessary. Cut into chunks, coins, dice, long quarters, or strips.

■ Zucchini, golden zucchini, ribbed Roman zucchini, Middle Eastern–type zucchini, pattypan, yellow crookneck: Trim ends. Cut into chunks, coins, dice, long quarters, or in half lengthwise for strips. Leave baby zucchini and small pattypans whole.

Winter Squashes

Timing: Steam until very tender when pierced, 15 to 30 minutes.

■ Acorn, chayote, blue Hubbard, butternut, turban, sugar pumpkin, sweet dumpling, golden nugget, kabocha, spaghetti: Small squashes can be steamed whole (peel, halve, and clean out seeds and fibers after steaming); for large squashes, peel, cut in half lengthwise, and clean out seeds and fibers before steaming. Squashes are also good cut into 1½-inch pieces, seeds removed.

Roots and Tubers

Timing: Steam until completely tender when pierced, 4 to 15 minutes. Steam all potatoes until completely tender, 18 to 30 minutes, depending on size of pieces.

■ Beets: Trim ends and peel. Leave whole (baby beets can have some of the stem left on) or cut into slices or quarters.

■ Carrots: Trim ends, peel, if desired, and cut into chunks, coins, or strips. Baby carrots should be left whole.

■ Daikon radish: Trim ends and peel. Cut into chunks, coins, or strips.

■ Jerusalem artichokes: Same as for potatoes.

■ Jicama: Same as for potatoes.

■ Parsnips: Trim ends and peel. Cut into chunks, coins, or strips.

■ Potatoes (russet or Idaho bakers, red or white boilers, baby creamer new potatoes, purple potatoes, Yukon Gold): Scrub whole potatoes in their jackets or peel, as desired. Steam whole, quartered, or sliced.

■ Turnips and rutabagas: Same as for potatoes.

■ Water chestnuts: Trim ends, peel, and slice.

■ Yams and sweet potatoes: Trim ends and peel. Cut into chunks or slices.

Thistles

Timing: Steam until tender, 20 to 45 minutes, depending on size.

■ Artichokes: See recipe on page 233.

■ Cardoon: Discard outer ribs and trim away spines and strings if tough. Cut off stalk end and cut ribs like celery.

asparagus with hollandaise sauce

A classic dish; once you have this version of hollandaise you will never be without a luscious butter sauce again. The sour cream stabilizes it, allowing the sauce to sit in a warm water bath for hours before serving without breaking or you can make the sauce while the asparagus steams. Use on all sorts of steamed vegetables, including broccoli. The best!

MACHINE: Large (10-cup) rice cooker; on/off only

CYCLE: Regular

YIELD: Serves 5 (1¼ cups hollandaise)

2 pounds fresh asparagus, bottoms snapped off

SAUCE

4 large egg yolks

1 tablespoon fresh lemon juice

Dash of salt

Dash of ground white pepper

1 cup (2 sticks) unsalted butter, melted and still hot

¹⁄₃ cup sour cream (lowfat or Imo imitation sour cream acceptable)

1. Fill the rice cooker bowl about one-quarter full of hot water. Close the cover and set for the regular cycle.

2. Coat the steamer basket with nonstick cooking spray and place the asparagus in the basket. When the water comes to a boil, place the steamer basket in the cooker and close the cover. Steam until tender, 8 to 15 minutes, depending on the thickness of the stalks.

3. While the asparagus steams, make the sauce. Place the yolks, lemon juice, salt, and pepper in a food processor. Process to combine. With the motor running, add the butter in a slow, steady stream, drop by drop at first, until the sauce is creamy and emulsified. Add the sour cream and pulse to incorporate. Pour the sauce into a heat-resistant deep container. Stand the container in a deep saucepan half-full of hot water over low heat until ready to serve, for 1 to 2 hours.

4. Arrange the asparagus on a serving platter and drizzle with the hollandaise.

asparagus with raspberry vinaigrette

Raspberries should not be relegated to desserts or cereal toppings. They can be used as a tart flavor accent for savory dishes as well. This raspberry-based vinaigrette is so good you might be tempted to drink it!

MACHINE: Large (10-cup) rice cooker; on/off only

CYCLE: Regular

YIELD: Serves 5 to 6

2 pounds fresh asparagus, bottoms snapped off

VINAIGRETTE

One 10-ounce package frozen raspberries, thawed

3 tablespoons raspberry vinegar

2 tablespoons fresh lemon juice

²⁄₃ cup canola oil

¹⁄₄ teaspoon salt

1. Fill the rice cooker bowl about one-quarter full of hot water. Close the cover and set for the regular cycle.

2. Coat the steamer basket with nonstick cooking spray and place the asparagus in the basket. When the water comes to a

boil, place the steamer basket in the cooker and close the cover. Steam until tender, 8 to 15 minutes, depending on the thickness of the stalks.

3. While the asparagus steams, make the vinaigrette. Puree the raspberries in a food processor. Press through a fine sieve to remove the seeds. Return the raspberries to the food processor and add the vinegar, lemon juice, canola oil, and salt. Process until creamy and emulsified. The vinaigrette can be made a day ahead and stored, refrigerated, in a covered container.

4. Arrange the asparagus on a serving platter and drizzle with the vinaigrette.

broccoli with lemon sauce

This lemon sauce is really a mayonnaise and a favorite one at that. It is the perfect sauce for fresh broccoli. Once you make homemade mayo, you will understand why this sauce is one of the most beloved in the kitchen. You can substitute orange juice for the lemon. Because the lemon sauce contains raw egg, make sure you use the freshest egg possible, that you keep it refrigerated until ready to serve, and that you eat this the day you make it. Also, because of the possibility of salmonella, it's best not to serve this to small children, the elderly, or anyone with a compromised immune system.

MACHINE: Large (10-cup) rice cooker; on/off only

CYCLE: Regular

YIELD: Serves 6

2 pounds broccoli, cut into equal-size florets and stems peeled and cut into pieces the size of the florets

SAUCE

1 small clove garlic, peeled

1 large egg

2 teaspoons Dijon mustard

2 tablespoons fresh lemon juice

1/4 teaspoon salt

Pinch of cayenne pepper

1/4 cup olive oil

1/2 cup canola or vegetable oil

1. Fill the rice cooker bowl about one-quarter full of hot water. Close the cover and set for the regular cycle.

2. Coat the steamer basket with nonstick cooking spray and place the broccoli in the basket. When the water comes to a boil, place the steamer basket in the cooker and close the cover. Steam until crisp-tender, 12 to 18 minutes.

3. While the broccoli steams, make the sauce. In a food processor with the motor running, drop the garlic in through the feed tube to chop. Stop the machine and add the egg, mustard, lemon juice, salt, and cayenne; pulse a few times to combine. With the machine running, slowly drizzle in the oils through the feed tube; the mixture will thicken and be smooth. If you are not using the sauce right away, transfer it to a covered container and refrigerate until ready to serve.

4. Serve small spoonfuls of the lemon sauce on the warm broccoli.

orange-glazed carrots

Carrots are extremely versatile and popular. They can be served with a pistachio butter (just grind up some nuts in the food processor with some softened butter), our Balsamic Vegetable Marinade (page 242), or a vinaigrette with some fresh chives added, and every version will be as delightful. Here they are tossed with orange marmalade, one of the finest jams for cooking.

MACHINE: Large (10-cup) rice cooker; on/off only
CYCLE: Regular
YIELD: Serves 4 to 5

1 1/2 pounds baby carrots

GLAZE
5 tablespoons unsalted butter
2/3 cup orange marmalade
2 1/2 tablespoons dry sherry or Grand Marnier

Pinch of salt

1. Fill the rice cooker bowl about one-quarter full of hot water. Close the cover and set for the regular cycle.
2. Coat the steamer basket with nonstick cooking spray and place the carrots in the basket. When the water comes to a boil, place the steamer basket in the cooker and close the cover. Steam until tender, 7 to 10 minutes.
3. While the carrots steam, make the glaze. Melt the butter in a medium-size skillet over medium heat. Add the marmalade and sherry and stir until the marmalade is melted. Keep warm.
4. Remove the carrots from the steamer and add to the skillet. Toss the carrots with the glaze and add the salt. Transfer to a warm serving dish and serve immediately.

carrot and rutabaga puree

Pureed vegetables are a joy to eat. You can certainly make one vegetable, such as peas or beets, and puree it, serving the puree on the side of the dinner plate with perhaps another steamed vegetable. Purees are brightly colored and incredibly tasty because of the intensity of the vegetable flavor. They are simple to prepare; just steam, then process in the food processor until smooth. Beth's mom introduced her to this melange of two root vegetables, along with another favorite, mashed carrots and potatoes, which is made in the same manner as this one, proportions of half and half. The rutabaga, like the turnip, is a strong root, so it needs another flavor to mute it. This is a vegetable dish you will not be able to stop eating.

MACHINE: Large (10-cup) rice cooker; on/off only
CYCLE: Regular
YIELD: Serves 6 to 8

1 pound carrots, cut into 2-inch chunks

1 pound rutabagas, peeled and cut into
2-inch chunks

3 tablespoons unsalted butter

Salt

Freshly ground black pepper

1. Fill the rice cooker bowl about one-quarter full of hot water. Close the cover and set for the regular cycle.

2. Coat the steamer basket with nonstick cooking spray and place the carrots and rutabagas in the basket. When the water comes to a boil, place the steamer basket in the cooker and close the cover. Steam until tender enough for mashing, 20 to 30 minutes.

3. Transfer the vegetables to a large bowl. Mash them with the butter using a potato masher or an electric mixer or process until smooth in a food processor. Season with salt and pepper to taste and serve immediately.

steamed corn on the cob

There is fresh, white, and very young (oh Silver Queen) corn or corn picked a bit later, yellow and less juicy. Early season, mid-season, or late season, corn on the cob is summer incarnate. On a summer visit to Wisconsin, Beth had a corn feast: an old flatbed truck, filled with local men and boys, drove out to the fields in the early afternoon for picking. Others set up 50-gallon drums, with wood fires built inside and metal bowls that fit on top, filled with water and ready to heat. The fresh-picked corn was boiled in its husks, then put in old insulated coolers to keep until eating. Large coffee cans were filled with melted butter. You got your ear, pulled down the husks, and, holding it like a lollipop, dipped it upside down into the melted butter. Dripping with butter, it was hard to stop eating at four ears. The best ever and Beth grew up in Jersey! Shuck the ears by holding the stem end over the garbage can and discard the messy silks and husk before this simple steaming.

MACHINE: Large (10-cup) rice cooker; on/off only

CYCLE: Regular

Corn on the cob bought at a farmer's
market or roadside stand, 1 to 2 ears
for each diner, husked

Unsalted butter

Salt or salt-free herb blend, such as
Mrs. Dash

1. Fill the rice cooker bowl about one-quarter full of hot water. Close the cover and set for the regular cycle.

2. Coat the steamer baskets with nonstick cooking spray or line with a layer of corn husks. Arrange the whole ears of corn in the steamer baskets, side by side, with a bit of room in between and broken in half to fill the ends, if desired. When the water comes to a boil, place the steamer baskets in the cooker and close the cover. Steam until tender, 10 to 15 minutes, depending on the size and age of the corn.

3. Remove the corn from the steamer and serve immediately with butter and a shaker of salt.

cauliflower with a puree of peas

If a cauliflower is not perfectly fresh, it can be pretty unappetizing after cooking. So look for a pure creamy head of cauliflower with no spots, which are a sign that it has been around for a while. Sauced with this puree, it is, by our standards, one of the tastiest ways to serve the beautiful flower of the cabbage family. Adapted from one of the best Junior League cookbooks, *San Francisco à la Carte* (Doubleday, 1979).

MACHINE: Large (10-cup) rice cooker; on/off only

CYCLE: Regular

YIELD: Serves 6 to 8

1 large or 2 small heads cauliflower, broken into large florets with 2 inches of stem

PUREE

Two 10-ounce packages frozen petite peas

2 small carrots, halved lengthwise

2 green onions

1 tablespoon sugar

$1/2$ teaspoon dried thyme

$1/4$ cup water

$1/4$ cup ($1/2$ stick) unsalted butter

$1/3$ cup half-and-half

Salt

Freshly ground black pepper

1. Fill the rice cooker bowl about one-quarter full of hot water. Close the cover and set for the regular cycle.

2. Coat the steamer basket with nonstick cooking spray and place the cauliflower in the basket. When the water comes to a boil, place the steamer basket in the cooker and close the cover. Steam until tender, 14 to 18 minutes.

3. While the cauliflower steams, make the puree. In a medium-size saucepan, combine the peas, carrots, onions, sugar, thyme, and water. Cook over medium-high heat, partially covered, for 3 minutes (This can also be done in the top steamer basket, lined with lettuce leaves.) Discard one of the carrots and the onions. Place the peas, the carrots, and the remaining pan juices in a food processor. Add the butter and half-and-half, and process until the mixture is thick and smooth. Season with salt and pepper to taste. Use the puree immediately or transfer to a deep container that can stand in a water bath until serving.

4. Arrange the hot cauliflower on a shallow serving platter, drizzle with the puree, and serve.

herbed green beans

These are the very best green beans. Diners say "ho-hum" when they think about having green beans for dinner, but one taste of these savory herbed vegetables and, trust us, they will be all eaten up.

MACHINE: Large (10-cup) rice cooker; on/off only

CYCLE: Regular

YIELD: Serves 4

1 pound fresh green beans, ends trimmed

2 tablespoons unsalted butter

2 tablespoons olive oil

$1/2$ cup minced onion

$1/4$ cup minced celery

$1/4$ cup minced fresh Italian parsley leaves

1 teaspoon chopped fresh rosemary leaves
  or $1/4$ teaspoon dried rosemary leaves,
  crumbled

$1/4$ teaspoon dried basil leaves, crumbled

$1/2$ to 1 medium-size red bell pepper
  (depending on whether you want just a
  touch of color or some to eat with each
  bite), seeded and cut into strips

Salt

1. Fill the rice cooker bowl about one-quarter full hot of water. Close the cover and set for the regular cycle.

2. Coat the steamer basket with nonstick cooking spray and place the beans in the basket. When the water comes to a boil, place the steamer basket in the cooker and close the cover. Steam until crisp-tender, 7 to 10 minutes.

3. Meanwhile, in a medium-size skillet, heat the butter and olive oil together over medium heat until the butter melts. Add the onion and celery and cook, stirring a few times, until just softened, about 2 minutes. Add the parsley, rosemary, basil, and pepper strips, cover, and cook for 5 minutes; don't let the pepper strips get too soft. Add salt to taste.

4. Add the steamed beans to the skillet and toss to combine. Transfer to a shallow 1-quart casserole that is ovenproof or microwave-safe. Serve immediately, or make a few hours ahead, cover, and reheat in the oven or microwave to serve.

pommes vapeur with tarragon butter

These are simply steamed new potatoes in their jackets with a fresh herb butter. The evocative licorice flavor of the tarragon makes for a great accompaniment to fish or chicken. This dish is adapted from a recipe from one of our favorite food writers, confirmed Francophile Faye Levy.

MACHINE: Large (10-cup) rice cooker; on/off only

CYCLE: Regular

YIELD: Serves 4

$1 3/4$ to 2 pounds small white or red new
  potatoes, scrubbed and left whole
  (unpeeled, partially peeled, or peeled)

6 tablespoons ($3/4$ stick) unsalted butter

$1 1/4$ tablespoons chopped fresh tarragon
  leaves

Salt

Freshly ground black pepper

1. Fill the rice cooker bowl about one-quarter full of hot water. Close the cover and set for the regular cycle.

2. Coat two steamer baskets with nonstick cooking spray and divide the potatoes between the baskets. When the water comes to a boil, place the steamer baskets in the cooker and close the cover. Steam until very tender when pierced with the tip of a knife, about 20 minutes.

3. While the potatoes are steaming, melt the butter in a small saucepan. Remove from the heat and add the tarragon; let stand at room temperature.

4. Transfer the steamed potatoes to a serving bowl, toss with the herb butter, and season with salt and pepper to taste. Serve immediately.

spiced yams with ginger and pears

Although yams, as far as we are concerned, are great just plain with butter, here is one step beyond in case you need a special holiday dish. The pears give it a lot of sweetness, so balance with another vegetable, such as green beans or zucchini, in your menu.

MACHINE: Large (10-cup) rice cooker; on/off only
CYCLE: Regular
YIELD: Serves 6

2 pounds ruby yams or sweet potatoes, peeled and cut into 2-inch chunks
2 teaspoons peeled and grated fresh ginger
1 teaspoon ground cardamom
Pinch of salt
3 firm ripe pears, peeled, cored, diced, and drizzled with the juice of 1 small lemon to prevent discoloration

1. Preheat the oven to 350°F. Fill the rice cooker bowl about one-quarter full of hot water. Close the cover and set for the regular cycle.

2. Coat the steamer basket with nonstick cooking spray and place the yams in the basket. When the water comes to a boil, place the steamer basket in the cooker and close the cover. Steam until soft enough to mash, 10 to 15 minutes.

3. Transfer the yams to a large bowl. With a fork, coarsely mash the yams with the ginger, cardamom, and salt. Fold in the pears. Spoon into a shallow 1½-quart gratin dish and smooth the top. (At this point, you can cover the dish and refrigerate for up to 4 hours.) Bake until heated through, 15 to 20 minutes. Serve immediately.

artichokes with caper aioli

Aioli is an infamous garlic mayonnaise that is an integral part of the cuisine of Provence in southern France. There exist some knock-you-out versions made with what seems the equivalent of heads of garlic, but a delicious, and not so deadly, aioli is made here with simply one clove. It is an appetizer supreme, stuffing a giant artichoke with the aioli and letting guests nibble on the leaves. Aioli is great on *all* steamed vegetables, room temperature or cold.

Because the aioli contains raw egg, make sure you use the freshest egg possible, that you keep it refrigerated until ready to serve, and that you eat this the day you make it. Also, because of the possibility of salmonella, it's best not to serve this to small children, the elderly, or anyone with a compromised immune system.

MACHINE: Large (10-cup) rice cooker; on/off only
CYCLE: Regular
YIELD: Serves 6 to 8 (1¹/₂ cups aioli)

6 to 8 medium-size artichokes, plus 1 very large artichoke

AIOLI

1 large clove garlic, peeled
1 cold large egg
1 tablespoon capers, rinsed
1 cup extra virgin olive oil

1. Set the steamer plate into the bottom of the rice cooker bowl and fill the bowl about one-quarter full of hot water. Close the cover and set for the regular cycle.
2. Cut off the stems and break the largest leaves off the artichoke bottoms. Cut off the top of the leaves with the thorns. Snip the tips of the leaves with kitchen shears.
3. Coat the steamer basket with nonstick cooking spray. When the water comes to a boil, place the largest artichoke on the steamer plate; there will be 2 to 3 inches of boiling water around it (this artichoke is slightly submerged). Place the other artichokes on their sides in the steamer basket. Place the basket on top of the cooker, over the large artichoke, and close the cover. Steam until the leaves easily pull off, 20 to 25 minutes. Remove the artichokes from the cooker and cool to room temperature.
4. While the artichokes are steaming, make the aioli. In a food processor with the motor running, drop the garlic in through the feed tube to chop. Stop the machine and add the egg and capers; pulse a few times to combine. With the machine running, slowly drizzle in the oil through the feed tube; the mixture will thicken and become smooth. Transfer the aioli to a covered container and refrigerate until serving.
5. To serve, pull open the inner leaves on the large artichoke and remove them, leaving the outer leaves intact like a shell. Scrape the choke clean. Fill the artichoke with the aioli and place in the center of a serving platter. Cut the remaining artichokes in half and clean out the chokes, or pull off all the leaves and arrange them around the aioli artichoke. Clean the artichoke bottoms, cut them in half, and arrange with the leaves.

himmel und erde

Himmel und Erde is German for "heaven and earth." It is a traditional holiday side dish that combines turnips, potatoes, and apples—stalwart fresh winter food that is delicious served with Thanksgiving turkey or pork roast.

MACHINE: Large (10-cup) rice cooker; on/off only
CYCLE: Regular
YIELD: Serves 8 to 10

1 pound turnips, peeled and cut into 2-inch chunks

1 pound russet potatoes, peeled and cut
   into 2-inch chunks
1 pound tart cooking apples, peeled,
   cored, and cut into uneven chunks
3 tablespoons unsalted butter
Salt
Freshly ground black pepper
4 slices bacon, cooked until crisp, drained
   on paper towels, and crumbled, for
   garnish

1. Fill the rice cooker bowl about one-quarter full of hot water. Close the cover and set for the regular cycle.

2. Coat the steamer basket with nonstick cooking spray and place the turnips, potatoes, and apples in the basket. When the water comes to a boil, place the steamer basket in the cooker and close the cover. Steam until tender enough for mashing, 20 to 30 minutes.

3. Transfer the vegetables to a large bowl. Mash them with the butter, using a potato masher or electric mixer, or process until smooth in a food processor. Season with salt and pepper to taste.

4. Transfer to a serving bowl, sprinkle with the bacon, and serve immediately.

steamed kabocha squash with ginger dressing

From Elizabeth Schneider, exotic vegetable and fruit maven, we learned that steaming winter squashes is the best way to cook them. The flesh turns out like velvet, with no tough skin to peel off the cut side, wasting the precious innards. The green kabocha is one of the nicest tasting squashes; you can prepare butternut and acorn in this same manner. All winter squashes taste great with just butter and a wedge of fresh lemon, a compound butter, or butter and pure maple syrup, but here the squash is served hot, with a Japanese-style dressing.

MACHINE: Large (10-cup) rice cooker;
on/off only
CYCLE: Regular
YIELD: Serves 4

DRESSING
1/3 cup fresh lemon juice
2 tablespoons sugar
2 tablespoons tamari (a thick, strong soy
   sauce)
1 tablespoon peeled and grated fresh
   ginger
3 tablespoons dry sherry or sake

1 or 2 kabocha winter squashes (2 to 2 1/2
   pounds total)

1. Make the dressing. Mix all the dressing ingredients together in a small bowl. Cover and let stand at room temperature for an hour or refrigerate for a few hours.

2. Fill the rice cooker bowl about one-quarter full of hot water. Close the cover and set for the regular cycle.

3. Meanwhile, wash the squashes and halve with a cleaver or large, heavy knife. Scoop out the seeds and fibers. Peel or partially peel, as desired. Cut into quarters or eighths.

4. Coat the steamer basket with nonstick cooking spray and place the squash cut side down in the basket. When the water comes to a boil, place the steamer basket in the cooker and close the cover. Steam until tender when pierced, 12 to 16 minutes.

5. Transfer the squash to a serving plate and serve hot, drizzled with the dressing.

spaghetti squash alfredo

Beth learned this recipe in the 1980s from Louise's Pantry Cooking School in Menlo Park, California. Spaghetti squash had just hit the market and no one knew quite what to do with the football-shaped squash with a stringy interior. People who are allergic to wheat and can't eat pasta go for this rendition in a big way. Steaming is the best way to cook this squash that ends up looking so very much like spaghetti, so the delicate insides don't get mushy. Spaghetti squash is also good with a tomato vinaigrette, or mixed with half spinach or plain angel hair pasta.

MACHINE: Large (10-cup) rice cooker; on/off only
CYCLE: Regular
YIELD: Serves 2

1 spaghetti squash (2 to 2½ pounds)
2 tablespoons unsalted butter
⅓ cup heavy cream
½ cup freshly grated Parmesan cheese
2 fresh basil leaves, cut into thin strips
Salt
Freshly ground black pepper

1. Fill the rice cooker bowl about one-quarter full of hot water. Close the cover and set for the regular cycle.

2. Meanwhile, wash the squash and halve with a cleaver or large, heavy knife. Scoop out the seeds and fibers. Halve each piece again.

3. Coat the steamer basket with nonstick cooking spray and place the squash cut side down in the basket. When the water comes to a boil, place the steamer basket in the cooker and close the cover. Steam until your finger leaves an indentation when pressed into the squash, 20 to 30 minutes.

4. Remove the basket from the cooker. Gently pull the strands from the shell with a large spoon until only the thin skin remains. Place the squash in a warm serving bowl and toss with the butter, cream cheese, basil, and salt and pepper to taste. Serve immediately.

cold vegetable platter with sauce verte

For summer entertaining or an extra-special vegetable dish. The creamy green sauce is easy to make, and perfect paired with all sorts of cold steamed vegetables. Serve with fresh crusty French or Italian bread and butter.

MACHINE: Large (10-cup) rice cooker; on/off only

CYCLE: Regular

YIELD: Serves 8 (about 1³/₄ cups sauce)

SAUCE

1 cup mayonnaise

¹/₂ cup sour cream

One 3-ounce package cream cheese

2 tablespoons fresh lemon juice

3 sprigs fresh Italian parsley, leaves only

2 green onions, cut into pieces

1 teaspoon seasoned salt-free blend, such as Parsley Patch

¹/₂ teaspoon dried tarragon, crumbled

³/₄ cup frozen spinach, thawed, drained, and squeezed dry before measuring

VEGETABLES

1 head cauliflower, broken into equal-size florets, steamed, and chilled

1 pound baby carrots, steamed and chilled

1 pound fresh green beans, ends trimmed, steamed, and chilled

1 pound baby zucchini, steamed and chilled

1 pound fresh asparagus, bottoms snapped off, steamed, and chilled

1¹/₂ pounds baby creamer potatoes or purple potatoes, whole if small, cut in half if larger, steamed, and chilled

6 ripe tomatoes, cut into wedges

1. Make the sauce. Place all the sauce ingredients in a food processor. Pulse to combine and coarsely puree. Transfer to a covered container and refrigerate until serving. Can be made a day ahead.

2. Arrange the vegetables on a serving platter. Transfer the sauce to a small bowl and place it in the center of the vegetables. Diners serve themselves.

fondutta with vegetables

When Beth was learning about Italian cuisine thirty years ago, pasta was spaghetti or ravioli and sauce was red. On a visit to her friend and gourmand Robert Barker, who lived in San Francisco's North Beach, she was treated one evening to an Italian take-out meal. Out of the carry-out containers came four different shapes of pasta, including angel hair and bows of tortellini, and myriad sauces, all in different colors. There was alfredo cream sauce, smooth red marinara, green pesto, and a yellowish Italian fontina cheese sauce called *fondutta*. This northern Italian version of Swiss fondue, using milk instead of wine, was the first new sauce she mastered. It is beautifully simple, tastes divine, and is a snap to make. Here is the recipe she has been making for what seems centuries. Serve over a pile of hot steamed vegetables and fresh cooked rice (or polenta) for a spectacular meatless meal with crusty bread, or as a side dish with simple roast chicken.

MACHINE: Large (10-cup) rice cooker; on/off only

CYCLE: Regular

YIELD: Serves 6 (4 cups *fondutta*)

FONDUTTA

1 pound Italian fontina cheese, diced (about 4 cups)

1¹/₂ to 2 cups whole milk, as needed

6 large egg yolks

1 tablespoon unsalted butter

Salt

Ground white pepper

Pinch of freshly grated nutmeg

VEGETABLES

4 baby leeks, washed well and cut in half lengthwise

1 head broccoli, broken into equal-size florets

4 stalks celery, cut into chunks

1 pound fresh asparagus, bottoms snapped off

1 pound fresh green beans, ends trimmed

1 pound zucchini, cut on the diagonal into 1-inch-thick rounds

One 12-ounce package frozen artichoke hearts, thawed

Your favorite rice (such as basmati, jasmine, short-grain brown, Japanese-style medium-grain, Wehani, or Jasmati) to serve 6, freshly cooked

1. Make the *fondutta*. In a large bowl, combine the cheese with 1½ cups of the milk. Cover and refrigerate for 4 hours to soak.

Place the cheese-milk mixture, egg yolks, and butter in the top of a double boiler over simmering water. Slowly cook, stirring occasionally, until the cheese is melted and the sauce has thickened, about 15 minutes. Thin with the extra milk, if a thinner sauce is desired. Season to taste with salt, pepper, and nutmeg. Keep hot.

2. Meanwhile, fill the rice cooker bowl about one-quarter full of hot water. Close the cover and set for the regular cycle.

3. Coat the steamer baskets with nonstick cooking spray and arrange the leeks, broccoli, and celery in the bottom tier of the baskets. Arrange the asparagus, green beans, zucchini, and artichoke hearts in the top tier. When the water comes to a boil, place the baskets in the cooker and close the cover. Set a timer and steam for 12 to 15 minutes. Check for doneness.

4. Arrange the vegetables on a serving platter, place the rice in a mound in the center, drizzle all over with the hot *fondutta*, and serve immediately. Serve the extra *fondutta* with a ladle.

steamed vegetables with port beurre rouge

The New York Times ran a story about a four-star French chef who serves only vegetables in his restaurant. "The taste!" he exclaimed. "The scent! It is so satisfying and delicious." Here is a dish you might encounter in this type of establishment, with the thick and luscious port *beurre rouge*, the red butter sauce, combining vinegar and port wine, that is a variation of one of the foundations of the French saucier art. We first had this dramatic-tasting sauce at Greens Restaurant, in the Fort Mason complex of San Francisco, where it is served with grilled vegetables during the fall and winter.

MACHINE: Large (10-cup) rice cooker; on/off only
CYCLE: Regular
YIELD: Serves 8 (1¹/₂ cups sauce)

SAUCE

¹/₃ cup plus 1 tablespoon balsamic vinegar
¹/₃ cup port wine
2 shallots, minced
1 cup (2 sticks) cold unsalted butter, cut into pieces
Salt
Freshly ground black pepper

VEGETABLES

1 pound baby carrots
8 baby beets, stems trimmed 2 inches above the beet, leaves reserved
1 pound baby creamer potatoes or purple potatoes, whole if small, cut in half if larger
2 pounds baby winter squashes, such as delicata or yellow acorn (4 squashes), halved and seeded
1 pound fresh shiitake mushrooms, stems removed
³/₄ pound fresh haricots verts, green beans, or sugar snap peas, ends trimmed
¹/₃ pound shallots or pearl onions, peeled and left whole
4 stalks celery, cut into 3-inch lengths and lengths cut into thin strips

1. Make the sauce. Combine ¹/₃ cup of the vinegar, the port, and shallots in a medium-size, heavy-bottomed nonaluminum saucepan. Cook over medium-high heat until reduced by half; this happens quite quickly, within a few minutes, so keep a close eye. Turn the heat down to medium, add the cold butter pieces, one at a time, and whisk, waiting until each piece is melted and incorporated before adding the next one. The sauce will thicken. Season with salt and pepper to taste and add the remaining 1 tablespoon vinegar. Pour into a deep container that can stand in a water bath until serving.
2. Fill the rice cooker bowl about one-quarter full of hot water. Close the cover and set for the regular cycle.
3. Coat the steamer baskets with nonstick cooking spray. Arrange the carrots, beets,

potatoes, and 4 squash halves in the bottom tier of the baskets. Arrange the mushrooms, haricots verts, shallots, remaining squash halves, and the celery in the top tier. When the water comes to a boil, place the steamer baskets in the cooker and close the cover. Set a timer and steam for 18 to 25 minutes. Check for doneness. (Or steam the vegetables in two batches if you have a single steaming tray.) 4. Arrange the vegetables on a serving platter, drizzle with the hot sauce, and serve immediately. Serve the extra sauce with a ladle.

A little bit of a good sauce or marinade goes a long way toward enhancing a simple plate of steamed vegetables. Imaginative butters or oils from your pantry, or freshly made sauces and marinades, add flavor. The butters keep nicely in the freezer, the oils last for weeks, and the Balsamic Vegetable Marinade tastes good on hot or cold vegetables.

Wine Butter

YIELD: 1/2 cup

1/2 cup (1 stick) unsalted butter, softened
1 shallot, minced
2 tablespoons dry white wine or flat champagne
1 tablespoon minced fresh Italian parsley leaves

1. In a small saucepan, melt 1 tablespoon of the butter over medium heat. Add the shallot and cook, stirring a few times, until softened, about 2 minutes. Add the wine and cook for 15 seconds. Add the parsley and stir. Remove from the heat and set aside to cool to room temperature.
2. In a food processor, combine the remaining 7 tablespoons butter and the wine mixture; pulse a few times to combine. Scrape the butter out onto a piece of plastic wrap and, using your hands through the plastic wrap, shape it into a thick log. Roll up and twist the ends to seal. Store in the refrigerator or freezer for up to 2 months.
3. Before serving, cut the log into 1/2-inch-thick slices to top hot steamed vegetables.

Orange-Chive Butter

YIELD: 1/2 cup

1/2 cup (1 stick) unsalted butter, softened
2 tablespoons finely chopped fresh chives
Grated zest of 1/2 orange

1. In a food processor, combine the butter, chives, and zest; pulse a few times to combine.
2. Scrape the butter out onto a piece of plastic wrap and, using your hands through the plastic wrap, shape into a thick log. Roll up and twist the ends to seal. Store in the refrigerator or freezer for up to 1 month.
3. Before serving, cut the log into 1/2-inch-thick slices to top hot steamed vegetables.

Fresh Herb Butter

YIELD: $^1/_2$ cup

$^1/_2$ cup (1 stick) unsalted butter, softened
1 tablespoon finely chopped fresh herb leaves, such as marjoram, sage,
    rosemary, basil, tarragon, dill, or thyme
Grated zest of $^1/_2$ lemon

1. In a food processor, combine the butter, herb, and zest; pulse a few times to combine.
2. Scrape the butter out onto a piece of plastic wrap and, using your hands through the plastic wrap, shape into a thick log. Roll up and twist the ends to seal. Store in the refrigerator or freezer for up to 1 month.
3. Before serving, cut the log into ½-inch-thick slices to top hot steamed vegetables.

Balsamic Vegetable Marinade

YIELD: 1 cup

$^1/_3$ cup balsamic vinegar
$^1/_3$ cup reduced-sodium soy sauce
$^1/_3$ cup cold-pressed or Asian sesame oil

Whisk the ingredients together in a small bowl. Pour over warm steamed vegetables and let stand for 1 hour at room temperature to meld the flavors. If not serving the vegetables within an hour, cover and refrigerate.

Cilantro Pesto

YIELD: $^1/_2$ cup

2 cloves garlic, peeled
1 cup packed fresh cilantro leaves
4 fresh basil leaves
Salt
Freshly ground black pepper
$^1/_2$ cup light olive oil

1. In a food processor with the motor running, drop the garlic in through the feed tube to chop. Stop the machine and add the cilantro, basil, and a sprinkle of salt and pepper; pulse a few times to combine. With the machine running, slowly drizzle in the olive oil; the mixture will become smooth.

2. Right before serving, thin the pesto with a few tablespoons of hot vegetable steaming water. Serve the pesto drizzled over hot or cold steamed vegetables. Store, covered, in the refrigerator for up to 1 day.

Asian Spiced Oil

YIELD: 1 cup

1 cup cold-pressed peanut oil
1¹/₂ tablespoons Asian sesame oil
1 tablespoon red pepper flakes
4 cloves garlic, quartered
1 tablespoon peeled and minced fresh ginger
Grated zest of ¹/₂ lemon
Few grinds of freshly ground black pepper or ¹/₄ teaspoon cracked black
    peppercorns

1. In a small saucepan, combine all the ingredients. Warm over low heat for 5 minutes. Do not overheat or let come to a boil.
2. Remove from the heat and let stand at room temperature for 30 minutes.
3. Place a fine strainer or double layer of cheesecloth over a 2-cup measuring cup; strain the oil into the cup and discard the solids. Pour the oil into a cruet with a cover or cork, or a pint spring-top jar. Store in the refrigerator for up to 3 months.
4. Drizzle the oil on hot or cold steamed vegetables.

Savory Vanilla Oil

While vanilla is usually associated with sweet flavors, it is a marvelous savory accent. Drizzle over your warm or room temperature steamed vegetables.

YIELD: 1 cup

1 cup light olive oil or canola oil
1 vanilla bean (3 to 4 inches), split lengthwise to expose the seeds

1. In a small saucepan, combine the olive oil and vanilla bean. Warm over medium-low heat for 10 minutes. Do not boil, but let the oil get very hot.
2. Remove from the heat and let stand at room temperature for 8 hours or overnight, lightly covered.
3. Remove the vanilla bean and discard. Pour the oil into a cruet with a cover or cork, or a pint spring-top jar. Store in the refrigerator for up to 3 months.
4. Drizzle the oil on hot or cold steamed vegetables, especially artichokes, or hot steamed rice.

Tofu-Miso Mayonnaise

This is such a wonderful sauce for vegetables. If you use the soft or silken tofu, the dressing will be pourable; if you use firm tofu, it will be more like regular mayonnaise. You can find miso at the supermarket, health food store, or Asian market.

YIELD: 1^1/$_2$ cups

^{1}/$_2$ small clove garlic, peeled
^{1}/$_2$-inch-thick coin-size chunk fresh ginger, peeled
3 tablespoons rice vinegar
1 tablespoon white miso (light)
1 teaspoon honey
2 teaspoons Colman's dry mustard
^{1}/$_2$ pound (1 cup) soft or silken tofu
2 tablespoons olive oil or Asian sesame oil

1. In a food processor with the motor running, drop in the garlic and ginger through the feed tube to mince. Stop the machine and add the vinegar, miso, honey, and mustard; pulse a few times to combine. Add the tofu and pulse until smooth. With the machine running, slowly drizzle in the olive oil. Process for 30 seconds; the mixture will be smooth and thick.
2. Refrigerate for at least 1 hour to chill and meld the flavors. Store, covered, in the refrigerator for up to 1 day.
3. Serve the mayonnaise spooned over hot or cold steamed vegetables.

whole-meal steam
CUISINE

Once you get comfortable using the steamer tray and baskets of your on/off rice cooker for vegetables, the next step is to create whole meals in the unit. Cuisines that utilize steam all have full-course steamed meals that are low in fat and quite quick to prepare. Rice (especially sticky short-grain *japonicas*) is traditionally steamed in a basket over hot water. Indian brass or tin steamers allow a full meal to be made at one time: the dal in the bottom bowl, the vegetables in the first level, and the basmati steamed on top. Our Steamed Ginger Salmon and Asparagus in Black Bean Sauce (page 253) has the rice in the bottom layer and the salmon and vegetable above. The simplicity of it all is ingenious. It is an addictively convenient form of cooking and if you have limited space, you will adore it and end up creating your own versions. If you use the tiered plastic baskets, you can even carry them to the table (with the lid on!) and serve or eat directly from them.

Use the information in the previous chapter about vegetables and work within your seasonal availability to prepare meals that combine one or more mixed vegetables, Asian noodles, Italian pasta, or leftover cooked rice, and tofu, poultry, shellfish, or fish, all arranged in the steamer baskets.

First the vegetables, which usually take up most of the space. Think of it as a seasonal assortment—whatever was nice at the farmer's market or produce section. You need only a few pieces of each (this method of cooking is very economical), so you can easily clean out the bottom drawer in the refrigerator. Spring is asparagus, green onions, the tiniest new potatoes, chopped ruby chard, and fresh peas, even some fiddlehead fern fronds. Winter finds carrots, cauliflower, fennel bulb chunks, whole baby carrots, a turnip, or other roots. During the summer you can splurge on baby vegetables: zucchini with their blossoms still attached, the tiniest beets, baby spinach leaves, string beans the size of a baby's finger. Remember that the harder the vegetable, the thinner the slice or wedge you want to cut, while softer vegetables can be in thick chunks or spears so that they all cook in the same amount of time. Balance not only the type of vegetable, but the color and different shapes to give the eye, as well as the palate, a delightful experience.

Then the protein. Four to eight ounces per person of fish, chicken, sausage, or turkey breast is all that is needed; less if you are dieting. You can mix and match here as well—a few ounces of chicken breast and a few large prawns or scallops, for example (a wonderful combination, by the way). Tofu, plain or one of the seasoned pressed varieties, is excellent steamed. Cut the poultry into thick strips rather than leaving it whole; it cooks more efficiently, with greater surface area for the steam to reach. Fillets of fish, such as sole and snapper, can be rolled up; a strip of halibut or sea bass fillet is perfect. You can steam them as is or soak for a short time in a light marinade first; our favorite for both fish and poultry is a bit of oil, lime juice and grated zest, and some onion or garlic powder.

You can certainly serve your basket meal with some plain fresh steamed rice, but steaming works well with other types of starch. Use partially precooked Asian noodles such as buckwheat soba or fresh udon; rice noodles (that soften by soaking in water for 30 minutes) or spelt noodles; or Italian pasta, such as fettuccine. Any leftover cooked grain fits well, from rice and couscous to quinoa and wheat berries. Mound the grains like a scoop of ice cream or make the pasta into a round nest, taking care to include only enough for the number of portions you are serving rather than letting it take over the whole basket.

You have prepped everything; now, for assembly. This is the fun part, arranging everything in the baskets. It is different every time. When you take off that lid, you want a little work of art; there are only a few rules. The longest-cooking vegetables need plenty of space around them for steam to get at all sides; place them around the outside of the basket. Quicker-cooking foods, such as soft vegetables, tofu, shrimp, and noodles, can be mounded nearer to the center, getting the lesser amount of steam.

Fill the rice cooker bowl one-quarter full of hot water and close the cover. Set for the regular cycle to bring the water to a boil, which happens within 5 to 10 minutes; you can be arranging the baskets at this time. Line the steamer baskets with a single layer of chard or Napa cabbage leaves or just a piece of parchment paper. Place the filled baskets over the vigorously boiling water and cover immediately. The rice cooker will keep the water at a steady boil. Avoid peeking; you don't want to disturb the buildup of the steam. Set a timer and steam for 10 to 20 minutes, depending on what you have in those baskets. When you do open the lid, open it away from yourself, so the steam won't burn you. Check for doneness by first evaluating the color and look of the meat or fish; it should be plump, moist, and have lost that translucent raw look. If you are using shellfish such as clams or mussels, the shells will open. You know your preference as to how you like your vegetables, softer or more crisp-tender. Make notes as to combinations and timing so you can repeat your favorite meals in a flash.

You can serve a cold or hot sauce, salsa, spiced oil, compound butter, even fresh lemon mayonnaise (the vegetable chapter has lots of suggestions) with the meal, but this is purely optional.

steamed chicken breasts on wild rice with gingered tomato relish

Although this recipe employs two rice cookers, it is terribly simple, which is why it gets made so often. Originally a "gourmet-lite" recipe from former Sonoma Mission Inn chef Larry Elbert using broiled chicken breast, the recipe made the leap perfectly for the chicken breast to be marinated and steamed. A steamed chicken breast is wonderfully tender and juicy. Use this recipe as a basic one; if you don't have time to marinate, just wash the breast in lots of fresh lemon juice and a tablespoon of olive oil. Serve on a bed of plain, fresh cooked wild rice, with a bit of the tomato relish on top.

MACHINE: Medium (6-cup) and large (10-cup) rice cookers; on/off only
CYCLE: Regular
YIELD: Serves 4

MARINADE AND CHICKEN

$1/3$ cup Dijon mustard

3 tablespoons red wine vinegar

3 tablespoons fresh lemon juice

1 clove garlic, pressed

$1 1/2$ teaspoons herbes de Provence or dried basil leaves, crumbled

$2/3$ cup olive oil or vegetable oil

4 boneless chicken breast halves, with skin on

RELISH

2 medium-size ripe tomatoes, blanched for a few seconds in boiling water, peeled, seeds squeezed out, and diced

3 tablespoons chopped green onions, white and green parts

1 tablespoon extra virgin olive oil

1 tablespoon champagne vinegar

$1/2$ teaspoon peeled and grated fresh ginger

Splash of Tabasco sauce

Pinch of salt or nonsalt alternative, such as Vegit or Spike

RICE

$1 1/4$ cups wild rice

$2 3/4$ cups water

Pinch of salt

2 to 3 large chard leaves, stems discarded, or Napa cabbage leaves, for lining steamer basket (optional)

1. *Make the marinade:* Place the marinade ingredients in a shallow bowl; whisk to combine. Place the chicken, skin side up, in the marinade. Cover and refrigerate for at least 2 hours.

2. *Make the relish:* Place the relish ingredients in a small bowl; stir to combine. Cover and refrigerate until serving.

3. *Make the rice:* Place the wild rice in the rice cooker bowl of a medium (6-cup) or large (10-cup) rice cooker. Add the water and salt; swirl to combine. Close the cover and set for the regular/Brown Rice cycle. When the machine switches to the Keep Warm cycle, stir with a wooden or plastic rice paddle or wooden spoon to dissipate the heat and prevent overcooking. Close

the cover and let the rice steam for 10 minutes. This step will take close to 1 hour, so plan accordingly.

4. Fill a large (10-cup) rice cooker bowl one-quarter full of hot water, close the cover, and set for the regular cycle. Line one steamer tray or basket with a single layer of chard or cabbage leaves or a piece of parchment paper. Remove the chicken from the marinade and arrange on the steamer tray or basket. If you are having steamed vegetables with the chicken (like some zucchini), you can arrange them in the top tier if you are using baskets. When the water comes to a boil, place the tray or basket in the cooker and close the cover. Set a timer and steam for 20 to 25 minutes. Check the chicken for doneness; it should no longer be pink in the center.

5. To serve, divide the rice among 4 dinner plates, place a chicken breast on top, and spoon some relish in a mound on top. Serve immediately.

OTHER GREAT MARINADES FOR STEAMED CHICKEN BREASTS AND FISH

Teriyaki Marinade

YIELD: About 2 cups

²/₃ cup soy sauce
¹/₃ cup honey
2 teaspoons peeled and grated fresh ginger
1 clove garlic, pressed
3 tablespoons dry sherry or sake
¹/₂ cup vegetable oil
¹/₂ cup chopped green onions, white and green parts

Place all the ingredients in a shallow bowl; whisk to combine.

Cumin-Yogurt Marinade

YIELD: About 2 cups

1¹/₂ cups plain yogurt
¹/₃ cup fresh lemon juice
2 teaspoons ground cumin
Pinch of mixed dried herbs, such as Parsley Patch
1 clove garlic, pressed
1 tablespoon olive oil

Place all the ingredients in a shallow bowl; whisk to combine.

steamed chicken breasts with warm mango sauce and coconut rice

This is a chicken recipe contributed by our local Mexican food expert and cooking teacher Marge Poore, the author of *365 Easy Mexican Recipes* (HarperCollins, 1997) and *1,000 Mexican Recipes* (HarperCollins, 2001). She also leads very popular food tours of Mexico. Here Poore combines tropical mangos with steamed chicken breasts and we couldn't be more excited about the combination. Mangos, usually served as a sweet fruit rather than the savory version here, have become a popular mainstream fruit and are widely available just about everywhere. We serve this dish from the steamer baskets with coconut rice and steamed asparagus and/or chayote squash, a vegetable that often is served steamed or sautéed as a side vegetable in Mexico.

MACHINE: Large (10-cup) rice cooker; on/off only
CYCLE: Regular
YIELD: Serves 4

2 1/2 cups basmati rice or other aromatic long-grain rice, such as jasmine or Jasmati
Two 14-ounce cans unsweetened coconut milk (can be light)
1/4 cup water
1/8 teaspoon salt (optional)
4 skinless, boneless chicken breast halves
1 pound thick asparagus spears, tough bottoms discarded, and/or 2 chayote squashes, peeled, seeded, halved, and cut into 1 1/2-inch-thick slices

SAUCE
1 large ripe mango, peeled, seeded, and cut into neat 1/2-inch pieces
1/4 cup dry white wine
2 tablespoons rice vinegar
2 tablespoons sugar
2 teaspoons peeled and minced fresh ginger
1/8 teaspoon ground allspice

Salt
Freshly ground black pepper
3 tablespoons minced fresh cilantro leaves, for garnish

1. Rinse the rice in a fine strainer until the water runs clear. Place the rice in the rice cooker bowl. Add the coconut milk, water, and salt, if using; swirl to combine.
2. Coat the steamer baskets with nonstick cooking spray and arrange the chicken in one basket. Place the asparagus and/or chayote in the other basket or arrange it around the chicken. Place the steamer baskets in the rice cooker. Close the cover and set for the regular cycle.
3. Make the sauce. In a medium-size sauce-pan, combine the mango, wine, vinegar, sugar, ginger, and allspice. Bring to a boil over medium heat, stirring to dissolve the sugar. Reduce the heat to low and simmer, uncovered, for 5 minutes. Remove from the heat and set aside.

4. When the machine switches to the Keep Warm cycle, check to make sure the chicken is no longer pink inside and the vegetables are tender. Fluff the rice with a wooden or plastic rice paddle or wooden spoon.

5. To serve, transfer the rice to a serving platter and top with the chicken. Arrange the vegetables around the rice and season with salt and pepper to taste. Reheat the mango sauce and spoon a small amount over the chicken. Garnish with cilantro. Pass the remaining sauce at the table.

steamed halibut steaks and scallops with sweet red pepper sauce

This is one of Beth's catering entrées. The red pepper sauce is delightful on the halibut (it is also good on lingcod) and scallops. We like to use Della long-grain white rice here.

MACHINE: Large (10-cup) rice cooker; on/off only

CYCLE: Regular

YIELD: Serves 4

Four 6- to 8-ounce halibut steaks (1 inch thick)
$^3/_4$ to 1 pound large scallops
2 tablespoons olive oil
Salt

Freshly ground black pepper
2 tablespoons dry white wine
1$^3/_4$ cups domestic aromatic long-grain rice, such as Della or Jasmati
2$^3/_4$ cups water
Pinch of salt
2 to 3 large chard leaves, stems discarded, or Napa cabbage leaves, for lining steamer basket (optional)
4 sprigs fresh thyme
1 pound fresh green beans, ends trimmed

SAUCE

4 large red bell peppers, seeded and cut into pieces
2 large yellow onions, chopped
3 to 4 tablespoons olive oil
3 tablespoons balsamic vinegar
Pinch of fresh or dried thyme leaves
Pinch of cayenne pepper
$^1/_3$ cup sour cream or crème fraîche
Salt
Freshly ground black pepper

1. Rinse and pat dry the halibut and scallops. Place on a plate and sprinkle with the oil, salt and pepper to taste, and the wine. Refrigerate while preparing the rice.

2. Place the rice in the rice cooker bowl. Add the water and salt; swirl to combine.

3. Line the two steamer baskets with a single layer of chard or cabbage leaves or a sheet of parchment paper. Arrange the fish on two tiers (2 steaks per basket) of the steamer basket in a single layer and top with the thyme sprigs. Loosely arrange the green beans around the outside of the steaks. Place the steaming baskets in the rice cooker. Close the cover and set for the regular cycle.

4. Make the sauce. Combine the peppers and onions with the oil in a sauté pan over medium heat. Cook until soft, 5 to 10 minutes. Add the vinegar, thyme, and cayenne. Transfer the mixture to a food processor and process until smooth. Add the sour cream and pulse to combine. Season with salt and pepper to taste. Transfer the sauce to a saucepan and keep warm until serving.

5. When the machine switches to the Keep Warm cycle, let steam for 10 minutes. Check for doneness: The halibut and scallops should be opaque and firm to the touch, and the vegetables should be cooked through. Fluff the rice with a wooden or plastic rice paddle or wooden spoon.

6. Serve immediately. Divide the fish, rice, and beans among 4 dinner plates and pass the sauce at the table.

steamed salmon steaks with pineapple salsa

Salmon steaks, now readily available because of farm-raised fish, are a sure thing for a fast dinner. This marinade is wonderful; we keep sake around just for this. Serve with some hot jasmine rice.

MACHINE: Large (10-cup) rice cooker; on/off only

CYCLE: Regular

YIELD: Serves 4

MARINADE AND SALMON

$^3/_4$ cup dry sake

$^3/_4$ cup reduced-sodium soy sauce

$^1/_3$ cup sugar

Four 6- to 8-ounce salmon steaks ($^3/_4$ inch thick)

SALSA

1 $^1/_2$ cups diced fresh pineapple

$^1/_3$ cup seeded and minced red bell pepper

$^1/_4$ cup minced red onion

$^1/_4$ cup minced fresh cilantro leaves

Juice and grated zest of 1 large lime

2 $^1/_2$ teaspoons seeded and minced jalapeño chile

2 to 3 large chard leaves, stems discarded, or Napa cabbage leaves, for lining steamer basket (optional)

1. *Make the marinade:* Place the marinade ingredients in a shallow bowl; whisk to combine. Place the salmon in the marinade, coating both sides well. Cover and refrigerate for 1 to 2 hours; turn once.

2. *Make the salsa:* Place the salsa ingredients in a small bowl; stir to combine. Cover and refrigerate until serving.

3. Fill the rice cooker bowl one-quarter full of hot water, close the cover, and set for the regular cycle.

4. Line the steamer baskets with a single layer of chard or cabbage leaves or a piece of parchment paper. Remove the salmon steaks from the marinade and arrange on one or two tiers of the steamer basket. (If you are steaming vegetables with the salmon, you can arrange them around the sides of the tiers.) When the water comes to a boil, place the steamer baskets in the cooker and close the cover. Set a timer and steam for 18 to 23 minutes. Check for doneness; the fish should be opaque and firm.

5. Serve the salmon immediately, with the salsa.

steamed ginger salmon and asparagus in black bean sauce

A full Asian-style meal in the rice cooker! The rice is cooked below while the salmon and asparagus steam above.

MACHINE: Large (10-cup) rice cooker; on/off only

CYCLE: Regular

YIELD: Serves 3 to 4

2¼ cups (3 rice cooker cups) Japanese-style or domestic medium-grain white jasmine rice

3 or 3¼ cups water (see directions)

SAUCE

2 tablespoons black bean garlic sauce (available in Chinese markets or well-stocked supermarkets)

2 teaspoons sake

1 teaspoon sugar

1 pound fresh asparagus, bottoms snapped off and stalks cut on the diagonal into 1½-inch-long pieces

2 to 3 large chard leaves, stems discarded, Napa cabbage leaves, or lettuce leaves, for lining steamer basket

One ¾- to 1-pound salmon fillet, rinsed and patted dry

6 thin slices peeled fresh ginger

2 green onions, white and tender green parts, slivered, for garnish

1. Wash or rinse the rice, if desired. Place it in the rice cooker with the water; add 3 cups water for Japanese-style rice, 3¼ cups for domestic.

2. Make the sauce. In a small bowl, stir together the black bean garlic sauce, sake, and sugar. Place the asparagus in a medium-size bowl and toss with half of the sauce.

3. Line the steamer basket with a single layer of chard, cabbage, or lettuce leaves. Place the salmon in the center of the basket. Cut 6 slits in the fish; insert a ginger slice into each slit. Spread the remaining sauce over the fish. Arrange the asparagus around the fish. Place the steamer basket in the rice cooker. Close the cover and set for the regular cycle.

4. When the machine switches to the Keep Warm cycle, let steam for 10 minutes. Check for doneness; the salmon and asparagus should be cooked through. If not, cover again and allow the fish to finish cooking, checking at 10-minute intervals.

5. Garnish with the green onions and serve.

steamed whole fish

We always see these wonderful whole snappers at the Asian market and they look so inviting. Have the fishmonger clean, scale, and trim the fish, leaving the head and tail on. Here is the Chinese method for steaming a whole fish in the steamer basket; it retains the texture of the delicate flesh and the flavor is fantastic. If you are having more guests, steam two fish, one on each tier. Serve with hot Chinese-style long-grain rice.

MACHINE: Large (10-cup) rice cooker; on/off only

CYCLE: **Regular**

YIELD: Serves 4

1 yellow snapper, whitefish, or sea bass
    (2¹/₂ to 3 pounds)

Salt

3 tablespoons dry sherry or Shaoxing wine
    (available in Chinese markets)

¹/₂ teaspoon sugar

2 cloves garlic, minced

Freshly ground black pepper

1 heaping tablespoon peeled and grated
    fresh ginger

2 tablespoons Chinese fermented black
    beans

2 to 3 large chard leaves, stems
    discarded, or Napa cabbage leaves,
    for lining steamer basket (optional)

¹/₄ cup chopped green onions, white and
    green parts, for garnish

3 tablespoons soy sauce mixed with
    2 tablespoons red wine vinegar and
    ³/₄ teaspoon sugar, for serving

1. Place the fish in a shallow bowl large enough to hold it. Sprinkle salt on both sides. Cover and refrigerate for 1 hour.

2. Wash the salt off the fish with cold water and pat dry with paper towels. Rinse the bowl and place the fish back in it. Make diagonal slashes, 1 inch apart, down both sides of the fish to allow for even cooking with the steam.

3. In a small bowl, stir together the sherry, sugar, garlic, a few grinds of pepper, the ginger, and black beans in a small bowl. Pour over the fish. Cover and refrigerate for 30 minutes.

4. Fill the rice cooker bowl one-quarter to one-third full of hot water, close the cover, and set for the regular cycle.

5. Line the steamer basket with a single layer of chard or cabbage leaves or a piece of parchment paper. Place the fish on one tier of the steamer basket. (If you are having steamed vegetables, you can arrange them in the top basket.) When the water comes to a boil, place the baskets in the cooker and close the cover. Set a timer and steam for 18 to 23 minutes. Check for doneness; the fish should be opaque and firm to the touch when pressed.

6. Serve immediately. Transfer the fish to a platter, garnish with the green onions, and serve the soy sauce–vinegar mixture on the side for drizzling.

steamed shrimp and jasmine rice

Shrimp is an excellent seafood for the rice cooker because it cooks so quickly. If your cooker has a glass lid, it's easy to tell when the shrimp are cooked by their bright orange-pink color; if you have to lift the lid to check the shrimp, do so with care to avoid the steam. If the shrimp is finished before the end of the rice cooking cycle, carefully remove the shrimp and green onions, either by removing the whole steaming tray or transferring the ingredients with a spatula or tongs.

Timing this recipe takes a little practice, but the whole dish couldn't be easier. Chopping up and mixing in the steamed green onions gives great flavor and texture to the cooked rice. You might try this with baby leeks instead of green onions. This is a light meal, suitable for lunch or Sunday night supper. This recipe comes from the kitchen of our literary agent, Martha Casselman.

MACHINE: Medium (6-cup) or large (10-cup) rice cooker; on/off only
CYCLE: Regular
YIELD: Serves 4

1 pound medium-size shrimp
1¹/₃ cups Thai jasmine rice
2²/₃ cups water
Pinch of salt
8 green onions, trimmed to fit steaming tray
2 pinches of dillweed
Ground white pepper

Sprigs of fresh Italian parsley, basil, or sage, for garnish

1. Peel and devein the shrimp, taking care to leave on the tails. Rinse the shrimp and pat dry with paper towels.
2. Rinse the rice. Place it in the rice cooker bowl with the water and salt; swirl to combine. Close the cover and set for the regular cycle.
3. Place the green onions on the steamer tray and lay the shrimp on top in a single layer. Sprinkle with the dill weed and white pepper to season.
4. About 8 minutes before the end of the regular cycle (depending on brand and size, about 15 minutes into the cycle), place the steaming tray in the cooker and close the cover. Steam the shrimp for about 6 minutes, until the color has changed to orange-pink. Do not overcook the shrimp, or they will become tough. Remove the steaming tray and place the shrimp in a warm covered dish. Let the onions cool, then chop them enough to stir them into the rice when it is done; you will have about ⅓ cup.
5. When the machine switches to the Keep Warm cycle, stir the green onions into the rice with a plastic or wooden rice paddle or wooden spoon.
6. To serve, mound the rice on a serving platter or 4 individual plates, place the shrimp on top, and garnish with the herb sprig.

vegetable pasta with prosciutto and olives

Once we learned how efficient it is to cook the vegetables, either in the boiling water along with the pasta or up top in the steamer basket, a meal can be on the table in 15 minutes. This recipe calls for dried pasta, since it takes about the same amount of time to cook as the vegetables.

MACHINE: Large (10-cup) rice cooker; on/off only

CYCLE: Regular

YIELD: Serves 4 as a main course, 6 as a first course

SOFT VEGETABLES

1 medium-size leek, white part only, washed well, cut in half, and thinly sliced

6 ounces pencil-thin asparagus, trimmed bottoms, sliced on a diagonal into 1-inch pieces

1 medium-size zucchini or yellow crook-neck summer squash, cut into thin strips

1 cup fresh or frozen petite peas

12 canned whole baby corn, drained and cut in half lengthwise

1/2 pound firm, fresh white mushrooms, thinly sliced

1 medium-size red or orange bell pepper, halved, seeded, and cut into thin strips

2 to 3 large chard leaves, stems discarded, or Napa cabbage leaves for lining steamer basket (optional)

1 pound fettuccine

1 carrot, cut into thin strips

1/2 head cauliflower, broken into florets

1/4 cup olive oil, or mixture of olive oil and walnut or hazelnut oil

4 paper-thin slices prosciutto, cut into thin strips

3 tablespoons pitted black olives

2 tablespoons minced fresh basil leaves or other fresh herb, such as oregano, marjoram, chives, or savory

1/2 cup freshly grated or finely shredded Parmesan cheese, plus more for sprinkling

Salt

Freshly ground black pepper

1. Prepare the vegetables and place them on a plate (this can be done 2 to 4 hours in advance). Cover and refrigerate until serving.

2. Fill the rice cooker bowl half-full of hot water, close the cover, and set for the regular cycle. Line two steamer baskets with a single layer of chard or cabbage leaves or coat with nonstick cooking spray. Arrange the soft vegetables in the baskets.

3. When the water comes to a boil, add the pasta, carrot, and cauliflower to the rice bowl. Place the steamer baskets over the boiling water and close the cover. Set a timer and steam for 10 minutes. Check for doneness; both the vegetables and the pasta should be tender. Remove the baskets and set aside. Carefully remove the bowl with oven mitts and drain the pasta, carrots, and cauliflower in a colander.

4. To serve, place the pasta and vegetables in a warm shallow serving bowl. Drizzle with the olive oil. Sprinkle with the prosciutto, olives, basil, cheese, and salt and pepper to taste; toss to combine. Serve immediately, with extra Parmesan on the side.

steamed flank steak and sweet potatoes

Rice ground up with spices (and sometimes hot pepper) is a popular Chinese coating for steamed flank steak or spare ribs. We got the idea for this presentation right off the box of rice powder that we bought at a local Asian market. If you can't find rice powder, you can make your own as follows: In a dry, heavy skillet, toast 1 cup washed and drained long-grain white rice, or 1 cup soaked and drained glutinous rice, over medium heat until it is lightly toasted, 7 to 10 minutes. Let cool, then whirl the rice in a blender with 1 star anise or 1 teaspoon five-spice powder until powdered. Feel free to double this recipe if you have a very large steamer rack (or a tier basket model); otherwise, just steam it in two batches. This is a wonderful meal: The steamed sweet potatoes will be meltingly tender and gently flavored by the meat.

MACHINE: Large (10-cup) rice cooker; on/off only
CYCLE: Regular
YIELD: Serves 2

1/2 pound flank steak, trimmed of fat
1 tablespoon soy sauce
1/2 teaspoon sugar
1/8 teaspoon ground white pepper
2 small to medium-size sweet potatoes (not yams), peeled and sliced 1/2 inch thick
About half of a 50-gram box spiced rice powder or about 1/4 cup homemade spiced rice powder (see headnote)

1. Cut the steak into bite-size pieces or slice thinly on the diagonal. Toss the steak with the soy sauce, sugar, and white pepper; let marinate for 20 to 30 minutes at room temperature.
2. Fill the rice cooker bowl one-quarter to one-third full of hot water, close the cover, and set for the regular cycle. Coat the steamer tray with nonstick cooking spray and arrange the sweet potatoes on it in 2 layers.
3. Sprinkle the rice powder over the meat; stir gently to combine and evenly coat. If the rice coating seems sparse, add a bit more. Arrange the meat on top of the sweet potatoes. When the water comes to a boil, place the steamer basket in the cooker and close the cover. Set a timer and steam for 25 minutes. Check for doneness; the meat and its rice coating should both be tender.
4. Serve immediately, dividing the meat and potatoes between two plates.

steamed sausages and sauerkraut with champagne

With the advent of the healthier sausages, it is now easy to eat them once a week. Here is an incredibly easy entrée. The amount of sauerkraut depends on your diners; anyone from Europe will eat a hearty serving. You can brown the sausages first in a skillet if you like, but that is optional. Serve with a variety of mustards and some butter and dill weed on the potatoes. We like to serve it with a tossed green salad with sliced cucumbers or cole slaw.

MACHINE: Large (10-cup) rice cooker; on/off only
CYCLE: Regular
YIELD: Serves 4

2¹/₂ to 3 pounds fresh sauerkraut, rinsed
¹/₃ cup dry champagne or sparkling white wine

8 fully cooked sausages, such as smoked chicken-apple or bockwurst with chives
12 medium-size red or white new potatoes, cut in half or quarters, or 24 baby creamer potatoes, left whole and unpeeled
¹/₄ cup (¹/₂ stick) unsalted butter, for serving
2 teaspoons dillweed, for serving

1. Fill the rice cooker bowl one-quarter full of hot water, close the cover, and set for the regular cycle.
2. Line two steamer baskets with a single sheet of parchment paper each. Divide the sauerkraut in half and arrange it like a bed in the center of both baskets; drizzle with the champagne. Place 4 sausages on each bed of sauerkraut, then loosely arrange the potatoes around the sauerkraut. When the water comes to a boil, place the baskets in the cooker and close the cover. Set a timer and steam for 30 to 40 minutes. Check for doneness: the potatoes should be tender when pierced with the tip of a knife and the sausages nice and hot.
3. Serve immediately, with each diner having 2 sausages, sauerkraut, and some potatoes with 1 tablespoon butter and ¹/₂ teaspoon dillweed sprinkled on.

dim sum, dolmas, and tamales:
LITTLE BITES

One of the delights of the on/off rice cookers is the ability to steam-cook foods like dim sum, dolmas, and tamales, all of which require special equipment if done on the stovetop. These out-of-hand little bites ended up being one of our favorite, and exceptionally convenient, ways to use the rice cooker. Whether as a before-dinner snack, as a buffet item, or a light meal, these tidbits are the best offerings from a variety of traditional world cuisine foods.

DIM SUM

Yum cha, or "to drink tea," is a morning tea and snack ritual in Chinese teahouses. The snacks are called dim sum, steamed or fried foods in diminutive, bite-size proportions served fresh and hot. Dim sum translates into the eloquent Cantonese saying, "touched by the heart." It is a buffet served from carts stacked with steamer baskets in teahouses that specialize in serving dim sum. The finger-food appetizers include steamed dumplings, vegetables, bits of fish and meat savories, shrimp, pearl rice balls, spring rolls, and pastries. Dim sum is also served in larger portions with salad and rice as the traditional Sunday morning meal that would be a brunch in the United States.

Although rice is served in the south of China, bread is a staple in the north, where fields of wheat, corn, and millet grow. Once the Chinese learned the art of milling over 2,000 years ago, they began to make noodles and steam breads made with a natural sour starter, since they did not have enclosed ovens, except for the occasional tandoori-style one. For dim sum, breads are steamed into rolls or filled with some sort of meat filling. Steamed breads have always been esteemed products of the kitchen; the Imperial Mings made a different bread every day of the month to take to the temples in honor of their ancestors. These steamed breads are now part of the dim sum kitchen.

Since many dim sum specialties are steamed, the on/off rice cooker is a perfect tool for them. Many rice cookers come with a metal steamer tray that fits into the top of the cooker. One of Beth's cookers came with a stack of three transparent plastic baskets, which mimic the traditional bamboo ones. These are really ideal for dim sum, but either type works fine. The water in the steamer should be boiling vigorously when the food-laden baskets are set in place and the timing for the cooking begins. The filled baskets should be situated well above the surface of the hot water so that the water doesn't touch or bubble up over into it. The tight-fitting heat-resistant glass cover is put on top to close the unit and efficiently enclose the steam (no mismatched covers, please). You can fill one or both of the stacked steamer baskets to cook at one time. We don't recommend using a third tier; rather, cook in a second batch so that all the food is cooked thoroughly and evenly. If your cooker came with only a single metal tray, you will be steaming dim sum in batches.

The medium or large rice cooker is advised for steaming dim sum, because it is important to have as large a pot as possible to hold enough water to create a lot of intense steam to circulate around the food. You want a steady volume of steam to be released during the entire cooking time, so the right amount of water in the bowl is important. If you must, add only boiling water to replenish.

dumpling blossoms

The delicate steamed dumplings known as dumpling blossoms (*shao mai* in Mandarin and *siu mai* in Cantonese) are named such because of the shape, like a little pouch with frilly edges and a peek at the filling. It is a favorite shape for dim sum, along with ones shaped like half-moons, closed pouches, and an origami-like double fold enticingly called a phoenix eye. The chicken-and-ginger filling is a very flavorful, lowfat version.

MACHINE: Medium (6-cup) or large (10-cup) rice cooker; on/off only
CYCLE: Regular
YIELD: 30 dumplings

DUMPLINGS
1¹/₂ pounds ground chicken
1 large egg white, lightly beaten
3 tablespoons chopped fresh cilantro
    leaves
3 green onions, finely chopped
1 clove garlic, pressed
2 tablespoons soy sauce
1 tablespoon peeled and minced fresh
    ginger

2 teaspoons sugar
¹/₄ teaspoon freshly ground white pepper
2 to 3 large lettuce or Napa cabbage
    leaves, for lining steamer basket
30 wonton or *siu mai* wrappers

DIPPING SAUCE
¹/₄ cup soy sauce
3 tablespoons cider vinegar
1 tablespoon chicken stock or water
2 teaspoons peeled and finely grated
    fresh ginger
1 teaspoon sugar
¹/₄ teaspoon Chinese hot chile sauce

1. In a medium-size bowl, combine the dumpling ingredients except the lettuce leaves and wrappers; mix well with a fork. Refrigerate for 4 hours to chill and firm up the mixture.

2. Fill the rice cooker bowl one-quarter full of water, close the cover, and set for the regular cycle. If the water boils before you are ready to cook the *siu mai*, flip the switch to the Keep Warm position (switch back for cooking).

3. Line two steamer baskets with a single layer of the lettuce or cabbage leaves. Place the wrappers on the side of your workspace, covered with damp paper towels to prevent drying. If using wonton wrappers, trim the edges to form circles. Take one wrapper and brush with some cold water (this helps the wrapper to stick to the meat mixture). Place 1 heaping teaspoon of filling in the center of each wrapper, spreading it around the center. Use your fingers to gather up and pleat the wrapper around the filling to form an open-topped cup; carefully squeeze the middle to give it

If you are new to cooking Asian-style food, there will be some ingredients, basic staples to these styles of cooking, with which you will want to become familiar. They are used in the following recipes and throughout this book. Shop in the Asian section of your supermarket or visit a specialty grocery, which is an experience every serious cook should entertain (you will come home with all sorts of wonderful foods and condiments). This section is also a useful reference when making any of our fried rices (pages 318–327).

Asian sesame oil: A toasted oil that is thick and brown and used more as a seasoning than a cooking oil. Store in the cupboard, or refrigerate if you use it slowly.

Black beans with garlic sauce: This pungent and addicting sauce is found in jars in Asian markets.

Chile oil: The same as hot sesame oil, only it says "vegetable oil" instead of sesame oil.

Chinese mustard: A spicy, smooth mustard.

Cilantro: An herb also known as fresh coriander or Chinese parsley, since it is used so much in their cooking. It has a fragile flat, fringed leaf with an intense peppery aroma and a flavor that is positively addictive, sort of citrus-like.

Dried shrimp: Sun-dried and salted golden orange shriveled-up shrimps are a prized ingredient and used as a seasoning. Sold in plastic bags; store, tightly closed, in the refrigerator or freezer.

Fermented black beans: These are sold on the shelf in plastic pouches. A little goes a long way in flavoring foods.

Fish sauce: Pungent *nam pla* in Thai is extracted from salted anchovies or shrimp and used as a cooking condiment. Thai and Vietnamese fish sauces differ slightly.

Ginger: Fresh ginger should be peeled before using. It doesn't keep well, so don't buy more than a week's worth. Pickled ginger is colored deep red and used as a garnish or flavoring.

Hoisin sauce: Made from soybeans, flour, sugar, salt, garlic, and chiles, hoisin is a thick, dark red sauce with a piquant flavor beloved in Chinese cooking. It can be used as an ingredient in dim sum, as a seasoning, or in the dipping sauce. Store in the refrigerator indefinitely.

Hot sesame oil: Made by steeping hot red chiles in sesame oil, this has a reddish tinge and comes in small bottles because you need only a little dab as a condiment or ingredient. Store in the refrigerator indefinitely.

Mirin: A Japanese sweet rice cooking wine, it is used to add sweetness to a recipe. Pale dry sherry with a dash of sugar added can be substituted.

Miso: A Japanese ingredient high in protein, it is a sticky, thick soybean paste made from fermented soybeans and salt, and is used as a flavoring agent or diluted into broth for soup. It comes in many varieties, each with its own hue and flavor, from mild to strong. Store in the refrigerator indefinitely.

Napa cabbage: Also called Chinese cabbage, it is a looser, oblong head of crinkly edged leaves that has an especially mild flavor and is a favorite ingredient, as well as a perfect liner for steamer baskets, along with butter lettuce and green chard leaves. Usually sold next to the regular heads of cabbage in the produce section.

Oyster sauce: A thick brown condiment, like Worcestershire sauce, made from a large array of ingredients—including fermented oyster extract, salt, and soy sauce—it adds color and a salty flavor to a dish. Beth loves a vegetarian oyster sauce (found only in specialty markets) with the oyster extract replaced with shiitake mushroom extract; it is fantastic! Pay the bit more for "premium" oyster sauce; it is worth it. Store in the refrigerator.

Rice vinegar: A distilled clear, straw-colored vinegar with a mild sweet flavor made from fermented white rice and used in cooking as a seasoning, and for pickling.

Rice wine: See Shaoxing wine, Sake, Mirin.

Sake: A Japanese rice wine that is not sweet like mirin. Stronger than American wine, it is used for cooking as well as for drinking. Hakusan is a good inexpensive domestic brand.

Shaoxing wine: The popular Chinese dark amber rice wine used for cooking, found in Asian markets, sometimes labeled with the older spelling Shao Hsing. A medium-dry sherry (not sake) is a good substitute.

Soy sauce: Made from fermented soybeans, salt, and wheat, soy sauce is a full-flavored salt substitute and premier ingredient in Asian cooking. It is used as an ingredient, a condiment, and a marinade. There are different brands, both Chinese and Japanese, ranging in degree of quality, saltiness, and flavor. There is a light, or thin, soy sauce, used in these recipes, and a dark, or thick, soy sauce that is more viscous and stronger in flavor. Beth uses tamari, a Japanese soy sauce that is more like Chinese dark soy sauce. Julie favors regular Japanese-style soy sauces called *shoyu*; they are thinner, a dash sweeter, and less salty than the Chinese ones. Reduced-sodium brands, catering to the health-conscious market and changing tastes, are excellent.

Szechuan pepper: Tiny red-brown peppercorns with a strong, hot flavor. This is a regional product of Szechuan province.

Tofu: Also known as bean curd, tofu is a pressed block made from curdled soybean milk. It is quite bland, but is favored as a vegetarian alternative to meat because of its high protein content. It comes in soft, silken, medium, firm, and extra firm styles, and is custardlike in texture. Store tofu in the refrigerator (except for the kind packed in juice box containers, which can be stored unopened at room temperature; once opened, they, too, must be refrigerated). After opening, store any leftover tofu in a water-filled plastic or glass container with a tight-fitting lid. Change the water daily and the tofu will stay fresh for days.

Wonton or siu mai wrappers: Look for these small, $3^1/_2$-inch square or round thin pasta sheets in plastic pouches in the produce or refrigerator section. Freeze unused wrappers for up to a month. They can be steamed, fried, or boiled after filling.

a waist and flare it to make a slightly open end. Tap each dumpling on the work surface a few times to flatten the bottom so it will stand upright in the steamer basket. (Alternatively, you can use your fingers to fold the wrapper into a half-moon and pleat the edge to seal.) Set the filled *siu mai* in the lined steamer baskets, at least an inch apart; cover with a damp cloth while filling the remaining wrappers.

4. Place the steamer baskets over the boiling water in the rice cooker and close the cover. Set a timer for 15 to 20 minutes and steam until the filling is cooked through (cut one open to test).

5. While the dumplings are steaming, make the dipping sauce. Place the dipping sauce ingredients in a small bowl; stir to combine.

6. Serve the dumplings hot, with little individual bowls of dipping sauce.

note: The uncooked filled dumplings can be frozen, close together, but not touching, on a lined baking sheet. After 6 to 8 hours, remove them from the sheet and store in plastic freezer bags. Freeze for up to 2 months. To cook, just remove from the bag and arrange in the lined steamer baskets. Steam frozen, doubling the cooking time.

steamed vegetarian siu mai

We feel really lucky to have this delicious, delicious, delicious vegetarian dim sum recipe from Master Chef Martin Yan, the celebrated host of more than 1,500 TV cooking shows and author of *Martin Yan's Feast: The Best of Yan Can Cook* (Bay Books & Tapes, 1998), his definitive work to date. Born in Guangzhou, in the Canton region of China (the birthplace of the art of dim sum), Yan entered the culinary world at age 13 with his apprenticeship at a Hong Kong restaurant. These *siu mai* dumplings are hearty and flavor-packed. We dare you to stop eating them once you have started! They are filled with tofu, but you'd never guess. It's important to steam them filled side down; otherwise, they'll stick to the steamer plate. Serve with soy sauce or Chinese mustard for dipping, if desired, or make a simple dipping sauce from soy sauce, rice vinegar, and chile oil.

MACHINE: Medium (6-cup) or large (10-cup) rice cooker; on/off only
CYCLE: Regular
YIELD: 30 dumplings

DUMPLINGS
1 pound (1 package) firm tofu, drained and mashed
2 green onions, white and green parts, finely chopped
1/4 cup coarsely chopped water chestnuts
1 1/2 tablespoons soy sauce
1 tablespoon Shaoxing wine (available in Chinese markets) or medium-dry sherry

2 teaspoons cornstarch

2 teaspoons peeled and minced fresh
   ginger

1 1/2 teaspoons Asian sesame oil

1 teaspoon sugar

1/4 teaspoon freshly ground white pepper

30 wonton or *siu mai* wrappers

DIPPING SAUCE

1/4 cup soy sauce

1/4 cup rice vinegar

3/4 to 1 teaspoon hot sesame oil, to your
   taste

1. Cut the tofu into 4 sections and place in a linen dish towel. Gather the towel edges together and twist to remove as much water as possible. Transfer the tofu to a medium-size bowl and mash with a fork until smooth. Add the remaining dumpling ingredients except the wrappers and mix well. Set aside for 30 minutes.

2. Fill the rice cooker bowl one-quarter full of water, close the cover, and set for the regular cycle. If the water boils before you are ready to cook the *siu mai*, flip the switch to the Keep Warm position (switch back for cooking).

3. Place the wrappers on the side of your workspace, covered with damp paper towels to prevent drying. If using wonton wrappers, trim the edges to form circles. Place 1 heaping teaspoon of the filling in the center of each wrapper. Use your fingers to gather up and pleat the wrapper around the filling to form an open-topped cup; carefully squeeze the middle to give it a waist, and flare it to make a slightly open end.

4. When all the dumplings are made, arrange them, filling side down, without crowding, on a lightly greased glass pie plate (or other heatproof plate or shallow dish) that will fit inside your steamer basket with some clearance all around. Set the plate on the steamer basket. Place the steamer basket over the boiling water in the cooker and close the cover. Set a timer for 12 minutes and steam until the filling in heated through (cut one open to test).

5. While the dumplings are steaming, make the dipping sauce. Place the soy sauce, vinegar, and sesame oil in a small bowl; whisk to combine.

6. Serve the dumplings hot, with little individual bowls of dipping sauce.

ming-man's pearl balls

These steamed meatballs covered with sticky rice (the pearls) are tasty additions to a dim sum meal. They also make great party food. Traditionally made with ground pork, we prefer a lighter version made with ground chicken. A mix of ground beef and ground turkey breast is another lower-fat yet flavorful choice. Pearl balls were the first thing Julie's friend Ming-man Hsieh learned to cook as a girl in Taiwan. We adapted the recipe only slightly.

MACHINE: Medium (6-cup) or large
(10-cup) rice cooker; on/off only

CYCLE: Regular

YIELD: About 20 rice balls

1 cup sticky rice, soaked in cold water for
several hours or overnight

2 dried shiitake mushrooms

1 tablespoon dried shrimp

1 large carrot

1 whole canned bamboo shoot or $1/4$ cup
sliced canned bamboo shoots

1 pound lean ground chicken, lean ground
pork, or half lean ground beef and half
lean ground turkey

1 teaspoon ground ginger

$1/2$ teaspoon salt

$1/4$ teaspoon freshly ground black pepper

$1/4$ teaspoon freshly ground white pepper

1 tablespoon soy sauce

2 teaspoons Asian sesame oil

1 tablespoon Shaoxsing wine (available in
Chinese markets) or medium-dry sherry

Pinch of sugar

2 to 3 large lettuce, Napa cabbage, or
chard leaves (stems discarded), for
lining steamer basket

1. Drain the rice thoroughly. Spread it on a plate and set aside.

2. Place the mushrooms and dried shrimp in a microwave-safe container just large enough to hold them. Barely cover them with water, then cover the container tightly with plastic wrap. Microwave on high for 2 minutes. Let cool and drain, reserving the soaking liquid. (Or let the mushrooms and shrimp soak in hot water for 30 minutes to 1 hour.)

3. Fill the rice cooker bowl one-quarter full of water, close the cover, and set for the regular cycle. If the water boils before you are ready to cook the pearl balls, flip the switch to the Keep Warm position (switch back for cooking).

4. Meanwhile, peel the carrot, cut into chunks, and finely chop in a food processor. Measure $1/4$ cup and reserve the rest to use as a garnish. Chop the bamboo shoot in the same manner. Measure $1/4$ cup and reserve the rest for another use.

5. When the mushrooms are cool enough to handle, trim off and discard the tough stems. Chop the mushrooms and puree them in a food processor with the shrimp and 2 tablespoons of the reserved soaking liquid. Add an additional tablespoon of the soaking liquid, if needed, to obtain a chunky puree.

6. Place the ground meat in a medium-size bowl. Add the chopped carrot and bamboo shoot and the mushroom-shrimp puree. Add the remaining ingredients except the rice and lettuce leaves. Gently mix with a wooden spatula or a large spoon to blend the mixture thoroughly without packing it down.

7. Line the bottom of the steamer basket with the lettuce, cabbage, or chard leaves. Shape the meat mixture into small meatballs, each about the size of a walnut or smaller. As each meatball is shaped, roll it in the rice so that it is covered as thoroughly as possible. Arrange as many meatballs as can fit, without touching, on the lettuce leaves in the steamer tray. (Leave a little space between the meatballs. Their rice coating expands as it cooks, and they will stick together if they touch.) Place a pinch of the reserved chopped carrot on top of each pearl ball.

8. Place the steamer basket over the boiling water in the rice cooker and close the cover. Set a timer for 12 minutes, and steam until the meatballs are cooked

through; cut into one meatball to test (the exact cooking time will depend on the size of your meatballs). Repeat until all of the meatballs are formed and cooked. Serve hot.

barbecued pork buns

(char siu bau)

Bau buns, encasing a filling of *char siu* pork, are a popular dim sum item in Cantonese restaurants. They were a specialty in the nineteenth-century Cantonese dim sum restaurants catering to the tastes of English merchant traders and Russian immigrants. The traditional way to cook them is to steam them until fluffy white, a snap in the stacked rice cooker baskets. For that real Chinatown flavor, you must buy the meat ready-made from an Asian grocery in the deli department (hanging next to the Peking ducks), where it is cooked the traditional way—in a hanging oven. There is an age-old technique to shaping the buns, usually made with a homemade yeast dough, and it will take you a few tries to get them right. In lieu of the homemade yeast dough, we used commercial frozen bread dough and it was a smash hit! These buns will be a bit smaller than those you buy in Chinatown bakeries.

MACHINE: Large (10-cup) rice cooker; on/off only
CYCLE: Regular
YIELD: 24 buns

SAUCE
1 1/2 cups chicken stock
1 1/2 tablespoons oyster sauce
1 tablespoon Shaoxing wine (available in Chinese markets) or medium-dry sherry
1 tablespoon hoisin sauce
1 tablespoon soy sauce
2 teaspoons ketchup
1 teaspoon sugar
2 tablespoons cornstarch

FILLING
4 cups finely diced prepared *char siu* (Chinese barbecued pork)
1/2 cup diced yellow onion

Two 27-ounce packages Bridgeford frozen dinner rolls (each package has 3 loaves of 6 pull-apart rolls), thawed
1 large egg white beaten with 1 teaspoon water and 1/4 teaspoon sugar until foamy, for egg glaze

1. *Make the sauce:* Place the stock, oyster sauce, wine, hoisin sauce, soy sauce, ketchup, and sugar in a heavy saucepan; stir to combine. Place 1/4 cup of the mixture in a small bowl and whisk in the cornstarch; pour back into the saucepan. Cook over medium-high heat, stirring constantly, until thickened and smooth. The sauce should be the consistency of thin mayonnaise. Remove from the heat and cool in the refrigerator.
2. *Make the filling:* Place the pork in a medium-size bowl. Add the onion and sauce and mix with a spoon. Cover and refrigerate for at least 4 hours but no longer than overnight.
3. Meanwhile, let the bread dough rise according to the package directions. Turn the

risen bread dough out onto a clean wooden work surface. Use 1½ dinner rolls for each bun, flattening them together into a thick round. Place the round of dough on the work surface (don't shape on cool marble or ceramic because it will stiffen the dough). With the palm of your hand, press down on the center and rotate your palm, spiraling out from the center. The dough will grow into a 3- to 4-inch-diameter circle (not lopsided, please) with a pretty spiral pattern radiating from the center like a flower. Don't use any flour. Repeat with the remaining rolls.

4. *Assemble the buns:* Cut twenty-four 3-inch squares of parchment paper and place them on a large baking sheet to hold the filled *bau*. Place a heaping tablespoonful (we use an oversized spoon that holds about 2 tablespoons) of the chilled filling in the center of a round of dough; don't overfill or the filling will fall out. Bring the dough up over the filling and, holding the two sides between your thumb and third finger, twist the edges to encase the filling. Place the bun, twist side down, on a parchment square on the baking sheet. Repeat with the remaining dough rounds and filling, spacing them at least 4 inches apart. Cover loosely with a damp tea towel and let rise at room temperature until puffy, about 45 minutes.

5. Fill the rice cooker bowl one-quarter full of water, close the cover, and set for the regular cycle. If the water boils before you are ready to steam the buns, flip the switch to the Keep Warm position (switch back for cooking), but you want a vigorous boil with lots of steam for these.

6. Brush each *bau* with the egg glaze. Arrange the *bau*, each on its own square of parchment, in two steamer baskets; we do the steaming in two batches, so it is 6 *bao* per basket. Place the stacked baskets over the boiling water in the rice cooker and close the cover. Set a timer to 18 minutes and steam until the *bao* are big and puffy. Don't remove the cover before 15 minutes have elapsed; open the cover away from yourself to prevent burns. Remove the *bau* from the steamer basket by slipping a spatula under the parchment paper; place on a wire cooling rack.

7. Serve the *bau* the day they are cooked, warm or at room temperature, or freeze in plastic freezer bags for up to 2 months. Reheat in a microwave (no need to thaw) for 2 to 3 minutes for a quick dinner.

honey flower rolls

Plain steamed breads are good served with roasted Peking duck, roast ham, roast or fried chicken, and even roast suckling pig. Being a breadmaker, Beth couldn't resist trying a steamed bread in the tiered baskets of the rice cooker, just like she has seen in Chinatown. While the rolls cook, you can watch the steam swirl around and the rolls rise into a piece of edible sculpture. This flower reminds us of a chrysanthemum. Be sure to use bleached white flour—since that will make the whitest rolls—in combination with some bread flour, which will make a springy dough suitable for the steaming. Since the rolls are not baked in an oven, there will be no crust. The rolls are pure white, fluffy, and tender-soft from the first bite to the last. You can mix the dough in a bread machine, as it is written here, or by hand. While these are usually eaten with other dim sum, they are also good with jam and a cup of tea. Vital wheat gluten is sold in supermarkets near the flour as a bread dough enhancer.

MACHINE: Large (10-cup) rice cooker; on/off only

CYCLE: Regular

YIELD: 10 steamed rolls

1 cup plus 2 tablespoons water

1¹/₂ tablespoons vegetable oil or Asian sesame oil

¹/₂ cup bread flour

2³/₄ cups bleached all-purpose flour

3 tablespoons mild honey

1 tablespoon vital wheat gluten

1 teaspoon salt

1¹/₂ teaspoons bread machine yeast, fast-acting yeast, or SAF fast-acting yeast, or 1 teaspoon active dry yeast

Unbleached all-purpose flour, for dusting

1 teaspoon baking powder

2 teaspoons Asian sesame oil or nonstick cooking spray

1. Place everything except the last 3 ingredients in a bread machine according to the order in the manufacturer's instructions. Program for the Dough cycle; press Start. When the full rising cycle has finished and the machine beeps, open the lid and gently deflate the dough. Close the lid and let the dough rise a second time (set a timer for 45 minutes); this second rise makes for a nice light texture.

2. Gently deflate the dough and turn it out onto a work surface sprinkled with a few teaspoons of unbleached flour and the baking powder. Flatten the dough slightly with your palms and begin gently kneading it; the dough will effortlessly pick up the flour–baking powder mixture from the work surface. The flour mixture will be incorporated quickly while you knead and the dough will be smooth and springy to the touch. Cover the dough ball with a clean tea towel and let rest on the work surface for 15 minutes to relax the dough.

3. Cut ten 3½-inch squares of parchment paper. Divide the dough into 2 equal portions. Cover one portion with the tea towel. With a rolling pin, roll 1 portion of dough into a 12 x 8-inch rectangle. Leaving a 1-inch border all around the edges, brush the surface evenly with 1 teaspoon of the sesame oil or coat it with a film of the cooking spray. Roll up jelly-roll fashion, starting from the long edge, and pinch the seam to seal. The cylinder will be only 1½ to 2 inches in diameter. Using a sharp chef's knife, with a gentle sawing motion, cut the cylinder into 10 equal portions, each separate portion being about 1⅛ inches thick, taking care not to squash the cylinder. Repeat with the remaining portion of dough.

4. To shape the flower rolls, press 2 separate slices side by side with the cut sides facing front and back, rather than up and down. Hold a chopstick horizontally and gently press it down the center of the two slices, all the way down to the work surface; you will push out and fan the rolled edges (this area will puff and expand more during the steaming to create the open

flower petal effect) while attaching the two slices at the same time. Place each roll on a square of parchment and set in the steamer basket, leaving at least 1 inch of space between them on all sides; 6 flower rolls will fit easily in each basket. Cover loosely with the tea towel draped over the basket while forming the other rolls.

5. Let the rolls rise at room temperature until puffy and doubled in bulk, 30 to 40 minutes. (The rolls can be refrigerated on a baking sheet before this last rise, covered tightly with a double layer of plastic wrap, leaving the rolls to rise slowly and be steamed up to 8 hours later, if necessary. Bring the pans to room temperature and let rest for 20 minutes while preheating the water in the rice cooker.)

6. Fifteen minutes before cooking the rolls, fill the rice cooker bowl one-quarter full of water, close the cover, and set for the regular cycle. If the water boils before you are ready to steam the flower rolls, flip the switch to the Keep Warm position (and switch back for cooking), but you want a vigorous boil with lots of steam for cooking these.

7. Place the steamer baskets over the boiling water in the cooker and close the cover. Set a timer for 20 minutes and steam until the rolls are puffy and dry to the touch. When done, remove the cover quickly so that no drops of water drip into the baskets, and remove the baskets from the cooker. Using a spatula, transfer the flower rolls to a wire rack or serving platter, if serving immediately.

8. If not serving immediately, let cool completely on the racks and store in plastic bags in the refrigerator for up to 5 days, or in the freezer for up to 2 months. To reheat, steam the cold rolls for 7 to 10 minutes or microwave for a few minutes on high. Eat immediately.

sticky rice in lotus leaves

This is a most extravagant dim sum! These fragrant and savory packets are rustic in appearance, thanks to their all-natural covering: dried lotus leaves, which can be purchased in Chinese markets. Lotus leaves are surprisingly large, especially when you realize that in the package, they are folded in half! Some people never cook sticky rice (glutinous rice, also called sweet rice) in their rice cookers, believing it must be steamed in a tray over boiling water for the best texture. This is generally true, but in this case, the rice is mixed with so many other ingredients that we feel it is all right. If you wish, feel free to steam the soaked rice in a cheesecloth-lined steamer tray for about 25 minutes instead of using the rice cooker. Dried shrimp has a rather strong flavor; if you don't like it, use 1/4 pound shelled fresh shrimp instead, adding it to the skillet when the chicken is almost cooked. Chinese dried sausages are available in Asian markets; use another cooked sausage (like kielbasa) if you can't find them. If you can't find dried chestnuts, and don't feel up to shelling fresh ones, you can leave them out. They are a frill, though a tasty one. Making these is a bit of a production, like making tamales. Also like tamales, these freeze well. Reheat in a steamer or in the microwave.

MACHINE: Large (10-cup) rice cooker;
on/off only

CYCLE: **Regular**

YIELD: Serves 6 to 12 as an appetizer or
snack

2¹/₄ cups (3 rice cooker cups) sticky rice

2³/₄ cups water

6 lotus leaves

2 tablespoons dried shrimp or ¹/₄ pound
 raw shrimp, shelled and deveined

¹/₄ pound boneless, skinless chicken
 (about ¹/₂ breast or 1¹/₂ thighs),
 trimmed of fat

2 teaspoons plus 2 tablespoons soy sauce

1 teaspoon plus 2 tablespoons Shaoxing
 wine (available in Chinese markets) or
 medium-dry sherry

1¹/₄ teaspoons Asian sesame oil

1 clove garlic, minced

1 teaspoon peeled and minced fresh
 ginger

10 dried chestnuts (available in Asian
 markets) or cooked and peeled fresh
 chestnuts (optional)

1 to 2 ounces Chinese dried sausage
 (about 1 sausage) or cooked smoked
 sausage such as kielbasa

¹/₂ cup diced ham

1 green onion, white and tender green
 parts, thinly sliced

¹/₄ cup grated carrot

¹/₄ teaspoon salt, or to taste

¹/₈ teaspoon ground white pepper or
 freshly ground black pepper, or to taste

1. Up to 4 hours ahead and at least 1 hour ahead, wash the rice in a bowl or strainer until the water runs almost clear. Place the rice in the rice cooker with the water. Let the rice soak for 1 to 4 hours.

2. At the end of the soaking time, set the rice cooker for the regular cycle. When the machine switches to the Keep Warm cycle, let the rice steam for 10 to 15 minutes. Stir the rice gently but thoroughly with a wooden or plastic rice paddle or wooden spoon. Hold the rice on Keep Warm until you are ready to use it.

3. One hour ahead, soak the lotus leaves in hot water. They are large and you may have to do this in a large stockpot or a scrubbed and well-rinsed sink. Let them soak for 1 hour.

4. Half an hour ahead, put the dried shrimp in a small cup or bowl with hot water to cover. Let the shrimp soak for 30 minutes, then drain and coarsely chop.

5. Cut the chicken into ¾-inch cubes. Place it in a small bowl with 2 teaspoons of the soy sauce, 1 teaspoon of the wine, ¼ teaspoon of the sesame oil, the garlic, and ginger; stir to combine. Let the chicken marinate for 30 minutes.

6. Place the dried chestnuts in a small saucepan with water to cover. Bring to a boil and boil them for 15 to 20 minutes. Drain and cut into quarters. Slice the sausage about ¼ inch thick. If you are using kielbasa or another thick sausage, cut the slices into half-moons.

7. Transfer the rice to a large bowl. Wash out the rice cooker bowl and fill it one-quarter to one-third full of water, close the cover, and set for the regular cycle. If the water boils before you are ready, flip the switch to the Keep Warm position.

8. Coat a small nonstick skillet with nonstick cooking spray. Heat the skillet over medium-high heat. Add the chicken with its marinade to the skillet and stir-fry until it is just barely cooked through. Transfer the chicken to the bowl with the rice. Add the sausage to the skillet and stir-fry until it gives up some of its fat. Transfer the sausage to the bowl and add the ham, green onion, carrot, and remaining 2 tablespoons soy sauce, 2 tablespoons wine, and 1 teaspoon sesame oil. Stir gently with a plastic or wooden rice paddle or wooden spoon to mix thoroughly. Taste and adjust the seasoning, if necessary, with salt, pepper, soy sauce, wine, or sesame oil.

9. Prepare a large work surface. Lift the lotus leaves carefully out of the soaking water. Open them carefully and cut one in half along the fold line. Place a lotus leaf half on your work surface, green side down, rounded side facing away from you. Put about ½ cup of the rice mixture in a small mound in the center of the leaf. Fold in first one side, then the other. Then fold the bottom and roll up the leaf into a small square or rectangular packet. Some people tie the packets with twine, but this isn't necessary if you handle them carefully. Place the packet seam side down on a plate. Repeat with the remaining lotus leaves and filling.

10. Stack as many leaves as you can in your steamer basket or tray, resting them seam side down or leaning them against each other so they don't unwrap. (We can fit 6 lotus leaf bundles in one steamer tray.) Place the tray over the boiling water in the rice cooker and close the cover. Steam for 30 minutes. Remove the bundles with tongs.

11. Unwrap the bundles to eat the sticky rice; the leaf is not edible.

DOLMAS

Dolma translates from the original Arabic as "something stuffed." While this word can refer to anything stuffed, from a vegetable to a fruit, the most recognizable dolma is rice-stuffed grape leaves braised in a lemony bath. Dolmas are a very popular little bite in Mediterranean and Middle Eastern cuisines.

Grape leaves make a flavorful wrapper. Consider them as a Mexican cook regards a corn husk, a Thai looks at banana leaves, the Polish look at cabbage, and the Japanese cook looks at seaweed. Grape leaves end up clinging to the foods they envelop, lending a special flavor. You can buy jars of commercially preserved grape leaves in brine or, if you have access to a vineyard or a lone grapevine in your backyard, preserve your own. Use fresh ones in spring and summer and your preserved canned leaves during the winter.

herb and rice dolmas

While many dolma fillings contain lamb or lentils, this recipe has a great rice, vegetable, herb, goat cheese, fruit, and nut filling. No matter what filling you decide on, this is the basic procedure to use for preparing the grape leaves and filling and steaming them.

MACHINE: Large (10-cup) rice cooker; on/off or fuzzy logic
CYCLE: Quick Cook and/or regular
YIELD: 28 dolmas; serves 6 to 8 as an appetizer

YOUR OWN PRESERVED GRAPE LEAVES

Pick the tender leaves early in the summer for the best tasting and most palatable leaves, and leave at least an inch of stem attached (you will use the stem to handle the wet leaves). Tasters say the best varieties of grape for their leaves are Thompson Seedless, Chardonnay, and Emperor.

Sort the leaves (rounded lobes are better than deeply lobed; they are more tender) and discard ones that have holes or are torn. Gently rinse under cold running water.

In a large saucepan filled with water, add 2 tablespoons of fine salt per quart of water. Bring to a boil. Slide the leaves into the boiling water and blanch for 2 to 3 minutes. Lift out with a large slotted spoon or pour through a large colander to drain. Remove each leaf, one at a time, pat dry with a paper towel, and uncurl the edges. The grape leaves are now ready for stuffing.

If you want to preserve them for up to 2 weeks, combine 1 cup water and 1 cup lemon juice in a saucepan; bring to a boil. Stack the wet leaves in piles of 10 and roll up like a cigar. Pack into a sterile pint canning jar. You will be able to pack quite a few rolls into each jar. Pour the hot liquid into each jar, covering the leaves completely. Cover and store in the refrigerator for up to 2 weeks or pressure-can for longer storage.

RICE

3/4 cup basmati rice

3 tablespoons olive oil

1 small yellow onion, finely chopped

1 clove garlic, minced

1 cup water

Pinch of salt

One 4-inch cinnamon stick

1/4 cup dried currants

2 tablespoons minced fresh Italian parsley
    leaves

1 tablespoon minced fresh mint leaves or
    dill

Grated zest of 1/2 small lemon

3 tablespoons pine nuts or chopped
    blanched almonds, toasted
    (page 68)

DOLMAS

1 jar (35 + loose leaves) grape leaves

5 ounces goat cheese

2 cups water

2 tablespoons olive oil

1/4 cup fresh lemon juice

Lemon wedges or cold plain yogurt, for
    serving

1. Place the rice in a fine strainer or bowl, rinse with cold water two to four times, and drain. The water will be chalky and slightly foamy. Spread the wet rice out with your hands on a clean tea towel on the counter. Let air-dry for at least 1 hour, until cooking time.

2. *Make the rice:* Set the rice cooker for the Quick Cook or regular cycle. Place the olive oil in the rice cooker bowl. When hot, add the onion and garlic and cook, stirring a few times, until softened, about 2 minutes. Add the rice and cook, stirring, until all the grains are evenly coated and hot. Add the water, salt, cinnamon stick, and currants; stir just to combine. Close the cover and let the rice complete the cycle. When the machine switches to the Keep Warm cycle, let the rice steam for 10 minutes.

3. Rinse the grape leaves under cold running water and drain on layers of paper towels. With kitchen shears, cut off the stems. Set aside.

4. Open the cover, remove the rice bowl, discard the cinnamon stick, and fluff the rice with a wooden or plastic rice paddle or wooden spoon. Stir in the parsley, mint, lemon zest, and pine nuts.

5. *Make the dolmas:* To fill, place a perfect leaf, shiny side down, rib side up, on your work surface. Place a tablespoon of the rice mixture and a piece of goat cheese (about ½ teaspoon) on top in the center of the leaf. Fold the sides in as for an envelope and roll up jelly-roll fashion to make a small, plump cylinder. If you have any tears, snip off a lobe and patch from the inside. Fill all the leaves in the same fashion. You will have enough filling for about 28 leaves.

6. Wash and dry the rice cooker bowl and return it to the machine body. Spray with nonstick cooking spray and line with the extra grape leaves, in an overlapping pattern. Place the dolmas in a single layer, seam side down and close side by side, on the bed of grape leaves. Add a second layer of dolmas.

7. In a measuring cup, combine the water, olive oil, and lemon juice. Pour over the dolmas in the rice cooker; the liquid should not come more than halfway up the sides (you may have extra). Close the cover and set for the regular cycle. After the cooking liquid comes to a simmer, cook the dolmas until they are firm to the touch and the leaf is tender when cut in half, 20 to 25 minutes.

8. Remove the cover carefully and let the dolmas cool slightly.

9. Serve the dolmas warm or at room temperature, with lemon wedges or plain yogurt. Or let them cool, place in a flat covered container, refrigerate overnight, and serve chilled or at room temperature.

dolmas stuffed with lamb, rice, and almonds

This is a hearty version of the ever-popular stuffed grape leaves, made slightly sweet by the addition of raisins. We like to serve it with tart plain yogurt for balance. Because these dolmas are made with raw meat and rice, they are not steamed but cooked in water to cover.

MACHINE: Large (10-cup) rice cooker; on/off or fuzzy logic
CYCLE: Regular
YIELD: About 35 dolmas; serves 8 to 10 as an appetizer, 6 as a main dish

FILLING

1 pound lean ground lamb

1/2 cup long-grain white rice

1/4 cup minced onion

1/2 cup dark raisins

1/2 cup slivered blanched almonds

1 tablespoon finely chopped fresh mint
   leaves or 1 teaspoon dried mint leaves,
   crumbled

1 1/2 teaspoons salt

1/2 teaspoon ground cinnamon

1/2 teaspoon ground allspice

1/2 teaspoon freshly ground black pepper

DOLMAS

1 jar (8 to 10 ounces) preserved grape
   leaves

2 tablespoons olive oil

2 cloves garlic

2 to 3 sprigs fresh mint (optional)

Cold plain yogurt, for serving

1. *Make the filling:* In a large bowl, gently blend the lamb, rice, onion, raisins, almonds, mint, salt, cinnamon, allspice, and pepper. You can do this with your hands or with a fork or mixing spoon, but take care not to mash the meat.

2. Remove the grape leaves from the jar and carefully unroll the stack. Gently rinse the grape leaves with cool water and allow them to drain. Cover the bottom of the rice cooker bowl with 1 or 2 grape leaves. This is a good use for any leaves that tore as you removed them from the jar.

3. *Make the dolmas:* To stuff the grape leaves, put 1 leaf on a plate, vein side up, stem end nearest you. Place about 1 table-spoon of filling on the center of the leaf and use your fingers to gently shape it into

a little log, arranged horizontally across the leaf. Fold both sides of the leaf in over the filling, then roll up the leaf. Place the rolled leaf, seam side down, in the bottom of the rice cooker bowl. Continue to stuff and roll leaves until you run out of filling. Arrange the dolmas in neat layers in the rice bowl. Top with the olive oil, garlic, and mint sprigs, if using.

4. Cover the dolmas with a small, heavy, heatproof plate to keep them from un-rolling during the cooking. Add water to the rice cooker bowl, pouring around the plate to cover. Close the cover and set for the regular cycle. Set a timer for 45 minutes. Add more water as necessary to keep the dolmas covered during the cooking time. Test for doneness, the dolmas should be tender; cook a bit longer if they are not.

5. When the timer sounds, turn off the cooker and allow the leaves to cool some-what in the liquid before removing them.

6. Serve the dolmas warm or at room tem-perature, with plain yogurt for dipping.

dolmas with figs and sun-dried tomatoes

These are the most intensely flavored dolmas we have ever eaten. Five cups sounds like a lot of chopped onion, but don't skimp. Their long simmer in fragrant olive oil leaves the onion soft and mild—a perfect complement to the tang of the tomatoes and gritty sweetness of the figs. This recipe is from Washington, D.C., freelance writer Joyce Gemperlein, a friend from her days at the *San Jose Mercury News*, where she was both food editor and the author of a wildly popular food column in the Sunday magazine.

MACHINE: Large (10-cup) rice cooker; on/off or fuzzy logic

CYCLE: Quick Cook and/or regular

YIELD: Serves 10 to 12

FILLING

1 cup extra virgin olive oil

5 cups finely chopped onion (about 5 or 6 large onions)

3 tablespoons pine nuts

1 cup long-grain white rice

1/2 cup minced dehydrated sun-dried tomatoes (not marinated)

3 tablespoons chopped fresh mint leaves

1 tablespoon chopped fresh dill

3/4 teaspoon ground cinnamon

1/4 teaspoon ground allspice

1/4 teaspoon freshly grated nutmeg

1/8 teaspoon ground cloves

3 tablespoons chopped dried figs

3/4 cup hot water

6 tablespoons fresh lemon juice

Salt

1 jar (8 to 10 ounces) preserved grape leaves, rinsed and drained

1. Make the filling. Set the cooker for the Quick Cook or regular cycle. Place ¾ cup of the olive oil in the rice cooker bowl. When hot, add the onion and pine nuts, stirring to combine with a plastic or wooden rice paddle or wooden spoon. Close the cover and cook for about 20 minutes.

Stir in the rice, close the cover, and cook for about 5 minutes. Stir in the tomatoes, close the cover, and cook for a few more minutes. Stir in the herbs, spices, and figs. Add the hot water, 2 tablespoons of the lemon juice, and salt to taste; stir to combine. Close the cover and let the cycle complete.

2. When the machine switches to the Keep Warm cycle, let the rice steam for 10 minutes. Open the cover and fluff the rice with a plastic or wooden rice paddle or wooden spoon. Transfer the filling to a bowl and let cool. Meanwhile, wash the rice cooker bowl and set aside.

3. Stuff the grape leaves as directed in the recipe on page 275 until you have used up all of the filling. Place some unused leaves on the bottom of the rice cooker bowl and arrange the stuffed dolmas side by side in layers. Mix 1 cup water, a little salt, and the remaining ¼ cup olive oil and pour over the dolmas. Place a small heatproof plate over them to keep them in place. Close the cover and set the cooker for the Quick Cook or regular cycle. Set a timer for 45 minutes. Check for doneness; the leaves should be tender. You may have to add water if it cooks away.

4. When the dolmas are done, open the rice cooker and transfer the rice bowl to a heatproof surface. Add the remaining 4 tablespoons lemon juice and let the dolmas cool, uncovered, in their liquid. Drain off the liquid and refrigerate. These will keep up to 1 week, if tightly covered. Serve at room temperature.

TAMALES

Tamales are the epitome of Mexican food and one of the classic tastes of the Hispanic kitchen. Tamales are "mother" food. The dough is made from masa harina or masa flour, ground corn that has been soaked in lime to make the corn kernel softer and more cohesive than regular cornmeal. It is the flour used to give tortillas and tamales that wonderful strong corn flavor that is so characteristic. The dough is made by kneading the masa harina with fat into a dough called masa.

Fillings for tamales are often made from shredded chicken or pork flavored with chile and spices, but once you become familiar with tamales, or have traveled in Mexico, you can find as many meat or vegetable fillings as there are cooks. One of the most luscious and satisfying fillings is made from fresh corn, green chiles, and cheese, but other fillings include beans, pumpkin, quinoa, diced cooked potatoes, mushrooms, roasted peppers, and shrimp. There are versions with fruit, coconut, and nuts, although savory ones are the most common. Tamales are little individual packages of filling and dough wrapped in dried corn husks, then steamed. You can also use fresh banana leaves or fresh corn husks for wrapping, if available. Your choice of wrapping contributes to the flavor of the tamale, serves as part of the covering during storage, and keeps the tamale warm while serving. Tamales can be perfectly steamed by laying them down tightly side by side (not standing up; the insides of the tamale will drain out during the steaming into the water) in the steamer baskets of the large 10-inch rice cooker, well above the simmering water bath.

Tamales were made by the Aztec Indians and served for religious celebrations, but most of the North and South American Indians have steamed cornmeal breads. Today, tamales are an essential food for Christmas holiday parties, weddings, fiestas, and family gatherings among Mexican-Americans. One of Beth's favorite feasting memories is of a Christmas Day brunch at her friend chef Oscar Mariscal's house. Homemade tamales, guacamole, and fresh salsa were laid out picnic style on the living room floor, complete with lace tablecloth and silver candelabra. Consider it an honor being invited to a *tamalada*, the tamale fest where a group of family and friends make tamales together.

Tamales have a reputation for being tricky and time-consuming. The tricky part is mastering the technique for rolling and tying them, and the time-consuming part is that everything is accomplished in a logical sequence over a few days. Making tamales is a task often done by groups of seasoned tamale veterans, where the atmosphere is spontaneous and jocular. It is an opportunity to make dozens of tamales, which keep well in the freezer.

The Tamale Schedule

1. Assemble the ingredients and purchase pure masa (wet masa dough) or dried masa harina (the flour) from a Mexican grocery or tortilla factory.

2. The day before making the tamales, make the meat filling and sauce. If you are making a vegetable filling, the filling and assembly can happen on the same day. Prepare the desired tamale filling according to your recipe. Place the filling in a container, cover, and refrigerate until ready to use.

3. The day of making the tamales, start by soaking the corn husks. These come in plastic packages available in specialty food stores or the Latin food section of your supermarket. Carefully remove the brittle husks from their packages and separate the individual husks; there may be dust and grit. You will usually be using 2 husks per tamale (plan on 3 to 5 tamales per person, depending on the size), so plan on a few extra in case some are too small. Place the husks in a large bowl or the sink and cover with hot water; put a plate on top to keep the husks submerged. Soak for 1 to 3 hours, until the husks have absorbed the water and are pliable. Drain in a colander and lay out on layers of clean tea towels or paper towels. Tear a few of the husks into long, thin strips for use as ties if you're not using twine.

4. Prepare the masa dough according to your recipe. While masa tamale dough is best used the day it is made, it can also rest overnight, covered, in the refrigerator, then be resoftened by whipping it in a food processor or electric mixer. Use home-rendered or top-quality lard, never hydrogenated *manteca*, the lard sold in red boxes in the supermarket; it has no flavor. In place of lard, you can use a combination of butter and vegetable shortening.

5. Fill and roll the tamales according to your recipe.

6. Steam the tamales. If using a metal rack instead of steaming baskets, place the rack in the rice cooker bowl. Fill the bowl with at least 2 inches and no more than 5 inches of water. If using the rack, the water should come to just below the rack; you do not want the rack submerged in the boiling water. Close the cover and set for the regu-

lar cycle. Place the tamales in single layers in the top and bottom steamer baskets, or on the rack. It is important that the tamales do not touch the water during steaming, or they will be soggy. There should be some space between the rack or baskets and the water to provide enough room to create the steam for cooking.

Lay the tamales, seam side down, tightly side by side (rather than standing them upright) to prevent them from absorbing too much steam and getting soggy. If there is a lot of extra space around the sides, pack with extra corn husks. Cover the tamales with a layer of 4 or 5 corn husks. Set the second steamer basket on top, filled in the same manner. When the water comes to a boil, place the baskets in the rice cooker and close the cover. Set a timer for 1 hour; the tamales will steam for 1 to 1½ hours, depending on their size. Make sure to check the water level periodically and refill as necessary by pouring in hot water on the sides of the tamales, never directly over them. This is important since the tamales will taste scorched if the water evaporates.

After 1 hour, remove a tamale with metal tongs and peel back the husk to check for doneness. Or you can pierce the tamale with a bamboo skewer. The dough should be firm and no longer sticky or mushy, and separate easily from the husk wrapping. Break off a section of dough to check the filling. Using metal tongs, remove the tamales from the basket. Let fresh tamales rest for 15 minutes at room temperature before serving to set the dough and meld the flavors.

7. The tamales can be cooled in the steamer baskets, then stored in zipper-top plastic bags in the refrigerator for up to 4 days. You can freeze the cooked tamales or even freeze the raw tamales for up to 1 month and steam later before serving (after thawing them overnight in the refrigerator in their wrappings).

8. To reheat cooked tamales, fill the rice cooker bowl with 5 inches of hot water and

There are never enough vegetable fillings for tamales, so here are a few extra.

Winter Squash and Cilantro Tamales

2 tablespoons unsalted butter
$1/2$ medium-size white onion, chopped
$1/2$ medium-size red bell pepper, seeded and chopped
$3^1/2$ cups peeled, seeded, and diced pumpkin or other winter squash, such as butternut or blue Hubbard
1 teaspoon salt
Dash of ground white pepper
1 cup chicken or vegetable stock
$1/4$ cup chopped fresh cilantro leaves

1. In a large skillet, melt the butter over medium heat. Add the onion and bell pepper and cook, stirring, until softened. Add the squash, salt, white pepper, and stock and simmer, partially covered, until the squash is tender.
2. Remove the cover, increase the heat to high, and cook until the liquid is evaporated. Mash a few times (leave some chunks) and stir in the cilantro. Let cool to room temperature or refrigerate.

Corn and Black Bean Tamales

2 cups fresh or frozen (and thawed) baby corn kernels
$1^1/4$ cups cooked black beans, drained and rinsed
One 7-ounce jar roasted sweet red peppers, drained on paper towels and minced, or 2 red bell peppers, roasted, peeled, seeded, and minced
2 teaspoons ground cumin
2 teaspoons chili powder
$1^1/2$ teaspoons salt
6 ounces goat cheese, crumbled

1. Place the corn, beans, roasted peppers, cumin, chili powder, and salt in a medium-size bowl; stir to combine. Refrigerate until needed.
2. When you fill the tamales, sprinkle them with some goat cheese before wrapping.

bring to a boil. Place the tamales in the steamer basket, close the cover, and steam for 15 to 20 minutes. You can also microwave individual tamales in their wrappers for 1 minute on high.

jacquie's rancho tamales

This exceptional recipe for tamales comes from food writer and California rancho cooking expert Jacquie McMahan, our very own tamale princess. Rancho tamales are the *grandes* of the genre—nice and big. You will be buying freshly ground masa, which is a wet dough, rather than masa harina, the flour that needs to be reconstituted before making it into dough. Be sure to buy your masa as fresh as you can get it, not *masa preparada*—the already prepared tamale dough, which is often in similar packaging, as it already has cheap lard and seasonings added; read the label carefully. You can get fresh masa in a specialty market, but some supermarkets carry fresh masa during the Christmas holidays. Set aside two days for preparation so that all you have to do is cook the tamales when you want to serve them. You will be using the rice cooker to steam the dried chiles for the sauce, as well as for cooking the finished tamales.

MACHINE: Large (10-cup) rice cooker; on/off only
CYCLE: Regular
YIELD: 30 large tamales

FILLING

3¹/₂ pounds boneless pork butt, trimmed of most of the fat
2 tablespoons vegetable oil
1 large yellow onion, cut into quarters
2 cloves garlic, cut in half
1 tablespoon dried oregano
Freshly ground black pepper

CHILE SAUCE

15 dried California or New Mexico chiles
About 1¹/₂ cups water
2 tablespoons vegetable oil or lard
2 tablespoons all-purpose flour
1 clove garlic, minced
1 teaspoon salt
1 tablespoon cider vinegar
2 teaspoons dried oregano
1 teaspoon cumin seeds

FOR MAKING THE TAMALES

2 packages wide dried corn husks
1¹/₂ cups pitted black olives

DOUGH

3 cups fresh leaf lard (1¹/₂ pounds), or a combination of 1¹/₂ cups vegetable shortening and 1¹/₂ cups (3 sticks) unsalted butter, softened
¹/₄ cup fruity olive oil
4 pounds freshly ground masa (not *masa preparada*)
2 tablespoons fine sea salt
³/₄ cup beef stock
2 teaspoons baking powder

1. Preheat the oven to 350°F.
2. *Make the filling:* Pat the pork butt dry with paper towels. Heat the oil in a large Dutch oven over medium heat and brown the

pork on all sides. Cover with cold water and add the onion, garlic, oregano, and pepper. Put on the lid and bake for 2 hours.

3. Let the pork butt cool for 1 hour in its broth. Drain, reserving the cooking liquid, and cut the meat into cubes. Set aside in the refrigerator until needed.

4. *Make the chile sauce:* Using kitchen shears, cut off the chile stems and cut the chiles in half. Shake out and discard the seeds. Fill the rice cooker bowl with 2 to 5 inches of water, close the cover, and set for the regular cycle. Place the chiles in the steamer basket. When the water comes to a boil, place the steamer basket in the rice cooker and close the cover. Steam the chiles for 30 minutes to soften them.

5. Place the warm chiles in a blender or food processor and puree in batches, adding about ½ cup water to each batch to liquify. Set aside ¼ cup of the chile puree in a separate container and refrigerate, covered, for use in the tamale dough later.

6. Heat the oil in a large skillet over medium heat and sprinkle in the flour. Brown the flour, stirring constantly, to a light golden roux, about 2 minutes. Whisk in the chile puree, garlic, salt, vinegar, oregano, and cumin seeds. If the sauce is too thick, thin it with more water or a bit of reserved cooking liquid from the meat. Simmer for 10 minutes over medium-low heat. Add the meat and simmer, uncovered, for 30 minutes. Remove from the heat and let cool to room temperature, then transfer to a covered container and refrigerate until tamale-making time.

7. The next day, remove the corn husks from the package and soak them in a sink filled with hot water for 30 minutes. Choose the widest and longest husks and rinse off any corn silk. Drain the husks on several layers of paper towels.

8. *Make the dough:* In a heavy-duty electric stand mixer fitted with the paddle attachment, whip the lard until it looks like fluffy butter, dribbling in the olive oil when it is whipped. Reduce to low speed and add dollops of masa so that it is slowly incorporated. Stir the salt into the stock and drizzle it into the dough. Increase the speed to medium and whip for 3 minutes. To test if the dough is made properly, drop ½ teaspoon of batter into a glass of cold water; if it floats to the top of the water, it is nice and light. If it sinks, continue to whip the dough for another few minutes. Add the reserved ¼ cup chile puree, which will turn the dough rose-pink. On low speed, sprinkle in the baking powder.

9. *Assemble the tamales:* To form the tamales, spread about ½ cup of the tamale dough inside the curve of a husk, leaving a ½-inch border along one side. Place a spoonful of the filling on top and 2 olives in the center. Fold the sides of the dough into the center. Spread 2 tablespoons more of the dough on a second husk and wrap it around the filled tamale. Tie off both ends with a piece of kitchen twine about 6 inches long. Continue to fill and wrap individual tamales. You will make about 30.

10. Fill the rice cooker bowl with 2 to 5 inches of water, close the cover, and set for the regular cycle. Arrange the tamales in the steamer baskets, 15 in each one, laying them side by side (not standing up), touching each other (don't worry if you fit fewer). Cover the tamales with a layer of 4 or 5 corn husks. When the water comes to a boil, place the steamer baskets in the cooker and close the cover. Set a timer for 1 hour and steam the tamales. Check for doneness. Using tongs, remove one tamale and pull back the husk. If it pulls away easily, it is done; if it sticks, continue to steam in 10-minute intervals.

11. When fully cooked, transfer the tamales to a serving platter with a pair of tongs. Allow the tamales to rest for 15 minutes before serving. See steps 7 and 8 of The Tamale Schedule section (pages 278–279) for storage and reheating instructions.

green corn tamales

While your mother might have bragged about her meat loaf, Mexican-American grand-mothers do the same about their tamales. Inspired by Jacquie McMahan, this is a vege-tarian tamale. The dough is made with masa harina, the dried hominy corn flour that is usually associated with tortilla making, although tamales take a coarser grind. It is also made with oil in lieu of the lard. They are filled with zucchini, green chiles, Monterey Jack cheese, and corn. Serve hot with some *crema doble* (Mexican sour cream) or sour cream and salsa.

MACHINE: Large (10-cup) rice cooker; on/off only
CYCLE: Regular
YIELD: 24 tamales

FILLING

1 cup roasted and peeled green Anaheim or New Mexico chiles or two 7-ounce cans whole roasted green chiles
1/4 cup water
3 pounds zucchini, grated
1 tablespoon minced garlic
Salt
1 cup fresh or frozen (and thawed) baby corn kernels

DOUGH

5 ounces Monterey Jack cheese, shredded
24 wide dried corn husks
6 cups masa harina, such as Quaker
1 2/3 cups canola or vegetable oil
5 1/2 cups water
1 tablespoon salt

1. *Make the filling:* Place the chiles and water in a medium-size saucepan. Simmer over medium-low heat until the chiles have darkened and most of the liquid has evaporated. Set aside to cool.

Place the chiles, zucchini, garlic, and salt to taste in a large bowl. Turn into a mesh sieve and press on the vegetables to extract any liquid. Add the corn and set aside.

2. Remove the corn husks from the package and soak in a sink filled with hot water for 30 minutes. Choose the widest and longest husks and rinse off any corn silk. Drain the husks on several layers of paper towels.

3. *Make the dough:* In a heavy-duty electric stand mixer fitted with the paddle attach-ment, combine the masa harina, oil, water, and salt. It will have the consistency of a moist cookie dough. Add more water, by the tablespoonful, if necessary, to adjust the texture.

4. *Assemble the tamales:* To form the tamales, spread about 2 tablespoons of the tamale dough inside the curve of a husk, allowing for a ½-inch border along one side. Place 2 heaping tablespoons of the filling on top of the dough and sprinkle with a bit of the shredded cheese. Fold the sides of the dough into the center. Tie off both ends with a piece of kitchen twine or some husk. Continue to fill and wrap individual tamales. You will make about 24.

5. Fill the rice cooker bowl with 2 to 5 inches of water, close the cover, and set for the regular cycle. Arrange the tamales in the steamer baskets (put 12 in each level), laying them side by side (not standing up), touching each other. Cover the tamales with a layer of 4 or 5 corn husks. When the water comes to a boil, place the steamer baskets in the cooker and close the cover. Set a timer for 1 hour and steam the tamales. Check for doneness. Using tongs, remove one tamale and pull back the husk. If it pulls away easily, it is done; if it sticks, continue to steam in 10-minute intervals.

6. When fully cooked, transfer the tamales to a serving platter with a pair of tongs. Allow the tamales to rest for 15 minutes before serving. See steps 7 and 8 of The Tamale Schedule (pages 278–279) for storage and reheating instructions.

tamale tarts

Inspired by Southwest chef and food writer Stephen Pyles, here is a little individual tart mold with a removable bottom, like the ones used for sweet French pastry, lined with tamale dough and filled like a quiche. The tarts are steamed in the rice cooker steamer baskets and are oh so very good. Since only three molds fit in the basket at once, you will be steaming in two or three batches, depending on whether you have one or two steamer baskets, staggering the cooking time. Serve warm or at room temperature, with a dab or *crema doble* (Mexican sour cream) or sour cream and salsa.

MACHINE: Large (10-cup) rice cooker; on/off only
CYCLE: Regular
YIELD: 8 tamale tarts

FILLING

1 tablespoon unsalted butter
1 medium-size onion, chopped
8 ounces fresh mushrooms, sliced; 4 medium-size zucchini; one 12-ounce package frozen spinach, thawed and squeezed dry; or 1 basket cherry tomatoes, halved
1 cup black olive halves, drained

DOUGH

2 cups masa harina, such as Quaker
1 teaspoon baking powder
1 teaspoon salt
1/3 cup fresh leaf lard, or a combination (half and half) of vegetable shortening and softened unsalted butter
1/2 cup canola or vegetable oil
1 1/2 tablespoons pureed canned chipotle chiles in adobo sauce (seeds removed, if less heat is desired)
1 1/4 cups hot chicken stock, plus more if needed

CUSTARD

2¹/₂ cups half-and-half

6 large eggs

1 teaspoon salt

Freshly ground white pepper

Dash of garlic powder

1 cup shredded cheese, such as Swiss,
   cheddar, mozzarella, or Monterey Jack

1. *Make the filling:* In a large sauté pan, melt the butter over medium heat. Add the onion and cook, stirring a few times, until softened, about 2 minutes. Add the mushrooms or zucchini and cook, stirring, until tender, or add the spinach or tomatoes and cook until just warm. Remove from the heat and let cool to room temperature.

2. *Make the dough:* In a heavy-duty electric stand mixer fitted with the paddle attachment, combine the masa harina, baking powder, and salt. On low speed, cut in the lard; the mixture will be crumbly like a pie dough. Then drizzle in the oil. When that is incorporated, add the pureed chiles and chicken stock in a slow stream. You want a soft, but not sticky or liquid, dough. You want to be able to pat this dough into the pans. Beat for 2 minutes on medium-high speed until light and fluffy, adjusting the texture with a tablespoon or two more of the chicken stock, if needed.

3. Divide the dough into 8 equal portions. Press evenly into the bottoms and sides of eight 4-inch tin tartlet pans with removable bottoms and fluted edges. The dough will be between ⅛ and ¼ inch thick.

4. Fill the rice cooker bowl with 2 to 5 inches of water, close the cover, and set for the regular cycle.

5. Divide the filling among the lined tartlet pans; sprinkle with the olives.

6. *Make the custard:* In a bowl with a whisk or immersion blender, beat together the half-and-half, eggs, and seasonings until smooth. Stir in the cheese. Pour the custard over the filling in the pans, filling only three-quarters full, leaving some headroom. Cover each pan with some plastic wrap and twist underneath to seal airtight. Place the pans in the steamer baskets, being careful not to tip the pans from side to side, or the custard will leak.

7. When the water comes to a boil, place the steamer baskets in the cooker and close the cover. Steam for 15 to 18 minutes, or until the custard is set. Remove each pan with a metal spatula and place on a wire rack. Remove the plastic wrap by snipping with some kitchen shears and peeling off. Let cool for at least 10 minutes before removing the sides of the pans. Steam the remaining batch of tartlets. The tartlets should be re-covered with plastic wrap individually and refrigerated after 1 hour.

8. These are best served the day they are made, or refrigerate overnight and reheat for 10 minutes in the steamer basket or for about 1½ minutes in a microwave oven.

While we often think of rice as just a dinner side dish or in rice pudding for dessert, rice is so beloved that an old-fashioned dessert of European royalty was to eat freshly steamed plain long-grain rice with spoonfuls of cherry or strawberry preserves and whipped cream or sour cream on top.

The Porridge cycle on the fuzzy logic machines, with its gentle, even heat source, makes beautiful, creamy, sweet dessert puddings such as tapioca and rice pudding, delightful desserts that have starch at their heart. It also makes lovely fruit desserts such as applesauce, compotes, and poached fruit. This is pure comfort food, softly cooked, warm, sweet. These are not elaborate desserts, just soothing simplicity. The Porridge cycle is essential to the success of these recipes. Please note that these recipes cannot be made in the on/off machines, because the heat is just too high.

TAPIOCA

Real old-fashioned tapioca pudding made from pearl tapioca, the whole pellets of dried cassava root, is a nuisance to make on the stove—such a nuisance, in fact, that it is hardly ever made from scratch anymore. There are recipes for it in early colonial cookbooks that call for hours of soaking and then cooking in sugar and wine. But in the rice cooker, tapioca becomes a simple one-step process that yields a delicious, creamy, nutritious dessert. Whole pearl tapioca can come in really large or small shapes. We prefer the small pearl tapioca (which is ground into smaller pellets), since it works much like quick-cooking minute tapioca by cooking a lot faster. These products are not the same as instant tapioca, which is what is used in presweetened mixes.

tapioca pudding

This pudding uses the whole pearl tapioca, a food that most Western cooks have never used, but it is a staple in tropical countries where flour would clump and spoil in short order. The flavor of this made-from-scratch pudding trounces that of ready-made or packaged tapioca mixes. If desired, fold in fresh or frozen berries, sliced peaches or mangos, poached pears, or other fruit, and top with whipped cream.

MACHINE: Medium (6-cup) rice cooker; fuzzy logic only
CYCLE: Porridge
YIELD: Serves 3 to 4

3 tablespoons small pearl tapioca (not minute or instant tapioca)
2 cups milk (lowfat or nonfat is fine)
1 large egg
1/2 cup sugar
Pinch of salt
1 teaspoon pure vanilla extract

1. Place the tapioca in the rice cooker bowl. In a 4-cup measuring cup or small bowl, whisk together the milk, egg, sugar, and salt. Pour the milk mixture over the tapioca; stir to combine. Close the cover and set for the Porridge cycle.
2. When the machine switches to the Keep Warm cycle, remove the bowl from the cooker and stir in the vanilla. Pour the pudding into a large bowl or individual dessert dishes. Let cool. Serve warm, if desired, or refrigerate, covered with plastic wrap.

coconut tapioca pudding

We knew tapioca pudding from childhood as "fish eye pudding." Here it is made with a twist, coconut milk instead of regular milk, just like it would be prepared in some place like Thailand. We like Cook's Cookie vanilla extract; it is a combination of vanillas that is especially flowery and delicate in flavor. Canned coconut milk is available in Asian specialty markets. Coconut-based puddings are nice with some chopped tropical fruit, such as pineapple or mango, on top.

MACHINE: Medium (6-cup) rice cooker; fuzzy logic only
CYCLE: Porridge
YIELD: Serves 6

3 1/4 cups canned unsweetened coconut milk
3/4 cup small pearl tapioca or quick-cooking tapioca
3/4 cup sugar
1 large egg
Pinch of salt
2 1/2 teaspoons pure vanilla extract, preferably Tahitian

1. Place the coconut milk, tapioca, sugar, egg, and salt in the rice cooker bowl; stir to combine. Close the cover and set for the Porridge cycle. Open the cover and stir about every 20 minutes for a few seconds, then close the cover.
2. When the machine switches to the Keep Warm cycle, remove the bowl from the

cooker and stir in the vanilla. Pour the pudding into a large bowl or individual dessert dishes. Let cool. Serve warm, if desired, or refrigerate, covered with plastic wrap.

RICE PUDDING

Anywhere in the world that there is rice, there is some sort of rice pudding. The use of leftover starch, such as rice or bread, as an ingredient in a sweet concoction is as old as cooking mush. It is important to note that different rices—long-grain, short-grain, medium-grain, brown, white, wild—all make different textured puddings. The different amounts of starch in the rices break down during the cooking process and, along with eggs, thicken the mixture. Long-grain rice has the least amount of starch, so recipes often call for short- and medium-grain rices such as Italian Arborio, Spanish Valencia, or Japanese glutinous rice to make a nice creamy pudding. Here we have included rice puddings made with apple juice and honey, as well as regular milk. Each has its own character and charm. Serve your rice puddings warm. As with regular rice, chilling hardens the starch in the rice kernel and you end up with a stiffer pudding after refrigeration.

old-fashioned
rice pudding

Here is the quintessential rice pudding of everyone's childhood. It is sweet and creamy, no fancy or exotic ingredients. Whole milk is best, but 2 percent works fine. It is slowly simmered in the rice cooker and ready to eat as soon as it cools. Remember that rice pudding thickens considerably when chilled as the starch in the rice sets up.

MACHINE: Medium (6-cup) rice cooker; fuzzy logic only
CYCLE: Porridge
YIELD: Serves 6

$^2/_3$ cup medium-grain white rice, such as Arborio, Calriso, or other California-grown rice
4 cups milk
1 large egg
$^1/_3$ cup sugar
1 teaspoon pure vanilla extract

1. Place the rice and milk in the rice cooker bowl; stir to combine. Close the cover and set for the Porridge cycle.

2. When the machine switches to the Keep Warm cycle, combine the egg, sugar, and vanilla in a small bowl and beat with a whisk. Open the rice cooker, spoon a few tablespoons of the rice milk into the egg mixture, and beat with a wooden spoon. Beating the rice milk constantly, pour the egg mixture into the rice cooker bowl. Stir for a minute to combine. Close the cover and reset for a second Porridge cycle. Stir every 15 to 20 minutes until the desired thickness is reached.

3. Pour the pudding into 6 custard cups or ramekins. Serve warm or let cool slightly and refrigerate for at least 1 hour. When cold, cover with plastic wrap and store for up to 4 days.

arborio rice pudding

This is a great slow-cooked, unbaked rice pudding. It uses medium-grain white rice and is enriched with cream and cream cheese or another dairy product. Some folks like raisins or other chopped dried fruit in their rice pudding, but we like this one without. It is very good with fresh fruit, such as chopped strawberries or mangos, or a pool of raspberry sauce spooned over before you top it with some whipped cream.

MACHINE: Medium (6-cup) rice cooker; fuzzy logic only
CYCLE: Porridge
YIELD: Serves 6

$3/4$ cup Arborio rice
4 cups milk
$1/2$ cup sugar
$1/2$ teaspoon salt
1 large egg, well beaten
$3/4$ cup heavy cream or milk
3 tablespoons cream cheese, cut into chunks, or mascarpone, sour cream, or ricotta cheese
2 teaspoons pure vanilla extract
$1/2$ teaspoon freshly grated nutmeg or ground mace

1. Place the rice, milk, sugar, and salt in the rice cooker bowl; stir to combine. Close the cover and set for the Porridge cycle.
2. When the machine switches to the Keep Warm cycle, briskly stir in the beaten egg, heavy cream, cream cheese, vanilla, and nutmeg with a wooden spoon. Close the cover and reset for a second Porridge cycle. Stir every 15 minutes until the desired consistency is reached. You can stop the cycle anytime after the first 15 minutes up to the end of the cycle, depending on how soft you like your pudding.
3. Let stand to cool slightly, then spoon into bowls. Or cool to room temperature, cover, and refrigerate for up to 2 days.

tahini–brown rice pudding

Here's a great-tasting milk-free pudding that's based on brown rice and sweetened naturally with dates, apple juice, and a small amount of honey. Sliced bananas are the perfect topping. The secret ingredient is tahini; in fact, we adapted this recipe from one on a brochure that the Arrowhead Mills company distributed with jars of tahini.

MACHINE: Medium (6-cup) rice cooker; fuzzy logic only
CYCLE: Regular/Brown Rice and Porridge
YIELD: Serves 8

$1^1/2$ cups medium-grain brown rice
$2^1/4$ cups water
$1/4$ cup sesame paste (tahini)
$2^1/2$ cups apple juice
2 tablespoons honey or brown rice syrup
$1/2$ cup chopped unsalted cashews
1 cup chopped dates
2 large ripe bananas, peeled and sliced, for serving

1. Wash and drain the rice.

2. Place the rice in the rice cooker bowl and add the water. Close the cover and set for the regular/Brown Rice cycle.

3. When the machine switches to the Keep Warm cycle, open the cover and add the sesame paste, apple juice, honey, cashews, and dates; stir with a wooden spoon. Reset for the Porridge cycle.

4. When the machine switches to the Keep Warm cycle, turn off the machine. Serve the pudding hot or cold, with sliced bananas on top.

kheer
(indian rice pudding)

The Indian rice pudding *kheer* fills the house with the heady aromas of basmati rice, cardamom, and that elusive hint of rose water. One of the glories of the Indian kitchen, it is smooth, creamy, not overly sweet, and good warm or cold. A sprinkle of nuts adds crunch. *Kheer* is traditionally made by boiling lots of milk and a small quantity of rice on the stove until the milk is reduced and the pudding thick. How much milk? Recipes vary, but the ratio of rice to milk can be as high as 1 part rice to 24 parts milk! No wonder the process can take more than an hour, with frequent stirring an absolute necessity. Worse, the pot with milk residue stuck to the bottom is no fun at all to clean. In your rice cooker, you can make authentic-tasting *kheer* with no fuss at all. A gentle swish in cold, soapy water cleans the pot. After months of experimentation, we

settled on this recipe, adapted from one on the website of the Tilda Company, which sells excellent imported basmati rice. The whipped cream is not essential, but a lovely touch. You can find rose water in gourmet markets or Indian or Middle Eastern markets.

MACHINE: Medium (6-cup) rice cooker; fuzzy logic only
CYCLE: Porridge
YIELD: Serves 6 to 8

$2/3$ cup white basmati rice

4 cups whole milk

$2/3$ cup sugar

4 green cardamom pods

2 teaspoons rose water

$1/3$ cup heavy cream

$1/3$ cup dark raisins

2 tablespoons roughly chopped unsalted pistachios

1. Rinse the rice and drain it well.

2. Place the rice, milk, sugar, and cardamom pods in the rice cooker bowl. Stir briefly with a wooden or plastic rice paddle or wooden spoon. Close the cover and set for the Porridge cycle.

3. When the machine switches to the Keep Warm cycle, open the cover and remove the bowl. Let the *kheer* cool for about 30 minutes, stirring occasionally to prevent a skin from forming on the surface of the pudding. Remove the cardamom pods. Stir in the rose water. Transfer the pudding to a serving bowl, if desired, and cover tightly with plastic wrap. Chill in the refrigerator until cool but not cold, about 1 hour.

4. Whip the cream with an electric mixer until soft peaks form. Gently fold the

cream into the pudding along with the raisins and most of the pistachios. Sprinkle a few chopped pistachios atop each serving.

chocolate rice pudding

Chocolate in rice pudding is not traditional, but oh so perfect for dessert. This is a great recipe to use up leftover rice. Serve straight out of the rice cooker with some whipped cream or nondairy whipped topping, as desired.

MACHINE: Medium (6-cup) rice cooker; fuzzy logic only
CYCLE: Porridge
YIELD: Serves 4

$^1/_2$ cup sugar
1$^1/_2$ tablespoons cornstarch
1$^1/_4$ cups milk
1 cup half-and-half
1 large egg, beaten
1 cup cooked medium-grain white rice
4 ounces bittersweet chocolate, coarsely chopped, or $^3/_4$ cup semisweet chocolate chips
1 teaspoon pure vanilla extract

1. In a medium-size bowl, combine the sugar and cornstarch. Whisking constantly, beat in the milk, half-and-half, and egg. Pour the mixture into the rice cooker bowl. Add the rice and chocolate; stir to combine. Close the cover and set for the Porridge cycle, stirring every 15 minutes,

if you remember (it works perfectly well without!).

2. When the machine switches to the Keep Warm cycle, open the cooker and stir in the vanilla. Spoon the pudding into 4 custard cups or ramekins. Let cool slightly and serve warm or at room temperature.

FRUIT DESSERTS

Poached fresh and dried fruit have a charm all their own. Depending on the type of fruit, they can be poached whole, halved, or in pieces, in a thick or thin sugar syrup. You can make a compote out of a single fruit or combination of two or more fruits, called a compote compose. They are just plain gorgeous in a serving bowl surrounded by their syrup. While poached prunes are the most familiar cooked dried fruit, relegated sadly to the breakfast table, all sorts of other dried fruits lend themselves well to the gentle cooking and sweet aromatic bath required for a nice compote.

The Porridge cycle on the fuzzy logic machines serves us well again, keeping the shape of the fruit intact and giving the time necessary to mull the cooking juices to perfection without extra soaking or fuss. Fruits can be poached in water, wine, or fruit juice, or a combination thereof. While the fruits are poached in a varying amount of sugar syrup, you never want to add too much sugar or honey; it will detract from the natural flavors and sweetness inherent in the fruit, as well as contribute to breaking down the fruit, unless, of course, that is what you want, as in the case of applesauce.

Compotes are so popular that there is a special glass or porcelain raised footed bowl just for serving them called a compotier. Using a slotted spoon, place the fruits in the bowl and pour the syrup over them. Poached fruits are traditionally served still gently warm with whipped cream, but are also good cold, served over ice cream or as a garnish to vanilla cheesecake and a battery of plain old-fashioned cakes such as angel food cake, sponge cake, gold cake, and pound cake. Try one of our poached fruit recipes and we think you will be delightfully surprised.

homemade applesauce

Who doesn't love homemade applesauce? Canned just doesn't come close. The Porridge cycle on the rice cooker makes great fruit sauce. We love our applesauce with lots of cinnamon. You can add the sugar or not; Julie likes hers sweet, Beth likes hers without sugar. Serve for breakfast with yogurt, alongside pork chops for dinner, or warm with a scoop of vanilla ice cream for dessert.

MACHINE: Medium (6-cup) rice cooker; fuzzy logic only
CYCLE: Porridge
YIELD: About 3 cups

8 large, firm, tart green apples (2¹/₂ to 3 pounds)
¹/₂ cup water or apple juice
¹/₄ cup sugar (optional)
1 to 2 teaspoons ground cinnamon, to your taste
¹/₄ cup (¹/₂ stick) unsalted butter

1. Peel, core, and coarsely chop the apples. Place in the rice cooker bowl. Add the water, sugar (if using), cinnamon, and butter. Close the cover and set for the Porridge cycle.
2. When the machine switches to the Keep Warm cycle, carefully open the cover, allowing the steam to escape. Stir the cooked fruit and its liquid with a wooden or plastic rice paddle or wooden spoon. The applesauce should be soft and chunky (you can puree it in a food processor or with an immersion blender if you like it smooth). Let stand to cool.
3. Transfer the applesauce to a covered container and refrigerate. Keeps for up to 2 weeks in the refrigerator (if it lasts that long), or freeze.

pear applesauce: Use 4 apples and 4 large, firm ripe pears, peeled, cored, and cut into chunks. Proceed with the recipe as directed.

black cherry applesauce: Use 6 apples and add one 16-ounce bag frozen unsweetened pitted dark sweet cherries. Proceed with the recipe as directed.

apricot applesauce: Add 4 to 6 fresh apricots, pitted and chopped, or 6 to 8 dried apricot halves to the apples. Proceed with the recipe as directed.

rhubarb applesauce: Use 5 apples and 2 cups fresh rhubarb cut into 1-inch pieces (¹/₂ pound). Substitute grated orange zest for the cinnamon. Increase the sugar to ¹/₂ cup. Proceed with the recipe as directed.

ginger applesauce: Add 2 heaping tablespoons chopped crystallized ginger. Proceed with the recipe as directed.

cranberry applesauce: Use 6 apples and 1½ cups fresh cranberries, picked over for stems. Increase the sugar to ⅔ cup. Proceed with the recipe as directed.

mango applesauce: Use 6 apples and add 1 to 2 fresh mangos, peeled, pitted, and chopped. No sugar is necessary, as the mangos are very sweet. Proceed with the recipe as directed.

plum applesauce: Use 4 apples and 6 firm ripe purple plums, pitted and cut into chunks. Proceed with the recipe as directed.

poached dried figs in spiced red wine

During the holidays it is really special to end up at a party where a simmering kettle filled with red wine and whole spices is on the stove for guests. That heartwarming flavor was the inspiration for this delightful and fantastic poached winter fruit compote known as *compote de figues seches* in France. Everyone who tastes it asks for more. While it looks like you have a lot of juice just as the compote completes its Porridge cycle, the fruit will absorb more and become syrupy when chilled. Serve gently warm over vanilla gelato or ladled on the side of a slice of New York–style cheesecake.

MACHINE: Medium (6-cup) rice cooker; fuzzy logic only
CYCLE: Porridge
YIELD: About 4 cups

1½ cups dry red wine, such as Merlot
1½ cups apple juice or pear juice
⅓ cup honey
3 cloves
3 allspice berries
One 4-inch cinnamon stick
One 12-ounce package dried Calimyrna figs, left whole
⅔ cup golden raisins (or use half dried tart cherries)

1. Place all the ingredients in the rice cooker bowl. Close the cover and set for the Porridge cycle. Carefully open the cover twice during the cooking to allow a burst of steam to be released from the wine burning off its alcohol.

2. When the machine switches to the Keep Warm cycle, carefully open the cover, allowing the steam to escape. The fruit should be plump and tender. Stir with a wooden or plastic rice paddle or wooden spoon. Remove the bowl from the cooker and let cool. Pour the figs into a storage container, cover, and refrigerate overnight. Keeps for up to 2 weeks in the refrigerator.

poached dried apricots

Poached dried apricot compote is a must for a quick dessert that will not only delight, but surprise the taste buds. It is delicious! Serve cold with a spoonful of sour cream on top or with a slice of pound cake. Use the largest, moistest apricot halves you can find.

MACHINE: Medium (6-cup) rice cooker; fuzzy logic only
CYCLE: Porridge
YIELD: About 3 cups

1 1/2 cups white wine, such as
    Gerwurztraminer or Riesling
1 1/2 cups water
3/4 cup sugar
3 or 4 strips orange zest
One 4-inch cinnamon stick
One 12-ounce package dried apricot
    halves

1. Place all the ingredients in the rice cooker bowl. Close the cover and set for the Porridge cycle. Carefully open the cover twice during the cooking to allow a burst of steam to be released from the wine burning off its alcohol.
2. When the machine switches to the Keep Warm cycle, carefully open the cover, allowing the steam to escape. The fruit halves should be plump and tender. Remove the bowl from the cooker and let cool. Pour the apricots into a storage container, cover, and refrigerate overnight. Keeps for up to 2 weeks in the refrigerator.

pruneaux pinot noir

Prunes poached in burgundy wine is a traditional country dessert in France, where prunes have a better reputation than they do in America. In the seventeenth-century *Culpeper's Herbal*, a compilation of foods and their properties, prune plums are defined as the fruit of Venus, and the dried fruit of the meaty Italian plum has lived up to its reputation. Serve this intensely flavored compote cold with a spoonful of whipped cream and grated semisweet chocolate on top, alongside angel food cake, or over chocolate ice cream. You can even tuck a few next to sautéed pork chops or roast lamb.

MACHINE: Medium (6-cup) rice cooker; fuzzy logic only
CYCLE: Porridge
YIELD: About 6 cups

3 cups Pinot Noir
1 cup water
1/2 cup sugar
1 1/2 pounds pitted jumbo prunes

1. Place all the ingredients in the rice cooker bowl. Close the cover and set for the Porridge cycle. Carefully open the cover twice during the cooking to allow a burst of steam to be released from the wine burning off its alcohol.
2. When the machine switches to the Keep Warm cycle, carefully open the cover, allowing the steam to escape. The fruit should be delightfully plump. Remove the bowl from the cooker and let cool.

Pour the prunes into a storage container, cover, and refrigerate overnight. Keeps for up to 1 month in the refrigerator.

brandied prune sauce

Adapted from an elegant restaurant dessert menu, this is an entirely different interpretation of prunes than the ones poached in wine. It is a heady, luscious, and decadent relative. For your fancy dinner party, serve this sauce over vanilla ice cream with some butter cookies on the side.

MACHINE: Medium (6-cup) rice cooker; fuzzy logic only
CYCLE: Porridge
YIELD: About 2¹/₂ cups

³/₄ cup Armagnac or Cognac
1¹/₄ cups water
1¹/₂ cups sugar
2 star anise
1 vanilla bean, split
One 4-inch cinnamon stick
One 1-inch piece fresh ginger, peeled
1 pound pitted jumbo prunes

1. Place all the ingredients in the rice cooker bowl. Close the cover and set for the Porridge cycle. Carefully open the cover twice during the cooking to allow a burst of steam to be released from the brandy burning off its alcohol.

2. When the machine switches to the Keep Warm cycle, carefully open the cover, allowing the steam to escape. The fruit should be plump and tender. Stir a few times with a wooden or plastic rice paddle or wooden spoon. Remove the bowl from the cooker and let cool. Remove the whole spices. Pour the sauce into a storage container, cover, and refrigerate overnight. Keeps for up to 1 month in the refrigerator.

stewed dried fruit

Great for kids, great for the buffet table with baked ham, great over pancakes or cottage cheese for breakfast, even great with a square of plain cake or ice cream for dessert. Any combination of dried fruit will do—prunes, apricots, apples, pears, peaches, light or dark raisins, dried cranberries, cherries, or currants. We especially like dried apples in this. You can also leave out the honey, if your diet dictates, and the compote will still be excellent.

MACHINE: Medium (6-cup) rice cooker; fuzzy logic only
CYCLE: Porridge
YIELD: About 8 cups

5¹/₂ cups water
¹/₃ cup honey
3 slices lemon
One 4-inch cinnamon stick
1 vanilla bean, split
1¹/₂ pounds mixed whole dried fruit of your choice

1. Place the water, honey, lemon, and spices in the rice cooker bowl. Close the cover and set for the Porridge cycle. Set a timer for 15 minutes; when the timer sounds, add the dried fruit. Close the cover and let the cycle complete.

2. When the machine switches to the Keep Warm cycle, carefully open the cover and allow the steam to escape. The fruit should be delightfully plump. Stir with a wooden or plastic rice paddle or wooden spoon. Remove the bowl from the cooker and let cool. Pour the fruit into a storage container, cover, and refrigerate overnight. Keeps for up to 1 week in the refrigerator.

stewed blueberries

Blueberries are a common sight on American tables from May to September. They grow wild in the pastures and meadows in the temperate regions of the Northern Hemisphere, and are part of diets in Scandinavia and near the Arctic Circle. Think of references to "gathering berries" and it usually is in reference to the blueberry. Blueberries, also known as bilberries or whortleberries, can be made sweet, in jams and pies, or savory, as an accompaniment to game and meats. Blueberries have been cultivated only since the early twentieth century and mass cultivated since the 1950s, so we have nice big, plump berries not only fresh, but frozen. Blueberries take well to being stewed; just look at the blue lips and teeth with all of the smiles after eating a bowl of these with yogurt. This is a favorite recipe for use with the extra-large frozen berries.

MACHINE: Medium (6-cup) rice cooker; fuzzy logic only
CYCLE: Porridge
YIELD: About 4 cups

4 cups fresh or frozen blueberries, picked over for stems
1/2 cup sugar
1/2 cup orange juice
3 slices lemon
1 tablespoon orange liqueur, such as Grand Marnier
1/4 teaspoon freshly grated nutmeg or ground mace

1. Place the blueberries, sugar, orange juice, and lemon slices in the rice cooker bowl. Let stand at room temperature for 15 minutes or in the refrigerator for an hour to give the berries a chance to exude some liquid (this is especially important for the frozen berries).

2. When ready to cook, place the bowl in the rice cooker. Close the cover and set for the Porridge cycle. Set a timer for 35 minutes; when the timer sounds, add the orange liqueur and nutmeg, stirring quickly with a wooden or plastic rice paddle or wooden spoon. Close the cover and let the cycle complete.

3. When the machine switches to the Keep Warm cycle, carefully open the cover, remove the bowl from the cooker, and let cool. Serve the blueberries warm or at room temperature, or pour into a storage container, cover, and refrigerate overnight to serve chilled, ladled into dessert bowls. Keeps for up to 5 days in the refrigerator.

poached rhubarb and strawberries

Don't have time to make a strawberry-rhubarb pie? Well, this early summer fresh fruit compote has all the flavor and pretty color without any of the fuss. The best loved fruit in the world, the delicate strawberry, is paired with the thick pink stems of rhubarb, a flowering rhizome that is much more appreciated in European cookery than American. Note that the recipe says to be careful with the stirring, so that the fruits do not get stringy and mushy. The flavor is so very delightful and especially good with vanilla gelato.

MACHINE: Medium (6-cup) rice cooker; fuzzy logic only
CYCLE: Porridge
YIELD: About 4 cups

1 cup water
1 cup sugar
1 vanilla bean, split
1 pound fresh rhubarb stems, cut into
    1 1/2-inch chunks (about 4 cups)
1 1/2 pints fresh strawberries, rinsed,
    hulled, and halved

1. Place the water, sugar, vanilla bean, and rhubarb in the rice cooker bowl. Close the cover and set for the Porridge cycle. Set a timer for 30 minutes; when the timer sounds, add the strawberries and stir once to distribute. Close the cover and let the cycle complete.

2. When the machine switches to the Keep Warm cycle, carefully open the cover, remove the bowl from the cooker, and let cool. Do not stir. Serve the compote warm or at room temperature, or pour into a storage container, cover, and refrigerate overnight to serve chilled, ladled into dessert bowls. Keeps for up to 4 days in the refrigerator.

poached pears with grand marnier custard sauce

Poaching pears is sometimes a hit-or-miss procedure; if the heat is too high, you have mashed pear floating in liquid when you want a perfect whole pear for display. Poaching them in the rice cooker was a pleasant surprise. The low, even heat is just right for the gentle cooking that the pear needs to stay whole. This is a favorite recipe, adapted from the now-defunct *Cuisine* magazine, poaching the pears in a lemon-water syrup and serving them with a divine custard sauce spiked with orange liqueur. Be sure to buy your pears hard, under-ripe, not close to the consistency you would want if you were to eat them out of hand. Use these same proportions to poach peeled peach halves (also buy them under-ripe).

MACHINE: Medium (6-cup) rice cooker; fuzzy logic only

CYCLE: **Porridge**

YIELD: Serves 4 to 5

3 cups water

1 cup sugar

Juice of 1 lemon

4 to 5 under-ripe Bartlett, Comice, Anjou, or Bosc pears, peeled and stem left intact

One ¹/₂-inch piece vanilla bean

1 slice lemon

Grand Marnier Custard Sauce (recipe follows; optional)

1. Place the water, sugar, lemon juice, and pears in the rice cooker bowl. The pears will be floating in the liquid. Close the cover and set for the Porridge cycle. Set a timer for 30 minutes. Do not stir at any time during the cooking. Check the consistency of the pears at 30 minutes by piercing their flesh with the tip of a small knife; you want them firm, but slightly soft. Remember, they will soften a bit more as they cool.

2. When the pears are the desired consistency, remove the bowl from the cooker. Transfer the pears to a storage container with a slotted spoon and let cool. Leave the poaching liquid in the bowl, add the vanilla bean and lemon, and let cool separately. When cooled, pour the poaching liquid back over the pears, cover, and refrigerate for at least 4 hours and up to overnight.

3. To serve, using a slotted spoon, transfer each pear to a dessert plate. Serve chilled, plain, or in a pool of the custard sauce. Can be made ahead and refrigerated.

grand marnier custard sauce

YIELD: 2 cups

1 cup heavy cream

1 cup half-and-half

¹/₃ cup sugar

3 large eggs

3 to 4 tablespoons Grand Marnier or other orange liqueur

1. In a medium-size saucepan or a glass measuring cup in the microwave, scald the cream and half-and half, heating them just until bubbles begin to form all along the edge of the saucepan or cup. Remove from the heat.

2. In a medium-size bowl or food processor, combine the sugar and eggs. Beat hard with a whisk or process briefly until light colored and foamy. Whisking constantly, or with the food processor running, gradually add the hot cream to the egg mixture.

3. Pour the sauce back into the saucepan and place over medium heat. Cook gently, stirring constantly with a whisk, until the sauce is just slightly thickened and coats a spoon; do not boil.

4. Pour the sauce into a storage bowl and stir in the liqueur. Cool to room temperature. Refrigerate, covered, until serving time. Serve cold.

poached fresh cherries

Is there anyone who doesn't love cherries? While the season for fresh cherries is, sadly, very short and the large orchards of the past are on the wane, cherries still are the most coveted of fruits, whether in jam, pies, or this compote, because of their exceptionally flavorful pulp.

MACHINE: Medium (6-cup) rice cooker; fuzzy logic only
CYCLE: Porridge
YIELD: 4 cups

3 cups cranberry-raspberry or unsweetened cherry juice
1 cup water
2/3 cup sugar
1 tablespoon pure vanilla extract
2 pounds sweet cherries, stems removed and pitted

1. Place all the ingredients in the rice cooker bowl. Close the cover and set for the Porridge cycle. Set a timer for 30 minutes. Check the consistency of the cherries at 30 minutes by piercing their flesh with the tip of a small knife; you want them firm, but slightly tender. Remember, they will soften a bit more as they cool.
2. When the cherries are the desired consistency, remove the bowl from the cooker. Transfer the cherries and their poaching liquid to a storage container and let cool. Cover and refrigerate for at least 4 hours and up to overnight. Serve chilled, with some of the liquid. Keeps for up to 3 days in the refrigerator.

poached fresh apricots

Alexander the Great supposedly introduced the apricot, along with the peach, to the Greco-Roman world after one of his military forays into the East, although it was centuries before cultivating the beautiful flowering tree became popular. Apricots make the best preserves and canned fruit, so with these easy-to-make poached fruits, you delightfully have a cross between the two. You will poach these apricots whole with their pits still in and store them in their lovely syrup, giving credence to their Eastern name, Moon of the Faithful, a reference to their fragrant, perfect moon shape.

MACHINE: Medium (6-cup) rice cooker; fuzzy logic only
CYCLE: Porridge
YIELD: Serves 3

3 cups water
1 cup sugar
Juice of 2 lemons
1 pound (8 to 10) small, firm fresh apricots

1. Place all the ingredients in the rice cooker bowl. Close the cover and set for the Porridge cycle. Set a timer for

30 minutes. Check the consistency of the apricots at 30 minutes by piercing their flesh with the tip of a small knife; you want them firm, but slightly soft. Remember, they will soften a bit more as they cool.

2. When the apricots are the desired consistency, remove the bowl from the cooker. Transfer the apricots and their poaching liquid to a storage container and let cool. Cover and refrigerate for at least 4 hours and up to overnight. Serve chilled, with some of the liquid.

pink wine quinces

Yellow-green and shaped like a knobby apple, the quince is an elusive fruit. It lives in old-fashioned backyards, where once it was a staple fruit in the autumn kitchen for poaching and jams. Although now a specialty item, the quince has lost none of its delightful flavor. With its hard, rather dry flesh, it must be slow cooked with plenty of sugar to transform it into the haunting apricot-orange hue. Quince is fruit that takes well to poaching. Here it is cooked in a spiced wine syrup made with slightly sweet blush wine (formerly rosé), which is a luscious pink. Perfect with sponge cake.

MACHINE: Medium (6-cup) rice cooker; fuzzy logic only
CYCLE: Porridge
YIELD: About 6 cups

4 cups fruity blush wine, such as White Zinfandel or Blanc de Pinot Noir, or imported rosé from Portugal, such as Lancer's or Mateus
1/4 cup fresh lime juice
1 3/4 cups sugar
5 cloves
Pinch of freshly grated nutmeg
Two 4-inch cinnamon sticks
2 slices candied ginger
3 medium-size quinces (about 1 1/2 pounds)

1. Place the wine, lime juice, sugar, spices, and ginger in the rice cooker bowl.

2. Quarter and peel the quinces with a sharp paring knife. With a melon baller or knife, remove the entire core area, cleaning out all the hard bits. Cut each quarter into 4 slices. Place the quince slices in the wine mixture. Close the cover and set for the Porridge cycle. Carefully open the cover twice during the cooking to allow a burst of steam to be released from the wine burning off its alcohol.

3. When the machine switches to the Keep Warm cycle, carefully open the cover, allowing the steam to escape. The fruit should be very tender; if it is not, reset for a second Porridge cycle and check every 15 minutes until the desired texture is achieved.

4. Remove the bowl from the cooker and let cool. Pour the quinces into a storage container, cover, and refrigerate overnight. Keeps for up to 2 weeks in the refrigerator.

custards and steamed
PUDDINGS

CUSTARDS

A custard is probably one of the most comforting and luscious of desserts. It is a combination of milk, sugar, eggs, and flavoring, cooked with very low heat until the eggs thicken the mixture and create the creamy texture as it sets.

There are two categories in the custard world. One is the small individual dish of custard called a *petit pot de crème*, or little pot of cream, with lots of egg yolks. The second is a custard, like a flan, that is turned out of its mold. The first type of custard is represented here.

Custards are either cooked on the stovetop in a double boiler or baked in a water bath in the oven. The rice cooker steamer tray or baskets meld both methods. The slow cooking ensures that the custards cook slowly and evenly, without giving the eggs a chance to curdle or get rubbery. They don't dry out either. These individual desserts look so pretty in their beautifully made ceramic dishes. Steamed custards are a real joy. You can steam them one day, chill overnight, and then have them ready and perfect to serve ice-cold the next day. Test to see if the custard is finished cooking by piercing close to the edge; you want the center to be quite moist or else it will be overcooked.

Custards can be kept, covered, in the refrigerator for up to three days before serving.

Please note that these custards can be made *only* in on/off machines fitted with a steamer tray or baskets, not in the fuzzy logic machines. Because the machine will always contain boiling water, it will not automatically turn off. You must set a timer for cooking, then unplug the machine to turn it off after the custards are done.

WHAT IS THE BEST DESSERT CUSTARD CUP?

There are three main types of heatproof individual dishes suitable for steaming custards. The following recipes are designed to be used in these types of containers.

Apilco and Emile Henri brands, available from specialty cookware stores, come in 3½-inch-diameter ramekins with a ½-cup (4-ounce) capacity. Four of these will fit comfortably in the 10-inch-diameter steamer basket. If you are using a smaller rice cooker with the metal steamer tray insert, you will only be able to fit three at one time. The Apilco ramekin, really a miniature soufflé dish, is always made of plain white French porcelain, while Emile Henri ceramics come in a range of earthy colors.

Pyrex custard cups, easily available in most supermarkets and hardware stores, are 4 inches in diameter with a ¾-cup (6-ounce) capacity. One-half cup of custard fits in this size as well. Three of these will fit comfortably in the 10-inch-diameter steamer basket (in the large rice cooker). If you are using a smaller rice cooker with the metal steamer tray insert, you will only be able to fit two custard cups at one time; cover and refrigerate the extra custard, steaming in batches.

If you use the stacked 10-inch-diameter steamer baskets, you can double any recipe and steam a double rack of custards at one time. That means you can place two Pyrex cups on each level to steam the entire recipe at one time.

steamed banana custards

This is a wonderful home-style, nurturing dessert adapted from a recipe by Jesse Cool in her book, *Your Organic Kitchen* (Rodale, 2000). Kids go nuts!

Machine: Large (10-cup) rice cooker; on/off only

CYCLE: Regular

YIELD: Serves 4

2 medium-size ripe bananas, peeled and
    cut into thick slices
1/2 cup whole milk
1/2 cup half-and-half or heavy cream
1/4 cup sugar
2 large eggs
1 large egg yolk
1 teaspoon pure vanilla extract
1/2 teaspoon pure coconut extract

1. Coat the inside of 4 custard cups or ramekins with butter-flavored nonstick cooking spray. Divide the banana chunks among the cups.
2. In a medium-size bowl, beat together the milk, half-and-half, sugar, whole eggs, egg yolk, and extracts with a whisk or handheld immersion blender until smooth. Pour the custard over the bananas, filling the prepared custard cups three-quarters full. Cover each cup with a small square of aluminum foil and crimp the edges to seal airtight.
3. Add 4 cups hot water to the rice cooker bowl, close the cover, and set for the regular cycle. When the water comes to a boil, arrange the cups in the tray or baskets (this works best steaming a double rack of custards at one time). Place the tray or baskets in the cooker and close the cover. Steam until the custards are just set and slightly wobbly in the center, 35 to 40 minutes. Unplug the machine to turn it off.
4. Remove the custards from the rice cooker with metal tongs. Remove the foil covers. Let cool, then refrigerate until ready to serve.

steamed lemon custards

We love this custard! Use an organic heavy cream, if you can, for a taste sensation you thought might not exist ever again—just like your grandma might have made, only better. Use the sumptuous pure citrus oils from Boyajian; the flavors are the edible perfume of the food world. You can find them in large supermarkets and gourmet stores.

MACHINE: Large (10-cup) rice cooker; on/off only

CYCLE: Regular

YIELD: Serves 4

1 cup heavy cream
1/4 cup sugar
2 large eggs
2 large egg yolks
1 teaspoon lemon oil or pure lemon
    extract

1. Coat the inside of 4 custard cups or ramekins with butter-flavored nonstick cooking spray.

2. In a small, deep bowl, beat together all the ingredients with a whisk or handheld immersion blender until well blended. Pour the custard into the prepared custard cups. Cover each cup with a small square of aluminum foil and crimp the edges to seal airtight.

3. Add 4 cups hot water to the rice cooker bowl, close the cover, and set for the regular cycle. When the water comes to a boil, arrange the cups in the tray or baskets (this works best steaming a double rack of custards at one time). Place the tray or baskets in the cooker and close the cover. Steam until the custards are just set and slightly wobbly in the center, 35 to 40 minutes. Unplug the machine to turn it off.

4. Remove each pudding from the rice cooker with metal tongs. Remove the foil covers. Let cool, then refrigerate until ready to serve.

steamed chocolate custards

A delectable chocolate custard that begs for some whipped cream on top.

MACHINE: Large (10-cup) rice cooker; on/off only
CYCLE: Regular
YIELD: Serves 4

1 1/2 cups whole milk
1/2 cup semisweet chocolate chips
2 tablespoons Dutch-process unsweetened cocoa powder, such as Droste
1/4 cup firmly packed dark brown sugar
Pinch of salt
1 large egg
2 large egg yolks
1/2 teaspoon pure vanilla extract

1. Coat the inside of 4 custard cups or ramekins with butter-flavored nonstick cooking spray.

2. In a small saucepan, whisk together the milk, chocolate chips, and cocoa over medium heat just until the chocolate melts, stirring occasionally.

3. In a medium-size bowl, combine the brown sugar and salt. Whisk in the whole egg, egg yolks, and vanilla until smooth. Whisk in about a quarter of the chocolate mixture, beating vigorously. Slowly pour in the remaining chocolate mixture in a steady stream, whisking constantly to avoid curdling. Pour the custard into the prepared custard cups. Cover each cup with a small square of aluminum foil and crimp the edges to seal airtight.

4. Add 4 cups hot water to the rice cooker bowl, close the cover, and set for the regular cycle. When the water comes to a boil, arrange the cups in the tray or baskets (this works best steaming a double rack of custards at one time). Place the tray or baskets in the cooker and close the cover. Steam until the custards are just set and slightly wobbly in the center, 35 to 40 minutes. Unplug the machine to turn it off.

5. Remove each custard from the rice cooker with metal tongs. Remove the foil covers. Let cool, then serve at room temperature or refrigerate until ready to serve.

country french prune custards

This is a lowfat version of a French custard. The prunes are a traditional addition to country desserts and a favorite with many diners. Be sure to get the moist-pack prunes; otherwise, soak regular prunes for a few hours in hot water or hot water with some Cognac or brandy added. Drain before placing them in the ramekins.

MACHINE: Large (10-cup) rice cooker; on/off only
CYCLE: Regular
YIELD: Serves 6

8 ounces (1 cup) pitted moist-pack prunes
One 12-ounce can evaporated skim milk
3 tablespoons unbleached all-purpose flour
3 tablespoons sugar
$1/4$ teaspoon salt
2 large eggs
1 teaspoon pure vanilla extract

1. Coat the inside of 6 custard cups or ramekins with butter-flavored nonstick cooking spray. Line each cup with the prunes, dividing them equally among the cups.

2. In a small, deep bowl, combine the remaining ingredients and beat with a whisk or handheld immersion blender until well blended. Pour ⅓ cup of the custard into each custard cup over the prunes. Cover each cup with a small square of aluminum foil and crimp the edges to seal airtight.

3. Add 4 cups hot water to the rice cooker bowl, close the cover, and set for the regular cycle. When the water comes to a boil, arrange the cups in the tray or baskets (this works best steaming a double rack of custards at one time). Place the tray or baskets in the cooker and close the cover. Steam until the custards are just set and slightly wobbly in the center, 22 to 25 minutes. Unplug the machine to turn it off.

4. Remove each custard from the rice cooker with metal tongs. Remove the foil covers. Let cool, then serve at room temperature or refrigerate until ready to serve.

steamed ginger custards

The bits of candied ginger, known as *gingembre* in France, melt into little pools throughout the custard.

MACHINE: Large (10-cup) rice cooker; on/off only
CYCLE: Regular
YIELD: Serves 6

2 cups half-and-half

1 teaspoon ground ginger

2 large eggs

3 large egg yolks

$^{1}/_{3}$ cup sugar

1 tablespoon crushed candied ginger

1. Coat the inside of 6 custard cups or ramekins with butter-flavored nonstick cooking spray.

2. In a small saucepan with a whisk, beat together the half-and-half and ground ginger until smooth. Bring to a boil over medium heat, stirring occasionally. Remove from the heat.

3. In a medium-size bowl, gently whisk the whole eggs, egg yolks, and sugar together just until blended. Whisk the warm half-and-half into the mixture, beating with the whisk constantly. Stir in the candied ginger. Pour the custard into the prepared custard cups. Cover each cup with a small square of aluminum foil and crimp the edges to seal airtight.

4. Add 4 cups hot water to the rice cooker bowl, close the cover, and set for the regular cycle. When the water comes to a boil, arrange the cups in the tray or baskets (this works best steaming a double rack of custards at one time). Place the tray or baskets in the cooker and close the cover. Steam until the custards are just set and slightly wobbly in the center, 22 to 25 minutes. Unplug the machine to turn it off.

5. Remove each custard from the rice cooker with metal tongs. Remove the foil covers. Let cool, then serve at room temperature or refrigerate until ready to serve.

chocolate pots de crème

The classic French dessert is steamed in the rice cooker steamer basket rather than being baked in the oven. This is rich, rich, rich. Make it in the morning and serve, gently chilled, that night, for the best texture. If you like your chocolate with the flavor of orange, add $^{1}/_{2}$ teaspoon Boyajian orange oil (or more to taste) in place of the vanilla.

MACHINE: Large (10-cup) rice cooker; on/off only

CYCLE: Regular

YIELD: Serves 6

2 cups half-and-half

4 ounces semisweet chocolate, cut into chunks

1 large egg

4 large egg yolks

$2^{1}/_{2}$ tablespoons sugar

Pinch of salt

2 teaspoons pure vanilla extract

1. Coat the inside of 6 custard cups or ramekins with butter-flavored nonstick cooking spray.

2. In a small saucepan over low heat, combine $^{1}/_{2}$ cup of the half-and-half and the chocolate, whisking occasionally until smooth. Warm the remaining $1^{1}/_{2}$ cups half-and-half in the microwave or in a small saucepan on the stove.

3. In a medium-size bowl, gently whisk the whole egg and egg yolks together just until blended.

4. Whisk the warm half-and-half into the hot chocolate mixture, beating constantly. Whisk in the sugar and salt. Slowly pour the chocolate mixture in a steady stream into the eggs, whisking constantly to avoid curdling. Whisk in the vanilla. Pour the custard into the prepared custard cups. Cover each cup with a small square of aluminum foil and crimp the edges to seal airtight.

5. Add 4 cups hot water to the rice cooker bowl, close the cover, and set for the regular cycle. When the water comes to a boil, arrange the cups in the tray or baskets (this works best steaming a double rack of custards at one time). Place the tray or baskets in the cooker and close the cover. Steam until the custards are just set and slightly wobbly in the center, 22 to 25 minutes. Unplug the machine to turn it off.

6. Remove each custard from the rice cooker with metal tongs. Remove the foil covers. Let cool, then serve at room temperature or refrigerate until ready to serve.

steamed cappuccino custards

The unique, complex flavor of coffee is a natural infused into a cream mixture for this custard. This is a favorite!

MACHINE: Large (10-cup) rice cooker; on/off only
CYCLE: Regular
YIELD: Serves 6

2 cups half-and-half
1 1/2 tablespoons instant espresso powder, such as Medaglia D'oro
6 large egg yolks
1/2 cup sugar
Pinch of salt

1. Coat the inside of 6 custard cups or ramekins with butter-flavored nonstick cooking spray.

2. In a small saucepan, whisk together the half-and-half and espresso until smooth. Bring to a boil over medium heat, stirring occasionally. Remove from the heat.

3. In a medium-size bowl, gently whisk the egg yolks, sugar, and salt just until blended. Whisk the warm half-and-half into the mixture, beating with the whisk constantly to keep it from curdling. Pour the custard into the prepared custard cups. Cover each cup with a small square of aluminum foil and crimp the edges to seal airtight.

4. Add 4 cups hot water to the rice cooker bowl, close the cover, and set for the regular cycle. When the water comes to a boil, arrange the cups in the tray or baskets (this works best steaming a double rack of custards at one time). Place the tray or baskets in the cooker and close the cover. Steam until the custards are just set and slightly wobbly in the center, 22 to 25 minutes. Unplug the machine to turn it off.

5. Remove each custard from the rice cooker with metal tongs. Remove the foil covers. Let cool, then serve at room temperature or refrigerate until ready to serve.

STEAMED PUDDINGS

Popular since medieval times in Britain and later in the New England colonies, a "pud" is a must for ending winter holiday meals. Once heavy with suet, today's steamed puddings are more like a steamed sponge or sweet quick bread, light and flavorful from fall fruits such as pumpkin and persimmon. They can be steamed in the medium or large on/off rice cookers with amazing efficiency and ease. We consider the large rice cooker the appliance of choice when steaming puddings.

The mold is of paramount importance here. We use beautiful covered fluted metal pudding molds, readily available from Williams-Sonoma, La Cuisine, or Sur La Table in three- and six-cup capacities. While traditional recipes can call for a fluted tube pan or one-pound coffee can, these are not suitable for steaming in the rice cooker because they are too tall. For the best fit, we recommend the 1½-quart (6-cup) round melon shape, Corinthian column, or a 6½-inch metal kugelhopf mold (you will need to cover this with aluminum foil and secure it with a rubber band in lieu of the lid) for the large (10-cup) rice cooker and the 3-cup fluted with wreath top and center tube for the medium (6-cup) rice cooker.

There are some smaller 2-cup molds (the Corinthian column is adorable) or English china pudding basins that will fit in the small or medium rice cooker, but the following recipes are designed for a 1½-quart (6-cup) mold. If you use a 3-cup mold, just cut the recipe in half. While so many other of the metal molds are beautiful, they may be too tall for the rice cooker cover to sit properly and enclose the steam.

The technique for steaming is simple. The mold is buttered and never filled past two-thirds to allow for expansion. Snap on the lid or cover. It is set on a rack or trivet in rapidly simmering water that should come halfway up the sides of the mold. In the large rice cooker, that is at the 5-cup line on the side of the bowl. It is important to check periodically in case the water has boiled off and needs to be replenished, but we found the rice cooker to be very efficient here; about 1½ inches of water boiled off every 25 to 30 minutes.

Warm steamed puddings should have a complementary sauce, ice cream, or liqueur-flavored whipped cream to proclaim them ready to eat.

How to Make Individual Steamed Puddings

Spoon the batter into well-buttered ceramic ramekins, china pudding basins, Pyrex custard cups, or even ovenproof coffee cups, filling them two-thirds full. Securely cover each with a piece of buttered aluminum foil and crimp the edges to seal. Set the steaming rack in place in the bottom of the cooker or place a wire rack in the bottom of the cooker and arrange the molds on the rack (they can be touching); you will probably have to steam in two batches. Pour in 1 to 2 inches of hot water, reaching only halfway up the molds. Turn on the cooker and bring the water to a boil. Steam until set, 25 to 35 minutes, depending on the size of the cups. Remove from the cooker with metal tongs and place on a wire rack. Remove the foil cover, run a knife around the sides to release the pudding, and turn out onto the rack. Serve warm or at room temperature with a sauce of choice. The small puddings are great to douse in a teaspoon of brandy and ignite (carefully) at serving time.

english pudding with cranberries and walnuts

This is an Americanized version of the very traditional, very beloved English pudding called spotted dick, which originally called for shredded suet and raisins. We discovered this recipe while researching recipes to run with a newspaper story on the food eaten by Harry Potter and his cohorts. This pudding is unusual because there are no eggs or butter in the ingredients and it still makes a luscious, nicely textured pudding. It takes literally minutes to combine. Serve with a package of Bird's custard sauce made according to the package instructions, if you want to be very English, or else use the following recipe for old-fashioned boiled custard.

MACHINE: Large (10-cup) rice cooker; on/off only
CYCLE: Regular
YIELD: Serves 8 to 10

1/2 cup hot water
1/2 cup light molasses
2 teaspoons baking soda
1/4 teaspoon salt
1/4 teaspoon ground ginger
1/4 teaspoon ground cinnamon
1 1/2 cups all-purpose flour (Beth uses White Lily bleached all-purpose flour, a southern favorite, unsifted right out of the bag)
2 cups fresh or frozen (and thawed) cranberries
1/2 cup chopped walnuts
English Custard Sauce (page 310; optional)

1. Set up the rice cooker for steaming by placing a small trivet or wire cooling rack in the bottom of the rice bowl. Fill the bowl one-quarter to one-third full of hot water, close the cover, and set for the regular cycle. If the water boils before you are ready to steam the pudding, flip the switch to the Keep Warm position (switch back for cooking). Generously grease or coat the inside of a 1 1/2-quart (6-cup) round melon-shaped tin pudding mold with a clip-on lid with butter-flavored nonstick cooking spray.
2. In a large bowl, combine all the ingredients in the order given with a large rubber

spatula. Stir well with a folding motion until evenly moistened.

3. Scrape the batter into the prepared mold, filling it two-thirds full; snap on the lid. Set the mold on the trivet or wire rack in the bottom of the cooker, making sure it is centered and not tipped. Close the cover and reset the cooker for the regular cycle to bring back to a rolling boil, if necessary. Set a timer and steam for 1 hour, checking a few times to be sure the water doesn't boil off. Check the pudding for doneness; it should feel slightly firm to the touch, yet slightly moist. It should be puffed, rising to fill the mold, and a cake tester inserted in the center should come out clean. Unplug the machine to turn it off.

4. Using oven mitts, carefully transfer the mold from the steamer to a wire rack and remove the lid. Let stand for a few minutes, then turn upside down to unmold the pudding onto the rack or a serving plate.

5. Serve still warm, cut into wedges, or at room temperature, with custard sauce, if you like.

english custard sauce

YIELD: 2 cups

2 cups whole milk

$1/4$ cup sugar

1 teaspoon cornstarch

5 large egg yolks

$1 1/2$ teaspoons pure vanilla extract or $1 1/2$ tablespoons Amaretto

1. In a medium-size saucepan over medium heat, scald the milk. Set aside.

2. In a large bowl or food processor, combine the sugar and cornstarch. Whisk in the egg yolks and vanilla. Beat hard with a whisk or process briefly until light colored and foamy. Whisking constantly, or with the food processor running, add the hot milk gradually to the egg mixture. Pour the custard back into the saucepan.

3. Cook the sauce gently over medium-low heat, stirring constantly with a whisk, until just slightly thickened and smooth, and the sauce coats a spoon, about 5 minutes; do not boil. Pour the sauce into a storage bowl and let cool to room temperature. Refrigerate, covered, until serving time. Serve cold, pouring a little vanilla extract or Amaretto around each wedge of pudding.

persimmon pudding with brandy sauce

The apple of the Orient is our orange globe of fall called the persimmon, a sign that the holidays are here in California. The neighborhoods are dotted with trees outfitted with the fetching pointed ovals. It's easy to beg a few because most trees are so abundant and it is a much misunderstood old-fashioned fruit. You want the goopy Hachiya persimmon, which is pointed at the base, not the crisp, flatter Fuyu, which is good in salads. You can freeze the ripe fruit whole or store the pulp in plastic storage containers, so you can have persimmon pudding, bread, or cookies in the summer. If someone says they don't like persimmons, just serve them a slice of this spicy-sweet pud; they will love it.

MACHINE: Large (10-cup) rice cooker; on/off only
CYCLE: Regular
YIELD: Serves 8 to 10

3 to 4 very ripe Hachiya persimmons (jelly-like)
1¹/₄ cups sugar
¹/₄ cup (¹/₂ stick) unsalted butter, melted
3 tablespoons Cognac
2 large eggs
1¹/₄ cups unbleached all-purpose flour
1 tablespoon ground cinnamon
¹/₄ teaspoon salt
³/₄ cups chopped pecans
³/₄ cup dark raisins or dried cherries
1 tablespoon fresh lemon juice
2 tablespoons hot water
2 teaspoons baking soda
Brandy Sauce (page 312)

1. Set up the rice cooker for steaming by placing a small trivet or wire cooling rack in the bottom of the rice bowl. Fill the bowl one-quarter to one-third full of hot water, close the cover, and set for the regular cycle. If the water boils before you are ready to steam the pudding, flip the switch to the Keep Warm position (switch back for cooking). Generously grease or coat the inside of a 1½-quart (6-cup) round melon-shaped tin pudding mold with a clip-on lid with a butter-flavored nonstick cooking spray.

2. Remove the stems and skins from the persimmons (we slit them open and squeeze out the gooey pulp). Mash the pulp to make 1 to 1¼ cups. In a large bowl, whisk together the pulp, sugar, butter, Cognac, and eggs; beat until smooth. Switching to a large rubber spatula, stir in the flour, cinnamon, salt, pecans, raisins, and lemon juice; beat until combined. In a small bowl, stir together the hot water and baking soda. Pour into the batter and stir until well mixed.

3. Scrape the batter into the prepared mold, filling it two-thirds full; snap on the lid. Set the mold on the trivet or wire rack in the bottom of the cooker, making sure it is centered and not tipped. Close the cover and reset the cooker for the regular cycle to bring back to a rolling boil, if necessary. Set a timer and steam for 1 hour and 10 minutes, checking a few times to be sure the water doesn't boil off. Check the pudding for doneness; it should feel slightly firm to the touch, yet slightly moist. It should be puffed, rising to fill the mold, and a cake tester inserted in the center should come out clean. Unplug the machine to turn it off.

4. Using oven mitts, carefully transfer the mold from the steamer to a wire rack and remove the lid. Let stand for a few minutes, then turn upside down to unmold the pudding onto the rack or a serving plate.

5. Serve still warm, cut into wedges, or at room temperature, with spoonfuls of the Brandy Sauce.

brandy sauce

YIELD: 3 cups

1 large egg
$1/3$ cup unsalted butter, melted and still hot
1 cup sifted confectioners' sugar
Dash of salt
2 teaspoons Cognac
2 teaspoons Amaretto
1 teaspoon pure vanilla extract
1 cup cold heavy cream, whipped to soft peaks

In a medium-size bowl, beat the egg until light colored with an electric mixer. On low speed, drizzle in the butter, which will cook the egg; beat on medium-high speed for 15 seconds to thicken. Beat in the sugar, salt, Cognac, Amaretto, and vanilla, then fold in the whipped cream. Refrigerate in a covered container up to 2 hours before serving. Stir gently with a whisk, if necessary, before serving.

mohr im hemd

Mohr im Hemd, or Moor in a shirt, is a Viennese steamed chocolate and ground nut pudding topped with whipped cream to make a pure black-and-white dessert. It emerges as a delicate spongy cake with an almost oozy center, which is exactly the way it should be. Pure elegance. If you use a very bittersweet chocolate like Sharffen Berger, you don't have to use the two different chocolates, just 5 ounces of the one. This is a recipe Beth got from one of her all-time favorite cooking teachers, baker and pastry artist Diane Dexter.

MACHINE: Large (10-cup) rice cooker; on/off only
CYCLE: Regular
YIELD: Serves 8 to 10

4 ounces semisweet chocolate, chopped
1 ounce unsweetened chocolate
$1/2$ cup (1 stick) unsalted butter
2 slices dried-out white bread (sweet French bread or egg bread), crusts removed and pulled into pieces
1 cup (4 ounces) whole almonds
$1/2$ cup warm heavy cream
$1/4$ teaspoon pure almond extract
2 tablespoons all-purpose flour
$2/3$ cup plus 2 tablespoons granulated sugar
4 large eggs
Pinch of salt
$1 1/2$ cups cold heavy cream
3 tablespoons sifted confectioners' sugar
1 teaspoon pure vanilla extract

1. Place the chocolates and butter in the top of a double boiler and melt over simmering water.

2. Place the bread in a food processor and grind to coarse crumbs. You will have about 1 cup coarse-ground fresh bread crumbs. Add the almonds and process with the bread crumbs until finely ground. Place the mixture in a medium-size bowl and add the ½ cup warm cream and almond extract. Stir and let stand for 5 minutes.

3. Set up the rice cooker for steaming by placing a small trivet or 5-inch-diameter wire rack in the bottom of the rice bowl. Fill the bowl one-quarter to one-third full of hot water, close the cover, and set for the regular cycle. If the water boils before you are ready to steam the pudding, flip the switch to the Keep Warm position (switch back for cooking). Generously grease or coat the inside of a 1½-quart (6-cup) round melon-shaped tin pudding mold with a clip-on lid with butter-flavored nonstick cooking spray. Combine the flour and 2 tablespoons of the granulated sugar and dust the mold.

4. In a medium-size mixing bowl, beat the eggs, the remaining ⅔ cup granulated sugar, and the salt, using an electric mixer on high speed, until thick and light colored, about 3 minutes. Meanwhile, with a large rubber spatula, add the melted chocolate to the soaked crumbs. Fold the egg mixture into the crumb-chocolate mixture.

5. Scrape the batter into the prepared mold, filling it two-thirds full; snap on the lid. Set the mold on the trivet or wire rack in the bottom of the cooker, making sure it is centered and not tipped. Close the cover and reset the cooker for the regular cycle to bring back to a rolling boil, if necessary. Set a timer and steam for 1 hour, checking a few times to be sure the water doesn't boil off.

6. Meanwhile, whip the 1½ cups cold cream with an electric mixer in a medium-size bowl until just thickened; add the confectioners' sugar and vanilla. Beat until soft peaks form. Refrigerate until serving.

7. Check the pudding for doneness; it should feel slightly firm to the touch, yet slightly moist. It should be puffed, rising to fill the mold, and a cake tester inserted in the center should come out clean. Unplug the machine to turn it off. Using oven mitts, carefully transfer the mold from the steamer to a wire rack and remove the lid. Let stand for a few minutes, then turn upside down to unmold the pudding onto the rack or a serving plate.

8. Serve the pudding still warm, cut into wedges, or at room temperature, with spoonfuls of the whipped cream. Pass the extra whipped cream in a separate bowl.

Once you get comfortable with your rice cooker, you will find how easy it is to make and enjoy fresh rice on a daily basis. With that comes the inevitable: left-over rice. While rice is fluffy and moist when hot, the same component that keeps it this way "retrogrades" (a technical term to describe the hardening of the starch in the center of each grain) when chilled. The degree of retrograda-tion is slightly different in each rice, depending on how much starch is in the rice. A lot of cooks especially like jasmine rice for its ability to stay a bit softer after refrigeration than other white rices. Short- and medium-grain rices, ones that end up with a lot of starch surrounding the grain after cooking, will retro-grade into a solid mass (risotto is a good example here). A dish like fried rice or a stuffing is perfect with hardened, crunchy rice; it holds its shape during secondary cooking. The best rice salads are made with rice that has not been refrigerated first. Just let the rice sit on the counter, covered, as long as overnight before adding the other ingredients; the rice is perfectly safe and will not spoil quickly. Of course, after adding the other ingredients, you must refrigerate the salad.

We keep leftovers in small plastic freezer bags, ready to be defrosted overnight in the refrigerator or in the microwave, to add to recipes. The first preparation that comes to mind for leftover rice is fried rice, impro-vised in the kitchen and made anew with each batch. Rice is also a great ingredient in other recipes, such as in soups, fried rice, rice salads, and pancakes, just to name a few. We have assembled a selection here to get you inspired, but remember your leftover rice for stuffings, casseroles, muffins, and yeast breads as well.

plain rice and green tea (ochazuke)

Ochazuke is as simple as it gets: plain cooked rice warmed up with brewed green tea, in roughly the same proportions as cereal and milk. *Ochazuke* is such popular Japanese-American family food that it even has a baby talk name: *cha-cha gohan* (*cha-cha* refers to the tea; *gohan* is rice). The rice can be fresh from your rice cooker's Keep Warm cycle or at room temperature. If it has been refrigerated, you may wish to reheat it slightly, either in the rice cooker (page 49) or in the microwave. At the very least, remove it from the fridge while you prepare the tea. It can be a snack, a quick, light meal, or a way to end a family supper. If you wish, you can eat your tea rice with Japanese pickles (page 200) or a pickled plum (umeboshi).

YIELD: Serves 2

1¹/₂ cups cooked Japanese-style white rice
1 cup freshly brewed hot green tea

Divide the rice between two bowls. Pour the hot tea over the rice and serve.

japanese-style leftover rice soup

This is a type of *zosui*, the quick Japanese rice porridge made with cooked rice (as opposed to *okai* or *okayu*, which is made on the Porridge cycle or on the stove with raw rice). It is a great fridge-emptier for lunch the day after you've fixed a chicken dinner and have just one or two pieces left over. This recipe is from Julie's friend Sharon Noguchi, who learned to make it when she lived in Tokyo.

YIELD: Serves 2

2 large or 3 small dried or fresh shiitake
    mushrooms
3 cups water
One 1-inch square kombu (the seaweed
    used to make Dashi; page 349)
¹/₂ cup grated carrot
¹/₂ cup cooked skinless chicken cut into
    small chunks (or use another type of
    rather plain cooked meat)
1 cup sliced Napa cabbage leaves cut
    crosswise ¹/₂ inch thick
¹/₄ cup frozen petite peas
1¹/₂ cups cooked Japanese-style white rice
1 or 2 large eggs
Salt (optional)
Prepared chile sauce, chile paste, or
    chile oil, or a few drops of soy sauce
    (optional)

1. If you are using dried mushrooms, soften them by soaking in hot water to cover for 30 minutes, or microwave them.

To microwave, place the mushrooms in a container just large enough to hold them and add water just to cover. Cover the container tightly with plastic wrap and microwave on high for 2 minutes. Let the mushrooms rest until they are cool enough to handle. Drain.

2. Meanwhile, place the water in a medium-size saucepan. Gently clean the kombu square by wiping it with a damp paper towel, but do not remove the white powder, which adds flavor. Place the kombu in the water. Turn the heat to high. When the water boils, turn off the heat.

3. To prepare the softened mushrooms, trim off the tough stems and discard. Slice the caps as thinly as possible. If you are using fresh mushrooms, simply trim away the stems and thinly slice the caps. Add the mushrooms to the pan with the kombu, along with the carrot and chicken, and turn the heat to high again. Stir in the cabbage and peas. When the mixture comes to a boil, stir in the rice. Gently pour in the beaten egg in a swirl pattern, letting it set for a few seconds before stirring. The result will be threads of egg. Cook 2 to 3 minutes more, until the rice begins to soften.

4. Serve immediately, seasoned (if you wish) with salt to taste; a dash of chile sauce, paste, or oil; or just a few drops of soy sauce.

FRIED RICE

Giving recipes for fried rice is like giving recipes for tossed green salad. Yes, you can go to the store, buy specific items, and follow a recipe if you wish, but few salads are actually made that way. In reality, salad-makers open their crisper drawers and toss in what's there. Leafy greens, yes, and the rest depends on what's on hand.

It's pretty much the same with fried rice, which is popular in many Asian countries, and in the United States, too. "Fried rice for dinner is a staple for me," says Judith Dunbar Hines, cultural liaison for the city of Chicago and former cooking teacher and recipe development consultant. "I always make double the amount of rice, usually Thai jasmine, keep two-inch chunks of bacon in the freezer, then mix and match with what is in the refrigerator—bits of raw or cooked vegetables and leftover chicken or pork. It is a different dish every time." To make fried rice, you need rice, of course, some kind of onion, and whatever else you like—eggs, garlic, vegetables, bits of meat or seafood; all of these are good. Using some of these ingredients—or none of these—is also fine. Your seasoning can be as plain as a dash of salt and pepper or a splash of soy sauce or fish sauce, or you can use more elaborate bottled condiments such as oyster sauce and chile paste.

Usually cookbooks have only one or two fried rice recipes at best, so we took it upon ourselves to gather a few favorite recipes from friends who are fried rice lovers. In the pages that follow, you can find some really special recipes. But first, here are some general tips for making fried rice. After reading them, you'll be ready to clean out your own refrigerator!

■ **The pan:** You don't need a wok to make good fried rice; a good sauté pan or cast-iron skillet will do just as well, maybe better. We find a large nonstick skillet the best tool for making fried rice. A 10-inch skillet is large enough to make fried rice for one or two hungry people; a 12-inch skillet is needed to serve three or more.

■ **Nonstick cooking spray or vegetable oil:** A thorough spray of Pam or a similar product is generally enough to keep the rice from sticking to the pan. We usually spray the pan twice. (If you encounter sticking during the cooking, you can always add a few drops of oil.) The more traditional method is to use oil. Let your conscience be your guide, but if your pan has a good nonstick coating, 1 to 2 teaspoons of oil per serving is really enough. If you don't have a nonstick pan, you'll need 2 tablespoons or more.

■ **The rice:** Fried rice was invented for leftover cooked rice. Cold cooked rice works best in fried rice dishes because the grains remain separated. You can use almost any kind of plain cooked rice. While we recommend the type of rice to use in the ingredient lists, any variety of leftover rice can be substituted.

Cold, hard rice straight from the refrigerator is just fine and, in fact, is less likely to stick together than fresh cooked rice. One of the secrets to good fried rice is the rice itself: the colder the rice, the better. Use it directly out of the refrigerator or use just-thawed frozen rice that you let rest on the counter for an hour. (Some people freeze cooked rice just for fried rice.) When using cold rice, be sure to break up any clumps with your fingers as you add it to the skillet.

If you don't have any cold rice on hand, go ahead and steam some rice in the rice cooker just for your fried rice. Spread the steamed rice in a single layer on a baking sheet and let it cool to room temperature. Place the uncovered baking sheet in the refrigerator for up to eight hours or overnight before using the rice. If necessary, the rice may be used after one hour in the refrigerator, if you run your fingers through it to break it up before using.

■ **Aromatics:** Sliced green onion (white and green parts) is a popular ingredient in fried rice. Some sauté it at the beginning of cooking; some sprinkle it on top at the end. Garlic, too, makes frequent appearances. Be careful not to burn the garlic. Chopped or sliced onion works nicely, too.

■ **Vegetables:** Quick-cooking vegetables can be added raw. The list includes Napa cabbage, bok choy, fresh or dried (and already reconstituted) mushrooms, celery, zucchini, green peas (these can be used straight from the freezer), shredded carrot, and many more. For veggies that take longer to cook, such as broccoli or carrots cut into larger pieces, you might want to cook them crisp-tender first. Don't use too many vegetables, or too much of one kind; you don't want to overwhelm the rice. It is amazing how good fried rice can be with just a small amount of vegetables. When adding raw vegetables, you may want to sprinkle on a few teaspoons of water to help them cook.

■ **Eggs:** Scrambled eggs are a very common addition to fried rice. Some people scramble them, remove them from the pan so they don't overcook, and add them back later. Others just clear a space on one side of the pan (or in the center) by pushing away any ingredients that are already there, pour in the eggs, let them sit till they are about half-set, then toss or scoop the rice on top, folding and scrambling the eggs to break them up and mix them with the rice. It's an easy skill to master. You'll want no more than one egg per person, and less than that is fine.

■ **Meat and fish:** Raw or cooked, many kinds of meat, poultry, fish, and shellfish can be tossed into your fried rice with great results. Something smoked, such as bacon, a bit of smoked sausage, or ham, is nice; the smokiness adds an extra dimension of flavor. Here's where you can use up leftover bits of this or that. Be careful not to overload the rice with meat, though. The rice should always be the most prominent element of the dish.

■ **Finishing touches:** Finish off your fried rice with nothing more than a dash of salt, if you wish. Or go the next step and add soy sauce and a sprinkle of pepper, or use a couple of teaspoons or more of one of the many savory or spicy sauces on the shelf in the Asian section of your market. Black bean sauce, fish sauce, oyster sauce, chile paste—these or others will change the character of your fried rice. Curry powder is also good. Even ketchup is not unheard-of! Be sure to add your final touches while the rice is still on the stove. You want the seasonings to have a chance to warm up and gently blend with the rice and other ingredients. And, of course, don't go too wild. One type of sauce plus soy sauce, salt, and pepper is probably enough!

a note about msg: Many Asian home cooks add a seasoning containing the flavor-enhancer MSG to their fried rice: *Ajinomoto* (the Japanese name for MSG) is popular, as are Asian bouillon powders or powdered dashis. Feel free to sprinkle in one of these seasonings sparingly, if you wish. We've left them out of our recipes because some people have unpleasant reactions to MSG, and because we find fried rice very tasty without them.

fried shrimp brown rice

This recipe is adapted from one in *All-American Waves of Grain* by Barbara Grunes and Virginia Van Dynckt (Henry Holt, 1997), one of Beth's favorite books. The recipe has had a few transmutations with every making, but it is a delightfully savory fried rice with small shrimp (we like to use the 51/60 count). The omelet is a snap to cut into strips with a nice pair of kitchen shears, such as ones made by KitchenAid, with blades that are as sharp as a paring knife and used only for food. We use the authors' tip to use very cold rice (made the day before), even frozen rice that has just been taken out of the freezer before stir-frying, which seems to be especially important when using tender brown rices.

YIELD: Serves 4 to 6

1/2 cup dried shiitake mushrooms

3 tablespoons vegetable oil or Asian sesame oil

2 large or extra-large eggs, lightly beaten

1 large egg white, beaten until foamy

2 teaspoons dry white wine

2 teaspoons cornstarch

1/2 pound small shrimp, shelled, rinsed, and patted dry

4 green onions, white parts and 3 inches of the green parts, chopped

1 heaping cup bean sprouts

1/2 cup coarsely grated carrot

1/2 cup finely diced celery

1/2 cup finely diced zucchini

2 ribs bok choy, chopped, or 1/4 cup chopped fresh green beans

1/4 cup reduced-sodium tamari (a thick, strong soy sauce)

4 cups cold cooked brown rice, such as long-grain brown Texmati, Wehani, or red rice

Asian sesame oil, for serving (optional)

1. Soak the mushrooms in boiling water to cover until nice and soft, about 30 minutes, or microwave, covered tightly with plastic wrap, for 2 minutes. Let cool before draining. Trim away and discard the stems. Mince the caps and set aside.

2. Heat 1 tablespoon of the oil in a 10-inch skillet or wok. Pour in the beaten whole eggs. When they have set, turn the omelet over with 2 spatulas; cook briefly on the second side, but do not brown. Slide the omelet out of the pan onto a plate; cut into thin strips with kitchen shears or a knife.

3. In a medium-size bowl, whisk together the egg white, wine, and cornstarch. Add the shrimp and toss to coat.

4. Wipe out the skillet or wok with a paper towel and add the remaining 2 tablespoons oil over high heat. Add the shrimp mixture and stir-fry until lightly cooked, about 30 seconds. Transfer the shrimp to a bowl, leaving any liquid in the pan. Add the mushrooms, green onions, sprouts, carrot, celery, zucchini, and bok choy; stir-fry until cooked and warmed through, a few minutes. Add the tamari and rice; stir-fry, breaking up any clumps of rice, until nice and hot, about 5 minutes. Stir in the shrimp and cook until hot.

5. Serve the rice immediately, with a drizzle of sesame oil over the top, if desired.

plain fried rice, egg, and peas

This is as plain as it gets. You can leave out the egg, the peas, or both and have an even simpler dish. Beth adds 1/2 cup or so of diced Chinese barbecued pork or honey-baked ham and a few sliced water chestnuts to this basic fry. Remember to use a very cold rice, such as Chinese-Style Plain Rice (page 35), so it will hold up during the cooking.

YIELD: Serves 2

1 green onion, white and green parts, sliced
1 clove garlic, minced
2 cups cold cooked rice
1 large egg, lightly beaten (optional)
1/4 cup frozen petite peas, thawed
1/2 teaspoon salt, or to taste (optional)
2 teaspoons soy sauce

1. Coat a 10- or 12-inch nonstick skillet or wok with nonstick cooking spray twice. Heat the skillet over medium-high heat. Add the green onion and garlic and stir-fry for a minute or two to soften the onion; do not let the garlic burn. Add the rice, breaking up any clumps; stir-fry the rice, allowing it to heat up and grow fragrant.
2. If using the egg, push the rice over to one side of the pan and pour the egg into the empty space. Don't worry if the edges of the egg run into the rice. Allow the egg to cook for a few seconds undisturbed; the bottom will begin to set. Then stir the rice into the egg, folding the rice and egg over and over to distribute the egg bits as evenly as possible throughout the rice. Add the peas and keep stirring. When the peas are almost hot, add the salt, if using, and soy sauce. Stir to combine and serve the rice immediately.

mushroom fried rice with walnuts and scallions

From creative recipe consultant Julia Scannel, here is one of her unique home recipes. She recommends serving this rice as a meal starter or appetizer piled into individual butter lettuce leaves with a drizzle of plum sauce— like the minced chicken dish served with lettuce leaves for rolling, burrito style, found at some Chinese restaurants. The fried rice should be hot so it contrasts with the cold lettuce leaf, a real sensory treat.

YIELD: Serves 2 as a light meal, 4 as part of a larger meal

1/4 cup fresh green beans cut on the diagonal into 1/2-inch lengths
2 tablespoons soy sauce
1 tablespoon oyster sauce
1 tablespoon Shaoxing wine (available in Chinese markets) or medium-dry sherry
1 tablespoon plus 1 teaspoon peanut oil

1/2 small white onion, diced

2 cups chopped fresh mushrooms (mix of cremini, oyster, and shiitake)

1 clove garlic, minced

2 large eggs, lightly beaten

1 1/2 cups cold cooked white rice

1 green onion, white and green parts, thinly sliced on the diagonal, for garnish

2 tablespoons coarsely chopped walnuts, toasted (page 68), for garnish

1. Blanch the green beans in a pot of salted boiling water for 1 minute; drain and set aside.

2. Combine the soy sauce, oyster sauce, and wine in a small bowl and set aside.

3. Heat 1 tablespoon of the oil in a 12-inch skillet or heavy wok over medium-high heat. Add the onion and cook until softened, about 2 minutes, stirring frequently to avoid burning. Add the mushrooms and stir frequently until they have cooked through, about 5 minutes. Add the garlic and beans and cook, stirring, for 1 minute.

4. Make a large well in the bottom of the skillet by pushing the mushroom mixture to the outside of the pan. Add the remaining 1 teaspoon oil to the middle of the skillet. When the oil is hot, add the eggs to the well. After the eggs begin to set, gently stir until they reach a crumbly stage. Add the rice to the skillet and stir to incorporate the eggs and rice into the mushroom mixture, breaking up any clumps in the rice. Add the soy sauce mixture and stir to combine.

5. Serve the rice immediately, sprinkled with the green onion and walnuts.

sausage and portobello fried rice

Atsuko Ishii, the source of so much of the information about Japanese cooking in this book, contributed this recipe. At home in Tokyo, Atsuko would make this fried rice with fresh shiitake mushrooms, but here in the States, the portobellos are always available and more reasonably priced. Choose oyster sauce for a mild dish, chile bean paste for a spicier one.

YIELD: Serves 4 to 6

2 medium-size to large portobellos or 1/2 pound fresh shiitake mushrooms

8 ounces Polish smoked sausage

3 large eggs, lightly beaten

4 cups cold cooked rice

4 green onions, white and green parts, sliced

1 tablespoon oyster sauce or 1 tablespoon chile bean paste

2 tablespoons soy sauce

1. Clean the mushrooms by wiping them gently with a damp paper towel. Break off and discard the stems. Slice the caps about 1/2 inch thick. Cut the larger slices in half or thirds crosswise.

2. Slice the sausage in half lengthwise, then into half-moon slices about 1/3 inch thick.

3. Coat a 12-inch nonstick skillet with nonstick cooking spray. Heat the skillet over medium-high heat. Add the mushrooms and cook, stirring gently so as not to break

them. When they begin to soften, add the sausage and stir-fry until the sausage is slightly browned, 3 to 5 minutes. Transfer the mushrooms and sausage to a plate.

4. Quickly rinse and dry the skillet with a paper towel, coat it with nonstick cooking spray twice, and heat it over medium-high heat. When hot, pour in the eggs. Allow them to cook undisturbed for about 1 minute, until they are about half-set. Working quickly, add the rice, breaking up any clumps with your fingers or the spatula, and green onions. Stir to combine. Return the sausage and mushrooms to the skillet, stir to combine, and reheat. Add the oyster sauce and soy sauce and stir to combine. Serve the rice immediately.

fried wild rice with chicken and vegetables

Wild rice may sound unusual as a base for Chinese-style fried rice, but it is just as good as any Asian rice. It is a great way to use up leftovers, but we prefer to use it in equal proportions with long-grain white or brown jasmine rice to cut the inherent intensity of the grain.

YIELD: Serves 4

2 teaspoons plus 2 tablespoons canola oil or Asian sesame oil

1 large or extra-large egg, lightly beaten

1 teaspoon peeled and minced fresh ginger

1 teaspoon minced garlic

3 fresh mushrooms, sliced, or one 4-ounce can straw mushrooms, drained and left whole

1 whole boneless, skinless chicken breast, trimmed of fat and cut into strips

2 green onions, white parts and some of the green parts, chopped

1 stalk celery, diced

1/2 cup frozen petite peas or blend of peas and carrots, thawed

1/4 cup diced cooked ham

4 cups cold cooked wild rice or white and wild rice blend

2 tablespoons oyster sauce or vegetarian mushroom oyster sauce

1 tablespoon soy sauce

2 teaspoons Asian sesame oil

Pinch of freshly ground white pepper

1/4 cup chicken stock

1. Heat a small nonstick skillet over medium heat. When hot, add 2 teaspoons of the canola oil and the egg; tip the pan to spread the egg over the bottom of the pan (like you are making a crepe). Cook the egg until barely set; turn once and cook the other side for about 30 seconds. Slide the egg out of the pan and let cool. Fold over and cut into thin shreds with kitchen shears or a knife.

2. In a 12-inch skillet or wok, heat 1 tablespoon of the canola oil over high heat. Add the ginger, garlic, and fresh mushrooms (if using straw mushrooms, add with the rice later in the recipe); stir-fry for 10 seconds. Add the chicken and stir-fry until cooked through, a few minutes.

Transfer the mixture to a bowl, leaving any juices in the pan.

3. Add the remaining 1 tablespoon canola oil to the pan and add the green onions and celery. Stir-fry until softened, a few minutes. Add the peas, ham, rice, and straw mushrooms, if using; stir-fry, breaking up any clumps of rice, until nice and hot, at least 5 minutes. Add the oyster sauce, soy sauce, sesame oil, pepper, and chicken stock. Stir the chicken mixture and egg threads back in and cook until hot and the stock is evaporated. Serve immediately.

poo khao phat supparot

(thai pineapple fried jasmine rice with crab)

This fabulously exotic recipe for fried rice comes from San Francisco food writer Joyce Jue. Although any long-grain rice can be used for Thai fried rice, long-grain jasmine rice works best. In Thailand, jasmine rice is also called fragrant or scented rice. While jasmine rice does not have an actual jasmine scent, or any fragrant flower petal for that matter, it does emit a pleasant floral aroma when cooked. The crab paste in soybean sauce is a prepared condiment. It is not crabby or fishy but it does bring a savory essence to the dish; it is easily found in Asian specialty markets.

YIELD: Serves 4 to 6

1 ripe fresh pineapple

2 tablespoons vegetable oil

1/2 teaspoon salt

3 cloves garlic, coarsely chopped

1/4 pound medium-size shrimp, shelled and deveined

1/4 pound cooked chicken, cut into 1/2-inch dice

2 large or extra-large eggs

1 1/2 tablespoons Thai crab paste in soybean sauce

1 to 2 tablespoons ketchup

3 green onions, white parts and 1 inch of the green parts, thinly sliced

4 cups cold cooked Thai Jasmine Rice (page 40), gently crushed to break up clumps

2 tablespoons Thai fish sauce (*nam pla*)

Fresh cilantro leaves, for garnish

2 ounces fresh lump crabmeat, picked over for shells and cartilage, for garnish

1 tablespoon crispy fried shallot flakes (a ready-to-use product), for garnish (optional)

1. Preheat the oven to 400°F.

2. Cut the pineapple in half lengthwise. Hollow out each half, leaving the shells intact. Place the hollow shells on a baking sheet and set in the oven for 10 minutes to dry out. When dried, remove from the oven and set aside. Coarsely chop 1 cup of pineapple; place in a bowl and set aside. Keep the remaining pineapple for another use.

3. Heat a wok over medium-high heat and add the oil and salt. When hot, add the garlic; stir-fry until light golden brown, about 30 seconds. Increase the heat to high and add the shrimp and chicken; stir-fry until the shrimp are bright orange-pink, about 1 minute.

4. Make a well in the center of the hot wok; crack the eggs into it. With the spatula, break up the egg yolks, but do not scramble. Let the eggs fry without stirring until the whites turn opaque, about 1 minute. Add the crab paste and ketchup, stir once or twice, then add the green onions, rice, and fish sauce. Toss quickly to warm the rice and incorporate the seasonings, about 2 minutes.

5. Add the reserved pineapple; toss and stir to heat, about 1 minute. Spoon the rice into the pineapple shells and garnish with the cilantro leaves, crabmeat, and shallot flakes, if using. Serve immediately.

smoky seafood fried rice

Julie's friend Feng-Chih "Lucy" Wuchen, who is from Taiwan, is the source of this glamorous recipe, so named because it has two smoked ingredients. If you live near a Chinese deli, you can find the crowning touch, smoked cuttlefish. If not, don't worry; it's good without it, too. Fish balls are sold refrigerated and frozen in Asian markets. Look for them in the meat, deli, or freezer case. You can freeze any leftover fish balls until next time. And if you can't find fish balls or smoked cuttlefish, just toss in a few more shrimp. Lucy is a health-conscious cook who made this with medium-grain brown rice, but you could use white rice, too.

YIELD: Serves 3 to 4

3 green onions, white and green parts, sliced, 1 teaspoon green parts reserved for garnish

1 large or 2 small cloves garlic, minced

2 slices bacon, cut into 2-inch squares

4 fish balls, cut into quarters

6 to 8 medium-size shrimp, shelled and deveined

1/4 cup sliced smoked cuttlefish (optional)

1 cup finely shredded cabbage or bok choy

1 tablespoon water

2 1/2 cups cold cooked rice

2 tablespoons soy sauce

1/4 teaspoon salt (optional)

1. Coat a 12-inch nonstick skillet with nonstick cooking spray twice. Heat the skillet over medium-high heat. Add the green onions (except the reserved green parts) and garlic and stir-fry until the onions soften a bit; don't let the garlic burn. Add the bacon and continue to stir-fry. When the bacon begins to look cooked, add the fish balls and shrimp; stir-fry for 30 seconds. Add the cuttlefish, if using, and cabbage; sprinkle the water over the cabbage and stir-fry until the cabbage begins to soften and lose volume, a minute or so.

2. Add the rice, breaking up any clumps; stir-fry until it is warm and fragrant. Add the soy sauce and salt, if using; stir-fry to combine. Serve immediately, garnished with the reserved green onions.

sauté of corn, brown rice, and fresh basil

Just when you thought you knew all there was to know about fried rice, here is a fried rice from a different part of the world using the same techniques, but different ingredients. Here fresh vegetables and basil are cooked with leftover rice. This is a rice Beth makes as a side dish for catering sit-down dinner parties and it is a smash hit with everyone. Originally fashioned by food writer James McNair after a dish at one of Beth's favorite hangouts, Christy Hill Restaurant in Lake Tahoe, it has had a few transmutations over the years. Make it with equal amounts of wild rice and long-grain brown rice, or cook up one of the brown rice blends from Lundberg Family Farms; you want a hearty-flavored rice, not white rice. Make this immediately!

YIELD: Serves 4

2 tablespoons unsalted butter
2 tablespoons olive oil
2 tablespoons minced shallots
Corn kernels from 6 to 7 medium-size ears
    fresh white corn or one 12-ounce bag
    frozen baby white corn kernels, thawed
    (3 to 3$^{1}/_{2}$ cups)
2 cups cold cooked blend of wild rice and
    long-grain brown rice
3 tablespoons drained and minced oil-
    packed sun-dried tomatoes
$^{1}/_{3}$ cup minced fresh basil leaves
Salt
Freshly ground black pepper

1. In a 10- or 12-inch nonstick skillet, heat the butter and oil over medium-high heat. When the butter melts, add the shallots and sauté for a minute or two, until softened. Add the corn and cook for 1 to 2 minutes.
2. Add the rice, breaking up any clumps with your fingers, if necessary. Sauté for 2 minutes, allowing the rice to heat up and grow fragrant. Add the tomatoes and basil; keep stirring. Cook for another few minutes to heat all the ingredients through, season with salt and pepper to taste, and serve immediately.

RICE AND GRAIN SALADS

A well-made salad is an irresistible delight. It is healthy eating at its best. Inspiration runs wild, whether it be a simple or more elaborate combination of rice and grains mixed with fruits, vegetables, shreds of poultry or ham, or beans and tossed with a variety of superb dressings.

If you are making a fair amount of rice in your cooker, you will inevitably have leftovers and can use them here, if you'd like. Rice salads, while not a commonplace dish in most households, are an absolute delight; they are fantastic as well as filling. You can make a small salad from whatever leftovers you have, or freeze your leftover rice in plastic storage bags and collect enough for a salad, or make rice especially for your salad (which is what we do). Rice doesn't spoil at room temperature after it is cooked, so you can leave it at room temperature, covered, as long as overnight, then assemble your salad with tender rice. Always refrigerate any salad containing meat or dairy ingredients.

You can make your reputation as a cook on distinctive salads and here is a selection of some of our most requested favorites—the best of the best. Black Bean, Corn, and Rice Salad (at right), Curried Rice Salad (page 331), and Wild Rice Salad with Cranberries and Berry Vinaigrette (page 335) come from Beth's catering files and have been made to feed up to a hundred people (just scale up all the ingredients proportionally). The others are served for small gatherings at home. Remember that once you have assembled the salad, refrigerate it, and the rice will absorb the flavors you have added.

French dining has a meal known as *déjeuner sur l'herbe*, the veritable *picque-nicque*, our outdoor midday meal known as a picnic or barbecue. Some wine or lemonade, bread and cheese, cornichons, fresh fruit, a wonderful cake or some cookies, and a hearty salad are all that are needed for a feast. Carry salads in a cooler to keep them chilled until serving.

black bean, corn, and rice salad with green chile vinaigrette

This is a dynamite combination of beans, rice, and veggies. The vinaigrette is not too spicy, so it appeals to all sorts of diners. This is a great picnic salad since it is best at room temperature.

MACHINE: Medium-size (6-cup) rice cooker; fuzzy logic or on/off
CYCLE: Regular
YIELD: Serves 10

RICE
2 cups converted rice
4 cups water
1 teaspoon salt

VINAIGRETTE
$2/3$ cup corn or vegetable oil
$1/4$ cup fresh lime juice
3 tablespoons cider vinegar
2 tablespoons firmly packed light brown sugar
One 4-ounce can minced roasted green chiles, drained
1 teaspoon chili powder
1 teaspoon ground cumin

SALAD

Three 16-ounce cans black beans, drained
    and rinsed
Two 12-ounce packages frozen baby corn
    kernels, thawed
1 bunch green onions, white parts and
    some of the green parts, chopped
1/2 cup chopped fresh cilantro leaves

1. *Prepare the rice:* Place the rice in the rice
cooker bowl. Add the water and salt; swirl
to combine. Close the cover and set for the
regular cycle.

2. When the machine switches to the Keep
Warm cycle, let the rice steam for 10 minutes. Fluff the rice with a wooden or plastic rice paddle or wooden spoon. Keep the
cover open and let the rice cool to room
temperature right in the cooker bowl.

3. *Make the vinaigrette:* In a food processor,
combine all the vinaigrette ingredients.
Process, pulsing, until mostly smooth and
emulsified. It is okay to have some chunks
of chile.

4. *Assemble the salad:* In a large bowl, combine the rice, beans, corn, green onions,
and cilantro and mix to combine well.
Pour the vinaigrette over the salad. Toss
to combine and evenly coat. Let stand at
room temperature for up to 4 hours, or
cover and refrigerate for up to 2 days
before serving. Serve the salad at room
temperature.

waldorf rice salad

This is Beth's version of Waldorf salad. The
rice makes it more filling. You can use a bit
more dried cherries and almonds if you like a
lot of these. We say this serves four, but be
prepared: It has often been totally consumed
by two. Serve cold with roast turkey breast
and steamed vegetables.

YIELD: Serves 4

SALAD

3 firm eating apples, such as Fuji or Red
    Delicious, cored and diced
Juice of 1 small lemon
2 cups room temperature cooked rice,
    such as basmati, Jasmati, or long-grain
    brown (or use half wild rice)
2 to 3 stalks celery, sliced
1/2 cup slivered blanched almonds
1/2 cup dried tart cherries

DRESSING

1/2 cup mayonnaise
1/3 cup plain yogurt

1. *Make the salad:* Combine the apples and
lemon juice in a large bowl (we use one
with a snap-on lid). Add the rice, celery,
almonds, and cherries; toss together.

2. *Make the dressing:* In a small bowl, whisk
together the mayonnaise and yogurt. Pour
over the salad and stir with a large rubber
spatula to combine and coat evenly with
the dressing. Store the salad in the refrigerator until ready to serve. This is best eaten
the day it is made.

lentil and brown rice salad

When Chez Panisse restaurant opened a café upstairs from the main dining room, it quickly became one of Beth's watering holes whenever she went to shop or visit friends in Berkeley. Since it was always so jammed, it was best to show up for lunch just after the doors opened at 11 A.M. Her favorite lunch was a lentil salad with soft fresh goat cheese crumbled on top, peasant French bread and sweet butter, and a Perrier mineral water, all for about five dollars. The café switched to taking reservations to relieve the crowds, so it is difficult to get in for a casual spur-of-the-moment lunch anymore. Here is Beth's version of her favorite salad with the addition of brown rice.

MACHINE: Medium (6-cup) rice cooker; fuzzy logic or on/off

CYCLE: Regular

YIELD: Serves 8

LENTILS

1 cup dried petite French lentils or green lentils

2 cups water

1 teaspoon salt

2 sprigs of fresh thyme or 1¹/2 teaspoons dried thyme

VINAIGRETTE

3/4 cup olive oil

1/3 cup red wine vinegar (a bit less if you use cabernet vinegar)

Salt

Freshly ground black pepper

SALAD

2 cups room temperature cooked Brown Jasmine Rice (page 54)

3 green onions, white parts and some of the green parts, chopped, or 1/4 cup minced fresh chives

1/2 cup finely chopped celery or seeded and finely chopped red bell pepper

1/3 cup finely chopped red onion

3 tablespoons chopped fresh Italian parsley leaves

3 tablespoons chopped golden raisins

3 tablespoons chopped walnuts

5 ounces goat cheese, crumbled

1. *Prepare the lentils:* Rinse and pick over the lentils. Place the lentils, water, salt, and thyme in the rice cooker bowl. Close the cover and set for the regular cycle and set a timer for 40 minutes. The liquid should all be absorbed. When the cycle ends or the timer sounds, unplug the machine, open the cover, and let the lentils cool to room temperature right in the cooker bowl.

2. *Make the vinaigrette:* In a small bowl, whisk together the oil, vinegar, and salt and pepper to taste. Set aside.

3. *Assemble the salad:* In a large bowl, combine the rice, lentils, green onions, celery, red onion, parsley, raisins, and walnuts. Toss with enough of the dressing to coat lightly; it is okay to have some vinaigrette left over. Let stand at room temperature for 1 hour before serving, or cover tightly and refrigerate for as long as overnight.

4. Serve the salad at room temperature, adding the goat cheese right before serving.

curried rice salad

This is a fantastic salad Beth originally learned from food writer Louise Fiszer when she had her cooking school in Menlo Park, California. The dressing evolved to this honey-curry version, which is so good, Beth often gives it by the jar for Christmas presents (it is just as nice on romaine or butter lettuce). Even if curry is not your thing, this dressing will have you licking your lips. You can use the imported white basmati or domestic brown basmati. Be sure to serve the salad nice and cold.

MACHINE: Medium (6-cup) rice cooker; fuzzy logic or on/off

CYCLE: **Regular**

YIELD: Serves 8

RICE

2 cups basmati rice

2¹/₂ cups water

1/2 teaspoon salt

1 cup chopped pecans or pistachios

DRESSING

2/3 cup mayonnaise

1/2 cup plain yogurt

1/3 cup sour cream

1/4 cup chutney of your choice

1 tablespoon fresh lemon juice

2 tablespoons honey

2 1/2 teaspoons curry powder dissolved in 1 tablespoon hot raspberry vinegar

SALAD

4 green onions, white parts and some of the green parts, chopped

2 stalks celery, chopped

1 large tart apple, peeled, cored, and chopped

1 cup chopped dried apricots

One 12-ounce package frozen petite peas, thawed

1. *Prepare the rice:* Place the rice in the rice cooker bowl and fill with cold water. Swish it around with your fingers. Carefully pour off the water, wash, and drain well a few times until the water runs clear. Add the 2½ cups water and salt; swirl to combine. Close the cover and set for the regular cycle. When the machine switches to the Keep Warm cycle, let the rice steam for 10 minutes. Fluff the rice with a wooden or plastic rice paddle or wooden spoon. Unplug the machine, keep the cover open, and let the rice cool to room temperature right in the cooker bowl.

2. Preheat the oven to 350°F.

3. Place the nuts on a baking sheet and toast just until they begin to color, 5 to 8 minutes. Remove from the oven, let cool to room temperature, and set aside.

4. *Make the dressing:* Place all the dressing ingredients in a food processor and pulse a few times to combine and chop the chutney. Scrape into a bowl, cover, and refrigerate.

5. *Assemble the salad:* In a medium-size salad bowl, combine the rice, green onions, celery, apple, apricots, peas, and nuts. With a large spatula, combine the salad ingredients with enough of the dressing to lightly coat, reserving any extra dressing in the refrigerator. Store the salad, covered, in the refrigerator and serve it chilled. It is best served the day it is made, or cover tightly and refrigerate no longer than overnight.

autumn rice and wheat berry salad

This recipe using wheat berries, wild rice, and two rices comes from friend and prolific food writer Peggy Fallon, who has impeccable taste buds. You will need to make the three different rices in shifts, even the day before, so plan accordingly. This is such a good salad.

MACHINE: Medium (6-cup) rice cooker; fuzzy logic or on/off

CYCLE: Regular

YIELD: Serves 6 to 8

WHEAT BERRIES AND CONVERTED RICE

$^1/_2$ cup wheat berries

Boiling water for soaking

$^1/_2$ cup converted rice

$^3/_4$ cup plus 2 tablespoons water

$^1/_4$ teaspoon salt

1 cup chopped walnuts

DRESSING

$^1/_2$ cup balsamic vinegar

1 tablespoon Dijon mustard

2 shallots, minced

Salt

Freshly ground black pepper

$^1/_4$ cup walnut oil

1 cup light olive oil

SALAD

$1^1/_2$ cups room temperature cooked Brown Jasmine Rice (page 54)

$1^1/_2$ cups room temperature cooked Basic Wild Rice (page 167)

1 cup seeded and chopped red bell pepper

1 cup seeded and chopped yellow bell pepper

$^1/_2$ cup chopped fresh Italian parsley leaves

$^1/_2$ pound fresh sugar snap peas or snow peas, strings removed, blanched for 1 minute in boiling water, and drained

1. *Prepare the wheat berries and converted rice:* Place the wheat berries in a bowl and cover with boiling water. Let soak at room temperature for 2 hours.

2. Place the converted rice in the rice cooker bowl. Add the water and salt; swirl to combine. Close the cover and set for the regular cycle. When the machine switches to the Keep Warm cycle, let the rice steam for 20 minutes. Fluff the rice with a wooden or plastic rice paddle or wooden spoon. Unplug the machine, keep the cover open, and let the rice cool to room temperature right in the cooker bowl.

3. Preheat the oven to 350°F.

4. Place the walnuts on a baking sheet and toast just until they begin to color, 5 to 8 minutes. Remove from the oven, let cool to room temperature, and set aside.

5. *Make the dressing:* In a small bowl or food processor, combine the vinegar, mustard, shallots, and salt and pepper to taste. Add the walnut oil and olive oil and whisk or process until thick. Set aside.

6. *Assemble the salad:* Place the three rices in a medium-size salad bowl. Drain the wheat berries well and add to the rice. Add the bell peppers and parsley and stir to combine. Toss with enough of the dressing to lightly coat, reserving any extra dressing in the refrigerator. Add the peas and walnuts right before serving the salad at room temperature. This salad is best eaten the day it is made.

barley salad with fresh dill and vegetables

This scrumptious salad is adapted from a recipe from *Jane Brody's Good Food Book* (Norton, 1985). It is one of our favorite ways to eat barley, a grain noted for its natural cholesterol-reducing qualities.

MACHINE: Medium (6-cup) rice cooker; fuzzy logic or on/off

CYCLE: **Regular**

YIELD: Serves 4

BARLEY

1 cup pearled barley

1 cup water

³/₄ cup plus 2 tablespoons chicken stock

Pinch of salt

VINAIGRETTE

¹/₂ cup olive oil

¹/₄ cup cider vinegar

1 clove garlic, flattened

Salt

Freshly ground black pepper

SALAD

1 large red bell pepper, seeded and diced

1 large carrot, coarsely grated

1 stalk celery, chopped

1 medium-size red onion, finely chopped

1 bunch radishes, ends trimmed and thinly sliced

¹/₄ cup chopped fresh dill

¹/₄ cup chopped fresh Italian parsley leaves

1. *Prepare the barley:* Place the barley in the rice cooker bowl. Add the water, stock, and salt; swirl to combine. Close the cover and set for the regular cycle. When the machine switches to the Keep Warm cycle, let the barley steam for 15 minutes. Fluff the barley with a wooden or plastic rice paddle or wooden spoon. Unplug the machine, keep the cover open, and let the barley cool to room temperature right in the cooker bowl.

2. *Make the vinaigrette:* In a small bowl, whisk together the oil, vinegar, garlic, and salt and pepper to taste. Let stand at room temperature.

3. *Assemble the salad:* Place the barley in a medium-size salad bowl or a decorative refrigerator bowl with a plastic cover. Add the vegetables, dill, and parsley. Remove the garlic from the dressing. Toss the salad ingredients with the dressing to lightly coat. Store the salad, covered, in the refrigerator and serve it chilled. Though this salad tastes best the day it is made, you can refrigerate it overnight.

quinoa tabboulé

In conversation with a friend in France, Beth was surprised one day when she mentioned tabboulé—the Middle Eastern salad made with bulgur—and said that it was very popular in Paris for school lunches. Having made so many variations of the satisfying staple salad over the years, here is one with quinoa substituted for the bulgur. You can also make this recipe substituting the same amount of bulgur cracked wheat for the quinoa.

YIELD: Serves 6

SALAD

1 recipe Basic Quinoa (page 162), cooled
    to room temperature

1/2 pound ripe tomatoes, seeded, if
    desired, and diced

1/2 pound cucumber, peeled, seeded if the
    seeds are watery, and diced

1/2 small red onion, thinly sliced and cut
    into 1/2-inch-wide strips

1/2 cup minced fresh Italian parsley leaves

DRESSING

1/4 cup fresh lemon juice

1/3 cup olive oil

Few drops of Tabasco sauce

1/2 teaspoon freshly ground black pepper

1. *Assemble the salad:* Place the quinoa in a large salad bowl. Add the tomatoes, cucumber, and onion; toss together.

2. *Make the dressing:* In a small bowl, whisk together the lemon juice, olive oil, Tabasco, and pepper. Pour the dressing over the salad, add the parsley, and stir with a large spoon to combine. Refrigerate the salad, covered, until ready to serve. Serve the tabboulé at room temperature. It is best served the day it is made.

japanese rice and cabbage salad

Beth's friend Susie Korngold has been making some version or another of this salad for decades. It consistently shows up at family potlucks and is always a welcome addition. When asked for the recipe, Beth received a card with just the ingredients, no measurements. "You know, I never wrote that down, so I will try to give you an idea from memory," said Susie. "Each time I make it, I change it a little bit." New additions include toasted peanuts, mung bean sprouts, some grated daikon radish, or carrot. Luckily, Beth wrote down the version she had at Susie's parents' 40th wedding anniversary party and here it is. You can use Japanese-style medium-grain white rice or brown jasmine, if you like, instead of the short-grain brown.

YIELD: Serves 6

SALAD

4 cups room temperature cooked medium-
    grain brown rice

1/2 head Napa cabbage, cored and
    shredded

1 bunch green onions, white parts and
    some of the green parts, chopped

1/2 cup chopped fresh cilantro leaves

1 or 2 fresh shiitake mushrooms, stems
    removed and caps very thinly sliced

2 heaping tablespoons toasted Japanese
    sesame seeds (page 145)

DRESSING

1/4 cup cold-pressed sesame or vegetable oil (sesame is best)

1 tablespoon toasted sesame oil

1 tablespoon fresh lemon juice or rice vinegar

One 1-inch piece fresh ginger, peeled and pressed through a garlic press

2 tablespoons honey

3 tablespoons tamari (a thick, strong soy sauce)

1. *Make the salad:* Place the rice in a medium-size salad bowl. Add the cabbage, green onions, cilantro, and mushrooms and mix well to combine.

2. *Make the dressing:* In a small bowl whisk together all the dressing ingredients. Pour the dressing over the rice and vegetables, add the sesame seeds, and stir with a large spoon to combine. Store the salad, covered, in the refrigerator and serve chilled or at room temperature. You can make this a day ahead and refrigerate it overnight, but it tastes best the day it is made.

wild rice salad with cranberries and berry vinaigrette

This is Beth's most requested salad for catering. It has been made for 10 and for 100, with equal success. The fresh berries in the dressing make it thicker and help it coat the rice. You will be preparing two batches of rice, so plan accordingly; we just make extra basmati, jasmine, or converted rice (the white rice mellows the flavor of the wild rice) and keep it in the freezer, ready to be defrosted and tossed with the other salad ingredients. This can be made the day before to give time to meld the flavors.

MACHINE: Medium (6-cup) rice cooker; fuzzy logic or on/off
CYCLE: Regular
YIELD: Serves 8

RICE

1 1/2 cups wild rice

3 cups water

3/4 teaspoon salt

1 cup coarsely chopped walnuts

VINAIGRETTE

1/2 cup canola or vegetable oil

1/2 cup red or black raspberry vinegar

2 teaspoons Dijon mustard

4 to 5 fresh strawberries, rinsed and hulled

Salt

Freshly ground black pepper

SALAD

1 1/2 cups room temperature cooked white
   or brown rice

1 bunch green onions, white parts and
   some of the green parts, chopped

4 stalks celery, chopped

1 1/2 cups dried cranberries

Two 12-ounce packages frozen petite
   peas, thawed

1. *Prepare the rice:* Place the wild rice in the rice cooker bowl. Add the water and salt; swirl to combine. Close the cover and set for the regular cycle. When the machine switches to the Keep Warm cycle, let the rice steam for 20 minutes. Fluff the rice with a wooden or plastic rice paddle or wooden spoon. Unplug the machine, keep the cover open, and let the rice cool to room temperature right in the cooker bowl.

2. Preheat the oven to 350°F.

3. Place the walnuts on a baking sheet and toast until they just begin to color, 5 to 8 minutes. Remove from the oven, let cool to room temperature, and set aside.

4. *Make the vinaigrette:* In a food processor, combine the oil, vinegar, mustard, and strawberries. Process until smooth and slightly thick; if too thin, add another berry or two. Season with salt and pepper to taste. Scrape into a bowl, cover, and refrigerate.

5. *Assemble the salad:* Place the wild rice in a medium-size salad bowl. Add the white or brown rice, green onions, celery, cranberries, peas, and walnuts, stirring to incorporate. With a large spatula, combine the salad ingredients with enough of the vinaigrette to lightly coat, reserving any extra vinaigrette in the refrigerator. Store the salad, covered, in the refrigerator and serve at room temperature. This can be prepared up to a day ahead.

creamy rice salad with fresh fruits

Back in the early 1970s, a friend of Beth's was involved with the Vedanta Society, one of the first meditation groups in the United States based on ancient orthodox Indian Hindu philosophy. At the time, the group was based in Berkeley, California. They had evening lectures at different people's homes and after the swami spoke and told parable-like stories based on the principles of Eastern thought, they had tea and dessert. At one of these gatherings, this sweet rice salad was served, almost a simple uncooked rice pudding, a favorite of the swami's. What a delight! It was fresh cooked white rice with whipped cream and mixed fresh fruit—that night a combination of fresh pineapple, mandarin oranges, bananas, and papayas—folded in to make it a delightful and ever-so-slightly heavenly dessert.

YIELD: Serves 6

3 cups room temperature cooked basmati
   rice (page 38)

2 cups cold heavy cream

1 teaspoon pure vanilla extract

3 cups chopped or sliced ripe fruits,
   such as mangos, papayas, bananas,
   raspberries, strawberries, blackberries,
   pineapple, kiwifruit, Fuyu persimmons,
   Comice pears, or fresh or canned
   mandarin oranges (any seasonal
   combination)

1. Place the rice in a large serving bowl.

2. In a chilled large bowl, whip the heavy cream and vanilla together with an electric mixer set at high speed until soft peaks form and just hold their shape. Fold the whipped cream into the rice with a large rubber spatula until evenly combined. Add the fruit (you want about equal amounts of fruit and rice) and gently fold in. Cover the salad and refrigerate for a few hours. It is best served the day it is made.

PANCAKES

Pancakes are one of the oldest foods, since they can be baked on a griddle rather than in an oven. Often thought of as only breakfast food, they make a wonderful grain-rich side dish or substitute for a sandwich. Pancakes are a perfect vehicle for leftover rice; you just stir in some leftover rice for flavor and texture. Here are four of our favorite renditions, all simple beyond belief, and very tasty and filling.

rice pancakes

Our dear friend, Washington, D.C. writer Joyce Gemperlein, created these nutritious and savory cakes for her young daughter Jocelyn's breakfast or lunch box. They are tasty hot or cold, and they can even be finger food (that is how Jocelyn eats them).

YIELD: 12 to 14 three-inch pancakes; serves 2 to 4

2 cups cold cooked white or brown rice

2 large eggs

2 to 3 tablespoons freshly grated Parmesan or other cheese

$1/4$ teaspoon salt, or more to taste

$1/8$ teaspoon freshly ground black pepper or splash of hot pepper sauce, or more to taste

1. In a medium-size bowl, using a fork, combine all the ingredients until evenly moistened with the egg.

2. Coat a large skillet or griddle with a bit of oil or nonstick cooking spray and heat over medium heat. Drop the batter into the skillet by tablespoonfuls, making pancakes about 3 inches in diameter and smoothing them out with the back of the spoon, if needed. Cook until golden brown and crisp, 3 to 4 minutes per side, turning once. Serve the pancakes hot or cold.

savory wild rice pancakes

The husky flavor and rustic texture of wild rice are delightful in these savory dinner pancakes. Beth makes these by the hundreds for special catering dinners and there is never a one left over. Serve with some chutney on the side or gravy drizzled over.

YIELD: 20 three-inch pancakes; serves 4 to 6

1/4 cup (1/2 stick) unsalted butter

2 small to medium-size shallots, minced

1 cup unbleached all-purpose flour or
   whole wheat pastry flour

1 tablespoon baking powder

1/2 teaspoon salt

3 large eggs

1 cup milk

1 1/2 cups room temperature or cold cooked
   wild rice

1. Melt the butter in a medium-size skillet over medium heat, add the shallots, and cook, stirring, until softened. Set aside.

2. In a large bowl or food processor, combine the flour, baking powder, and salt, and whisk or process or blend. Add the shallots, eggs, and milk; beat or process just until smooth. The batter will be thin, yet thicker than crepe batter. Stir in the wild rice.

3. Heat a griddle or heavy skillet over medium heat until a drop of water skates over the surface, then lightly grease with butter. Pour the batter onto the griddle, using 2 tablespoons batter for each pancake. Cook until bubbles form on the surface, the edges are dry, and the bottoms are golden brown, about 2 minutes. Turn once, cooking the second side until golden, about 1 minute. The second side will take half the amount of time to cook as the first side. Serve the pancakes immediately or keep warm in a preheated 200°F oven until ready to serve.

leftover risotto pancakes

Risotto does not reheat well, so if you have any left over, the best way to eat the day-old Italian rice dish is to make a pancake. Known as *risotto al salto* in Milan, it is traditionally made into one large pancake, then cut into wedges to serve. This recipe makes two over-sized six-inch pancakes.

You can make the one pancake if you wish in a larger skillet, but the cooking time will increase slightly. The best risotto pancake is cooked slowly to create a nice crust on both sides, so don't rush. Risotto pancakes are good for breakfast or lunch right out of the skillet, or as a room temperature picnic food or snack.

YIELD: 2 pancakes; serves 2

1 or 2 large eggs, beaten

1 3/4 cups cold cooked risotto

1 to 2 tablespoons tomato paste or tomato
   sauce, or pinch of minced fresh herb
   leaves, such as basil, Italian parsley, or
   marjoram (optional)

2 tablespoons plus 2 teaspoons unsalted
   butter or olive oil, or a combination

3 tablespoons freshly grated Parmesan or
   other cheese, for serving

Freshly ground black pepper, for serving

1. Depending on the consistency of the risotto, if you like a dry pancake, use 1 egg; if you want more of a frittata, use 2 eggs. Combine the egg and risotto in a medium-size bowl and mix well. Add the tomato paste, sauce, or herbs if you want to add some complementary flavoring to the risotto.

2. Heat a small, heavy 6-inch skillet until a drop of water skates over the surface, then add 2 teaspoons of the butter or olive oil, coating the entire surface. Place half of the mixture in the skillet, flattening with the back of the spoon or spatula to make an even pancake that fills the bottom of the skillet. Cook over medium heat until the edges are dry and the bottom turns golden and crusty, about 5 minutes. Loosen the bottom with a spatula and turn once by flipping with the spatula or sliding the pancake onto a small plate and sliding it off the plate to retain the large size.

Add the remaining 2 teaspoons butter or olive oil to the pan, return the pancake to the pan, and cook the second side until golden and crusty, about 5 minute longer. Remove from the pan and cook the second pancake using 2 teaspoons butter for each side.

3. Serve the pancakes immediately, sprinkled with the cheese and some black pepper, keep warm in a preheated 200°F oven until ready to serve, or let cool to eat later.

buttermilk rice breakfast pancakes

Leftover rice makes a great American-style breakfast pancake. If you are a pancake lover, consider investing in an electric griddle, so you can cook all the pancakes at one time. We like our pancakes served simply, with luscious grade B pure maple syrup and butter dripping down the sides, but sliced fruit, cottage cheese, or hot applesauce works as well. If you wish to make rice waffles, simply cut back the buttermilk by 1/4 cup to make a slightly thicker batter.

YIELD: 12 four-inch pancakes; serves 2 to 4

2 1/4 cups unbleached all-purpose flour
1 1/2 teaspoons baking powder
1 teaspoon baking soda
Large pinch of salt
2 1/2 cups buttermilk
2 large eggs
3 tablespoons unsalted butter, melted, or vegetable oil
1 cup cold cooked white or brown rice

1. In a large bowl, combine the flour, baking powder, baking soda, and salt. In a medium-size bowl, whisk together the buttermilk, eggs, and butter. Add the buttermilk mixture to the dry ingredients, stirring just until combined. Do not overmix; the batter should have small lumps.

Stir in the rice. Let the batter rest at room temperature for 5 minutes.

2. Heat a griddle or heavy skillet over medium-high heat until a drop of water skates over the surface, then lightly grease with butter. Pour the batter onto the griddle, using a ¼-cup measure for each pancake. Cook until bubbles form on the surface, the edges are dry, and the bottom is golden brown, about 2 minutes. Turn once, cooking the second side until golden, about 1 minute. The second side will take half the amount of time to cook as the first side. Serve the pancakes immediately or keep warm in a preheated 200°F oven until ready to serve.

the basics: homemade
STOCKS

Many of the recipes in this book call for the addition of a stock, a symbol of wholesome, healthful home cooking. A stock is made with a combination of raw, uncooked poultry, meat, or fish; aromatic vegetables; fresh water; and a bouquet garni, a bundle of herbs. These ingredients are simmered together until their essences have been extracted out into the water. Stock provides a depth of flavor not available from using just water. No salt is added so that you can season the final recipe to taste at its completion. Stocks are an important component of rice cookery and especially essential in pilafs and risottos. There's no doubt—homemade is definitely best here. You will never imitate the quality and flavor of homemade stock with a can of broth or a cube.

Making a stock (a word that is often used interchangeably with broth) is really very simple. A few minutes are needed to combine all the ingredients in the pot with enough water just to cover everything, and then it is left alone to simmer for several hours (the exception here are fish stocks, which are prepared in under an hour), until it develops its own sweet aroma. Vegetables from the supermarket produce section are as good as ones harvested from a home garden. Frankly, the simpler the ingredients, the better the stock, so resist throwing all those vegetable scraps into the pot unless you are making a vegetable stock.

While the water is coming to a boil for your stock, prepare your bouquet garni. The combination of parsley, thyme, bay leaf, and peppercorns is a classic in Mediterranean herb bouquets. Instead of tossing the herbs into the stock by themselves, the herbs are neatly placed in the center of a 10-inch square of cheesecloth and tied with some kitchen twine. If you don't have any cheese-cloth, just gather up the herbs in a small bunch and wrap with twine. A small bouquet garni will suffice in each of the following recipes. You can improvise with any combination of herbs you like—rosemary, sage, marjoram, curly or Italian parsley, even dried mushrooms and a hot little dried chile pepper. When you turn down the heat to a simmer, toss in the bouquet garni. During the final skimming, you will easily be able to discard it easily.

Hardcore stock makers use their "special" stockpot—usually made from stainless steel or anodized aluminum like Calphalon—a pot that is deeper than it is wide. Never use a cheap aluminum pot or cast-iron Dutch oven; your stock will taste very metallic. There are many sizes of stockpots, from small to large. Buy one that reflects the amount of stock you normally make in each batch. The following recipes make small amounts of stock, so a medium-size six-quart capacity stockpot will do nicely and be easy to lift when full.

Once your stock is done simmering, let it cool a bit (ideally to around 160°F); be aware, though, that you do not want your stock sitting around at room temperature for any length of time; otherwise, your nice, warm stock becomes a breeding ground for bacteria. Use a small saucepan or large ladle to transfer the still-warm stock to a cheese-cloth-lined colander sitting in a larger bowl. Do this procedure over the sink, since during the process of straining there is the chance of splashing. The solids will catch in the colander and, when you lift it out, you can admire your beautiful, clear stock. After straining, refrigerate the stock until cold. The fat will coagulate on top and be easy to remove.

Buy a variety of two- and four-cup freezer containers at the supermarket that stack easily in the freezer; the square ones are the most space efficient. The recipes in this book call for a variety of stocks, but please note that you can most certainly use what is at hand. Add a bit of salt and pepper and you can savor a bowl of stock on its own or pour it over toasted country bread for a great lunch!

A WORD ON COMMERCIAL STOCKS AND BROTHS

For the cooks who always wish they had luscious homemade stocks stashed in the freezer, but don't, fear not; here's what we've learned from extensive testing with canned broths.

In adapting your own recipes to the rice cooker, remember that canned broth is intense and salty and can easily overpower other flavors. If a risotto or other dish con-tains ingredients with delicate flavors—Butternut Squash Risotto (page 130) is one example—try it with half water, half broth, or search out a reduced-sodium or salt-free broth.

In general, you get what you pay for. The cheap brands taste it. Swanson's is available nationwide and is fine, and the new reclosable aseptic packaging is very handy (if you can stand the fact that those juice box–type containers can't be recycled in most parts of the country). Ready-made frozen commercial stocks have become increasingly available, a specialty food item that is almost an artisan craft, and though they are quite good, they tend to be very expensive.

In many parts of the world, including Italy, dry bouillon powder or cubes (such as Knorr) dissolved in water are essential constituents of the home pantry, contributing their distinctive flavors to many grain dishes. Bouillon cubes are considered a type of *glacé*, or stock that has been reduced to a thick, concentrated mass. Consommé falls in between and should be thinned with an equal amount of water, if using. Unfortunately, bouillons are all highly salted and often taste artificial in the finished dish. Use these or not, as you prefer, but know that if you use a bouillon broth in recipes calling for homemade or canned, you will definitely taste the difference.

chicken stock

If you make only one type of homemade stock, it should be chicken stock. Unsalted chicken stock is a cornerstone of good cooking and is called for in many recipes in this book. While many stocks call for a reduction, or boiling down, to concentrate the flavor, we have found that the best stock for cooking rice and grains in the rice cooker is more delicate in flavor and color. Many cooks use only the accumulated scrap parts (kept in the freezer) and make great stock; we like cutting up a whole chicken and adding the extra parts. Julie makes chicken stock in the pressure cooker; it is done after 35 minutes of pressure cooking.

YIELD: About 2¹/₂ quarts

5 pounds chicken backs, necks, wings, and carcasses, or one 5- to 7-pound chicken, cut up and fat removed (no liver)
2 medium-size yellow onions, cut into quarters
1 medium-size carrot, cut into chunks
5 stalks celery, with leaves
4 sprigs fresh Italian parsley, with stems
10 black peppercorns

1. Place the chicken in a large stockpot. Add water to cover by 2 inches. Partially cover and bring to a boil over high heat. Skim off the foam on the surface. Cover, reduce the heat to medium-low, and simmer for 2 hours, skimming as necessary.

2. Add the vegetables and peppercorns, cover, and simmer for 2 hours longer. Remove the cover and let the stock cool to lukewarm. Line a large colander or strainer with cheesecloth and set it over a large bowl; carefully pour the stock through to strain it. Press the vegetables to extract all the liquid.

3. Pick the meat off the chicken, then discard the skin, bones, and vegetables. Reserve the meat for soup, salad, or another purpose, if desired. Divide the stock into airtight plastic freezer storage containers, leaving 2 inches at the top to allow for expansion in the freezer. The stock is ready for use and can be refrigerated for up to 2 to 3 days, or frozen for 3 to 6 months.

turkey stock

Since roast turkey is so popular during the winter holidays, there always seems to be this big, old carcass all picked over a day or two after the big meal. Don't waste it, and use it as soon as possible! It is perfect for breaking up (separate the ribs from the backbone; it won't fit into the pot whole) and cooking into an aromatic stock that seems to make itself.

YIELD: About 1¹/₂ quarts

3 pounds roast turkey carcass bones with some meat left on, broken up, including the wings and skin
1 yellow onion, chopped

1 leek, white and green parts, washed well
   and chopped
1 carrot, cut into chunks
3 stalks celery, with leaves, chopped
6 sprigs fresh parsley, with stems
1 bay leaf
2 sprigs fresh thyme or 1 teaspoon dried
   thyme
6 black peppercorns

1. Place the turkey bones in a large stock-pot. Add water to cover by 3 inches. Partially cover and bring to a boil over high heat. Skim off any foam that floats to the surface. Add the vegetables, herbs, and peppercorns. Reduce the heat to medium-low, partially cover, and simmer for 3 hours. **2.** Remove the cover and let the stock cool to lukewarm. Line a large colander or strainer with cheesecloth and set it over a large bowl; carefully pour the stock through to strain it. Press the vegetables to extract all the liquid and discard. Discard the bones and meat. Divide the stock into airtight plastic freezer storage containers, leaving 2 inches at the top to allow for expansion in the freezer. The stock is ready for use and can be refrigerated for up to 2 to 3 days, or frozen for 3 to 6 months.

game stock

Game bird or rabbit stock is very much like poultry stock in flavor and viscosity. It is quite delicate and very delicious in pilafs and risottos. It is a must if a member of your family is a hunter, and game stock is a great way to use up the extra trimmings, flesh, and bones after

boning the breasts. Since most game birds are quite small, you can accumulate bones by keeping them in resealable plastic bags in the freezer. While here you will brown the vegetables first, never brown game or poultry bones; they will lose a lot of flavor. This stock is best made with only one type of game at a time to avoid muddling the flavor.

YIELD: About 2 quarts

3 tablespoons olive oil
2 yellow onions, cut into quarters
2 carrots, cut into chunks
4 stalks celery, with leaves
5 pounds duck, pheasant, or small game
   bird (like chukar or quail) backs, necks,
   wings, and trimmings, or rabbit carcass
   and bones
3 sprigs fresh parsley, with stems
1 bay leaf
2 sprigs fresh thyme or 1 teaspoon dried
   thyme
6 black peppercorns

1. In a large stockpot, heat the olive oil over medium-high heat. Add the onions, carrots, and celery and cook, stirring, until they begin to brown, about 10 minutes. Add the game, herbs, peppercorns, and water to cover by 2 inches. Partially cover and bring to a boil over high heat. Reduce the heat to medium-low and simmer for about 3 hours, skimming off any foam that rises to the surface a few times with a large spoon. **2.** Remove the cover and let the stock cool to lukewarm. Line a large colander or strainer with cheesecloth and set it over a large bowl; carefully pour the stock through to strain it. Press the vegetables to extract all the liquid and discard. Discard the bones and meat. Divide the stock into airtight plastic freezer storage containers, leaving 2 inches at the top to allow for expansion in the freezer. The stock is ready for use and can be refrigerated for up to 2 to 3 days, or frozen for 3 to 6 months.

white stock

White stock is made with veal and chicken bones, making a much more light-colored and delicately flavored stock than one made with beef. It is the savory delight of the country kitchen and can be used in place of chicken stock in recipes. Beth buys chicken breasts for dinner, bones them herself, and keeps the raw bones in plastic freezer bags until making the stock. This is a recipe adapted from the 1957 edition of *The Gourmet Cookbook* compiled by the original publisher and creator of the magazine devoted to good eating, Earle R. MacAusland.

YIELD: About 2¹/₂ quarts

3 tablespoons unsalted butter
1 yellow onion, cut into quarters
1 carrot, cut into chunks
1 leek, white and green parts, washed well
  and chopped
3 stalks celery, with leaves
2 veal knuckles
4 to 6 chicken half-breast bones (left over
  from boning breast fillets)
4 sprigs fresh parsley, with stems
6 black peppercorns

1. In a large stockpot, melt the butter over medium-high heat. Add the onion, carrot, leek, and celery and cook, stirring, for about 3 minutes. Add the veal knuckles, chicken bones, parsley, peppercorns, and water to cover by 2 inches. Partially cover and bring to a boil over high heat. Reduce the heat to medium-low and simmer for about 3 hours, skimming off the foam that rises to the surface.

2. Remove the cover and let the stock cool to lukewarm. Line a large colander or strainer with cheesecloth and set it over a large bowl; carefully pour the stock through to strain. Press the vegetables to extract all the liquid and discard. Discard the bones and solids. Divide the stock into airtight plastic freezer storage containers, leaving 2 inches at the top to allow for expansion in the freezer. The stock is ready for use and can be refrigerated for up to 2 to 3 days, or frozen for 3 to 6 months.

potager vegetable stock

If you thought that a pure vegetable stock is a new invention by vegetarians, think again. Known as *fond de légumes* in French, vegetable stock is a wonderfully old-fashioned aromatic combination of mild herbs and vegetables, with a decidedly neutral taste. When evaluating a vegetable stock recipe, note that vegetables that have assertive flavors—cabbage, turnips, green peppers, broccoli, and cauliflower, should be avoided; they will overpower your stock. Potatoes make a stock murky from their starch, and anything like beets or tomatoes will instantly tint your stock a brilliant, earthy color, which is usually undesirable. Use fresh vegetables; old vegetables will not make such a nice tasting stock.

YIELD: About 2 quarts

3 tablespoons olive oil

2 tablespoons unsalted butter or vegetable oil

3 medium-size yellow onions, chopped

2 leeks, white and green parts, washed well and chopped

1 medium-size carrot, cut into chunks

1 medium-size parsnip, peeled and cut into chunks

1 small bunch celery, with leaves, stalks pulled apart and bottoms trimmed

2 cups sliced fresh mushrooms

1 or 2 ears fresh corn (optional), husked, kernels cut off and reserved for another dish, and cobs broken into pieces

6 sprigs fresh parsley, with stems

Few strands fresh chives or green onions

1 head garlic, unpeeled and cut in half horizontally

1 bay leaf

2 sprigs fresh thyme or marjoram or 1 teaspoon dried thyme or marjoram

6 black peppercorns

1. In a large stockpot, heat the olive oil and butter over medium-high heat. When the butter melts, add the onions, leeks, carrot, parsnip, and celery and cook, stirring occasionally, until they begin to brown, about 10 minutes. Add the mushrooms, corn, parsley, chives, garlic, bay leaf, thyme, and pepper-corns. Add water to cover by 2 inches. Partially cover and bring to a boil over high heat. Reduce the heat to medium-low and simmer for about 1½ hours.

2. Remove the cover and let the stock cool to lukewarm. Line a large colander or strainer with cheesecloth and set it over a large bowl; carefully pour the stock through to strain it. Press the vegetables to extract all the liquid and discard. Divide the stock into airtight plastic freezer storage containers, leaving 2 inches at the top to allow for expansion in the freezer. The stock is ready for use and can be refrigerated for up to 3 to 4 days, or frozen for 3 to 6 months.

chinese vegetable stock

This is a variation on the plain vegetable stock, which I find very aromatic and perfect for making rice that will be served with prawns or chicken, even a Chinese-style paella. The addition of fresh-tasting cilantro (also known as Chinese parsley or fresh coriander), a few broken points of licorice-scented star anise (a favorite seasoning for Asian broths), and slices of spicy fresh ginger make a stock that is still quite delicately flavored. Aromatic Szechuan peppercorns, used in place of black peppercorns, are the dried berries of a shrub rather than a true pepper. They are pan-toasted to bring out their flavor and fragrance.

YIELD: About 2 quarts

3 tablespoons vegetable or peanut oil

2 yellow onions, chopped

1 bunch green onions, white and green
parts, chopped

1 head garlic, unpeeled and cut in half
horizontally

6 thin slices fresh ginger, unpeeled

3 carrots, cut into chunks

1 small bunch celery, with leaves, stalks
pulled apart and bottoms trimmed

1 cup sliced fresh mushrooms

3 tablespoons soy sauce

1 teaspoon Szechuan peppercorns

6 sprigs fresh cilantro, with stems

1/2 star anise

1 large or 2 small dried shiitake
mushrooms

1/2 teaspoon freshly ground white pepper

1. In a large stockpot, heat the oil over medium-high heat. Add the yellow onions, green onions, garlic, and ginger and cook, stirring, for about 2 minutes. Add the carrots, celery, fresh mushrooms, soy sauce, and water to cover by 2 inches. Partially cover and bring to a boil over high heat.

2. Meanwhile, place the peppercorns in a dry skillet over medium heat, shaking the pan frequently to prevent burning, until they smell fragrant, about 4 minutes. Add to the stock along with the cilantro, anise, dried mushrooms, and white pepper. Reduce the heat to medium-low and simmer for about 1½ hours, partially covered, skimming off any foam that comes to the surface.

3. Remove the cover and let the stock cool to lukewarm. Line a large colander or strainer with cheesecloth and set it over a large bowl; carefully pour the stock through to strain it. Press the vegetables to extract all the liquid and discard. Divide the stock into airtight plastic freezer storage containers, leaving 2 inches at the top to allow for expansion in the freezer. The stock is ready for use and can be refrigerated for up to 3 to 4 days, or frozen for 3 to 6 months.

fish stock

Fish stock is very fast to make; only about half an hour of simmering is needed to get a nicely flavored stock. Be sure to use only the bones of mild white fish, not oily fish like salmon, or else the stock will be too strong. A good alternative to homemade fish stock is to use one part bottled clam juice mixed with two parts chicken broth.

YIELD: About 1½ quarts

Heads and bones of 2 red snappers or
other mild white fish (about 2½
pounds), rinsed in cold water and gills
removed

2 tablespoons unsalted butter

1 medium-size yellow onion, sliced

1 leek, white and green parts, washed well
and chopped

3 stalks celery, with leaves, roughly
chopped

1 cup dry white wine

1/2 small bunch fresh parsley, with stems

2 bay leaves

2 sprigs fresh thyme or 1 teaspoon dried
thyme

10 black peppercorns

1. In a stockpot, combine the bones and butter over medium-high heat. Cover and steam for about 4 minutes. Add the vegetables, cover, and steam for another 4 minutes. Add water to cover by 2 inches, the wine, parsley, bay leaves, thyme, and peppercorns. Partially cover and bring to a boil over high heat. Reduce the heat to medium, cover, and cook at a rapid simmer for about 35 minutes. **2.** Remove the cover and let the stock cool to lukewarm. Line a large colander or strainer with cheesecloth and set it over a large bowl; carefully pour the stock through to strain it. Press the vegetables to extract all the liquid and discard. Divide the stock into airtight plastic freezer storage containers, leaving 2 inches at the top to allow for expansion in the freezer. The stock is ready for use and can be refrigerated for up to 2 to 3 days, or frozen for 3 to 6 months.

dashi

Dashi is a quick all-purpose quick clear stock that is the heart of Japanese-style cooking. Made properly it is described as tasting of the sea. It calls for kombu seaweed (also called kombu), which is a thick dried kelp that is an essential ingredient in Japanese broths, and bonito flakes, pale pink shavings made from dried bonito fish fillets. Look for the seaweed and bonito flakes in an Asian grocery or the Asian food section of a well-stocked supermarket. Dashi is so quick to make that you can make it fresh each time you need it. Beth likes her version with one dried shiitake mushroom added.

YIELD: About 1 quart

4 cups cold water
1 sheet (1 ounce) kombu seaweed 3 to 4 inches square, wiped clean with a damp cloth and soaked in cold water in the refrigerator overnight
1/3 cup dried bonito flakes

1. Place the water in a medium saucepan. Add the kombu. Bring to a low boil over medium-high heat. Reduce the heat to low (if the water continues to boil, the stock will not be totally clear) and simmer for 5 minutes. Add the bonito flakes and stir. Turn off the heat and let stand for 2 minutes to allow the bonito flakes to settle. Skim off any foam. **2.** Line a large colander or strainer with cheesecloth and set it over a large bowl; carefully pour the dashi through to strain it. Discard the kombu and bonito flakes. The stock is ready for use and can be refrigerated for up to 3 days, but is best used the day it is made.

sharon's dashi

Here is a simpler stock made with only kombu (the flat seaweed covered with a whitish powder).

YIELD: 4 cups

One 1-inch square dashi kombu
4 cups water

Wipe the kombu clean with a damp cloth, but don't remove the white powder. Place in a saucepan with the water. Bring to a boil; remove from the heat and let stand for at least 5 minutes before using.

The following all-purpose online and mail-order resources are assembled to give you the ability to shop for a wide variety of the best quality rices and whole grains, many of which are difficult to find even in the best stocked stores. Goldmine Natural Food Company and Bob's Red Mill are becoming bigger names in the mail-order grain business, and King Arthur's Baker's Catalogue and Walnut Acres are our favorite one-stop shopping resources.

Look for heirloom whole grains (such as buckwheat groats and hull-less barley), ancient grains (such as quinoa and spelt), hard-to-find regionally grown rice (such as Wild Pecan rice, Della basmati, and Bhutanese red rice), custom cereal and mixed grain blends, and Asian or Indian rices and ingredients. Most sources with equipment carry at least one type of rice cooker machine. Call the customer service departments or check online for complete catalogs and price lists.

Birkett Mills
16 Main Street
Penn Yan, NY 14527
(315) 536-3311
www.thebirkettmills.com
Buckwheat is readily available in natural food stores, in the supermarket with kosher foods, and by mail order. Birkett Mills is the major processor and source of the best buckwheat products sold in the United States today. Their buckwheat groats, grits, and kasha are marketed under the trademark of Pocono.

Bob's Red Mill
5209 SE International Way
Milwaukee, OR 97222
(503) 654-3215
www.bobsredmill.com
One of Beth's favorite sources for cornmeal and whole grains, available in almost a staggering assortment. Every bean you might want to cook, from *chana dal* and cannellini beans to petite French green lentils, soldier beans, and Tongues of Fire beans, used for making Portuguese recipes. Buckwheat, bulgur, brown rice, farina, polenta and organic cornmeals, couscous and granola, millet, long- and short-grain white and brown basmati, sushi rice and short-grain white rice, wild rice, rye berries, spelt berries, and sea salt. Try Bob's organic stone-ground Scottish oatmeal!

Butte Creek Mill
P.O. Box 561
Eagle Point, OR 97524
(503) 826-3531
www.buttecreekmill.com
Great stone-ground cornmeals, which come in different grinds, from an old water-powered stone mill. A treat!

The California Press
6200 Washington Street
Yountville, CA 94599
(707) 944-0343
www.californiapress.com
Virgin almond, pistachio, pecan, hazelnut, and walnut oils pressed by artisan craftspeople.

Chef's Catalog
P.O. Box 620048
Dallas, TX 75262
(800) 338-3232
www.chefscatalog.com
Quality kitchenware from brand names such as All Clad, Le Creuset, KitchenAid, and Cuisinart, to name but a few. Rice cooker machines.

cooking.com
www.cooking.com
The Baking Shop on this site features the finest in bakeware and handy utensils for the home baker. The Baking Ingredients section carries an impressive array of nine hard-to-find sugars, in addition to chocolate, extracts, and farro. Rice cooker machines.

EthnicGrocer.com
www.ethnicgrocer.com
Products found around the world, from Asia (Korea, Thailand, and the Philippines) and India to Latin America and countries in between. This is the place for Greek and Turkish foods (pickled grape leaves), *bulghol* crushed wheat, and specialty olive oils. Order rices, semolina, blue cornmeal, crystallized ginger, pomegranate molasses, and more.

Gibbs Wild Rice
10400 Billings Road
Live Oak, CA 95953
(800) 824-4932
www.gibbswildrice.com
Premium Minnesota and California wild rice that is organically grown, without chemical fertilizers, pesticides, or herbicides. Available in many grades, all delicious.

Goldmine Natural Food Company
3419 Hancock Street
San Diego, CA 92110-4307
(800) 475-FOOD
www.goldminenaturalfood.com
Organic and heirloom grains, rice, rolled oats, and a similar product line to Bob's Red Mill and The Grain and Salt Society.

Gourmet Rice/Ellis Stansel
P.O. Box 206
Gueydan, LA 70542
(318) 536-6140
www.stanselrice.com
Louisiana-grown long-grain white and brown aromatic rice under the moniker of Gourmet Popcorn Rice. A unique artisan rice bred from a basmati-type seed from Pakistan early last century.

The Grain and Salt Society
273 Fairway Drive
Asheville, NC 28805
(800) TOP-SALT
www.celtic-seasalt.com
A great family-run company that specializes in organic and macrobiotic food products. Excellent Celtic Sea Salt, miso, tamari, umeboshi plums, organic beans, quinoa, whole-grain rye and spelt, organic buckwheat kasha, pearled barley, organic long- and short-grain brown rices, organic white and brown basmati, and organic rolled oats.

Grain Millers
11100 NE Eighth, Suite 710
Bellevue, WA 98009
(800) 443-8972
A great family-run company that specializes in organic rolled oats.

Hodgson Mill, Inc.
P.O. Box 430
Teutopolis, IL 62467
(800) 525-0177
www.hodgsonmill.com
Hodgson is a well-known Midwest supermarket staple and produces a full line of stone-ground yellow and white cornmeal and grits, cracked

wheat, bulgur wheat with soy grits, barley, golden lentils, black beans, and split peas out of their three milling sites. One of Beth's favorite sources for cornmeal.

India Plaza
www.indiaplaza.com
Excellent online source for basmati and other Indian white rices, curry powders and other spices, such as mustard seeds, dozens of dals, and Indian pickles and condiments.

The Baker's Catalogue (King Arthur Flour)
P.O. Box 876
Norwich, VT 05055
(800) 827-6836
www.kingarthurflour.com
Brinna Sands has built her mail-order catalog to offer the best for the home baker and a wide variety of equipment; dried fruit and coconut; dried Michigan tart cherries, blueberries, and raspberries; nuts and nut oils; chocolate and cocoa; vanilla products; citrus extracts; saffron; sugars; and spices. We recommend the entire line of King Arthur flours from unbleached to whole wheat.

La Cuisine
323 Cameron Street
Alexandria, VA 22314
(800) 521-1176
www.lacuisineus.com
Valhrona chocolate, cocoa powders, Tahitian vanilla beans and extracts, glacéed fruits, candied citrus peels, dried berries, shelled pistachios, whole peeled hazelnuts. We like their India Tree sugars; we are hooked on the dark muscovado brown sugar.

Lotus Foods
El Cerrito, CA 94530
(510) 525-3137
www.lotusfoods.com or
www.worldofrice.com
Exquisite domestic white and brown jasmine rice from Lowell Farms, Bhutanese red rice, Chinese

Black Rice, Argentinean Carnaroli, and Kalijira baby basmati.

Lundberg Family Farms
P.O. Box 369
Richvale, CA 95974
(916) 882-4551
www.lundberg.com
This is an excellent source for domestic brown and specialty rices. Lundberg offers Wehani, American white and brown basmati, *japonica* short-grain black rice, short- and long-grain brown rices, and California white Arborio. They even sell a rice cooker.

McCormick & Co. Food Service Mail Order
226 Schilling Circle
Hunt Valley, MD 21031
(800) 322-SPICE
You can purchase bulk spices, usually in one-pound containers. Almond, vanilla, and anise extracts.

Mexican Grocer
7445 Girard Avenue, Suite 6
La Hoya, CA 92037
(858) 459-0577
www.mexgrocer.com
Latin American, Caribbean, and Spanish food items are a specialty here. Valencia medium-grain white rice and masa harina. From sausages to dried chiles and brick-red anchiote paste, even cheeses and spices. The site is in both English and Spanish.

Mountain Ark Trading Company
799 Old Leicester Highway
Asheville, NC 28806
(800) 643-8909
www.mountainark.com
Full line of organic grains and heirloom grains, such as soba gome and kibi millet, beans and rices, sea salt, miso, and macrobiotic supplies and condiments.

The Oriental Pantry
www.orientalpantry.com
Consider this site culinary Chinatown online. Over a thousand Asian food products, with the emphasis on Chinese ingredients. Here are your Shaoxing cooking wine, fermented black beans, delicious mushroom soy sauce, spices, and oyster sauces.

Penzeys Ltd. Spice House
P.O. Box 1448
Waukesha, WI 53187
(414) 574-0277
www.penzeys.com
If this resource is new to you, call immediately for their catalog. Penzeys has exemplary herbs and spices, both whole and ground, extracts, and spice blends. The spices are very specialized: true cinnamon from Ceylon and cassia cinnamon from Indonesia (Korintje), China (Tunghing), and Vietnam (our favorite). They also have chili powders, hot or sweet curry powders (try their Maharajah-style blend), mustard seeds, rosemary, saffron, and single- or double-strength vanilla extracts from Madagascar, Tahiti, and Mexico (hard to find). Their gift boxes defy description; one is an eight-jar Indian curry selection (hand-mixed to boot!) that includes hot and sweet curry powders, Punjabi Garam Masala, Maharajah Curry Powder, Tandoori Seasoning, Rogan Josh Seasoning (Pakistani-style spicy spices), Vindaloo (includes cinnamon, mustard, chili, Tellicherry pepper, and cardamom from the Malabar Coast), and Balti Seasoning, a spice mixture with Persian, Chinese, and Tibetan influences. Wow!

Quickspice.com
www.quickspice.com
An excellent resource for Asian food and cookware available direct from the supplier. Search the site by cuisine—Japanese, Chinese, or Thai—for tools, ingredients, and tableware to re-create your favorite dishes. Rice cooker machines.

RiceTec, Inc.
P.O. Box 1305
Alvin, TX 77512
(800) 232-RICE
www.riceselect.com
Texas-grown Texmati, Jasmati, Kasmati, Sushi Rice, and Risotto Rice under the RiceSelect label. These are excellent domestic rices.

Specialty Rice, Inc.
1000 West First Street
Brinkley, AR 72021
(870) 734-1233
www.dellarice.com
Della Gourmet is our homegrown Arkansas basmati and considered an American artisan rice. Also Basmati White and Natural Brown Rice, Jasmine White and Natural Brown Rice, Arborio White Rice, Indian Basmati, and Koshi Hikari White Rice. Limited distribution west of the Rockies. If you are a rice connoisseur, you will want to try these rices.

Sur La Table
www.surlatable.com
Distinctive cooking products sourced from suppliers throughout Europe that include an exclusive line of small appliances like rice cookers, cutlery, kitchen tools, tableware, hard-to-find gadgets, and seasonal and specialty foods. Rice cooker machines.

Tavolo
www.tavolo.com
High-quality cookware, baking and pastry tools, and specialty foods. Products include pure citrus oils, amaranth, Lotus Foods' Bhutanese Red Rice and Forbidden Rice, and Valrhona chocolate.

Uncle Ben's Gourmet Kitchen
www.unclebens.com
Uncle Ben's is the largest marketer of rice in the United States today. They carry a full line of specialty rices, such as basmati and jasmine, as well as American rices.

Walnut Acres
Walnut Acres Road
Penns Creek, PA 17862
(800) 344-9025
www.walnutacres.com

One of the first, and still excellent, mail-order resources for reliable organic rices, grains, cereals, dried fruits, nuts, herbs, and spices. Similar to Bob's Red Mill.

War Eagle Mill
Route 5, P.O. Box 411
Rogers, AK 72738
(501) 789-5343
www.wareaglemill.com

Excellent organic stone-ground corn grits, water-ground cornmeals, and cracked wheat.

Western Trails Food Products
P.O. Box 460
Bozeman, MT 59715
(406) 587-5489
www.cowboyfoods.com

Western Trails is a unique company offering the most innovative artisanal barley available today. The Black Buffalo and Bronze Nugget whole-grain barleys are a must.

White Lily Foods Company
P.O. Box 871
Knoxville, TN 37901
(615) 546-5511
www.whitelily.com

The flour of the South for making biscuits is a cross between pastry flour and regular all-purpose flour. One of our favorite flours for baking and Beth's choice for making steamed puddings.

Williams-Sonoma
P.O. Box 7456
San Francisco, CA 94120
(800) 541-2233
www.williams-sonoma.com

Offers an extensive selection of high-quality cooking-related merchandise from cookware to specialty and artisan foods. Arborio, Vialone nano, and Carnaroli rices imported from Italy, Calaspara and Bomba medium-grain rice imported from Spain (hard to find anywhere else!), Kumai Harvest Koshi Hikari imported from Japan, whole roasted chestnuts, Boyajian citrus oils, dried berries, Fini aceto balsamic vinegar, and olive oil. Rice cooker machines.

INDEX